40.95

D1174859

2

28 DAY BOOK

	DATE DUE		
7|13 |80.6|c4			©1986

JUN 25 1987

VENEZUELA

VENEZUELA

The Democratic Experience
revised edition

edited by
John D. Martz
David J. Myers

PRAEGER

PRAEGER SPECIAL STUDIES • PRAEGER SCIENTIFIC

New York • Philadelphia • Eastbourne, UK
Toronto • Hong Kong • Tokyo • Sydney

Library of Congress Cataloging-in-Publication Data
Main entry under title:

Venezuela : the democratic experience.

  Bibliography: p.
  Includes index.
  1. Venezuela – Politics and government – 1958-   –
Addresses, essays, lectures. 2. Representative
government and representation – Venezuela – Addresses,
essays, lectures. I. Martz, John D. II. Myers, David J.
JL3831.V45   1986   987'.0633   85-28268
ISBN 0-03-003464-7 (alk. paper)
ISBN 0-03-003467-1 (pbk. : alk. paper)

Published in 1986 by Praeger Publishers
CBS Educational and Professional Publishing, a Division of CBS Inc.
521 Fifth Avenue, New York, NY 10175 USA

© 1986 by Praeger Publishers

6789 052 987654321

Printed in the United States of America on acid-free paper

INTERNATIONAL OFFICES

Orders from outside the United States should be sent to the appropriate address listed below. Orders from areas not
listed below should be placed through CBS International Publishing, 383 Madison Ave., New York, NY 10175 USA

Australia, New Zealand
Holt Saunders, Pty, Ltd., 9 Waltham St., Artarmon, N.S.W. 2064, Sydney, Australia

Canada
Holt, Rinehart & Winston of Canada, 55 Horner Ave., Toronto, Ontario, Canada M8Z 4X6

Europe, the Middle East, & Africa
Holt Saunders, Ltd., 1 St. Anne's Road, Eastbourne, East Sussex, England BN21 3UN

Japan
Holt Saunders, Ltd., Ichibancho Central Building, 22-1 Ichibancho, 3rd Floor, Chiyodaku, Tokyo, Japan

Hong Kong, Southeast Asia
Holt Saunders Asia, Ltd., 10 Fl, Intercontinental Plaza, 94 Granville Road, Tsim Sha Tsui East, Kowloon,
Hong Kong

**Manuscript submissions should be sent to the Editorial Director, Praeger Publishers, 521 Fifth Avenue,
New York, NY 10175 USA**

Preface

Twenty-five years ago, even the most astute political observers of the Latin American scene were skeptical about the prospects of the fledgling democracy instituted in Venezuela. Although there seemed to be a diminution of dictatorships—as noted by the knowledgeable journalist Tad Szulc in his *Twilight of the Tyrants*— the birthplace of Simón Bolívar seemed an unlikely land for the evolution of pluralism and of representative government. There was little to suggest that Latin America's most vibrant, vigorous, and contentiously competitive democratic system was about to emerge. Yet, with the benefit of hindsight, that was precisely what loomed ahead. By 1984, six successive elected presidents had ascended to Miraflores Palace. Moreover, four consecutive elections had seen the defeat of the government candidate by the leader of the opposition. The record had become uncommon, but undeniable.

It is rather surprising, and in some ways shameful, that the Venezuelan political system has received very limited scholarly attention throughout these years. Indeed, we noted in the 1977 edition of this volume that "little significant social science research had been undertaken in Venezuela." Since that time, to be sure, there have been further serious analyses by both Venezuelan and North American students. Nevertheless, the flow of research has been little more than a trickle. Revolutionary socialism in Cuba, fading and failed military authoritarianism in Brazil and Argentina, the inhumanity of dictatorship in Chile, and the arbitrary antipopulism of the Mexican system have all seemed to hold greater interest than the evolution of a party-based reformist democracy in Venezuela. If this was true at the time of the first edition, it is even more striking today.

Little purpose is served by undertaking a strained or speculative inquiry. Suffice it to say that the essays that follow should suggest that the Venezuelan experience is intrinsically important, one with significance for its neighbors as well. We initiated the effort to prepare a totally new and updated volume, the first manifestation of which was an extended panel convened at the November 1983 conference of the Northeast Political Science

Association in Philadelphia, Pennsylvania. The papers constituted early versions of several of the chapters that, in fairly drastically revised form, are among the contributions presented here. They have all been completed since the conclusion of the government of Luis Herrera Campins and the inauguration of Jaime Lusinchi's presidency. Where the first edition ended chronologically in the early years under Carlos Andrés Pérez, the second has centered on more recent events.

The present chapters, in the majority of cases authored by the same scholars who contributed to the first edition, are entirely new. Their concern is with the past decade of the Venezuelan democratic experience, and thus are not merely updated restatements of the previous writings. In a number of instances circumstances required a change in authorship; the research interests of some collaborators had shifted during the intervening years. For others, the time constraints of diverse commitments made participation impossible. Such adjustments have been accommodated within the basic organizational structure of the first edition, which we found heuristically valid as a means of presenting the materials of contemporary Venezuelan politics.

The three basic sections therefore remain the same, beginning with an overview of those variables and environmental conditions that influence political behavior. John V. Lombardi provides the historical context out of which emerged the unexpected phenomenon of pluralistic democracy. This is followed by R. Lynn Kelley's discussion of legal rules and the shifting patterns of constitutional practice. Part I then proceeds with Enrique A. Baloyra's reassessment of Venezuelan political attitudes and concludes with a statement by John D. Martz and David J. Myers of the economic setting that informs and nourishes contemporary democracy. With these statements in mind, the reader may then proceed to the articulation and aggregation of interests that constitute the primary concern in Part II.

The party system, so central to all political activity in Venezuela, is examined by David J. Myers. He notes the realigning character of the 1973 elections, the hegemonic role assumed by COPEI and by Acción Democrática, and considers possible shifts in the years ahead. The modernizing role of the armed forces constitutes the emphasis for José Antonio Gil, who traces its development as a strongly supportive institutional pillar for the democratic system. Bureaucratic mechanisms are described by William S. Stewart in both their formal and actual functioning, while the marked expansion of the central state is depicted by Gene E. Bigler and Enrique Viloria.

In Part III the central concern is policymaking and its implications for the continuing evolution of the nation. Petroleum, of crucial significance since the 1920s, has entered upon a time of uncertainty. John D. Martz studies the growing threat of politicization, as well as the deleterious implications of world market conditions in the 1980s. Steve Ellner highlights the ever-influential role that falls to the university students and to their interrelated political and educational preoccupations. The long and continuing story of argicultural stagnation, and the diverse efforts to reenergize this sector of the economy, is traced by Donald L. Herman. The shifting character of municipal and local government as a grass-roots component of the democratic system attracts the attention of Ildemaro Jesús Martínez, and H. Dieter Hienen and Walter Coppens consider the ongoing struggle of the Venezuelan Indian for dignity and an improved standard of living. The nation's continuing effort to project itself as an influential middle-range power, especially in Caribbean affairs, emerges from the analysis of Charles D. Ameringer.

The broad overall reevaluation of Venezuelan democracy, which constitutes the preoccupation of all the contributors, is summarized and restated by the coeditors in their concluding chapter. The overall performance of the system is isolated under several different rubrics, after which a closing assessment is made. These remarks, and the projection for the future that is drawn, reflect the views of Martz and Myers in the light of the individual chapters. For the reader, of course, a similar exercise is both possible and desirable. Those who will, we hope, wish to seek a more profound knowledge of one or another aspect of Venezuelan politics may be guided in their search by the bibliographic essay. We thank our contributors for providing the necessary information, as well as for joining us in the present undertaking.

Contents

PART II. ARTICULATING AND AGGREGATING INTERESTS

PART III. POLICY AND PERFORMANCE

Tables, Figures, and Maps

xv

Glossary and Abbreviations

AD	Acción Democrática (Democratic Action)
adecos	Members of the AD
ALALC	Associación Latinoamericana de Libre Comercio (Latin American Free Trade Association, LAFTA; cf.)
ALMIL	Almacenes Militares (Military Stores)
AVECI	Venezuelan Association of Integrated District Councils
Bandera Roja	Red Flag, a guerrilla group
BAP	Banco Agrícola y Pecuario (Agricultural and Livestock Bank)
BCV	Banco Central de Venezuela (Venezuelan Central Bank)
BIV	Banco Industrial de Venezuela (Venezuelan Industrial Bank)
BND	Banco Nacional de Descuento (National Discount Bank)
BTV	Banco de los Trabajadores de Venezuela (Venezuelan Workers' Bank)
Bs	Bolivars; Venezuela's monetary unit
C.A.	Campañía Anónima (incorporated)
CADAFE	C.A. de Administración y Fomento Eléctrico (Electrical Administration and Development Company)
CANTV	C.A. Nacional Teléfonos de Venezuela (Venezuelan National Telephone Company)
CAP	Comisión de Administración Pública (Public Administration Commission)
caraqueño	Resident of the city of Caracas
CARICOM	Caribbean Community and Common Market

Casa Amarillo	The Venezuelan Foreign Ministry
CAVIM	C.A. de Industrias Militares (Venezuelan Military Industries Company)
CCN	Cruzada Cívica Nacionalista (Nationalist Civic Crusade)
CEN	National Energy Council, not to be confused with the National Executive Committee of AD
CENDES	Centro de Estudios del Dessarrollo, the social science research department at the Central University
CIN	Comisión Indígena Nacional (National Indian Commission)
CMA	Corporación de Mercadeo Agrícola (Agricultural Marketing Corporation)
CODESUR	Comisión para el Desarrollo del Sur (Commission for the Development of the South)
COLM	East Coast of Lake Maracaibo Communities
CONAC	Consejo Nacional de la Cultura (National Council of Culture)
CONAHOTU	Corporación Nacional de Hoteles y Turismo (National Corporation of Hotels and Tourism)
CONASEDE	Consejo Nacional de Seguridad y Defensa (National Council for Security and Defense)
CONSECOMERCIO	Consejo Comercio (Merchants' retail council)
COPEI	Comité de Organización Política Electoral Independiente (Committee of Independent Electoral Political Organization), the Christian Democratic party
copeyanos	Members of COPEI
CORDIPLAN	Oficina Central de Coordinación y Planificación (Central Office of Coordination and Planning)
CORPOANDES	Andean Development Corporation

CORPOINDUSTRIA	Corporación de Desarrollo de la Pequeña y Mediana Industria (Development Corporation for Small and Medium Industry)
CORPOMERCADEO	Corporación de Mercadeo Agrícola (Corporation for Agricultural Marketing)
CORPOORIENTE	Eastern Development Corporation
CORPOTURISMO	Corporación de Turismo (Tourism Corporation)
CORPOVEN	One of the four operating affiliates of PDVSA, formed around the old Venezuelan Petroleum Corporation (CVP)
CORPOZULIA	Zulian Development Corporation
CRIAP	Comisión para la Reforma Integral de la Administración Pública (Commission for Reform of Public Administration)
criollo	In colonial time, a person of purely Spanish descent, born in the New World
CSB	Centro Simón Bolívar, C.A.
CSE	Consejo Supremo Electoral (Supreme Electoral Council)
CTV	Confederación de Trabajadores de Venezuela (Confederation of Venezuelan Workers)
CUTV	Central Unitaria de Trabajadores de Venezuela (Unitary Confederation of Venezuelan Workers); small leftist rival to the CTV
CVF	Corporación Venezolana de Fomento (Venezuelan Development Corporation)
CVG	Corporación Venezolana de Guayana (Venezuela Guayana Corporation)
CVP	Corporación Venezolana de Petróleos (Venezuelan Petroleum Corporation), now part of CORPOVEN, S.A., a subsidiary of PETROVEN
DAI	Dirección de Asuntos Indigenas (Office of Indian Affairs)

DIANCA	The munitions producing corporations of the Navy
Digepol	Dirección General de Policía (the national police force)
DIM	Dirección de Inteligencia Militar (Military Intelligence Directorate)
DISIP	Dirección de Servicios de Inteligencia y Prevención del Estado (Intelligence and State Security Services Directorate)
DPA	Decentralized public administration
ECLA	UN Economic Commission for Latin America
EDELCA	Electrificacíon del Caroní, S.A. (Caroní Basin Electrification Company)
ELECAR	Electricidad de Caracas, Venezuela's largest nationally controlled private corporation
evangélicos	Converts to "born again" Protestantism
FACUR	Federación de Associaciones de Comunidades Urbanas (Federation of Associations of Urban Communities)
Faja Bituminosa	Orinoco Tar Belt
FALN	Fuerzas Armadas de Liberación Nacional (Armed Forces of National Liberation)
FAPO	Faja Petrolífera del Orinoco, the new Orinoco heavy oil belt
FCA	Fondo de Crédito Agropecuario (Agriculture and Livestock Credit Fund)
FCV	Federación Campesina de Venezuela (Venezuelan Peasant Federation)
FDP	Fuerza Democrática Popular (Popular Democratic Force)
FEDECAMARAS	Federación de Cámaras y Asociaciones de Comercio y Producción (Federation of Chambers and Associations of Commerce and Production), roughly comparable to U.S. Chamber of Commerce

FEDEPETROL	Federación de Trabajadores Petroleros (Oil Workers' Federation), Venezuela's richest and most important labor union
FIV	Fondo de Inversiones de Venezuela (Venezuelan Investment Fund)
FND	Frente Nacional Democratica (National Democratic Front)
FONDUR	Fondo Nacional de Desarrollo Urbano (National Fund for Urban Development)
FUNDACOMUN	Fundación para el Desarrollo de la Communidad y Fomento Municipal (Foundation for Community and Municipal Development)
FVM	Federación Venezolana de Maestros (Venezuelan Teachers Federation)
golpe de estado	Coup d'etat
hacendado	Large landowner
IAEDEN	Instituto de Altos Estudios de la Defensa Nacional (Institute of Advanced Studies for National Defense, the War College)
IAN	Instituto Agrario Nacional (National Agrarian Institute)
ICE	Instituto de Comercio Exterior (Foreign Trade Institute)
ICAP	Instituto de Crédito Agrícola y Pecuario (Agro-livestock Credit Institute)
IESA	Instituto de Estudios Superiores de Administracíon (Institute of Higher Administrative Studies)
IMF	International Monetary Fund
INAVI	Instituto Nacional de Vivienda (National Housing Institute)
INOS	Instituto Nacional de Sanitarias Obras (National Institute of Sanitary Works)
INCE	Instituto Nacional de Corporación Educativa (National Institute of Educational Cooperation)

INCIBA	Instituto Nacional de Cultura y Bellas Artes (National Institute of Culture and Fine Arts)
IPFN	Independent Electoral Front (forerunner of FND)
IPSFA	Instituto de Previsión Social de las Fuerza Armadas (Armed Forces Institute of Social Welfare)
IUPFAN	Instituto Universitario Politécnico de las Fuerzas Armadas (Armed Forces Poly-technic Institute)
IVIC	Instituto Venezolano de Investigación Científica (Venezuelan Institute of Scientific Investigation)
IVP	Instituto Venezolano de Petroquímica (Venezuelan Petrochemical Institute)
IVSS	Instituto Venezolano de Seguro Social (Venezuelan Social Security Institute)
JRC	Juventud Revolucionaria Copeyana (Copeyano Revolutionary Youth)
La Casona	Residence of the president
LAFTA	Latin American Free Trade Association
LAGOVEN	The operating affiliate of PDVSA formed out of Exxon's pre-nationalization sub-sidiary
llanero	Inhabitant of the llanos, or plains regions
LUZ	University of Zulia
MAN	Movimiento de Acción Nacional (Na-tional Action Movement)
maracucho	Resident of the second city of Mara-caibo
MAS	Movimiento al Socialismo (Movement Toward Socialism)
masistas	Members of the MAS
MARAVEN	The operating affiliate of PDVSA formed out of Shell's pre-nationalization sub-sidiary
MEP	Movimiento Electoral del Pueblo (People's Electoral Movement)

mepistas	Members of the MEP
MIR	Movimiento de la Izquierda Revolucionaria (Movement of the Revolutionary Left)
miristas	Members of the MIR
NIEO	New international economic order
OAS	Organization of American States
OAPEC	Organization of Arab Petroleum Exporting Countries
OCAI	Oficina Central de Asuntos Indigenas (Central Office of Indian Affairs)
OPEC	Organization of Petroleum Exporting Countries
OPINA	National Opinion (political movement)
Palacio Miraflores	Miraflores Place, the presidential palace
patrón	Literally patron, as involved in a master-servant relationship; *patrones* may be landlords, employers, political bosses, etc.
PCV	Partido Communista de Venezuela
PDVSA	Petróleos de Venezuela, S.A. (Venezuelan Petroleum Company), the nationalized oil holding company
PEQUIVEN	Petroquímica de Venezuela, S.A. (Venezuela Petrochemical Company)
plancha	Electoral slate of party candidates for congress, state and district council offices
PRODUZCA	Zulian Urban Development Corporation
PTJ	Policía Técnical Judicial (Judicial Technical Police)
rancho	Makeshift slum homes, in urban areas customarily constructed from discarded lumber, cartons, flattened tin cans, and the like
RECADI	Regimen de Cambio de Dinero, foreign exchange bureaucracy of the Central Bank

rosca	Network of old friends, families, and colleagues who support and are linked with one another in business, commerce, and/or politics
S.A.	Sociedad Anónima (incorporated)
SECONASEDE	Permanent secretariat of the National Council for Security and Defense
SELA	Sistema Económico Latinoamericano
SIDOR	Siderúrgica del Orinoco, C.A.(state steel corporation)
SIEX	Superintendencia de Inversión Extranjera (Superintendency of Foreign Investment)
situado	Constitutionally mandated grants from the national budget to state and local governments
STO	State-owned enterpise
SUTISS	Sindicato Unico de Trabajadores de la Industria Siderúrgica y Similares (Single Union of the Steel Industry)
UCV	Universidad Central de Venezuela (Central University of Venezuela)
URD	Unión Republicana Democrática (Democratic Republican Union)
urredistas	Members of the URD
USB	Universidad Simón Bolívar
VENALUM	Industria Venezolana de Aluminio, C.A. (Venezuelan Aluminum Industry, Inc.)
VIASA	Venezolana Internacional de Aviación, S.A. (Venezuelan International Airlines, Inc.)

VENEZUELA

NORTH
ATLANTIC
OCEAN

VENEZUELA   GUYANA
                        SURINAME
COLOMBIA

ECUADOR

BRAZIL

PERU

BOLIVIA

SOUTH
PACIFIC   PARAGUAY
OCEAN

URUGUAY

CHILE   ARGENTINA

SOUTH   SOUTH
AMERICA   ATLANTIC
                  OCEAN

Part One
The Environments

1

The Patterns of Venezuela's Past

John V. Lombardi

Located along the northernmost coast of the South American continent, Venezuela, a region shaped roughly like an inverted equilateral triangle, played a minor but nonetheless significant role in the grand drama of the conquest and settlement of America. For generations afterward, Venezuela searched for the riches that meant power, influence, and recognition within the Spanish imperial system.

Finally, in the second half of the eighteenth century, the region gained special prominence as a result of the economic experiment of the Basque-managed monopoly, the Caracas Company, and an imperial concern with the defense of the Caribbean. The innovative enthusiasm of Spain's Bourbon Monarchs, and especially their ministers, also brought Venezuela a dramatic reorganization of government institutions and economic administration. Accompanying this remarkable ferment came prosperity for some, reduced social status for others, and a sense of change—a relaxation of the traditions of authority, privilege, and control—for all. At the conclusion of this imperial reorganization, Venezuela found itself thrown into the midst of the long, expensive, and disruptive civil war for independence.

From a position of relative marginality within a declining Spanish Empire, the two or three generations following the establishment of the Caracas Company found themselves at the center of a continental civil war and became the agents for the dissolution of much of the Western world's greatest imperial venture. Venezuela provided a disproportionate number of soldiers and leaders for this effort, and paid a substantial price for political independence.

Throughout the next decades, Venezuela experienced only a brief moment of peace and tranquillity in the 1830s and 1840s when world markets for it crops provided sufficient economic prosperity to satisfy the country's competing factions. By the middle of the nineteenth century, however, Venezuela returned to a position at the fringes of Latin America's primary centers. While not quite marginal by comparison with some Central American countries, Venezuela's development in the postindependence era could never hope to keep pace with the dynamic growth of a Mexico or a divided but nonetheless powerful Argentina.

Pulled apart by the seemingly irreconcilable demands of local elites and North Atlantic commercial houses, Venezuela took most of the rest of the nineteenth century to guarantee foreign investors and merchants adequate security for their investments and to induce them to provide the credit and trade that spelled prosperity for the local economy. By the early twentieth century, Venezuela had accomplished this feat, but at a considerable cost to its internal development. Still, order had been established and maintained through the use of techniques perfected over at least a generation. Venezuela had learned how to pay its debts, how to keep its commercial products flowing to North Atlantic markets, and how to supply the imports needed by the local elite.

Venezuela, however, had little time to take much satisfaction in this smoothly functioning system, for the 1920s saw a petroleum boom sweep into the country, twisting and distorting an institutional structure designed to contain far less powerful forces. One short generation revised the terms of political, social, and economic exchange, modifying as well the country's physical landscape and economic possibilities.

Once again, some 150 years later, Columbus's Tierra de Gracia found itself at the center of hemispheric and global exchange. This time Venezuela appeared better prepared than ever before with the human and material resources needed to compete in a worldwide arena. If the opportunities for international preeminence and domestic felicity seemed abundant, the penalties for error or miscalculation had also increased. In the technologically sophisticated world of the 1960s, 1970s, and 1980s, with the media probing everywhere and the power of industrialized superpowers and financial conglomerates committed, Venezuela's fragile industrial, political, social, and economic institutions often seemed ill-equipped to meet the challenge of rapid economic development.

This chapter provides a historical counterpoint to the detailed contemporary analyses that follow. It locates Venezuelan democracy in space and time, tracing the major patterns of the country's history and outlining its principal structures. This understanding helps place the analyses of subsequent chapters within the context of Venezuela's history.

Venezuela's history resolves into three major patterns, each with an internal logic, a distinctive set of relationships, and a characteristic form of interaction with the outside world. Although these patterns emerge easily from the kaleidoscopic background of Venezuela's history, they prove more difficult to describe and analyze with precision. Part of this difficulty can be traced to the state of the historiography on a wide range of important topics. In spite of the efforts of Venezuelan and foreign scholars, much of Venezuela's past remains relatively opaque to our historical view. Although we may know with reasonable certainty something about the bare bones of the process, the names and public accomplishments of principal figures, the formal organization of institutions, and the visible structure of the economy, much of this process resists close inspection. The analysis presented here provides only preliminary hypotheses that will surely require adjustment and revision as our historiographical understanding increases.[1]

THE MAIN HISTORICAL PATTERNS

From the discovery of America and throughout the Spanish colonial period, Venezuela grew slowly until, with a final burst of energy and enthusiasm, it became a mature colonial society in the last quarter of the eighteenth century. The first Venezuelan pattern emerged early in the seventeenth century and prevailed well into the second half of the nineteenth century.

A second design appeared in response to a reorientation of the Venezuelan elite to serve the needs of an expanding North Atlantic commerce. This style, with its origins in the dying decades of the Spanish Empire in America, gained form and substance during the years of the first republican governments. In the last decades of the nineteenth century, the organizational genius and political subtlety of Antonio Guzmán Blanco brought this second pattern into its definitive form.

Once tuned to the North Atlantic market, Venezuela's internal rhythms became irrevocably tied to the development of the industrializing world; but with the discovery of commercially marketable petroleum in the 1920s, Venezuela once again had to change. While the petroleum boom encouraged Venezuela to pursue industrial development, and brought the country into a close interaction with North Atlantic political and social expectations, this third historical pattern has not yet stabilized. In part the time span involved has been rather short on a historical scale, and in part the new design, closely integrating Venezuela into the North Atlantic community, makes the country subject not only to the requirements of Venezuela's political and economic situation but also to the pressures that come from the more advanced and powerful societies of the developed world.[2]

In the rearrangements of Venezuela's history no new design ever completely obliterates a previous pattern. Motifs, styles, and elements of the mature colonial society appear in today's technologically sophisticated Venezuela. The old design blends easily into the new, and contemporary observers must take care to identify such enduring characteristics; for if such survivals remain vital, they must respond to some basic social or political requirement.

The identification and analysis of these constants in Venezuela's ever-changing past may well be the most important task for historians. Among these constants, one feature dominates every one of Venezuela's major patterns. From the middle of the seventeenth century to the present the primary focus of Venezuela's structures and functions never shifts from the central city of Caracas operating through an urban network consolidated in the late colonial period. Every significant activity required *caraqueño* validation before it could become part of the national plan.

Political revolution or social and economic changes, all could take place elsewhere; but before any of them could become part of the national destiny, they had to come under the influence and control of Caracas.

When Venezuela became integrated into the North Atlantic technological empire, or when earlier its elite reorganized itself to serve that community's needs for coffee and other materials, the country received this pattern via Caracas. For this reason no analytical framework can afford to ignore the primacy of Caracas in the process that created the Venezuela analyzed in detail by the contributors to this volume.[3]

THE MATURE COLONIAL SOCIETY: 1560–1830

Events in the sixteenth, seventeenth, and eighteenth centuries may seem remote and unrelated to the controversies of today and the planning for tomorrow, but a quick survey of the formation of Venezuela's urban landscape in the colonial period reveals a network of hamlets, villages, towns, and cities almost identical in form with the one displayed on Venezuela's modern road maps. To be sure, there are a few more places on modern map, many more people live within the boundaries of the network, and petroleum exploitation has created some urban conglomerates in unlikely places. When seen in a national perspective and in terms of communication, power, and wealth, today's network nonetheless closely matches the colonial network completed in Venezuela during the last years of the eighteenth century.

The two anchor points for the urban network during the first years of its formation in the sixteenth century—Cumaná-Margarita-Cubagua in the east and Coro in the west—served as the outposts for the generation of explorers and adventurers who spun out their years in the exhausting search for the gold of the imaginary chieftain, El Dorado. In Cumaná, the lure of fortune and the impulse for settlement came from the rich but quickly exhausted pearl fisheries beneath the waters of Margarita and Cubagua islands. Exploitative and extractive, the pearl fishing industry gave Spaniards reason enough to establish more or less permanent settlements along the mainland coast, places used to recruit pearl divers and to begin the introduction of cattle into the Venezuelan llanos (plains) through Barcelona and the Unare depression. With the early decline of the pearl boom before the middle of the seventeenth century, those Spaniards who stayed in the region turned inland and began a process of slow expansion and settlement that, with the addition of missionary towns built during the early eighteenth century, would complete the European conquest of eastern Venezuela above the Orinoco.

In the west, Coro, an early colonial capital, soon transferred to inland centers, such as El Tocuyo, the role of generator of settlement. The first generation of explorers, beginning under the control of the Welser commercial enterprise in Venezuela and then in Spanish-led expeditions, pushed into the Venezuelan Andes, crossed the trackless llanos to the Apure and beyond, and in general covered practically all of Venezuela west of the Unare and north of the Apure searching for gold or Indian settlements. By the beginning of the seventeenth century the descendants of those frenetic searchers for El Dorado had come to terms with an environment poor in precious minerals, devoid of large concentrations of tractable Indians, and rich in spectacular scenery well removed from the ports of call along the coast.

Proceeding in the typical Spanish manner, the European conquerors of Venezuela took control of the territory by creating towns linked together in the fledgling urban network we see filled out today. Because of its relative inaccessibility in the central mountains and the resistance of its determined native inhabitants, the Spaniards failed to settle the rich healthy valley of Caracas until near the end of the first expansion in the second half of the sixteenth century.

In the years following the founding of Caracas, the urban network expanded slowly until the early eighteenth century, when the missionary enthusiasm of Jesuits, Franciscans, Augustinians, and others spread villages throughout the plains and along the Orinoco and Apure river systems.[4]

Organizationally fragmented throughout much of the colonial period, the principal part of Venezuela focused on Caracas, an area outlined by the Unare and Apure rivers, the Segovia Highlands of Barquisimeto and El Tocuyo, and the Tocuyo River. Most of the Andes (Trujillo and Mérida) and the Coro-Maracaibo region, however, looked to Bogotá for direction and guidance. On the other side, to the east, Cumaná and Barcelona found their lines of communication drawn to the Caribbean centers of Puerto Rico and Santo Domingo. As the Caracas valleys and nearby regions prospered over the centuries from a trade based on cacao, indigo, and the cattle raised in the plains south of the mountains, their influence and commerce with the peripheral parts of Venezuela grew stronger. When the Bourbon monarchs chose to update their imperial organization in the late eighteenth century, they consolidated the area of present-day Venezuela into a single jurisdiction headed by an administration located in Caracas.[5]

In the last half of the eighteenth century, the Venezuelan colonial outpost finally came of age, and the pattern consolidated during that time has had a strong influence on the course of Venezuelan history. The mature colonial society of late eighteenth-century Venezuela coalesced around the region's central city. In an institutional sense, the creation of the captaincy-general of Venezuela and the audiencia or royal court—bureaucratic, military, and judicial constructs that brought together into unified administrative control the semiindependent provinces of the region—provided the most important symbols of this maturity. The audiencia and the captaincy-general tied the Cumaná, Maracaibo, and San Cristóbal-Merida-Trujillo regions firmly into the management bureaucracy of Caracas.

The consolidation of Venezuela around Caracas involved more than defense, administration, and justice. It also included fiscal and financial matters through the creation of an intendancy and an ecclesiastical administration with the elevation of Caracas to an archiepiscopal see including the bishoprics of Mérida de Maracaibo and Guayana.

This reordering of Venezuela's institutional structure offers a convenient series of symbols testifying to the high degree of complexity reached by the region, its integrated trade network, and its northward, Caribbean export orientation. The administrative and economic reforms of this period reinforced the centralizing tendency of Caracas. To be sure, not all regional identity disappeared, nor did the domination of Caracas sit well with the rich and powerful in other cities. But whatever their resentments or dreams of regional autonomy, no place in Venezuela could determine its destiny independently of the central city; no regional coalition could dominate the country except from within and through the city of Caracas.[6]

If the mature colonial society can be defined in one dimension by reference to an institutional structure managed by a central city, it can also be measured by its social and demographic structure. Thanks to a perennial shortage of labor and the resulting commerce in African slaves, blacks or pardos equaled almost 60 percent of the mature colonial society's population. Whites provided most of the elite and filled influential posts in the administrative bureaucracy.

Although the 25 percent of the population labeled white may have controlled an overwhelming proportion of the region's property, power, and privilege, by the late eighteenth century they nonetheless saw their social position weakened from above and attacked from below. Blacks, slave and free, appeared to be losing the traditional respect for the elite; some successful mulattoes even bought into the privileges and position formerly reserved only for whites. Equally disturbing, the Spanish metropolitan authorities gave little encouragement to the whites in their exclusivist pretensions and in some instances even supported the blacks' bid for social improvement.

Although the discussions of social tension in the mature colonial society used racial terms, the substance of the argument involved control of and access to important material resources. In earlier times, before the prosperity and growing complexity of Venezuela's agricultural and cattle-raising enterprises demanded more elaborate modes of organization, social control and structure were more easily managed. The expanded economy of the late eighteenth and early nineteenth centuries, and the growing administrative bureaucracy in Caracas, made the maintenance of old norms increasingly difficult. Some of the less privileged but prosperous individuals of darker color found possibilities for display and advantage in newly established militia companies. Others, whose skin color and wealth permitted, passed into the white category through the purchase of a royal patent certifying their newfound whiteness. Thus one of the characteristics of the mature colonial society was its social tension between white and black, a tension expressed in racial terms that reflected the majority's desire to participate in the minority's control of land, money, and other resources.[7]

The independence wars sorely tested Venezuela's fragile and late maturing institutional structure. In the epic struggle that liberated South America from Spanish control, Venezuela and Venezuelans contributed enormous stores of resources and sacrificed thousands of men. Even though Venezuela provided much of the treasure, soldiers, and officers for Simón Bolívar's crusade to create a new American empire, Venezuela itself refused to unite to follow the Caracas elite into independence. Blacks, free and slave alike, showed little interest in the war and less in liberating the white elite from Spanish rule. Most blacks recognized that any improvements in their condition that had occurred during the generation prior to independence had come principally from Spain and Spanish officials, not from the creole landlords who so jealously defended their privileges. Regional elites, resenting Caracas's assumption of leadership, refused to join the crusade. As a result, the *caraqueño* white elite found it necessary to reconquer much of its own territory before Bolívar's grand American design could be attempted elsewhere.[8]

Even though the analysis of the course and consequences of Venezuelan independence is beyond the scope of this chapter, this greatest of all Venezuelan civil wars altered the Venezuelan pattern. In the mature colonial society before the war, conflicts and disputes at all levels were settled through an elaborate, formal, and bureaucratized system. Whatever the problem—disagreements over land or authority, precedence and honor, concessions or profits—a formal procedure existed to resolve it. With remarkably few exceptions, individuals in this society accepted the constraints of the system and worked to maximize their advantages within the rules.

The existence of such a system does not, of course, imply that it treated people fairly, remained incorruptible, or protected the helpless. Frequently it did none of these. For all its failings and injustices, however, the system peacefully managed a complex society for several centuries. The wars of independence destroyed this system in the clash of bandit armies and the confiscation and reallocation of property. After ten to fifteen years of instability, violence, and destruction, old methods of defining legitimacy and right had been replaced by a new system based almost entirely on force and the favor of those who controlled force.

This modification of the colonial order came as a logical extension of the militarization of political authority, the other major contribution of independence to Venezuelan society. Under colonial rule, power and authority came from within an essentially civilian context, the symbol of Spanish authority being the notary and the lawyer, not the caudillo or instant general. Colonial officials came and went, their abuses might be punished and their successes rewarded, but whatever the issue, it took a lawyer or a notary or perhaps even a cleric to resolve it. Imperial Spanish military officers rarely ruled by virtue of their military experience alone, and then usually only during the defense of a frontier or coastline. Spanish colonials planned on appealing the injustices of a bad magistrate, not to the nearest petty chieftain but to the royal courts or the king's ministers. They took their neighbors' property, not with armed troops but with legal writs. They might attempt to bribe judges and officials but not remove or replace them by force.[9]

By 1830, then, the mature colonial society remained in many ways much as it had been in 1810. But while the organizing themes provided by the Spanish imperium had changed—mostly in terms of lower-level whites' taking positions previously occupied by higher-level whites—the basic pattern of resource allocation and control remained. The elite kept the independence movement from becoming a social war, although only by a small margin. The years of turmoil also reinforced the central role of Caracas, proving over and over that control of Venezuela meant control of Caracas. If the substructure of this new republic remained in the pattern generated by the mature colonial society, new forces directed that society toward different ends using different means.

THE COMMERCIAL-BUREAUCRATIC OUTPOST: 1830-1920

Venezuela's first century of independence often appeared as a chaotic, senseless struggle of picturesque nomad warriors, a shifting mosaic of petty conflicts and personal rivalries. Beneath the confusion of changing presidents, constitutional revisions, and erudite propaganda campaigns, Venezuela worked toward the reformation of its mature colonial society to cope with the new demands placed on the old organization by the gradual integration of Venezuela into the North Atlantic commercial system.

Venezuela, within this system, provided certain agricultural commodities to the rapidly industrializing nations in exchange for a mixed package of finished goods produced abroad. The control of this trade remained in the hands of entrepreneurs, financiers, and companies in the North Atlantic community, and Venezuela's elite had to adjust to the requirements of the new relationships. Because adjustments in the pattern of this mature colonial society could only benefit some at the expense of others, much of the civil strife characteristic of the nineteenth century can be traced to a contest over the allocation of burdens and benefits required by Venezuela's direct involvement in world trade.

The new system worked out during these years developed in response to external conditions defined by northern Europeans and implemented by Venezuelans. The mature colonial society had also come from outside, pressed on Venezuela and the rest of Spanish America during Spain's brief but spectacular moment of domination in the Western world, even though the centuries of gradual adjustment that turned the descendants of Spanish conquerors into Venezuelan creole elites tend to obscure the external source of Venezuela's colonial pattern. The success of the independence movement opened the mature colonial society to the new demands of North Atlantic commerce with little time for careful preparation.

In local terms, the reorientation required two or three stages to reach a logical conclusion by the beginning of the twentieth century. The adjustments of the first postindependence generation depended on a charismatic military chieftain, usually a hero from the wars for independence and always capable of rallying sizable groups of people to his standard in time of domestic turmoil. The Venezuelan hero from this mold took the shape of General José Antonio Páez. From obscure beginnings in the llanos during the years prior to 1810, Páez rose during independence to become the Venezuelan caudillo par excellence: military hero, master of the Venezuelan llaneros (plainsmen), arbiter of disputes between lesser chiefs, and guarantor of Venezuela's territorial integrity.

Until the 1850s this man symbolized the Venezuelan struggle to create and stabilize the new pattern required by the consequences of political independence and participation in modern world trade.

Although no attempt is made here at detailed chronological coverage, several political controversies help highlight the process taking place in Venezuela, and we may suppose elsewhere in Latin America, throughout the nineteenth century.[10]

During the first years after independence, much conflict turned on managing the advantages that could be derived from the new direct participation in North Atlantic trade. Between 1830 and at least 1850 this relationship involved one major crop: coffee. The external demand for coffee had raised its price to a favorable level for Venezuelan producers, but before profits could be reaped, certain conditions had to be met. Venezuela had to maintain peace and internal order if workers were to plant trees and harvest coffee. Merchants and planters needed credit, for few Venezuelans had the money to pay workers or finance coffee production. General Páez, clearly understanding the essentials of these requirements, accepted responsibility for maintaining peace and tranquility and wisely delegated the arrangement of credit and trade to the Caracas elite.

In the euphoric prosperity of the postwar years, Venezuela's landowners pledged their properties to commercial houses in exchange for the credit they needed to produce the coffee that would make them rich. Once the cycle of credit-financed export crop production began, a series of built-in consequences operated throughout Venezuelan society. Those supplying credit had little interest in Venezuela except for the planter's ability to pay his debts and provide sufficient quantities of coffee and other commodities at favorable prices.

In the early years, say, between 1830 and 1840, everyone benefited from the new arrangement. Páez maintained the peace. The Caracas elite quickly diversified into an active and qualified commercial bureaucracy serving as an intermediary between the sources of finance and commodity speculation and the producers of coffee, cacao, or hides. The planters spent borrowed fortunes rebuilding plantations and harvesting coffee. The Venezuelan elite revised an institutional structure inherited from the mature colonial society to conform to the requirements of North Atlantic commerce. Taxes, tariffs, and debt laws all took the form most likely to benefit the interests fueling the postwar prosperity.[11]

Venezuela, reacting to opportunities presented from abroad, controlled neither the terms nor the conditions of its participation in North Atlantic trade. When a shift in the world commodity market in the late 1830s and early 1840s brought the price of coffee down, Venezuelan coffee growers often found themselves unable to pay their debts or escape from the consequences of their overextension. Their government, structured to maintain order and guarantee the integrity of commercial contracts, offered little support, and the segment of the local elite serving as intermediaries for international trade found itself enforcing foreclosures and debt procedures against their friends and relatives in the landowning elite.

As foreign investors lost interest in Venezuela because of low returns on coffee and uncertain debt payments, the local elite fell to fighting among themselves over the best remedies for their situation. In Venezuela the years 1850–70 saw a readjustment in the organization of the local elites. During the 20 years of intermittent civil war and internal disorder, the commercial-bureaucratic pattern sketched in during Páez's ascendancy passed through several variations until another strongman stabilized it for several decades after 1865.[12]

General-President Antonio Guzmán Blanco possessed ideal credentials. A member of the Caracas elite, he grew to adulthood amidst the intense conflicts of the 1830s and 1840s over the best way to manage Venezuela's participation in North Atlantic commerce. His father Antonio Leocadio Guzmán spoke eloquently, if not always consistently, in favor of landowners and coffee growers and even championed an abortive social revolution in the 1840s. The son, Antonio Guzmán Blanco, through extensive travel and residence in Europe, especially France, improved his perspective on world affairs and educated himself in the intricacies of international commerce and finance. His own fortune, built in the service of his country, reflected a profound grasp of the details of international business. His participation in Venezuela's long civil unrest, known as the Federal Wars (1858–63), gave him the skills to deal with local reality. From every perspective,

Antonio Guzmán Blanco represented the ideal intermediary between the North Atlantic commercial centers and Venezuela.

Guzmán Blanco's task became easier as the Federal Wars exhausted and impoverished the contending factions. With the military control of Venezuela firmly in his hands after 1863, the "Civilizing Autocrat" set about reshaping Venezuela. The conditions influencing Guzmán Blanco's Venezuela differed very little from those facing General Páez's a generation earlier, but Guzmán Blanco's experience better equipped him to play the role of intermediary; he knew exactly how to create optimal conditions for such a role. Through a series of compromises and arrangements, he restored internal tranquility. Fully aware that North Atlantic commercial houses cared little about the domestic political balance within peripheral states, Guzmán Blanco permitted his regional satraps a relatively free hand as long as they delivered security of property and civil order. He guaranteed them a share of the lucrative spoils of commerce and trade, mostly in the form of graft and public works patronage, and in return they supported his regime.

With civil order secured, Venezuela could deliver its crops to the world market so that the country's landowning and bureaucratic elites would prosper. Through skillful operations in North Atlantic money markets, Antonio Guzmán Blanco gained the resources to finance Venezuelan recovery. Under this remarkable leader, landowners, merchants, financiers, and perhaps even a few peasants found peace and prosperity, and foreign merchants and lenders found security for investments, reasonable prices for commodities, and attractive profits for manufactured goods. In line with this approach, Guzmán Blanco also initiated a wide-ranging program of public works and beautification projects, every one of which made Venezuela appear as a more efficient provider of useful crops and more sophisticated market for manufactured goods.[13]

Given Venezuela's fragile political and institutional structures and the relative newness of the bureaucratic-commercial pattern—especially its dependence on the skills of a single strong-man—it is no wonder that Guzmán Blanco's departure in the late 1880s should have caused serious internal problems. In some ways, his self-imposed exile in Europe was the ultimate irony. Starting out as a small-scale caudillo dedicated to the conversion of his country to the efficient service of the North Atlantic community, Guzmán Blanco became so much a part of that community that he could no longer bear the thought of finishing his life amidst the imitation luxuries and reflected splendor of his native land.

If Antonio Guzmán Blanco superseded his intermediary role to become what he imitated, many of his countrymen had lesser dreams, and after a series of unedifying squabbles over the management of Venezuela, a new national symbol emerged at the turn of the century in the person of Juan Vicente Gómez, a shrewd and canny operator unimpressed with the sophisticated pleasures of such commercial centers as Paris, London, and New York and dedicated to the prosperity of Venezuela as reflected in his welfare and that of his family and friends.[14] Juan Vicente Gómez took the essential relationships inherent in Antonio Guzmán Blanco's regime and by applying a rigorous and ruthless logic, aided by a monopoly on communications and military technology, developed them to their conclusion. Along with the brutality and repression of his system, Goméz fixed the commercial-bureaucratic pattern in its final form before Venezuela succumbed to the overwhelming pressure of the petroleum-based technological imperium.

At the center of the commercial-bureaucratic pattern, in either the Antonio Guzmán Blanco or the Juan Vicente Gómez version, Caracas maintained and increased its central functions. Measured by any variable or mix of variables—population, revenues, functions, power, elites, or culture—Caracas gained disproportionately throughout the century after independence. If the civil disorders of the nineteenth century proved nothing else, they demonstrated time and time again the centrality of Caracas to Venezuela. Why this should have been so is relatively easy to understand.

Nineteenth-century Venezuela, as a part of the North Atlantic system, produced certain commodities, exchanged them for a limited package of manufactured goods, and in general served the commercial needs of the industrializing and industrialized nations. No member of the Atlantic community had much interest in the direct supervision or manipulation of Venezuela's social or political system, largely because the cost would have greatly exceeded the return, and partly because such complex control mechanisms were unnecessary anyway.

With the end of Spanish rule of this mature colonial society in the first half of the nineteenth century, Venezuela, or at least the local elites, desperately wanted to become a part of the North Atlantic community. For the nineteenth-century Venezuelan man of property, ability, or ambition, the only alternative to peripheral participation in this community was an unacceptable isolation. Through a long and often painful process, wasteful of lives and resources, Venezuela's controlled class settled their internal conflicts and fixed on a political and economic system centered on the bureaucratic establishment in Caracas. The urban nexus provided successive local leaders with the administrative and financial apparatus needed to maintain the country's vital connection to world trade and commerce. The North Atlantic center, in turn, had no interest in discriminating between rival urban bureaucracies and probably judged correctly that Venezuela could barely support one full-service capital city, certainly not two.

Caracas attracted foreign merchants and investors who transacted their business with local agents. Regional caudillos captured the city from time to time, exacting tribute but never seriously damaging the administrative machinery. In times of widespread civil unrest, international commerce withdrew until Venezuelans reestablished order, recognized outstanding debts, and promised a return to acceptable commercial behavior. Venezuelans in search of advancement, preference, prosperity, or advantage came to the city. Many stayed, of course, but others returned to their provincial enclaves with the best solution Caracas could provide.

The increasing stability of the commercial-bureaucratic pattern centered on Caracas during the course of the nineteenth century carried a variety of subsidiary developments. Those who settled in Caracas came because they wanted to participate in the benefits accompanying close ties to the North Atlantic center. They brought to this submetropolitan capital as many amenities as they could afford, and because Venezuela could afford very few, Caracas rarely had advantages to share with the rest of the country. University education, art, culture, social services, architectural and urbanistic grandeur—whatever the North Atlantic imitation— Caracas monopolized it to an ever-growing degree. As Caracas acquired the trappings of modernity while the rest of the country stayed much the same, the distance separating metropolis from province grew greater, until no other place could compare with the capital.[15]

Venezuela's commercial-bureaucratic system, for all its utility and rationality, could not withstand the changes brought to the country by the petroleum boom, especially coupled with the post–World War II technological revolution. After Juan Vicente Gómez, a new pattern had to emerge.

THE TECHNOLOGICAL EMPIRE: 1920–PRESENT

For most, contemporary Venezuela exists for, and is defined by, oil, and few pause to reflect on the newness of a petroleum bonanza now but a few generations old. Already, however, Venezuela has readjusted its commercial-bureaucratic structures to meet the new demands brought by close involvement with the North Atlantic technological and industrial world.

In the early years of the oil boom, General Juan Vicente Gómez cushioned the impact of massive foreign intervention in Venezuelan affairs by manipulating the commercial-bureaucratic pattern. His arrangement of the forces created during the century of independence since 1820 could barely contain the complexities and imperatives of the early stages of a technological empire forced on Venezuela by the opportunity of natural resources. As a result, there began another shifting, a redesign promising a new, complex, modern, and up-to-date Venezuela.

From one perspective, Gómez and his political successors needed to bring Venezuela rapidly into a closer relationship with the industrial societies. In less frantic times, Venezuela had produced its commodities in whatever old-fashioned and in-efficient way the local elite chose, with the costs of inefficiency paid by Venezuelans. The highly sophisticated process of petroleum exploitation, however, proved incompatible with the primitive technology available throughout most of the country.

So the consumers of energy sent their experts to establish enclaves at the necessary places to produce oil in sufficient quantities and with adequate efficiency. If the operation were to succeed, Venezuela, or at least certain parts of the bureaucratic and material subcultures, had to be brought up to the standards of the technological imperium. Furthermore, the oil bonanza created such incredible wealth and opportunity for the members of Venezuela's elite favorably situated in the national capital that these newly rich came to demand a higher level of comfort and modernity in their city. This elite could well afford to import all the external and some of the structural features of a developed country's existence.[16]

As every student of post-Gómez Venezuela has noticed, one of the striking consequences of the petroleum boom has been a dramatic expansion of Caracas. The city had prospered and grown as the administrator of the commercial bureaucracy required throughout the nineteenth century. After 1925 it blossomed into an imperial subcapital complete with industry, social services, mass transportation and communications, and a middle class grown increasingly sophisticated. As Caracas acquired the myriad advantages of being the administrative center of a technologically complex society, the poor, the rich, and the ambitious flocked to the capital in search of opportunities unavailable elsewhere in the republic.[17]

If Caracas quickly took on the attributes of modern imperial centers such as Los Angeles or Houston, its structures for conflict resolution and administration yielded to the modern style more slowly. General Gómez had built well when he consolidated the nineteenth-century pattern. After his death in 1935 his successors continued his system for almost a decade. In part, their success in delaying changes in the governing structure can be traced to their ability to satisfy the needs of the North Atlantic technocrats who managed the empire's oil resources. Concessions, public tranquility, and low taxes permitted the oil consortia to extract resources and profits and the Venezuelan elite to prosper.

Ironically, it proved impossible to modernize Venezuela in the petroleum enclaves without also permitting local entrepreneurs to profit from the growth of the technological society. As Venezuela acquired the wealth to purchase more and more of the North Atlantic community's goods and services, a host of imitation industries emerged within Venezuela, controlled from the core societies, but managed more and more by members of the growing local elites and the emerging middle class.

The dizzying pace of change accompanied by the elaborate

communications technology available in the mid-twentieth century made governments designed to manage the commercial-bureaucratic system increasingly untenable. The traditional military coalitions responded to change too slowly. Modern communications techniques provided opposition groups with a range of new, alternative tactics. The growing concentration of people in cities and industrial centers made mass populist movements possible, and sophisticated propaganda permitted opposition groups relatively free and rapid access to the population at large.

Venezuela's closer integration into the North Atlantic community implied increased intervention by foreign interest groups in Venezuela's internal affairs. Some of these interventions proposed the improvement of Venezuela as a market for manufactures and as a locus for capital investment. Others saw Venezuela's internal politics as a means of furthering international political goals. Whatever the cause, Venezuela's internal affairs rapidly became closely tied to, influenced by, and imitative of the politics of the principal industrial societies, while still maintaining many features of the country's traditional political patterns.[18]

Perhaps the best example of this occurred with the regime of General Marcos Pérez Jiménez. Carried to national prominence by a coup designed to bring a North Atlantic-style democratic government to Venezuela, Pérez Jiménez instituted a regime in 1952 patterned partly on Juan Vicente Gómez's authoritarianism and partly on Antonio Guzmán Blanco's developmentalism.

He employed all the technological resources of his environment to suppress and control Venezuela, he promised as much as possible to North Atlantic interests, but he operated his government in an anachronistic nineteenth-century style. He spent a fortune in petroleum revenue to modernize Caracas, encouraged massive foreign immigration to create a new Venezuela, and exalted the military establishment in an attempt to keep the peace.

Most of the characteristics of his regime are hauntingly familiar to students of Antonio Guzmán Blanco's grand design, but thanks to oil, Pérez Jiménez had the resources to put most of the plan into effect. In less complex times, this political throwback might have survived, but the newly created Venezuelan technological elite, the petroleum enclave society, and the Caracas masses put up with the economic extravagance and political regression represented by Pérez Jiménez for less than six years, when, in 1958, a coalition of military officers and concerned civilians joined to terminate the nostalgic interlude.

Since the fall of Pérez Jiménez, Venezuela has been restructuring its characteristic pattern. Two major variants of the technological society seem to be competing for dominance. One is based on a form of democratic conflict resolution and resource allocation. Within this pattern, the technologically capable new Caracas elite, dedicated to bringing Venezuela fully into the North Atlantic core as an equal partner, provides the primary design. A major element here has involved transferring the control of natural resources exploitation from foreign corporations to the local elite, who use those resources to purchase a place in the modern industrialized world.

Because this plan requires continuing high petroleum prices and a dynamic world economy, the events of the early 1980s have made it painfully obvious that success depends on petroleum revenues sufficient to pay the cost of constructing the new society. While Venezuela's progress had indeed been spectacular, the plan has saddled the country with an exaggerated continuing cost that must be borne at least until Venezuela fixes its place among industrialized societies. Because the country has worked almost entirely in a consumption mode, importing a tremendous amount of its material, social, and cultural goods, changes in the external demand for petroleum and declines in the world economy have a major and immediate impact. Many dimensions of this dilemma, made more obvious by recent events, are discussed extensively elsewhere.[19]

If the democratic conflict-resolution pattern dissolves under the pressure of popular unrest brought on by a collapse of the country's ambitious and expensive economic development plans, Venezuela could well turn to an authoritarian political system administered by a single political party or the military. The purpose of such a system would be the same, to keep Venezuela a part of the industrialized world, but with only minimal pretensions of democratic forms and styles. Such a pattern might be characterized by high standards of living for a reduced elite, the maintenance of serious technological imbalances among Venezuela's various regions, and the employment of petroleum revenues to maintain public order and subsidize an elite lifestyle.

In some ways this second variant would appear easier to maintain and cheaper to finance. However, because the technologically sophisticated middle class and elite in Venezuela have successfully supported the first, or democratic, variant in the face of a host of serious challenges, we may never see the authoritarian version.[20]

The present Venezuela design is by no means clear enough to permit firm pronouncements about developments to come. Much of what happens depends on rearrangements now taking place in the industrialized world. Should this dominant world pattern, which has shaped Venezuelan affairs for a century and a half, dissolve into some other arrangement of trade, commerce, or industry in which Venezuela's petroleum represents less value, the effects on Venezuela would be difficult to predict. Nevertheless, the overview of Venezuela's historical patterning presented here, in conjunction with the analyses that follow, should permit a careful reader to speculate about Venezuela's future with the best chance of success possible in our uncertain world.

NOTES

1.Students interested in an introduction to Venezuelan historiography could begin with John V. Lombardi et al., *Venezuelan History: A Comprehensive Working Bibliography* (Boston: G. K. Hall, 1977). General histories of Venezuela abound. The two classics are José Gil Fortoul, *Historia constitucional de Venezuela*, 5th ed., 3 vols. (Caracas: Librería Piñango, 1967), and Francisco González Guinán, *Historia contemporanea de Venezuela*, 15 vols. (Caracas: Presidencia de la República, 1954). An especially useful one-volume survey of Venezuela's past is J. L. Salcedo Bastardo, *Historia fundamental de Venezuela*, 7th ed. (Caracas: Fundación Gran Mariscal de Ayacucho, 1977). A more recent treatment is John V. Lombardi, *Venezuela: The Search for Order, the Dream of Progress* (New York: Oxford University Press, 1982). For a review of Venezuelan historiography, see Germán Carrera Damas, *Historia de la historiografía venezolana (textos para su estudio)* (Caracas: Universidad Central de Venezuela [UCV], 1961). General bibliographical guides to Venezuelan history are rare, but the work of Manuel Sequndo Sánchez, *Obras*, 2 vols. (Caracas: Banco Central de Venezuela 1964), is the classic. See also R. J. Lovera de-Sola, *Guía para el estudio de la historia de Venezuela* (Caracas: Academia Nacional de la Historia [ANH], 1982), and Angelina Lemmo

B., *Historiografía colonial de Venezuela* (Caracas: UCV, 1977). For specialized bibliographical guides, see Pedro Grases, *Investigaciones bibliográficas* 2 vols. (Caracas: Ministerio de Educación, 1968).

2. In preparing this chapter I have been greatly aided by the work of the research group headed by Germán Carrera Damas of the Centro de Estudios del Desarrollo (CENDES) of the UCV, CENDES, *Formación histórico-social de América Latina* (Caracas: UCV, 1982).

3.Caracas has long fascinated scholars. An ambitious effort is the multi-volume *Estudio de Caracas*, 15 vols. (Caracas: UCV, 1967–73), a project still underway. Most of these volumes deal with aspects of the modern city, but volume 2, *Marco histórico. Technología, economía y actitudes hacia el trabajo*, has some valuable historical material. See "Principales momentos del desarrollo histórico de Caracas," directed by Germán Carrera Damas, pp. 23–102. Other perspectives on the city can be seen in Antonio Arellano Moreno, *Caracas: su evolución y su régimen legal* (Caracas: Cuatricentenario de Caracas, 1967), and José Antonio de Armas Chitty, *Caracas: Origen y trayectoria de una cuidad*, 2 vols. (Caracas: Fundación Creole, 1967). The literature on various aspects of the history of Caracas is extensive, and some of the important and representative items are cited in later notes.

4. Venezuelan historians have been much taken with their colonial past, especially the periods of conquest and settlement and the missionary labors of the religious orders. Thanks to the Academia Nacional de la Historia's ambitious publications program, a series of valuable works on this period exists, including Pedro de Aguado, *Recopilación historial de Venezuela*, 2 vols. (Caracas: Academia Nacional de la Historia [ANH], 1963); Antonio Arellano Moreno, ed., *Relaciones geográficas de Venezuela* (Caracas: ANH, 1964); Buenaventura de Carrocera, *Misión de los capuchinos en Cumaná*, 3 vols. (Caracas: ANH, 1968); Joseph Cassani, *Historia de la provincia de la Compañia de Jesús del Nuevo Reino de Granada en la América* (Caracas: ANH, 1967); Antonio Caulín, *Historia de la Nueva Andalucía*, 2 vols. (Caracas: ANH, 1966); Lino Gómez Canedo, ed., *Las misiones de Píritu: documentos para su historia*, 2 vols. (Caracas: ANH, 1967); José Oviedo y Baños, *Historia de la conquista y población de la provincia de Venezuela* (Caracas: Ediciones Ariel, 1967).

For an excellent panoramic survey of Venezuela's formation with emphasis on human geography, see Pablo Vila et al., *Georgrafía de Venezuela*, 2 vols. (Caracas: Ministerio de Educación, 1960, 1965). Also helpful is Pablo Vila's *Visiones geohistóricas de Venezuela* (Caracas: Ministerio de Educación, 1969). For the preconquest period, see Angelina Lemmo B., *Esquema de estudio para la historia indígena de América* (Caracas: UCV, 1980). On the Welser episode, see Juan Friede, *Los Welser en la conquista de Venezuela* (Caracas: Ediciones Edime, 1961). The conquest and colonization of the Caracas valleys has stimulated a remarkable literature. Much of it focuses on disputes over the dates and personalities involved in the initial founding of the city. For some representative examples, see Manuel Pinto C., ed., *Los primeros vecinos de Caracas: recopilación documental* (Caracas: Cuatricentenario de Caracas, 1966); Demetrio Ramos Pérez, *La fundación de Caracas y el desarrollo de una fecunda polémica* (Caracas: Italgráfica, 1967); and Pedro Manuel Arcays U., *El cabildo de Caracas: período de la colonia*, 2nd ed. (Caracas: Libería Historia, 1968). On the El Dorado myth as an ingredient in the conquest mentality, see Demetrio Ramos Pérez, *El mito del dorado: su génesis y proceso. Con el Discovery de Walter Raleigh y otros papeles doradistas* (Caracas: ANH, 1973). A useful account of Indian resources and their exploitation is still Eduardo Arcila Farías, *El régimen de la encomienda en Venezuela*, 2nd ed. (Caracas: UCV, 1966).

5. Some general studies of Venezuela's colonial period may provide supplementary information of value. See, for example, Federico Brito Figueroa, *Historia económica y social de Venezuela: una estructura para su estudio*, 2 vols. (Caracas: UCV, 1966), and Jerónimo Martínez Mendoza, *Venezuela colonial: investigaciones y noticias para el conocimiento de su historia* (Caracas: Editorial Arte, 1965). Also interesting are Guillermo Morón, *Historia de Venezuela*, 5 vols. (Caracas: Italgráfica, 1971), and the elaborate critique in Angelina Lemmo, *De como se desmorona la historia* (Caracas: UCV, 1973).

6. On the administration reorganization of the late eighteenth century, see Caracciolo Parra Pérez, *El régimen español en Venezuela: estudio histórico*, 2nd ed. (Madrid: Cultura Hispánica, 1964); José L. Sucre Reyes, *La capitanía general de Venezuela* (Barcelona: Editorial R. M., 1969); Manuel Nunes Dias, *El Real Consulado de Caracas (1793-1810)* (Caracas: ANH, 1971); *Documentos para la historia de la iglesia colonial en Venezuela*, 2 vols. (Caracas: ANH, 1965); and Nicolás Eugenio Navarro, *Anales eclesiásticos venezolanos*, 2nd ed. (Caracas: Tipografía Americana, 1951). The first bishopric of Venezuela was founded in 1531 in Coro. In 1652, Caracas officially became the see. Margarita and Cumaná became part of the bishopric of Puerto Rico in 1588, Guayana joined in 1624-25. The bishopric of Mérida de Maracaibo dates from 1777 and that of Guayana from 1793. In 1804, Caracas became the seat of the archbishopric. The captaincy-general came into being by virtue of royal order in 1777 that included most of all of present-day Venezuela. The intendency dates from 1776. Caracas received a royal court or audiencia in 1786 and a consulado in 1793. Helpful for this period are Guillermo Boza, *Estructura y cambio en Venezuela colonial* (Caracas: Fondo Editorial Común, 1973), and Raúl Díaz Legórburu, *La Capitanía general de Venezuela (estudio histórico y documental)* (Caracas: Presidencia de la República, 1977). On the role of the Caracas Company, see Roland D. Hussey, *La Compañía de Caracas (1728-1784)* (Caracas: Banco Central de Venezuela, 1962).

7. Venezuela's social history has received considerable attention. On the history of Venezuela's slave system in the colonial period, see Miguel Acosta Saignes, *Vida de los esclavos negros en Venezuela* (Caracas: Ediciones Hespérides, 1967), and Ermila Troconís de Veracoechea, *Documentos para el estudio de los esclavos negros en Venezuela* (Caracas: ANH, 1969). Also valuable is Carlos Siso Maury, *La formación del pueblo venezolano (estudios sociológicos)*, 2 vols. (Madrid: García Enciso, 1953). Although much of our information on the racial tensions contained by colonial social structure comes from discussions during the independence period, James F. King's pioneer work provides a glimpse into the colonial mind in "A Royalist View of the Colored Castes in the Venezuelan War of Independence," *Hispanic American Historical Review* 33 (1953): 526-37. See also Pedro M. Arcaya, *Insurrección de los negros de la serranía de Coro* (Caracas: Panamerican Institute of Geography and History, 1949). The demographic

information on the colonial period has been incomplete at best. There are two major sources of generalizations about Venezuela's colonial population. The most frequently cited are the figures offered by Alexander von Humboldt, *Viaje a las regiones equinocciales del nuevo continente*, 5 vols. (Caracas: Ministerio de Educación, 1956). More detailed estimates can be derived from the records of Bishop Mariano Martí's visit to the parishes of his diocese in the last quarter of the eighteenth century: *Documentos relativos a su vista pastoral de la diócesis de Caracas (1771-1784)*, 7 vols. (Caracas: ANH, 1969), and Pablo Vila, *El Obispo Martí*, 2 vols. (Caracas: UCV, 1980-81). Some more detailed estimates are available in John V. Lombardi, *People and Places in Colonial Venezuela* (Bloomington: Indiana University Press, 1976).

8. Next to the colonial discovery and settlement, few topics claim such overwhelming historiographical interest for Venezuelans as the independence movement. One of the key figures has been Bolívar. For an illuminating study of the Bolivarian myth and its influence on Venezuelan historiography, see Germán Carrera Damas, *El culto a Bolívar: esbozo para un estudio de la historia de las ideas en Venezuela*, 2nd ed. (Caracas: UCV, 1973). The two-hundredth anniversary of Bolívar's birth in 1983 provided an opportunity for more publications related to that great Venezuelan hero. For a taste of that literature, see Manuel Pérez Vila, *Símon Bolívar (1783-1830): Bibliografía básica* (Bogotá: Centro Regional para el Fomento del Libro, 1983), and Simón Bolívar, *Al esperanza del universo* (Paris: UNESCO, 1983). Thanks to the Academia Nacional de la Historia, scholars have more than 50 volumes of texts and analyses available on the independence period. Especially valuable in that collection is Caracciolo Parra Pérez, *Historia de la Primera República de Venezuela*, 2nd ed., 2 vols. (Caracas: ANH, 1959). An excellent guide to independence historiography is in Pedro Grases and Manuel Pérez Vila, "Gran Columbia: referencias relatives a la bibliografía sobre el período emancipador en los paises grancolombianos (desde 1949)," *Anuario de Estudios Americano* 21 (1964): 733-77. An excellent review of the social aspects of independence is in Charles C. Griffin, *Los temas sociales y económicos en la época de la independencia* (Caracas: Fundación John Boulton and Fundación Eugenio Mendoza, 1962). For a discussion of the role of slaves and blacks in the independence movement, see John V. Lombardi, "Los esclavos negros en las guerras venezolanas de la independencia," *Cultura Universitaria* (Caracas) 93 (1966): 153-68. No survey of Venezuelan independence would be complete without mention of the work of Venezuela's foremost Bolivarianist, Vicente Lecuna. See especially his *Crónica razonada de las guerras de Bolívar*, 2nd ed., 3 vols. (New York: Fundación Vicente Lecuna, 1960). For the definitive edition of Bolívar's writings, see the Sociedad Bolivariana's ongoing series, *Escritos del libertador*, 12+ vols. (Caracas: Sociedad Bolivariana de Venezuela, 1964-). Also helpful is Augusto Mijares, *El Libertador*, 5th ed. (Caracas: Ministerio de Obras Públicas, 1969).

9. There are a variety of ways of approaching the changing modes of conflict resolution. For a fascinating glimpse of the Spanish colonial military establishment in Venezuela, see Santiago Gerardo Suárez, *Las instituciones militares venezolanas del período hispánico en los archivos* (Caracas: ANH, 1969). For the dissolution of traditional norms, see the documents in *Materiales para el estudio de la cuestión agraria en Venezuela (1800-1830)*, vol. 1 (Caracas: UCV, 1964), and the

royalist vision in *Anuario*, Instituto de Antropología e Historia, 1967–69, 2 vols. (Caracas: UCV, 1971). Both volumes carry important introductory studies by Germán Carrera Damas. In *Materiales* the essay appears in a separate publication, *Boves. Aspectos socio-económicos de la guerra de la independencia*, 3rd ed. (Caracas: UCV, 1972); and in the *Anuario*, see "La crisis de la sociedad colonial," pp.xiii–lxxxix. Also useful for the royalist view is Steven K. Stoan, *Pablo Morillo and Venezuela, 1815–1820* (Columbus: Ohio State University, 1974).

10. For students of nineteenth-century Venezuelan history, there are several significant document collections for the analysis of the commercial-bureaucratic outpost. First is the fine collection prepared by Pedro Grases and Manuel Pérez Vila, *Pensamiento político venezolano del siglo xix: textos para su estudio*, 15 vols. (Caracas: Presidencia de la República 1960–62). Also important for this period are *Las fuerzas armadas de Venezuela en el siglo xix*, 12 vols. (Caracas: Presidencia de la República, 1963–), and the useful *Historia de las finanzas públicas en Venezuela (1830–1857)*, ed. Tomás Enrique Carillo Batalla, 10 vols. (Caracas: Cuatricentenario de Caracas, 1969–). See, too, the collection published by the ANH under the series title of *Fuentes para la historia republicana de Venezuela*. This began in 1969 and to date has covered the Páez period into the Federal Wars in 15 volumes. On Páez, see José Antonio Páez, *Autobiografía del general . . .* , 2 vols. (Caracas: ANH, 1973), and *Archivo del general José Antonio Páez (1818–1823)*, 2 vols. (Caracas: ANH, 1973).

11. There is considerable literature on various aspects of this period of Venezuela's history. Especially helpful in understanding the dynamics of the Páez era are Ramón Díaz Sánchez, *Guzmán: elipse de una ambición de poder*, 5th ed., 2 vols. (Caracas: Editorial Mediterraneo, 1968); Robert Ker Porter, *Sir Robert Ker Porter's Caracas Diary, 1825–1842: A British Diplomat in a Newborn Nation* (Caracas: Instituto Otto and Magdalena Blohm, 1966); and Caracciolo Parra Pérez, *Mariño y las guerras civiles*, 3 vols. (Madrid: Ediciones Cultura Hispánica, 1958–60). Some of the best discussions of the issues of this period are in the contemporary polemics collected in the appropriate volumes of *Pensamiento político*. Two indispensable works on the conditions of Venezuelan agriculture and population are Giovanni Battista Agostino Codazzi, *Obras escogidas*, 2 vols. (Caracas: Ministerio de Educación, 1961), especially his geography of Venezuela in 1838; and Antonio Arellano Moreno, comp., *Las estadísticas de las provincias en la época de Páez* (Caracas: ANH, 1973). For a general survey of the slavery question, see John V. Lombardi, *The Decline and Abolition of Negro Slavery in Venezuela, 1820–1854* (Westport, Conn.: Greenwood Press, 1971). On the coffee industry in Venezuela, see Miguel Llorens Izard, "El café en la economía venezolana del siglo xix: estado de la cuestión," *Estudis* (Valencia, Spain) 1 (1973): 205–73; and his "La agricultura venezolana en una época de transición: 1777–1830," *Boletín Histórico* 28 (1972): 81–145.

12. The complexity of the Federal Wars has received historiographical attention in Lisandro Alvarado, *Historia de la Revolución Federal en Venezuela* (Caracas: Ministerio de Educación, 1956), and Ramón Diaz Sánchez *Guzmán* (Caracas: n. p., 1968). See, too, Jacinto R. Pachano, *Biografía del mariscal Juan C. Falcón*, 2nd ed. (Caracas: Imprenta Nacional, 1960). An excellent discussion of Venezuelan government and philosophy is in Laureano Vallenilla Lanz,

Cesarismo democrático: estudios sobre las bases sociológicas de la constitución efectiva de Venezuela, 4th ed. (Caracas: Tipografía Garrido, 1961). Other helpful items on this period are Federico Brito Figueroa, *Ezequiel Zamora: un capítulo de la historia nacional* (Caracas: Avila Gráfica, 1951); Luis Level de Goda, *Historia contemporánea de Venezuela. Política y militar(1858–1886)* (Caracas: Imprenta Nacional, 1954); José Santiago Rodriguez, *Contribución al estudio de la Guerra Federal en Venezuela*, 2 vols. (Caracas: Imprenta Nacional, 1960); José María Rojas, *Bosquejo histórico de Venezuela. Primera parte, 1830–1863* (Paris, 1888); and Dolores Bonet de Sotillo, *Crítica a la Federación. Campañas de prensa (1863–1870)* 4 vols. (Caracas: Imprenta Nacional, 1964–68). An interesting view of land policy can be seen in *Materiales para el estudio de la cuestión agraria en Venezuela (1828–1860). Enjenación y arrendamiento de tierras baldías* (Caracas: UCV, 1971), especially the study by Carmen Gómez R., "Política de enajenación y arrendamiento de tierras baldías (1830–858)," pp. vii–xxii. See also *Archivo del mariscal Juan Crisóstomo Falcón* 5 vols. (Caracas: Imprenta Nacional, 1957–60).

13. Antonio Guzmán Blanco served as vice-president in 1863–68 and as president in 1870–77, 1879–84, and 1886–88. His regime has attracted considerable historiographical attention. See especially Díaz Sánchez, *Guzmán*; Rafael Angel Rondón Márquez, *Guzmán Blanco, "El Autócrata Civilizador." Parábola de los partidos políticos tradicionales en la historia de Venezuela*, 2 vols. (Caracas: Tipografía Garrido, 1944); and George S. Wise, *Caudillo: A Portrait of Antonio Guzmán Blanco* (New York: Columbia University Press, 1951). See also Manuel Modesto Gallegos, *Anales contemporáneos: memorias del general... 1925* (Caracas: Tipografía Case de Especialidades, 1925–26), which covers in fragmentary fashion the years 1877–98. James Mudie Spence, *La tierra de Bolívar, o guerra, paz y aventura en la república de Venezuela*, 2 vols. (Caracas: Banco Central de Venezuela, 1966) is an excellent travel account of Guzmán Blanco's Venezuela. Julian Nava's "The Illustrious American: The Development of Nationalism in Venezuela under Antonio Guzmán Blanco," *Hispanic American Historical Review* 45, no. 4 (1965): 527–43, is a good survey of the period, rich in bibliographical detail. See also Ramón J. Velásquez, *La caída del liberalismo amarillo: tiempo y drama de Antonio Paredes*, 2nd ed. (Caracas: Cromotip, 1973). Two useful guides to this and subsequent periods are Francisco J. Parra's *Doctrinas de la cancillería venezolana. Digesto*, 6 vols. (New York: n. p. 1952–64), which catalogs the foreign policy positions of the Venezuelan government from 1830 to 1939; and Ulises Picón Rivas, *Indice constitucional de Venezuela* (Caracas: Editorial Elite, 1944), which covers Venezuela's constitutions from 1811 to 1936. On Guzmán Blanco see also Manuel Briceño, *Los Ilustres. O la estafa de los Guzmanes* (Caracas: Ediciones Fe y Cultura, 1954). One of the important consequences of Guzmán Blanco's modernizing impulse was a renewed interest in statistics. See especially Manuel Landaeta Rosales, *Gran recopilación geográfica, estadística, e histórica de Venezuela*, 2 vols. (Caracas: Banco Central de Venezuela, 1963). For church-state relations, see Mary Watters, *A History of the Church in Venezuela, 1810–1930* (New York: AMS Press, 1933).

14. The characteristic figure of this interlude was General Cipriano Castro, who served as president in 1899–1908. His failure to obey the rules of Atlantic trade led to the blockade of Venezuela's coast in 1903 by British, German, and

ultimately Italian warships to enforce payment of debts; see, for example, *Documentos británicos relacionados con el bloqueo de las costas venezolanas* (Caracas: FUNRES, 1982). A useful work on the entire period of 1830-1910 is Robert L. Gilmore, *Caudillism and Militarism in Venezuela, 1810-1910* (Athens: Ohio University Press, 1964). On Castro, see Carlos Brandt, *Bajo la tiranía de Cipiano Castro* (Caracas: Tipografía Vargas, 1952); Cipriano Castro, *Documentos del general...*, 6 vols. (Caracas: J. M. Herra Irigoyen, 1903-08); Enrique Bernardo Núñez, *El hombre de la levita gris (los años de la restauración liberal)* (Caracas: EDIME, 1953); Antonio Paredes, *Como llegó Cipriano Castro al poder*, 2nd ed. (Caracas: Ediciones Garrido, 1954), especially the introduction by Ramón J. Velásquez; and a good overall account in Mariano Picón Sales, *Los días de Cipriano Castro (historia venezolana del 1900)* (Caracas: Primer Festival del Libro Popular Venezolano, 1958). Especially helpful is Ramón J. Velásquez, ed., *Venezuela moderna. Medio siglo de historia, 1926-1976* (Caracas: Fundación Eugenio Mendoza, 1976).

15. The literature on Juan Vicente Gómez (president, 1909-10, 1910-14, 1915-22, 1922-29, 1931-35) is extensive. One of the best ways to view the *gomecista* system at work is through Mario Briceño Iragorry's historical novel *Los Riberas* (Caracas: Ediciones Independencia, 1957), and the essay on the novel by Germán Carrera Damas, "Proceso de la formación de la burgesía venezolana," in his *Tres temas de historia*, 2nd ed. (Caracas: UCV, 1974). Ramón J. Velásquez offers some fascinating insights in *Confidencias imaginarias de Juan Vicente Gómez* (Caracas: Ediciones Centauro, 1980). On the state of agriculture and landholding patterns, see Miguel Acosta Saignes' polemical but solid *Latifundio* (Mexico: Editorial Popular, 1938). Also interesting is Crisalida Dupuy, *Propiedades del General Juan Vicente Gómez, 1901-1935* (Caracas: Archivo Histórico, Contraloría General de la República, 1983). Other detractors of the Gómez regime are Daniel J. Clinton, *Gómez, Tyrant of the Andes* (New York: Morrow, 1941), and Domingo Albert Rangel, *Los andinos en el poder: balance de una hegemonía, 1899-1945* (Caracas, 1965), a study of the Táchira dynasty in Venezuela politics. Gómez had his adulators and defenders as well. See Pedro M. Arcaya, *The Gómez Regime in Venezuela and Its Background* (Baltimore: Sun Printing, 1936); Pablo Emilio Fernández, *Gómez, el rehabilitador* (Caracas: J. Villegas, 1956); John Lavin, *A Halo for Gómez* (New York: Pageant Press, 1954); and Juan Vicente Gómez, *El general... documentos para la historia de su gobierno* (Caracas: Litografía del Comercio, 1925). A quick source for information and statistics on a variety of economic and social indicators is Miguel Izard's valuable compilation *Series estadísticas para la historia de Venezuela* (Mérida: Universidad de los Andes, 1970).

16. As we approach modern times, the material on Venezuelan topics increases tremendously. In these notes I can only indicate some of the important and representative items from the range of possibilities. Two specialized guides for the period are Victor M. Badillo and Celestino Bonfanti's *Indice bibliográfica agrícola de Venezuela* (Caracas: Fundación Eugenio Mendoza, 1957), and supplements (Maracay, 1962, 1967); and Helen L. Clagett, *A Guide to the Law and Legal Literature of Venezuela* (Washington, D.C.: Library of Congress, 1947). On oil, the standard history is Edwin Lieuwen, *Petroleum in Venezuela: A History*

(Berkeley: University of California, 1954). A more recent comprehensive treatment is Franklin Tugwell, *The Politics of Oil in Venezuela* (Stanford, Calif.; Stanford University Press, 1975). See also Hector Malavé Mata, *Petróleo y desarrollo económico de Venezuela* (Havana: Publicaciones Económicas, 1964). Also valuable is Brian S. McBeth, *Juan Vicente Gómez and the Oil Companies in Venezuela, 1908–1935* (Cambridge: Cambridge University Press, 1984).

17. See the volume of the *Estudio de Caracas* for reflections on the oil boom's impact on the city. Also useful are Chi-Yi Chen, *Los pobladores de Caracas y su procedencia: resultados de una encuesta* (Caracas: Universidad Católica Andrés Bello [UCAB], 1970), and his *Movimientos migratorios en Venezuela* (Caracas: UCAB, 1968). Carlos Acedo Mendoza has two books of interest here. *Venezuela: ruta y destino*, 2nd ed. (Caracas: Fondo Editorial Común, 1971), and *Reforma urbana* (Caracas: Fondo Editorial Común, 1974), offer an analysis of Venezuela and a plan for urban reform. For a review of Marxist historiography and a guide to contemporary Venezuela historians, see Germán Carrera Damas, *Historiografía marxista venezolana y otros temas* (Caracas: UCV, 1967). An excellent survey of the sweep of Venezuelan history from a traditional perspective is Mariano Picón Salas et al., *Venezuela independiente, 1910–1960* (Caracas: Fundación Eugenio Mendoza, 1962).

18. Some useful insights into the turbulent period of 1930 to the present can be gained from the following: Banco Central de Venezuela, *La economíc venezolana en los últimos treinta años* (Caracas, 1971); Frank Bonilla and José Antonio Silva Michelana, eds., *A Strategy for Research on Social Policy* (Cambridge, Mass.: MIT Press, 1967); *Castro-Communist Insurgency in Venezuela: A Study of Insurgency and Counterinsurgency Operations and Techniques in Venezuela, 1960–1964* (Alexandria, Va.: Altantic Research Corp., 1964); John Friedmann, *Regional Development Policy: A Case Study of Venezuela* (Cambridge, Mass.: MIT Press, 1966); Henry Gómez, *La industria del mineral de hierro en Venezuela: experiencia y perspectivas* (Caracas: UCAB, 1970); Louis E. Heaton, *The Agricultural Development of Venezuela* (New York: Praeger, 1969); Manuel Vicente Magallanes, *Partidos políticos venezolanos* (Caracas: Tipografí Vargas, 1959); Venezuela, Oficina Ministerial de Transporte, *Estudios y proyección de la población del área metropolitana de Caracas y de Venezuela 1966–1990* (Caracas, 1967); Marco Aurelio Vila and Juan J. Pericchi L., *Zonificación geo-económica de Venezuela*, 4 vols. (Caracas: Corporación Venezolana de Fomento, 1968); John Duncan Powell, *The Political Mobilization of the Venezuelan Peasant* (Cambridge, Mass.: Harvard University Press, 1971); Stephen G. Rabe, *The Road to OPEC: United States Relations with Venezuela, 1919–1976* (Austin: University of Texas, 1982); Domingo Alberto Rangel, *La industrialización de Venezuela* (Caracas: Pensamiento Vivo, 1958); Talton F. Ray, *The Politics of the Barrios of Venezuela* (Berkeley: University of California Press, 1969); and Silva Michelena, *The Illusion of Democracy in Dependent Nations: Politics of Change in Venezuela* (Cambridge, Mass.: MIT Press, 1971). Other material on these themes can be found in the notes accompanying the rest of the chapters in this volume.

19. On Venezuelan politics and society in recent times, see the following for a start on the literature. Robert J. Alexander, *The Venezuelan Democratic*

Revolutions: A Profile on the Regime of Rómulo Betancourt (New Brunswick, N.J.: Rutgers University Press, 1964); Robert F. Arnove, *Student Alienation: A Venezuelan Study* (New York: Praeger 1972); Enrique Baloyra, "Oil Policies and Budgets in Venezuela, 1938–1968," *Latin America Research Review* 9, no. 2 (1974): 27–72; Enrique A. Baloyra and John D. Martz, *Political Attitudes in Venezuela: Societal Cleavages and Political Opinion* (Austin: University of Texas Press, 1979); Rómulo Betancourt, *Política y petróleo* (Mexico: Fondo de Cultura Económica, 1956; 2nd ed. rev., Caracas: Senderos, 1969); Winfield J. Burggraaff, *The Venezuelan Armed Forces in Politics, 1935–1959* (Columbia: University of Missouri Press, 1972); Susan Berglund and Humberto Hernández Calimán, *Estudio analítico de política inmigratoria en Venezuela* (Caracas: Ministerio de Relaciones Interiores, 1977); Tomás Enrique Carrillo Batalla, *Crisis administración fiscal* (Caracas: UCV, 1964); Steve Ellner, *Los partidos políticos y su disputa por el control del movimiento sindical en Venezuela, 1936–1948* (Caracas: UCAB, 1980); Judith Ewell, *The Indictment of a Dictator: The Extradition and Trial of Marcos Pérez Jiménez* (College Station: Texas A & M University Press, 1981); Ramón Fernández y Fernández, *Reforma agraria en Venezuela* (Caracas: Las Novedades, 1948); R. González Baquero, *Análisis del proceso histórico de la educación urbana (1870–1932) y de la educación rural (1932–1957) en Venezuela* (Caracas: UCV, 1962); George W. Hill et al., *La vida rural en Venezuela* (Caracas: Ministerio de Sanidad y Asistencia Social, 1960); Daniel H. Levine, *Religion and Politics in Latin America: The Catholic Church in Venezuela and Colombia* (Princeton, N.J.: University Press, 1981); Fred D. Levy, *Economic Planning in Venezuela* (New York: Praeger, 1968); Eleázar López Contreras, *Gobierno y administración (1936–1941)* (Caracas: Editorial Arte, 1966); John D. Martz, *Acción Democrática: Evolution of a Modern Political Party in Venezuela* (Princeton, N.J.: Princeton University Press, 1966); Domingo F. Maza Zavala, *Venezuela una economía dependiente* (Caracas: UCV, 1964); David J. Myers, *Democratic Campaigning in Venezuela: Caldera's Victory* (Caracas: Fudación La Salle, 1973); Luis Beltran Prieto Figueroa, *De una educación de castas a una educación de masas* (Havana: Universidad de la Habana, 1951); Domingo Alberto Rangel, *La revolución de las fantasías* (Caracas: Ediciones Ofidi, 1966); Philip B. Taylor, *The Venezuela Golpe de Estado of 1958: The Fall of Marcos Pérez Jiménez* (Washington, D.C.: Institute for the Comparative Study of Political System, 1968); Franklin Tugwell, "The Christian Democrats of Venezuela," *Journal of Interamerican Studies* 7, no. 2 (1965): 245–67; and Howard R. Penniman, ed. *Venezuela at the Polls: The National Elections of 1978* (Washington, D.C.: American Enterprise Institute, 1980).

20 The principal actors in the Venezuelan presidency since Gómez have been Eleazar López Contreras (1936–41), Isaías Medina Angarita (1941–45), Rómulo Betancourt (1945–48), Rómulo Gallegos (1948), Carlos Delgado Chalbaud (1948–50), Marcos Pérez Jiménez (1952–58), Wolfgang Larrazábal (1958), Rómulo Betancourt (1959–64), Raúl Leoni (1964–69), Rafael Caldera (1969–74), Carlos Andrés Pérez (1974–79), Luis Herrera Campíns (1979–84), and Jaime Lusinchi (1984–89).

2

Venezuelan Constitutional Forms and Realities

R. Lynn Kelley

In the late 1950s and early 1960s a new mode of political discourse emerged known as the literature of "development." This literature was spawned by the appearance of the new states of Africa and Southeast Asia, as well as by the fascination Westerners had with the direction of certain models of development, notably the dichotomy between Soviet-inspired regimes, on the one hand, and liberal-democratic regimes in the West European and North American tradition, on the other.

This literature was largely descriptive of regimes then in existence. But its pretension was to be explanatory and/or predictive. After 25 years of experience with this literature and that of behaviorist, quantitative political science, our ability to explain and predict change in whole systems does not seem to be notably better than what it was then. On the other hand, the descriptive vocabulary of political science has been enriched by the effort to produce models and paradigms.[1]

"Subsystems" of large-scale political units have been studied in great detail. Sometimes individual political behavior or political attitudes have been the focal point of these studies. Other times political institutions have come under scrutiny.

In this chapter I deal with the concept of "developing political institutions," a kind of hybridized concept. An institution has been defined as patterned human activity that has persisted for at least 25 years. Only if patterned behavior has existed for at least this long can there have been the possibility of the transfer of control from one elite generation to another. The presumption is, of course, that these elites share to such an extent the underlying attitudes upon which the patterned behavior is based that the behaviors will persist upon the passing of the "founding generation" with power wielded in a patterned way to a new generation that has continued to accept these norms of behavior.

If this occurs, the patterned behavior initiated by the old elite can be said to have become "institutionalized." Certainly what has been occurring in Venezuela in the past few years lends dramatic credence to the notion of the inevitability of change in the composition of the personalities who form the civilian political elite. It was fashionable throughout the 1960s to speak of the "Guardia Vieja" (the "old guard") of Acción Democrática in particular and the Generation of 1928 in general as if they were either venerable "has-beens" or ogres of reaction. In fact, however, these were men who very carefully were trying to consolidate their personal and/or partisan positions in the postdictatorial period for which they had worked, but into which they had been thrown by events not of their own choosing.

In recent times the "old guard" quite literally has become debilitated by age and eliminated through death from natural causes. The deaths of such prominent *adecos* as Raúl Leoni and Rómulo Betancourt, and luminaries associated with them like Juan Pablo Pérez Alfonso, have all occurred within the past decade. Several have taken place even more recently. These events, and the passing of personalities like Villalba and Prieto Figueroa from the center of political debate, call for a reexamination of the constitutional theory and operating realities of the formal political structures that were initiated in 1958. Are they surviving the tests of the transition? Can they be expected to persist into the intermediate future without considerable change in form and activity from what they have been and as they have evolved since 1958?

The 1961 constitution provides a benchmark of written norms against which we can seek to measure changes that have transpired since that time for national political institutions in the three branches of government. The Venezuelan system is nominally federal. However, for reasons peculiar to the unitary, centralist traditions of Hispanic and Roman Catholic constitutional development, the position of local government is much more intimately connected with national political patterns and performance than has been the case in the United States, Canada, and Australia. Any discussion of Venezuelan constitutional forms and realities entails understanding that this close relationship between federal executive, legislative, and judicial branches of government, on the one hand, and the local and state governments, on the other, is a primary fact of political theory and practice in the country.

CONGRESS

As in the language of the U. S. Constitution, the 1961 Venezuelan constitution[2] uses language that suggests that the font of all lawmaking in the country lies with the Congress. Composed of a Chamber of Deputies and a Senate, the Congress has the same constitutional and legal rules of membership in 1983 that applied to that body as conceived in 1958. Basically, these are that all congressmen—deputies and senators—must meet age requirements (21 and 30 years, respectively); that each body is elected at the same time with the same congressional ballot every five years; and that a party list system of proportional representation is the method of selection for both houses. (The Senate's membership also includes all former constitutional presidents of the republic.) The feature of alternates (*suplentes*) is a social convention ubiquitous in the Hispanic tradition. This allows for persons formally designated as alternates to hold the position to which a principal has been elected in the latter's excused absence. While public complaints are raised periodically about the personal and party irresponsibility associated with the system, it is so ingrained as a cultural pattern that the idea of eradicating it seems unlikely.

Historically, the public political institutions of the United States preceded and contributed to the development of political parties. Seymour Lipset[3] and others have recognized the importance of the American Congress in the formation process that led first to personalist caucuses around figures like Jefferson and Hamilton and later to the protoparties of the Democratic-Republicans and Federalists. In Venezuela, the process was reversed historically: The constitution and the Congress are both products of the great compromise of Punto Fijo in 1958 among the four organized political parties of the day—COPEI, AD, URD, and PCV. The character that the Congress has assumed ever since is a direct outgrowth of this historical relationship between the development of political parties and national political structures. The single most important unit of organization within the Congress today remains the *fracción*, or party caucus. It encompasses members of a party's elected delegation Chamber of Deputies and Senate. While it is presided over by a chairman (*jefe*), who is nominally elected by the members of the caucus, in fact he has been preselected and approved by the party's national central committee.

During the Carlos Andrés Pérez administration, the makeup of the Congress placed the president's party in command of large legislative majorities that complemented the orientation toward issues that the president normally supported. However, as the Pérez period (1973–78) drew toward an end, the AD congressional bloc began to mirror the conflict between Pérez and Betancourt backers over the issue of public corruption. This intraparty disharmony produced veiled criticism of the president by his own party adherents in the debates of the Congress, which was significant for two reasons. First, both AD and COPEI have maintained special support for the concept of "party discipline" with which the European parties have traditionally been associated. While voting in the Congress on issues was not affected, this departure in debate from a notion of absolute loyalty to the party line demonstrated something of the AD movement from its more ideologically pure past. Second, unlike previous periods of AD party history, the party did not produce splinter groups as a result of the widespread disparagement of its incumbent leader. This may have been a tribute to the fact that each side in the intraparty dispute could count in its corner a former AD president. Nevertheless, that it did not produce a splinter party suggests that both the party leadership and rank-and-file members recognized the legitimacy of the debate.

This intraparty dispute has debate counterparts in interparty disputes—for example, the calls for a moral reawakening of Venezuela by COPEI throughout the Pérez period or the debate over the mounting national debt which began under Pérez and escalated under Herrera Campins. What is significant is that the country looked primarily to the Congress for an airing of these issues. It can be concluded, therefore, that the Venezuelan Congress in the 1973–83 decade served the same political functions as its predecessors did from 1958–1973.

- *Legitimation*—the discussion of public policy prior to its implementation helps legitimate the policy in the eyes of the electorate.
- *Political catharsis*—the rhetoric of oftentimes highly emotive debate allows for the pacific airing of grievances in an open, legal, more or less dignified, articulate manner.
- *Delay*—debate in itself can force postponement of implementation of executive decisions. The delay itself can mean that the government of the day will lose, at least psychologically, on a particular issue.
- *Democratic socialization*—the demonstration effect of political adversaries cooperating or discussing issues openly provided an example to the electorate of the country's political parties' elites observing the norms of democratic pluralism.

None of these functions has changed since the first 15 years of the democratic experiment. What has changed, however, is the relative importance attached to each of the functions. As the governments of the past two administrations have been untroubled by noisy, anticonstitutionalist congressional minorities and have possessed either a large congressional plurality (Herrera Campins) or an official majority of its own supporters (Pérez), the idea of the Congress as the legitimizer of public policy initiatives from the executive has been relegated to a less important spot than that of political catharsis. Catharsis is possible and more compatible for an opposition—loyal or otherwise—than "legitimizing" by formally voting for the government's programs. For the president's ideas to become law, the Congress still must officially pass his bills. Nevertheless, the decree law power that presidents possess is considerable in its implications.

The North American analyst of Venezuela's political system will find nothing peculiar about the functions that the Venezuelan Congress has played for its entire postdictatorial period. Each of these is played also by the American Congress. What the American will find of significant difference is the relative lack of other functions that result from the lack of decisional autonomy of the Venezuelan Congress as the creature of the party system that created it. Many of the nominal relationships an American would expect to find in legislative bodies exist in the Venezuelan Congress. Foremost among these is the committee system. But with the lack of staff and budgetary resources, the committees of the Venezuelan Congress cannot presume to serve the same autonomous functions of interest group linking, agenda setting, and decision making that their American counterparts do.

In addition to the functions listed here Congress apparently has begun to perform another important function for the political system. One must ponder seriously the fact that the last two presidents of the republic, and three of the serious contenders for the presidency in 1983, had earlier served as elected members of the Congress. One of the most interesting developments for political personnel selection would have to be that both Carlos Andrés Pérez and Luis Herrera Campins gained their public prominence from the role each had as chairman of his party delegation in Congress. Viewed from this perspective, the advancement of the Venezuelan democratic experience over 25 years of history has meant that the official state structures (and especially the Congress as the official lawmaking unit) provide a highly desirable, if not "necessary," air of civility and visibility from which presidential candidates are cultivated.

This has had an impact on the cementing of interparty cooperation also. In the early years of the presidency of Rafael Caldera, a deal was finally cut to allow AD to control Congress while COPEI controlled the executive area. This allowed AD an instant entrée to the media through control of the process of debate. In 1978 another deal was effected between AD and several smaller parties in the Chamber of Deputies to permit AD to hold the presidency of the Chamber despite the fact that AD had two fewer deputies than COPEI, and the *copeyanos* had received close to a majority of votes cast on the congressional election card.

The systemic importance of the Congress is not found in any autonomous decisional functions but rather in its communicative and symbolic functions. That so much effort has been invested by the parties over the past 25 years to control and maneuver this structure to their own advantage suggests that it is the *visibility* of the Congress that is of such significant importance, both to the political parties as organizational entities and to individuals within them who are ready to advance their own political careers.

THE EXECUTIVE

To read any article on Venezuelan politics is to find allusion to the classic pattern of Latin American presidential hegemony. The presumption of psychological origins for this kind of paternalistic, strongman executive is reported by David C. McClelland et al. to be the low level of achievement motivation and an outstanding need for power.[4] Regardless of the motivation for the strong presidential pattern, it is inescapable. The 1961 constitution did not significantly try to sublimate the tradition of centralist strength in the executive; it did, however, attempt to shape that strength constitutionally by setting certain limits on what constituted legitimate presidential actions.

Much has been written about the delicacy of political behavior of the civilian party elites vis-á-vis the military during the first five years of constitutional development in the post-dictatorial period.[5] Likewise, a great deal has appeared in print about the relationship of the political parties to each other. In all of these writings there is evidence of the overwhelming importance of the tutelage of AD under Betancourt, Leoni, and Pérez and of COPEI under Caldera and Herrera Campins for the achievement of an interparty and party-military-business elite consensus to the rules of the game. The rules necessarily had to emanate from the president but required the acceptance of these other groups.

The powers of the president under the 1961 constitution are significant. The president is commander of the armed forces, can call special sessions of the Congress, and appoints all cabinet ministers and governors. He can also declare a state of siege and temporarily order the restriction or suspension of constitutional guarantees. Perhaps as important, the president is constitutionally empowered through his ministers to adopt all necessary regulations to bring laws into effect. Such regulations are neither subject to the approval of the Congress nor to the courts. Under such circumstances the Venezuelan president could be considered virtually unfettered in his use of power. In fact, the very tenuousness of the political situation from 1958 through 1968 made the political party elites—and especially the AD elite during Betancourt's administration—unwilling to risk the rupture of constitutionalism or the ouster of AD through acts that appeared arbitrary and capricious.

The role of the Venezuelan executive in the past 25 years has basically mirrored the relationship among the parties. In spite of periodic rumors of coup attempts, especially during times of economic recession, the military has become a decreasingly important factor of concern in the executive level political decisions for the system as a whole. Proportionately decreasing perquisites to the Ministry of Defense is one good measure of this change. Of course, it remains very much involved in certain policy areas, notably defense, internal security, and national infrastructure development.

The mechanism that is constitutionally outlined for the implementation of executive decisions is the ministry. Under Betancourt and Leoni the number of ministries remained stable at 13. Under Caldera and Pérez it increased to 15. Under Herrera Campins there were 25 ministers of state with 20 ministries. This suggests what one finds clearly documented elsewhere: There has been, especially since the quadrupling of oil prices in 1973, a tremendous increase in public payroll and a consequent mitosis of the centralized bureaucracy under the formal control of the president. To this proliferation of the ministerial bureaucracy must be added the number of state corporations, among which are PDVSA, CORPOANDES, CORPOZULIA, CORPOINDUSTRIA, plus the Instituto de Comercio Exterior and Superintendencia de Inversión Extranjera (SIEX) in trade and industry. While the president of the republic cannot be said to have the same control over the state corporations and military as with the civilian ministries, his power of appointment is significant. Although the president sits at the apex of this system, the accomplishment of his policy and political objectives depends increasingly upon his ability to appoint persons whose organizational talents of communication and administrative ability and specific expertise can reasonably assure the successful implementation of his ideas.

Politically, the last three presidents of Venezuela have not been completely successful in working with the Congress—this in spite of both the growing electoral strength of COPEI and AD, which have split nearly 90 percent of the vote between them in the last three elections, and of the decision of all parties in the Congress to act increasingly as protagonists for the constitutional system. Indeed, it is perhaps for this reason that Herrera Campins saw fit to create a minister of state for congressional relations as a member of his cabinet. The initiation of such a position lends credibility to the belief that the role of the Congress is not taken lightly by Venezuelan presidents.

Herrera Campins's creation of four other "ministers without ministries"—development of intelligence, science and technology, women's affairs, and president of the investment fund—is instructive for what it indicates not only about the predisposition of a particular incumbent but also for what it implies about the cutting issues in Venezuelan society. The executive branch, in order to strengthen and build consensus, has had to engage in dialogue with groups committed to certain issues of interest primarily to them and then to respond with actions designed to meet the needs of those groups by developing administrative bureaucracies and policy initiatives. Not to do so is to risk acrimonious congressional debate, social group disharmony, and future losses at the polls. By expanding the bureaucracy in an effort to address himself to those groups and issues, every Venezuelan president has placed recognized limits on his legitimate authority, as perceived by informal public opinion.

Much of the growth of the bureaucracy has been condemned by Venezuelans as self-serving and predatory, but its existence and growth cannot be questioned. Certainly, the long-range implications of such rapid, sustained bureaucratic growth may be harmful to the maintenance of political consensus. Under Herrera Campins a point had already been reached where 1.5 million government workers of a total labor force of 5 million could not be sustained in a period of economic recession. In the short run, however, this growth probably contributed to political consensus building and helps to explain AD's and COPEI's continued electoral successes. Further capping of this bureaucracy may occur because of recessionary pressures on public sector spending. Politically, the growth of the public bureaucracy in the ministries and the state corporations has helped to consolidate a sense of counterbalance to the parties that created much of both. In the process of this inefficient organizational development, dependence upon the public norms of the constitution has been increased.

The growth of the Venezuelan public sector is not merely the result of the parties' wasteful efforts to buy the allegiance of organized economic and social groups in the country. It also proceeds from solid bases in Hispanic and Roman Catholic social philosophy concerned with the state as the legitimate provider of all earthly essentials and the regulator of all group interests. Viewed from this perspective an issue such as the nationalization of oil companies is not a radical act but rather constitutes a fundamentally conservative act by moderate politicians. These same politicians by these acts have helped to bring the democratic experiment in Venezuela to a new level of maturity—one in which the institutions they have created, essentially for partisan reasons, have assumed a social character and institutional consciousness in their own right.

The Venezuelan executive branch has grown enormously since 1958. Several important social and economic reasons account for this growth. Many of them, and especially the public economy surplus, are no longer historically valid. Therefore such explosive growth cannot be sustained. Both elites and the general population are aware of this. Much of the public sector growth is either not germane to democratic constitutionalism or may be considered harmful to it in the long range. Yet, in the short or intermediate range, it has given the democratic processes time to mature, has given certain strata seeking employment a sense that government can help answer their employment problems, and has helped to build system affect by producing rules and a social system that (at least in some instances) go beyond the understanding and powers of the party elites.

If the new bureaucracies of the ministries and the state corporations can become more efficient and can be managed more effectively, they can become a real strength for the democratic system by providing goods and services rationally to a people who will look more toward government as an efficient provider. Even now, however, their very existence has constituted a check on purely partisan activities as the basis for decision making. They have also constituted something of a short-term guarantee of social stability and therefore of constitutional development and legitimacy. The 1961 constitution, and the form that political offices and systems have taken that have emerged with it, are themselves the product of the party system that preceded it. Unlike other chapters of this book that address the question of policies, here we focus on normative structures. From that perspective one can ask if there has been any discernible movement in the past 25 years tending toward the permanency of the constitutional structure and the autonomous role of the executive, legislative, and judicial branches of the government.

There is no doubt that the party system has become highly institutionalized, "polyclassist," and ideologically "re-formulative."[6] In other words, as the years have passed and the dominant parties have sustained and increased their electoral "take" and implemented their earlier progress, they have both ingrained themselves into the political culture and developed a need to have new answers for new questions created by successes of their earlier administrations.

The constitutional *forms* have provided a sense of legitimacy and continuity to the necessarily frothy developments of everyday politics. As a result, the structures of constitutional government, especially the executive and the legislative, have themselves developed a measure of autonomy from the parties that created them. This confirms what appears to be a common social psychological need in all modern political systems: the need for a sense that the *formal* institutions of the state legitimate, and stand apart from and above, those actions of the political actors organized into party life. This is certainly true of one-party systems, even those of the Soviet Union and its allies where in more recent years the party leader has sought the mantle of state president and premier, along with the party leadership title, which informally gave him command of the state in any case.[7]

It follows that if this "law" holds true in societies as relatively regimented and monolithic as those of the Soviet bloc of states, it should be even more important in a state such as Venezuela where the continuation of the openness of the post-Pérez Jiménez system necessarily depends upon the citizenry's acceptance of a sense of long-term legitimacy with respect to the state's formal institutions of government. The trend appears to be toward a measure of public institutional autonomy in the Venezuela of the 1980s. If the Venezuelan democratic experiment is not unduly hung up on the rocks of economic recession, it seems clear that the powerful twin forces of social-psychological symbolism and the progressive growth of the bureaucracy of the government ministries and state corporations will make this trend even more evident in the years to come.

THE JUDICIARY

In studies of Latin American politics generally the judiciary receives little mention. Venezuela is no exception to this rule. A variety of reasons exists to explain both the general rule and Venezuela's fit with it. These reasons are all related to the historic lack of real constitutionalism, that is, a real regard for regularized, pacific settlement of disputes by reliance on knowable, impartial rules. Only since the 1930s has there been any real effort in Venezuela to develop a literature on the theory of the law. Prior to that time, a few treatises were developed by ersatz jurists who utilized their talents to develop apologias for strongman rule as a kind of rule of law. Such theories inevitably had a kind of fascist quality to them, in that they relied upon the notion that the will of the society was somehow exemplified in the person of the president and that his pronouncements were therefore the law.

While such theories accord with a minimal criterion of the logical positivists (namely, the law can be said to exist if there can be determined to be a "will of the sovereign" from which there is no higher appeal),[8] they disregard notions of "knowableness," equity in application, and due process for regularized changes in the will of the sovereign. Postdictatorial Venezuelan legal theory has been developed slowly. Again, the primary reason is evident: Legal theory is difficult to develop in a vacuum of historical practice. Nevertheless, several jurists have emerged as theorists of the law in two areas of the law, constitutional and criminal. This appears to be significant because it suggests that an internal understanding in the society has emerged to the point that there needs to be a framework that will explain constitutional and criminal law matters to the interested, informed public in a way that is logically and historically consistent enough with juridical and political action to invite credible acceptance of those actions and the theory informing them or explaining them, as the case may be.[9]

These theories are tested by the actions of the court system, the political officials, and the police enforcers. In Venezuela the constitution is described as "federal" in the political arrangements of the postdictatorial period. On the other hand, the language of the constitution describes this federalism as existing in the "peculiar measure" that it has been lived historically in the country. Translated accurately, this means that the country is officially divided into twenty states, two national territories, and a federal district that conform fairly well to certain regionalist-based, and later administrative, realities of Venezuelan political history. On the other hand, the Venezuelan constitutional arrangements provide virtually no autonomy for these units. In spite of the existence of elected municipal councils (which had separate election from the president and the Congress for the first time on June 3, 1979) and state legislatures, these are not empowered to create and administer meaningful budgets or policies. All state governors are appointed by the president. Members of state legislatures are nominated by the parties, and the money for state budgets comes directly from the federal government as a constitutionally recognized small percentage of federal revenues.

This sense of Venezuelan federalism does not allow for state courts in adjudicating state law. The law is presumed in theory to be unitary through the national territory. All courts, all jurists, and virtually all legal officers—arresting and prosecutorial—are federal (that is, central government) officials. The Venezuelan justice system is capped by a Supreme Court of Justice that theoretically has the same power of judicial review and the same autonomy from the executive and legislative branches as does that in the United States. The system is composed of several types of courts, all of which have been conveniently categorized by Juan Mayorca into two major categories: special and ordinary jurisdictions.[10] The ordinary jurisdictions are of three types: civil, labor, and penal. Each of these areas is composed of a hierarchy of courts. The courts of special jurisdiction are also of three types: juvenile, fiscal, and military tribunals. The old Castilian tradition of the military *fuero* has been incorporated into the Venezuelan legal system to prevent the members of the military from being tried by civilian courts. Tax and juvenile offenses constitute other types of special cases that the "ordinary jurisdiction" courts do not oversee.

While the military personnel cannot be tried by civilian courts, the military nevertheless plays an important role in meting out constitutionally affirmed "justice" to the civilian sector. This occurs in several ways, but most notably through the workings of the various police forces of Venezuela. The Fuerzas Armadas de Cooperación (FAC), roughly the equivalent of the Spanish Guardia Civil, are a part of the army and are charged with the function of protecting all international borders and highways and of *prosecuting* contraband cases and all questions related to summary court proceedings due to contraband.[11] In effect, this makes the military responsible for the criminal prosecution of a large number of suspected civilian offenders.

The official independence of the postdictatorial judiciary from the legislative and executive powers is guaranteed by the constitution of 1961 in Article 203. However, this guarantee in political practice has been considerably more circumscribed than is true of the role of the U.S. judiciary. In addition to the historic tradition of strongman rule expectations in the presidency, the court system is hampered by the code law tradition itself, which casts the jurists in the system as confirmers of the written code rather than finders or makers of the law as is the case in common law analogical reasoning. That the judges in the system are selected for short periods of time by the minister of justice (for lower civilian courts) and by the Congress (for the Supreme Court of Justice) and that they receive their salaries not as a guarantee but as a line item from the Ministry of Justice's annual budget request to Congress have been cited as two other, very real constraints on the actual independence of the jurists in the Venezuelan system.

Taken together, these reasons help explain why the Supreme Court of Justice has not to this time made use of its official right to declare legislatively ordained law and executive decree law "unconstitutional." Yet, to assume that the Supreme Court has not played a part in regularizing constitutional processes would be misleading. In 1968 the court took dramatic action involving a case in which the out-of-power congressional party coalition referred a case to it, when the Leoni government appeared prepared to intervene on behalf of maintaining AD's official organizing control in the Senate during a tense election year. More recently, in early 1982 under the Herrera government the national retailers' association, CONSECOMERCIO, threatened to have the Ministry of Development sued in order to determine the constitutionality of its internal resolutions regarding price controls.[12]

The justice system in Venezuela is dependent for its quality upon the relationship among police officials, officers of the courts (especially judges), and three ministries (Justice, Defense and Interior). It is from the ministries that much of the webbing of ideas and regulations comes to set limits of acceptable behavior on the other two sets of actors. The other two major police forces are, like FAC, directly a part of one of the ministries. Like judges, their officials are paid from line items in these ministries' budgets. The old Dirección General de Policía, now renamed Dirección de Seguridad Público (DISEP), and the Policía Técnico Jurídico (PTJ) report to the Ministry of the Interior and the Ministry of Justice, respectively. DISEP is responsible for the security of the state, the surveillance of foreigners, and the carrying of arms. It reports through its director to the minister of interior.

On the other hand, the PTJ is not, theoretically, a part of the executive, but rather an "auxiliary body of the judicial power," according to the decree law of 1958 that created it. Necessarily, PTJ is politically sensitive to the Ministry of Justice, because of its financing. In terms of its functions, it differs from DISEP in that it is entrusted to investigate all "offenses" (the official term for crimes) as well as to prevent crime and to apprehend those responsible. In short, it is a kind of amalgam of a national FBI and local district attorney staff.

The Venezuelan police system has been criticized internally by jurists who find the three national bodies with police functions to be a problem for delivering justice. Calls have been heard in recent years for incorporating the two civilian national police units and requiring better integration of FAC in terms of functional responsibility with the two civilian units of police. Yet, with such calls has often come a countercomplaint that suggests bureaucratic integration of the justice system may do little more than create a larger system of a monopoly of force and therefore of "repression." Critics of the proposal for police force integration also suggest that the real issues of justice in the Venezuelan postdictatorial period lie in the social and economic conditions that create the seedbeds for crime.

It may be said of the justice system in postdictatorial Venezuela that it is not yet well established with its own, Venezuelan-inspired theory of the law, although there is evidence that this has begun to develop. The current justice system is a melange of democratic political system ideas superimposed over a code law background that evolved out of the country's Spanish colonial and dictatorial past.[13] The police forces, too, have strong links to the predemocratic period. There is no question that human rights have been more highly regarded in the past 25 years than at any time in the country's history. Constitutional guarantees clearly exist in the written constitution for due process and a form of habeas corpus. The country's press has reported a number of presumed violations of these fundamental rights and of political problems involving constitutional jurisdictions of the Congress and the executive. Nevertheless, the judiciary remains the least well known, the least autonomous, and consequently the least influential of political system actors after 25 years of democratic system experimentation.

ANALYZING CONSTITUTIONAL FORMS AND REALITIES

In this volume analyses of various aspects of the postdictatorial system have been incorporated. To gain some perspective on so much information, we can consider what it means by asking certain questions: *Procedurally,* is the system one of rules? Is there in the system an expectation and a meeting of basic guaranteed human needs, both *economically* and *politically* as identified by the actors in the system and those who constitute the governed? *Structurally*, is the system designed to be effectively *participatory* at levels considered desirable by its actors and subjects?

Looking at the basic constitutional structuring of the system first, it is clear that the roles of the executive, the Congress, and the judiciary have attained something of a hallowed place in the system after 25 uninterrupted years of the democratic experiment. The best evidence available of this is seen in the political fact that the country has undergone six open, contested presidential-congressional electoral campaigns since 1958 with high percentages of voter participation, increased levels of electoral support for parties adhering to democratic norms, and (in the past three elections) a larger percentage of the ballots being split between AD and COPEI, as distinct from the other parties.

In large measure this has been the outcome of adherence by the parties to the democratic norms to which they agreed under the Pacto de Punto Fijo as "amended" by the outcomes of each of the electoral outcomes since 1958. In the early years especially, the practice of giving ministries to particular parties and independents representing distinct, powerful, nonparty groups helped solidify a notion in the minds of many that fairness in procedure and access to the political system's rewards of power, money, and personnel were possible. This evolving sense of community grew out of a notion that the rules of the game constitutionally were knowable and were being applied with some degree of fairness in an effort to incorporate those previously disenfranchised (the poor, the illiterate). At the same time, the wealthy and powerfully entrenched political groups were assured that their interest would receive due process treatment and just compensation, monetarily, if government action was taken against them.

Similarly, the initial reticence of the Betancourt government to proceed aggressively against even anticonstitutional political actors made the rules of the new constitutional system easier to accept when the crackdowns on guerrillas and their congressional sympathizers began in 1961. The operations of the Congress as a national forum for the free expression of opposition opinion have been maintained even during the worst periods of the guerrilla war of the 1960s. The rules of congressional debate have given the voters awareness of new potential presidential contenders, several of whom have subsequently assumed the country's highest office.

The freedoms of the press and adherence to rule by the courts and—certainly much more than in the past, even during guerrilla warfare—of the police agencies again constitute solid evidence of procedural openness and fairness and a sense of "access" with respect to basic human rights. Although not all Venezuelan jurists even today are trained in the law, the organic law requires this in theory. This constitutes another challenge of the system in efforts to place persons of appropriate background in sensitive roles to assure outcomes—as well as procedures, that will be considered fair, equitable, and just. In systems that style themselves as "liberal democratic" this is perhaps easier to accomplish in the domain of human rights (that is, as *political* rights) than it is in the area of the redistribution of the economic benefits of the system in terms of "economic" rights.

It can be argued that the "success" of the Venezuelan postdictatorial democratic enterprise has been fired and sustained by the 20 years of oil-driven growth of the country's gross national product. Because of this growth, it is reasoned, the parties could afford to be the allocators of the economy's profits in ways that would satisfy entrenched political and economic groups and assuage the have-nots enought to incorporate some of them into the system and keep others pacified. A corollary of this theory is, of course, that with any sustained slowdown of growth in national income, the system will begin to wobble and/or fall apart because of its lack of commitment to, or internalization of, basic political norms. This argument is essentially materialist, for it assumes that economic substructures determine the type of political super-structure a country will develop and maintain.

Since 1980 the Venezuelan economy has experienced several years of no growth or actual negative growth. In that same time period the system has undergone severe financial problems based upon a large and growing international debt. In spite of this lugubrious economic record, the political system has managed to survive unscathed through the sixth national election in December 1983. What is more, AD and COPEI, the parties most responsible for the postdictatoral policies and system, were not destroyed by this election. Instead, power passed peacefully from the one to the other—from the former head of COPEI's congressional delegation to the former head of AD's congressional delegation—for the fourth time in the past 25 years.

Thus the argument of economic structural determinants for short-term Venezuelan political and constitutional outcomes seems at best too severe, if not naive. It overlooks an essential ingredient of any successful political system: the possibility that constitutional norms can be internalized within 25 years—a political generation—in a broad enough spectrum of political actors to preclude traditional tendencies toward anti-regime behavior during poor economic times. In life generally and especially in political life, perceptions are often the paramount reality. To the extent that the politically active, informed Venezuelan public perceives the current constitutional system as "acceptable under current conditions" that system is likely to be able to endure a considerably deep and long-term economic recession without necessarily creating the spectre of a political crisis on a constitutional-regime level.

Both in terms of Latin American and other developing countries, the argument has sometimes been advanced that the official Western liberal-democratic constitutional systems are not particularly useful to these states' political and social development. This kind of analysis has been prevalent among structural-functionalists. A counterargument can also be posed: that the formal political structures that are in place in countries like Venezuela have stood the test of time to such an extent and have been modified by internal political realities and processes enough that they now constitute effectively a system with deep roots in the country's political culture.

While a single generation is a short historical period, it does provide a minimum time period for a population in an open system, and the elites within it, to test out and either accept or reject notions about the franchise, human rights, institutional arrangements, and levels of efficiency. In structural-functionalist terminology, the Venezuelan political system in 1984 appears to have an acceptable functional fit between its formal structure and its political processes. The inputs of the system are accepted by recognized "gatekeepers" who may or may not be recognized by the formal language of the constitution, but all of whom increasingly argue for their roles and policy positions within the framework of that document.

The Chilean case of political culture disintegration and dysfunctionalism has been cited by some as a "proof" that in Latin America the institutionalization of democratic structures is not assured even after a period of two generations of successful implementation. Yet the Chilean case differs in great measure from that of Venezuela in a host of areas. The structure of elites, the product base of the economy and the consequent international network of political and economic communication set up by this base and its price structure, and the inordinate influence that the U. S. administration of that period took in actively destabilizing the public confidence of the Allende regime are all factors that need to be remembered in trying to draw worthwhile analogies between the Venezuelan and Chilean cases.

The inefficiencies of the Venezuelan political system are also cited both as reasons to question the chances for the longevity of the system and to suggest that the system is demonstrating inaccessibility to decision-making channels and a disregard for fundamental fairness in following the "rules." There is undoubtedly some truth in the observation that the system of bureaucratic favoritism, "*palanca*," creates tremendous tension and strain in a system that is officially "democratic" for those members of the public who are its clients. But if the bribery of officials can somehow be amalgamated to democratic theory as "essential" (or, at least, useful) for creating access for little people who otherwise would not have access available to them, then the existing tensions are unlikely to create constitutional crisis. Certainly, American urban political machines offer significant evidence of the ability of populations to accommodate social "pull" and corruption ideas in practice with the ideal of democratic access to decision-makers on the merits of an argument. It is not possible to give a simple answer to the question of difference that a formally democratic system makes in terms of access to decision making, the application of rules in a manner considered fair, and policy outcomes that are apt to raise various have-not groups in the society. As the earlier edition of this work pointed out, at least in the early years of the democratic experiment in Venezuela, there were areas of policy in which the democrats gave entrenched groups (like the officer corps) better treatment than the dictatorship had—and did so in the name of promoting constitutionalism.

Bernard Crick, like Burke two centuries earlier, has pointed out that both paradox and the unification of opposites are in the nature of politics.[14]

To make harmonious blendings of these opposites in peaceful, periodized, rule-oriented ways is the heart of constitutionalism in practice. There are different levels at which societies can be rule-oriented, and, of course, a society is more or less rule-oriented over periods of time. In Venezuela in 1984 it is fair to conclude that the society has never been more rule-oriented politically than it is now. It is also fair to say that because these rules were created to a great extent in time when the society was increasingly affluent and are being implemented currently during a time of economic stagnation, they will necessarily face some important tests. Laws will change; certain institutions (for example, the state corporations) may very well change their complexion greatly; and political careers will be affected for both individuals and parties. But, as Gil Yepes and others have pointed out, and as electoral results increasingly show, the parties that were largest in 1958 have grown even larger and have changed their socioeconomic complexion in the process to become "polyclassist" and less ideological.

In the process, their commitment to the current constitutional system has been the one factor that has continued to unite them. The economic recession has not changed this. Indeed, it can be said that it appears to have strengthened the bonding between elites and the constitutional arrangement. From this vantage point it can be fairly said that the constitutional arrangement has become institutionalized and should be expected to persist without significant change through the next generation of Venezuelan political actors.

NOTES

1. Gabriel A. Almond and James S. Coleman, *The Politics of the Developing Areas* (Princeton, N.J.: Princeton University Press, 1960), and Lucien Pye and Sidney Verba, eds., *Political Culture and Political Development* (Princeton, N.J.: Princeton University Press, 1965).

2. República de Venezuela, *Constitución promulgada el 23 de enero de 1961* (Caracas: Secretaría del Senado, 1961).

3. Seymour Martin Lipset, *The First New Nation* (New York: Doubleday Anchor, 1967).

4. Maria Eugenia de Currel, *Tres motivaciones en el niño venezolano y sus aplicaciones en la enseñanza primaria* (Caracas: Imprenta del Ministerio de Educación, 1971), footnoted in José Antonio Gil Yepes, *The Challenge of Venezuelan Democracy* (New Brunswick, N.J.: Transaction Books, 1981), p. 77.

5. Perhaps the most cogently written of these analyses is found in John D. Martz and David J. Myers, eds., *Venezuela: The Democratic Experience* (New York: Praeger, 1977), pp. 359–90.

6. David J. Myers, "The Elections and the Evolution of Venezuela's Party System," in Howard R. Penniman, *Venezuela at the Polls* (Washington, D.C.: American Enterprise Institute, 1980), p. 221. Also see Gil Yepes, *Challenge*, pp. 39–74.

7. The best and most recent case of this in Soviet bloc leadership circles is evidenced by Konstantin Chernenko, who, within one month's time of accepting the leadership of the Communist party, also assumed the title of president of the state.

8. H. L. A. Hart, *The Concept of Law* (London: Oxford University Press, 1961). pp. 18–25 especially.

9. Roberto Goldschmidt, *Nuevos estudios de derecho comparado* (Caracas: Facultad de Derecho, Universidad Central de Venezuela, 1963); Rafael Naranjo Ostty, *Doctrina y acción jurídicas* (Caracas: Gráfica Americana, 1963); and Juan Manuel Mayorca, hijo, "Venezuela,"in *Criminology: A Cross-Cultural Perspective*, ed. Dee H. Chang (Durham, N.C.: Carolina Academic Press, 1976), pp. 980–1039.

10. See Mayorca, "Venezuela."

11. Ibid., p. 1021.

12. "Venezuela," *Bank of London and South American Review* 16, no. I/82 (February 1982): 50.

13. Mayorca, "Venezuela," p. 1021.

14. Bernard Crick, *In Defense of Politics* (Baltimore: Penguin Books, 1964). See especially his discussion of Lincoln as the quintessential example of the effective politician able to unify these opposites in a principled way. It can be argued that the Venezuelan politicians of the Betancourt period and later have dealt with the military in much the same way as Lincoln spoke to the issue of slavery in American public life.

3

Public Opinion and Support for the Regime: 1973-83

Enrique A. Baloyra

Much has been written about the deterioration of the Venezuelan democratic regime during the last ten years. Critics and opponents of the regime have left no stone unturned searching for aspects of contemporary Venezuelan politics deserving condemnation. Even more sober students and observers share these concerns while posing the problem in a more measured tone. There is to be sure much about the Venezuelan democratic regime that deserves criticism. However, those who refuse to focus their criticism are no more effective, both in an intellectual and in a political sense, than the proverbial blindman lashing out with a walking cane. It is not enough to say that there is a crisis. After all the crisis of Venezuelan politics has been a topic of discussion since the early 1960s.[1] It behooves the analyst to specify what is in crisis, and there is a tendency to neglect this in favor of more sweeping generalizations concerning the shortcomings of political institutions and the unacceptable results of the political process.[2] Very frequently the crisis is linked to the dominant values of the contemporary political culture that cannot be expected to change abruptly.[3]

There are those who turn a Marxist parable on its head and insist that the Venezuelan state exists only to reproduce a party system that has proven incapable of administering abundance. Previous governments are castigated because of their corruption and their lack of any effective judicial action against most of those accused of corruption and graft.[4] Their identity is supposedly known to all Venezuelans.[5]

Some consider 1974 to have been a watershed year because many fiscal restraints were loosened up and the squandering of petroleum resources was legalized.[6] This produced a Venezuelan economic "countermiracle" that has created misery out of abundance.[7] More charitable versions of this theme complain about government providing little bread and much too much circus.[8] The bureaucracy is also blamed for not restraining the irresponsible policies of the government. Many see it paralyzed, or as a slowly turning machinery of government beset by defective decisional mechanisms, predominantly ideological criteria, and misinformation.[9] In essence the complaint here is about a colossal maladministration of abundance.

Inevitably, the two dominant political parties are put in the eye of the storm. They are allegedly controlled by inaccessible elites pejoratively described as *cogollos* or *cúpulas*, no longer representative or responsible, who have imposed corruption as a life norm.[10] The domination of these two parties has created a *partidocracy* that has turned politics into a business and a very profitable investment for their leaders.

These developments have turned the Venezuelan regime into an enormous and gigantic farce, a "democracy of parties" lacking any substantive content and terminally ill despite its populist pretentions.

Judging from these apocalyptic descriptions of the crisis one would imagine that the Venezuelan regime survives by an unparalleled act of political will and/or the imbecility of the population. Another interpretation is that those outside the mainstream of the two dominant parties have made a virtue out of invective and exaggeration.

Given the centrality of political parties in Venezuelan life, it would appear inevitable that if the system is in crisis the dominant political parties have something to do with it. The problem, as posed by some eminent students of Venezuelan politics, is whether these parties are capable of changing course or, lulled by their own electoral success and overwhelmed by their inability to resolve the contradictions that they have created, play for time.[11] As a matter of fact, the presidential candidates of the two dominant parties referred to the crisis during the electoral campaign of 1982–83 and, in addition, there is evidence of increasing discontent among the Venezuelan public.[12]

Readers familiar with Venezuelan politics will immediately detect that many of the works cited were utilized by the director of a news weekly to prepare his campaign for the presidency in the general election of 1983. Those readers might dismiss the arguments as blatantly self-serving. But however perverse and extreme these criticisms may be, they illustrate the kind of critical discourse found in contemporary Venezuelan politics.

I will utilize as a baseline results presented in the first edition of this book. I will compare data collected in 1973 and in 1983 to describe how the patterns of evaluations of the public have changed during the decade past. Finally, I will present additional information on the present mood of the Venezuelan public.

CONTINUITY AND CHANGE: 1973–83

Ten years ago I summarized the contradictory results of a similar inquiry as follows. Despite much discontent with the outcomes of the policies of the governments of the democratic era and with the performance of political parties, the bureaucracy, and the politicians, the level of support for the intermediary institutions of democracy remained very high.[13] More specifically, I found (1) higher levels of support and more favorable evaluations of the regime among middle-class citizens, (2) very high levels of support for democratic capitalism among the partisans of the Social Democratic (AD) and the Social Christian (COPEI) parties, (3) higher levels of criticism among Venezuelan leftists who are younger, better educated, and feel more efficacious than other voters, and (4) very high levels of support for political opposition, competitive elections, and multiparty politics.[14]

High discontent with the results of democratic politics and high levels of support for the democratic principles are not a uniquely Venezuelan phenomenon.[15] Apparently, even in the more authoritarian context of Mexico, it is possible to maintain high levels of "diffuse support" for the regime since "there is a persistent and widespread tendency for citizens to attribute failures of [regime] performance to the personal inadequacies of incumbents."[16] However, there is evidence that sustained dissatisfaction may lead to protest behavior by politically efficacious critics of the system.[17]

Intrigued by the absence of widespread protests and of civil disobedience in Venezuela following the settlement of the guerrilla question in 1968, I went back to the data trying to establish finer discriminations. I separated "critics" from "cynics," treating the latter as extreme critics, and trying to determine the sources and consequences of each type of discontent. I found that the relatively high "normal" levels of public criticism found in Venezuela were closely related to partisan and ideological considerations.[18] Cynicism, by contrast, was grounded in social inequality and interpersonal distrust and appeared relatively immune to partisan and/or ideological manipulation.[19] Finally, increasing levels of criticism and cynicism led to a decreased sense of personal political efficacy and to a greater propensity to withdraw from voting participation but not to greater support for more extreme partisan and ideological options or forms of protest behavior.[20]

How much have these patterns changed during the last ten years?

A summary of data based on identical questions administered in 1973 and 1983 offers partial answers.[21] The evidence consists of data on four different areas of opinion, including criticism of the governments of the last 25 years, of the role of politicians, of the institution of elections, and feelings of personal political efficacy. These data do not suggest an irresistible process of deterioration. While negative evaluation of the government has increased, evaluation of the role of politicians—the more negative aspect detected in 1973—is less unfavorable. Support for the institution of elections has held very firm. Finally, levels of personal political efficacy have not improved from the very low levels of the early 1970s (see Table 3.1).

In general, the performance of the governments of the democratic era is now viewed more disfavorably. More people believe that those governments have wasted public resources, that their policies have been harmful to them, that they really have served the interests of powerful groups and not those of the people, and that many of the officials of those governments were crooked.

TABLE 3.1. Public Discontent in Venezuela, 1973 and 1983

	1973	1983
Criticism of the government[a]		
Government action almost never right	28.0	26.4
Governments ... have wasted money	56.5	68.4
Impact of policy personally harmful	16.6	28.8
Governments have served powerful groups	60.3	68.0
Many government officials crooked	39.0	66.0
Government policy has been bad for nation	34.4	37.8
Criticism of elections		
Voting not important in politics	5.4	3.9
Democracy possible without elections	7.6	4.0
Elected candidates do not care about constituency problems	43.5	27.8
Elections do not make the government care about people's problems	25.8	23.4
Criticism of politicians		
Politicians always lie	81.1	77.7
Government better off without politicians	56.5	40.3
Politicians do not care about the problems of people like me	66.6	60.2
Politicians do not care about the problems of the nation	44.8	36.3
Politicians talk much and do nothing	81.6	72.3
Personal political efficacy:		
People in government do not worry about what people like me think	73.5	62.2
People like me cannot influence what the government does	65.9	62.8
Politics is so complex that people like me do not know what is going on	70.3	64.6
Voting is the only way that people like me can influence the government	64.7	69.9

All figures in percentages.

[a]All of these questions refer to the governments of the democratic era (1958–83).

Sources: VENEVOTE (*n* = 1,521), VENEDEMO (*n* = 1,789).

Additional evidence—not included in the table—shows that there is greater dissatisfaction with the performance of the more recent governments, particularly those of COPEI.

On a scale of 1 (very good) to 5 (very bad), the mean scores are as follows: 2.54 for Rómulo Betancourt (1959–64), 2.35 for Raúl Leoni (1964–69), 2.92 for Rafael Caldera (1969–74), 2.90 for Carlos Andrés Pérez (1974–79), and 3.66 for Luis Herrera Campins (1979–84). About 57 percent of those interviewed in 1983 said that "AD governments had done less than what was expected of them," and 70 percent held the same opinion with respect to those of COPEI. Luis Herrera's performance stands for its very negative ratings, but this does not suggest an irreversible decline. There were two previous occasions in which incumbents were rated better than their predecessors: Leoni over Betancourt and Pérez over Caldera. However, President Jaime Lusinchi (elected in 1983) may find it difficult to emulate this feat.

Despite this discontent with government there is nothing to indicate similar discontent with the method for selecting the government. If anything, the low level of criticism of the institution of elections has diminished even more. The aspect receiving more criticism—whether elected officials care about the problems of their constituents—improved substantially. In 1973, about 44 percent of the respondents thought that candidates no longer cared once elected; in 1983, only about 28 percent thought so.

Politicians were very much the lightning rod of public discontent a decade ago. Substantial majorities of the 1973 sample found themselves in agreement with all kinds of derogatory statements about politicians. Opinion continues to be rather negative about them, particularly with respect to deceit, indolence, and lack of regard for people's problems.[22] However, most people no longer believe that government would be better without politicians and that politicians do not care about national problems.

Feelings of personal political efficacy are another matter. Most Venezuelans continue to feel incapable politically, but fewer feel that government officials do not care about what they think or that politics is incomprehensible. The proportion of those who believe that the suffrage is the only way in which they can influence the government has increased.

In summary, Venezuelans remain very supportive of the manner in which their governments have come to office, are increasingly dissatisfied with what they do once they get there, and are imbued with the feeling that the suffrage is the only way to improve things.

The evidence on party loyalties and ideological preferences suggests little fluctuation during the last two presidential terms. Despite the negative patterns of evaluations of government performance and of the behavior of politicians, the level of support for the two dominant parties has not been eroded and the level of

TABLE 3.2. Party Preferences and Ideological Tendencies, 1973–83

| | Identify With | | | |
	AD	COPEI	None	Other
...in 1973...	22.3	26.8	34.8	14.8
...in 1978...	20.9	24.9	29.5	18.2
...in 1983...	36.6	22.1	26.5	11.3

| Feeling thermometer[a] | Degree of Sympathy | | | |
| | A Great Deal | | None Whatever | |
	AD	COPEI	AD	COPEI
...in 1973...	17.2	20.4	52.3	43.4
...in 1983...	19.3	10.1	32.6	46.3

Ideological tendency[b]	Left	Center	Right	None
...in 1973...	20.5	22.0	30.6	15.9
...in 1978...	19.5	28.2	27.3	15.6
...in 1983...	16.5	23.1	30.0	11.8

[a]Question: "... We would like you to tell us whether you feel *a lot, considerable, some, very little,* or *no sympathy whatsoever* toward ...."

[b]Question: "... where are you in Venezuelan politics, on the Right, the Center, or the Left?"

Sources: VENEVOTE and VENEDEMO. Date for 1978 from a survey of 1,000 respondents conducted by DATOS, C.A. in the seven largest cities for Dr. Juan Del Aguila, now at Emory University.

support for other partisan and ideological alternatives has remained relatively low (see Table 3.2).

The percentage of *adeco* identifiers dipped somewhat during the government of Carlos Andrés Pérez but rebounded rather strongly during the Herrera Campins presidency. AD identifiers increased from 22 to almost 37 percent of the public between the election campaigns of 1973 and 1983. COPEI, by contrast, suffered a reduction from almost 27 down to 22 percent. During this decade the proportion of nonidentifiers declined from about 35 to 26 percent, and all the combined total of those identifying with all other parties declined to 11 percent, despite a slight increase in 1978.

Data measuring the degree of professed sympathy for these parties are presented in Table 3.2. Party identifiers and ideological tendency results refer to all respondents; the thermometer includes only the two extreme categories, those expressing "a great deal" of sympathy and those averaging "none whatsoever." Gauged in these terms the partisan loyalties seem less robust as only 19 and 10 percent of those interviewed in 1983 expressed a great deal of sympathy for AD and COPEI, respectively. By contrast, level of antipathy toward AD declined substantially, whereas that expressed toward COPEI increased somewhat, compared to 1973 levels.

In essence, the data on party loyalties show an overall increase in the proportion of those identifying with the dominant parties; a marked increase in the proportion of *adeco* identifiers and a more receptive attitude toward the Social Democrats, suggested by the decline in the proportion of those expressing outright antipathy toward AD; and a gradual decline of *copeyano* identifiers accompanied by a substantial decrease in the proportion of the most intense sympathizers of COPEI.

Other data gathered in 1983, but not included in Table 3.2, offers some clues about the public's evaluation of the role of these two parties during the democratic era. On the negative side we find 35 percent without any faith in them, 55 percent saying they are the same thing, and 29 percent believing that their role has been, in the main, negative. These views are counterbalanced by 55 percent saying that at least one of them has played a positive role, 40 percent who do not believe that they are the same thing, and 62 percent who have faith in at least one of them. While these views are not completely favorable, they do not suggest that both parties stand together in disgrace.[23]

Turning back to the evidence presented in Table 3.2 we can see that the patterns of personal ideological tendencies did not change much during 1973–83. More people now hold specific ideological preferences, fewer people identify themselves as leftists, and centrists and rightists are about the same proportion of the public. This is hardly the harbinger of a major political upheaval about to be instigated from below.

In summary, the contrast between 1973 and 1983 shows sustained discontent with a number of political institutions that seems to be related more closely to the performance of the Social Christian governments and that has naturally affected levels of support for that party. The result has been an improvement in the fortunes of their Social Democratic rivals expressed in terms of party identification and party sympathy. Tentatively at least one can conclude that it is not the system but one of the dominant parties that is in crisis. The regime itself does not appear to be in serious trouble, at least as long as disenchantment with COPEI translates into support for AD and not for extreme and/or more drastic options. In order to determine whether this may be the case, we need to review some additional evidence.

POLITICAL CRITICISM IN 1983

Two conclusions that emerge from such a review can be advanced immediately: first, there is a very marked preference for democracy among the Venezuelan public but, second, there is a great deal of concern about the corrosive effect of corruption and about what this may ultimately do to the regime. The public continues to believe in the promise of democratic politics but is apprehensive about this being overwhelmed by moral deterioration.

Continued faith in the possibilities of the regime is manifested in the very substantial majorities of respondents agreeing that "a democracy like ours" can resolve the problems of unemployment (62 percent), the high cost of living (58 percent), the lack of housing (63 percent), the foreign debt crisis (60 percent), and even the dire living conditions of the poor (57 percent). This confidence is all the more remarkable, for it has been tested by shortcomings of the governments of the democratic era that have not escaped the attention of the public, as indicated above. However, this confidence in the regime's ability to resolve very complex problems is clouded by concern with corruption.

Even higher proportions of the public believe that there is a lot of corruption in politics (79.3 percent), that nothing or very little has been done to control it (75.4 percent), that political parties are largely responsible for it (76.8 percent), that its present level is intolerable (77 percent), and that so much corruption threatens the democratic regime (79.7). About one in three respondents, 35.5 percent, believe that if things continue to move along in this fashion a military coup would be very possible within two years.

But neither these majority opinions about corruption nor the minorities who believe and/or hope for a change have eroded the preference for democracy among the Venezuelan public. In the 1983 survey we asked a number of preference questions concerning democracy and dictatorship. The results are presented in Table 3.3. In only one out of five significant areas of opinion is democracy compared unfavorably to dictatorship, and this is precisely on the question of corruption. Democracy is rated more favorably in every other area, including being able to resolve the national problems better, producing more well-being, and being better for Venezuela. The magnitudes involved in the overall

TABLE 3.3. Public Opinion About Democracy and Dictatorship, 1983

Questions	DEMO	DICTA
Do you prefer a democracy like the one of the last 25 years or dictatorship?	82.2	10.2
Which one can resolve better the national problems...?	67.0	20.7
Which is more corrupt...?	47.0	23.3
Which produces more well-being?	68.7	16.0
Which is better for Venezuela?	76.1	14.2

Source: VENEDEMO.

preference for one or the other show an overwhelming preference for democracy by a margin of 82 to 10 percent.

As for the question of support for military coups one must remember that a military coup made possible the redemocratization of Venezuela in 1958. Therefore it is not surprising to find, even in 1983, that 53 percent of our respondents can conceive of situations in which military coups are justified—without this necessarily implying the inauguration of an authoritarian regime. The proportion of persons who believed that the situation justified a coup in 1983 was not insubstantial, at 34.2 percent. However, responding to a different question, only 23.8 percent thought that the regime should be replaced.[24] Among those who supported this kind of option, 9.7 wanted a socialist regime and 4.8 a military dictatorship. Therefore those who have a specific alternative to the regime, whether or not this is brought about by a coup, are about 15 percent of the public.

Once again we do find some disturbing patterns, particularly with regard to corruption, but not much by way of high levels of support for specific alternative to the status quo. We find concern and exasperation with the shortcomings of Venezuelan democracy coupled with an overwhelming preference for that democracy; we even find that dictatorship is considered less corrupt than democracy but most people say democracy is better for the country. In summary, therefore, democracy still gets the benefit of the doubt, but it cannot rest on its laurels.

PROFILE OF THE DISCONTENT

It remains to be seen how different segments of the population feel about these matters. Given limitations of space and the nature of the evidence, this can be accomplished by focusing on the more critical aspects of opinion and on how persons with different characteristics feel about them. Table 3.4 includes such personal attributes as age, class status, income and education, political self-image, and ideological tendency that produce statistically significant differences of opinion, as measured by the eta co-efficient.[25] The opinions are four items dealing with whether a military coup was justified at the time, whether the political system should be substituted, respondents' personal choice between democracy and dictatorship, and which one, democracy or dictatorship, is better for Venezuela. Although these are not the most extreme views one can hold about Venezuelan politics, they tap crucial aspects of allegiance to the regime.

In essence, the data are congruent with previous findings concerning discontent running in terms of differences between the haves and the have-nots, between younger and older voters, and between mainstream and more extreme partisan and ideological preferences. One finds wider discrepancies of opinion among persons in different social circumstances, but these differences involve only one or two of the items. By contrast, one finds differences for all four items among persons holding differences in political self-images and ideological preferences, but the disparities are not as great.

The young appear more supportive of a coup and somewhat more willing to substitute the system. By contrast, those over 50 years of age, who presumably know better because they experienced dictatorship, are least willing to change the system and least supportive of a coup. The difference between the youngest and oldest generations is about 15 percentage points in these two items. However, those most willing to substitute the system are between 25 and 34 years of age.

Viewed from the perspective of the haves versus that of the have-nots, opinion about whether a coup is justified is more divergent. Using class status we find differences of 46 to 19 percent between classes D and A; using income, the difference is of 60 to 22 percent between the lowest (less than Bs. 500 a month) and highest (more than 10,000) brackets; and using educational level the difference between illiterates and college graduates is of 47 to 18 percent (see Table 3.4). Those at the bottom of the socioeconomic ladder—in class D, below an income of Bs. 999, and without formal education—are more impatient.

However, we cannot detect statistically significant differences for the items measuring opinion about whether the system ought to be substituted, except among persons of different educational levels. In this case, those who had expressed more agreement with the desirability of a coup, the illiterate, were least willing to substitute the system. Evidently they saw the coup as a means of removing a government—that of Luis Herrera—and not of changing the regime.

TABLE 3.4. Democratic Disillusionment Among the Public, 1983

Age cohort

Personal Attributes/Opinions	18–24	25–35	35–49	50+	Eta	Sample Percent	Valid Cases
Coup justified now	45.0	39.2	32.1	30.9	.11	38.0	1,612
Substitute system	28.2	30.2	23.6	14.6	.18	25.2	1,693

Class status

	D	C	B	A	Eta	Sample Percent	Valid Cases
Coup justified now	46.4	40.4	25.9	19.1	.18	38.0	1,612

Monthly family income

	<500	<999	<1,999	<4,999	<9,999	10,000+	Eta	Sample Percent	Valid Cases
Coup justified now	60.5	49.3	44.7	36.1	26.3	21.8	.20	38.0	1,486

Educational level

	Illit.	Some Elem.	Elem.	Some Sec.	Sec.	Some College	College	Eta	Sample Percent	Valid Cases
Coup justified now	46.7	40.0	40.3	43.4	35.6	29.1	17.7	.15	38.0	1,607
Substitute system	18.4	18.9	25.9	31.4	22.8	24.5	19.6	.14	25.1	1,688

Political self-image	Apolitical	Independent	Sympathizer	Militant			
Coup justified now	46.1	38.4	34.7	27.9	.11	38.0	1,605
Substitute system	35.6	26.4	19.7	12.2	.19	25.3	1,685
Prefer dictatorship	15.9	11.7	6.9	4.2	.14	10.6	1,721
Dictatorship better for Venezuela	22.5	18.0	10.0	6.3	.16	15.5	1,637
Ideological tendency	None	Left	Center	Right			
Coup justified now	43.4	44.9	33.5	33.3	.10	37.1	1,352
Substitute system	25.3	46.3	25.3	15.4	.22	25.9	1,402
Prefer dictatorship	14.2	15.8	9.6	7.3	.19	10.7	1,415
Dictatorship better for Venezuela	19.8	24.0	12.1	10.5	.16	14.9	1,360

Note: Class status categories were assigned by the interviewer following criteria including type of dwelling, income, value of household items, and other status-related attributes of the interviewees. Each income category refers to the bracket above the previous one listed and below the figure listed.

Source: VENEDEMO.

Turning our attention to the data on political self-images and ideological preferences in Table 3.4, we can see that it is not those who have explicit preferences who are the most disloyal or problematic. Even though there are differences among independents, sympathizers, and militants, the independents are at or slightly above the sample mean. The apoliticals, by contrast, are relatively higher than the norm in terms of their antidemocratic opinions on all four items, and there are substantial differences between them and the militants. Therefore those who profess to have "no interest in politics" (the apoliticals) are a relatively authoritarian group in Venezuela. A similar proposition could be made with respect to those without specific ideological preferences except for the fact that they are not as impatient as the leftists.

Of the entire set of groups presented in Table 3.4 no group appears as impatient and ready to trash the Venezuelan democratic regime as the left. They may not be as far above the sample as some of the low-income groups, but leftists are above that norm in more areas of opinion. They would be followed by apoliticals and by persons without ideological identification. Next would be those under 24 years of age, persons with some secondary school education, and those between 25 and 34. One important qualification must be stressed once again, and that is that the numbers of people involved are not large.

RECAPITULATION

If the situation is neither as bad as some might have hoped and certainly less favorable than the professional optimists would like it to be, where does this mixed bag of evidence leave us? How serious really is the "crisis of democracy" in Venezuela?

The first point that we have to make is that democracy, whether the abstract ideal or the Venezuelan version, is not in trouble at the present time. There is little evidence to suggest that Venezuelans prefer authoritarianism and dictatorship, despite the serious drawbacks that they detect in the performance of the governments of the democratic era.

Second, the public was in a relatively foul mood at the time of our preelection survey of 1983, which covered the months of October and November. The administration of President Herrera received the lowest marks of any post-1958 administration, and a considerable minority was sufficiently exasperated with the situation that they would not mind deliverance through a coup.

Third, that coup would not have been, in the main and on the whole, linked to a substitution of the present system. Most of the people who believed that conditions justified a coup did not turn out to favor the installation of a dictatorship. Apparently, they felt that Herrera's lackluster performance justified a shortening of his term by whatever means.

Fourth, despite improvements in some of the areas being evaluated by the public, some deterioration is detectable. Concern with corruption in general and with the dishonesty of government officials is not to be taken lightly.

Fifth, the parties, and by implication "the center," can hold in the sense that the misfortunes of one improve the standing of the other. However, the unanswered question is what happens if or when the incumbent AD administration of President Jaime Lusinchi falters and is unable to address the policy agenda in any satisfactory way. My guess is that, even if this were the case, nothing dramatic would necessarily follow, for it is quite possible that the Social Christians would, in turn, benefit from this and get another chance.

Sixth, above and beyond the levels of discontent with the performance of politicians in general, the level of discontent with COPEI is unprecedented. It is here that one may speak more appropriately of a crisis that can have serious repercussions for Venezuelan democracy.

Finally, politics is the art of the possible and public opinion research deals with the realm of the probable. While at the level of the public the numbers are not there yet to talk about a crisis of Venezuelan democracy there is little in those numbers reviewed here that, taken together, suggests that what we see in Venezuela is "business as usual." Nothing could be farther off the mark, for the clear and present danger in today's numbers is that since they do not substantiate the thesis of a crisis of regime, they may lead to the erroneous inference that there is really not that much to worry about. I hope to have made an adequate case to the contrary.

NOTES

1. Among others, José Agustín Silva Michelena, *The Illusion of Democracy in Dependent Nations* (Cambridge, Mass.: MIT Press, 1971).

2. This tendency is evident even in some of the more sober appraisals written by Venezuelan scholars and public figures. See, for example, Allan Randolph Brewer-Carías, *Política estado y administración Pública* (Caracas: Editorial Ateneo, 1979); Luis Oropeza, *Tutelary Pluralism* (Cambridge, Mass.: Harvard Center for International Affairs, 1983); and Antonio Stempel Paris, *Venezuela, una democracia enferma* (Caracas: Editorial Ateneo, 1981).

3. I am referring here to a critical commentary concerning more specific aspects, such as the decentralized public enterprises, the university system, state legislatures, and municipal administration, which will not be dealt with here.

4. Gustavo Coronel, "Blanco, negro o gris: El dilema venezolano," *Resumen*, February 22, 1981, pp. 12–15.

5. Ibid., p. 12

6. "Habla el contralor: El país incontrolable," *Resumen*, May 2, 1982, pp. 11–15.

7. "Diálogo Olavarría-Ulsar Pietri: El contra-milagro venezolano ha creado miseria de la riqueza," *Resumen*, August 15, 1982, pp. 36–42.

8. "Monseñor Parra León: Los partidos no hacen sino hablar," *Resumen*, June 7, 1981, p. 6.

9. Diego Bautista Urbaneja, "Para una breve patología gubernamental," *Resumen*, September 27, 1981, pp. 14–15.

10. Jorge Olavarría, "La partidocracia venezolana," *Resumen*, July 5, 1981, and Domingo A. Labarca, "Venezuela: Partidocracia o estado de partidos?" *Resumen*, July 12, 1981, pp. 14–15.

11. See John D. Martz, "Los peligros de la petrificación," and Andrés Stambouli, "La democracia venezolana," in *Iberoamérica en los Años Ochenta*, ed. Enrique Baloyra and Rafael López-Pintor (Madrid: Centro de Investigaciones Sociológicas, 1983).

12. For illustration, see "Proyecto de bases del programa de gobierno del candidato socialcristiano," *Resumen*, September 12, 1982, pp. 17–22. See also Jaime Lusinchi's acceptance speech of July 29, 1982, reprinted in *Resumen*, August 8, 1982, pp. 4–8.

13. Enrique A. Baloyra, "Public Attitudes Toward the Democratic Regime," chapter 3 in John D. Martz and David J. Myers, *Venezuela: The Democratic Experience* (New York: Praeger, 1977), pp. 50–51.

14. Ibid., p. 62.

15. High levels of diffuse support and popular discontent are characteristic of many contemporary European democracies. See, for example, Richard Rose, "Public Confidence, Popular Consent: A Comparison of Britain and the United States," *Public Opinion* 7, no. 1 (February/March 1984): 9–11, 60.

16. Ann L. Craig and Wayne A. Cornelius, "Political Culture in Mexico: Continuities and Revisionist Interpretations," in *The Civic Culture Revisited*, ed. Gabriel A. Almond and Sidney Verba (Boston: Little, Brown, 1980), pp. 375, 371–78.

17. See Mitchell A. Seligson, "Trust, Efficacy and Modes of Political Participation," *British Journal of Sociology* 10, no. 1 (January 1980). Cited from draft version, pp. 34–41.

18. Enrique A. Baloyra, "Criticism, Cynicism, and Political Evaluation: A Venezuelan Example," *American Political Science Review* 73, no. 4 (December 1979): 997.

19. Ibid., pp. 994, 996.

20. Ibid., pp. 998–1000.

21. The 1983 data were collected through a national sample survey conducted by the Instituto Gallup de Venezuela and a team of investigators of the Coordinación de Estudios de Postgrado en Ciencia Política of Universidad Simón Bolívar during October and November of 1983, in collaboration with the author. The research design consisted of a progressively stratified random sample of 1,789 adult Venezuelans drawn from communities of 10,000 or more inhabitants. Hereafter I will refer to this study as VENEDEMO, to distinguish it from the 1973 survey identified as VENEVOTE elsewhere.

22. In 1983 about 48 percent of our respondents held a negative view of politicians that seems to be rooted in a perception of politicians as capable, albeit malevolent, individuals: 56 percent believed that they are corrupt, 78 percent that they lie systematically, and 69 percent that they are capable.

23. Once again we find COPEI evaluated less favorably. About 37 percent believed that both have played a positive role, 12 percent believe that AD's role has been positive but not COPEI's, and 5 percent hold the opposite view; and 19 percent have faith in both, 27 percent have faith in AD but not in COPEI, while 16 percent have faith in COPEI but not AD.

24. Responding to this question, 22.2 percent said they were "very happy" with the regime and 48.6 said they were "more or less satisfied" with it.

25. There are no such differences to report with respect to the sex of the respondent, that is, men and women did not really differ in how they viewed these matters. Two other variables, occupation and party identification, pose the problem of too many categories resulting in too many empty cells when they are cross-tabulated with other variables. This creates an additional problem pertaining to the validity of the results. Fortunately, class status and income and education yield the same results that occupation would have, and ideological tendency can be used as a proxy for partisanship.

4

The Politics of Economic Development

John D. Martz and David J. Myers

The intertwining of oil and politics has been a salient characteristic of twentieth-century Venezuela. Central to the economic outlook of Venezuelan political elites is the obvious if critical conviction that properly used petroleum wealth holds the key to national control over the economy, to progress in the realm of social justice, and to achieving balanced economic development. In the words of Juan Pablo Pérez Alfonzo, architect of modern Venezuelan petroleum policy:

> Venezuela has a great resource in its petroleum, but it is faced with great responsibility. It must not impede use of this resource to satisfy the needs of other people, but in protecting its own national interest, it must never let the industry become dilapidated.
> Petroleum is the principal of all indispensable fuels in modern life.... Venezuela needs to maintain and even to increase the income it receives from petroleum. With a policy of just participation, the exploitation of present concessions is enough for the country.[1]

While the concept of "sowing" petroleum to create industry and modernize agriculture has received lip service since the early 1940s, little was accomplished until the second Betancourt administration (1959–64). Indeed, General Pérez Jiménez (1953–58) followed a policy of benign neglect in relation to sowing petroleum. His advisers essentially viewed the growth of the oil industry, plus income from new concessions and sales, as a means to finance an ever-increasing volume of imports. Oil represented as much as 98 percent of the total value of exports while occupying a mere 3 percent of the economically active population. During the Pérez Jiménez years, such a shortsighted view of economic development even seemed defensible. As James Hanson reported in his analysis of post-1950 cycles of growth and structural change, the increase in domestic product averaged an extraordinary 9.4 percent per year. National income also grew rapidly, enjoying one of the highest per capita growth rates in the world—5.7 percent when adjusted for population growth. Petroleum constituted the basis for the expansion, as the nation "took advantage of a rapidly growing world market... to expand exports of crude oil at 7.4 percent and petroleum products at 14 percent per annum."[2]

During the 1950–57 period, overall growth in the national economy closely paralleled that of the petroleum sector. Expansion in industry, construction, textiles, and power was linked to to the performance of petroleum. The economy's growth was fundamentally capital-intensive, and it was accompanied by rapid urbanization. In the mid-1950s Caracas became the first Venezuelan city with more than 1 million inhabitants. So much attention was devoted to modernizing Caracas that the government ignored the lagging agricultural sector. Thus the condition of a dynamic enclave petroleum economy surrounded by inefficient agricultural production, a dualism that long characterized twentieth-century economic life, persisted as the dictatorship approached its demise. Also, a host of typically grandiose projects stood incomplete: the Simón Bolívar Center's rebuilding of central Caracas, the Morón petrochemical complex, the CONAHOTU hotel chain, and such white elephants as the futuristic Heliocoide and the impractical Humbolt Hotel. These projects were financed by short-term treasury bills that pushed the public debt to the limit of the government's ability to pay. The situation became critical after General Pérez Jiménez looted the treasury during the final weeks of his regime.

The provisional government of Admiral Wolfgang Larrazábal faced a grave economic situation when it hastily assumed power. During a year at the helm, it succeeded in further aggravating the economic situation. While the junta paid off $1.4 billion in short-term debt inherited from the dictatorship, an almost equal amount was disallowed. Influence and commissions became critical in determining whose billings were considered legitimate and whose were not. Larrazábal's "emergency plan" to build public works in Caracas was intended to relieve unemployment and attract popular support. In practice it became so costly and so corrupt that it was quickly abandoned. Consequently, by the time Rómulo Betancourt opened the democratic era with his February 1959 inauguration, economic crisis threatened political stability. The task of meeting immediate economic needs appeared over-whelming. Beyond that lay the imperative of formulating the basis for a consensus within which individual developmental policies might be defined and implemented.

PLURALISM AND STATE CAPITALISM

Initiating the Democratic Era

With the beginning of the democratic renewal, at least three ideologies or political doctrines existed that could help to set public policy objectives: the Social Democratic, the Social Christian, and the Marxist. Despite significant differences, especially concerning the latter's view of the Soviet Union, the three generally have concurred with one another over four policy objectives: nationalism, statism, populism, and developmentalism.[3] As concerns the economy, this was interpreted as rejection of Cuban-style authoritarianism to force a redistribution of wealth and status. Venezuela's democratic elite also rejected the Mexican and Brazilian models, which emphasized growth and overlooked problems related to the unequal distribution of wealth. Instead, stress was placed on utilizing petroleum income both to stimulate economic growth and close the gap between rich and poor. In addition, President Betancourt promised to "sow the petroleum"— use income from the sale of petroleum to create industries that would make the country less dependent on foreign manufactured goods. Betancourt spoke for the democratic political elites when he declared on 15 February 1961

> We must dispel the happy theory that the oil derricks are producing an inexhaustible quantity of dollars and bolivares. The truth is that we are spending the proceeds of unrenewable, perishable

wealth, and that we must spend it well, taking advantage of the extraordinary current situation of Venezuela to establish solid and durable bases for the Venezuelan nation. We are investing the funds that oil brings us to obtain increasingly greater returns from this wealth.[4]

Economic recession seriously hampered the Betancourt administration during its first three years. In addition to the legacy of Pérez Jiménez' extravagances and Larrazábal's emergency expenditures, petroleum prices dropped—resulting in a $150 million reduction in annual income. Capital flight, spurred by fears of devaluation and accompanying tax increases, also added to Betancourt's economic difficulties. In order to stabilize the economy, foreign loans were negotiated, exchange controls were imposed, and government salaries were reduced by 10 percent on two occasions. Not until late 1961 and early 1962 did deflationary policies begin to stem the flow of capital. Gross domestic product (GDP) rose only 3.1 percent between 1959 and 1961. Manufacturing and construction also suffered, and the goals of the First National Development Plan—which included 7 percent growth in GDP— had to be discarded in 1962.

Betancourt's economic advisers advocated creating new government entities for the purpose of import substitution. They also strengthened a number of existing autonomous institutes, especially the Corporación Venezolana de Fomento (Venezuelan Development Corporation—CVF) and the Corporación Venezolana de Guayana (Venezuela Guayana Corporation—CVG). The former sought out both foreign and domestic investment to promote industrial development. The latter was assigned the responsibility to stimulate and oversee development of the vast Guayana region, its resources, and the new town of Ciudad Guayana. Among the difficulties of import substitution, however, was the fact that foreign investors were increasingly relocated in Venezuela. Consequently, like their local counterparts, the subsidiaries of multinational enterprises came to depend on resource transfers from the government to finance their activities in Guayana. In addition, the high tariffs that protected most private sector activities in Venezuela led "to the concentration of capital, and pinched the Venezuelan consumer."[5]

If there was some inconsistency in its fiscal policy, the Betancourt administration was also constrained by the fact that petroleum income grew by only 2.7 percent annually from 1959 to 1963. At that juncture, a somewhat greater increase contributed to more rapid growth of the money supply, and economic commitments were expanded. By the time the Leoni team came to government in early 1964, the economy was slowly but undeniably on the road to recovery. The new president continued the basic policy emphases of his long-time colleague and predecessor, which were consistent with the character of the times. Given that petroleum production gradually was increasing in value, government revenue also rose. There were few new programs of major consequence, nor were there striking economic initiatives. Gross domestic product averaged 5.5 percent increase annually from 1963 to 1967—a healthy development, even if failing to meet the ambitious target of 7 percent set forth in the Third National Plan.

A major struggle during the Leoni years came with AD's attempted reform of tax policy. Both corporate and personal income taxes were to be augmented while, at the same time, oil company profits were to be taxed at a higher rate. When the private sector-oriented National Democratic Front, one of the three parties in President Leoni's governing coalition, came out in opposition to the tax increase, the government was paralyzed for several months. Nevertheless, an alliance of AD and the populist URD was ultimately successful in securing congressional approval for a watered-down version of the original proposal. Notwithstanding the successful negotiation of new terms with the multinational petroleum interests, however, the government was faced with the reality of lagging external income and the necessity of increasing the domestic economy's productivity. The rate of agricultural growth did exceed GDP expansion during these years, the recession came to an end, and import substitution helped the nation achieve annual growth rates of about 7 percent. The administration won an important symbolic battle by joining the Associación Latinoamericana de Libre Comercio (Latin American Free Trade Association—ALALC) in 1966 despite the angry opposition of Fedecamaras. Some years would pass, however, before Venezuela was able to participate in even a minimal fashion.

With the election of COPEI's Rafael Caldera in 1968, the

pluralistic system received a further test of the consensus over economic policy that had been solidifying during the preceding decade. The experience of a non-*adeco* administration—for Caldera did not invite members of the opposition party to join him—did indeed testify to the relative agreement that had emerged. With regard to petroleum itself, still the linchpin for national economic development, objectives and strategies were increasingly bipartisan. These included achievement of greater control over the industry, the "sowing" of profits to raise living standards and create ever more import substitution enterprises, the conservation of oil reserves, and the encouragement of global conditions that might assure stable markets and fair prices.[6] Thus the Social Christians were no less insistent than the Social Democrats that the state should be heavily involved in the quest for national development and that oil earnings must contribute to distributive justice.[7] In this context it is significant that the Caldera government found itself facing basically similar political-economic problems to those encountered by Raúl Leoni.

The benefits of import substitution policies were viewed with increasing skepticism during the second half of the Caldera administration. The domestic market was small and geared to the middle classes and the elites. Prospective entry into the Andean Pact, however, although strongly supported by the Social Christians, engendered active opposition from Venezuelan industrialists who feared competition from their low-wage neighbors. Perennially cautious Fedecamaras spokesmen argued that Pact membership would discourage investment, introduce greater domestic inflation, and place difficult strains on Venezuela's more affluent labor sectors. In spite of the private sector's opposition, Rafael Caldera convinced the Congress to approve Pact membership in February 1973. An important factor influencing Caldera's advocacy was his desire to unite Spanish South America in a way that would enable it to match Brazil's rapidly expanding economy. Also, over the long run Caldera hoped to decrease Venezuelan dependence on the United States as a market for its products. He had already repudiated the Venezuela-United States trade agreement in 1971. Such actions occurred within a context of modestly increasing petroleum revenues—although there had in fact been a temporary decline in 1969. Government income continued to rise throughout the remainder of Caldera's term; however, the rise also depended on revenue from iron ore and several nonmining products, as well as on oil.

In a sense, the experience of the Caldera administration was economically striking because of its domestic political implications. The Venezuelan private sector, although marginally less suspicious of Acción Democrática than in 1959, had nonetheless clung to the hope that the installation of a COPEI government would in effect produce a pro-business regime. Its illusions were dashed, for the government-private sector relationship proved, if anything, less harmonious than had been the case under Leoni. By way of illustration, consider the fact that the Congress in 1970 voted to limit the equity of foreigners in Venezuelan banks to 20 percent. This encouraged the availability of additional credit but limited the economic power of those who historically had acted as agents for overseas financial interests. Two years later, efforts to "democratize" by opening the ownership of domestic businesses to the Venezuelan public were perceived as signs of hostility by those who managed the entrepreneurial sector. It was ultimately unsurprising that, as José Antonio Gil reported, a 1973 survey found that only 38.3 percent of business leaders regarded the Caldera government as providing adequate representation for their views on public policy.[8] Again, citing Judith Ewell, it was evident that business was as disillusioned with COPEI and Caldera as it had been previously with the AD; by 1973, it "could see little difference between COPEI and AD on economic matters."[9]

The Petroleum Bonanza

Upon the return of Acción Democrática under Carlos Andrés Pérez in 1974, Venezuelan state capitalism was unleashed with a vengeance. The quadrupling of petroleum income in the 12 months preceding Pérez's inauguration resulted in a flood of new capital being available to the incoming administration. Even though Pérez spoke of the need to administer abundance with the criteria of scarcity, there were grounds for skepticism as the so-called petroleum bonanza began to permeate the economy. The new prosperity was entirely the consequence of international events over which Caracas had diminishing control. From 1958 to

1973 the state had remained heavily dependent on petroleum revenue, although reserves were shrinking and Venezuela was no longer the leading exporter in the world. Also, it was unclear that Venezuela's financial infrastructure was capable of managing wealth of the magnitude that flowed into the country beginning in 1974. The government did create the Fondo de Inversiones Venezolanas (Venezuelan Investment Fund—FIV) to hold dollars abroad and prevent inflation; the cost of goods and services, nevertheless, increased more rapidly than in the past.

Pérez preferred state capitalism as an organizational form to stimulate economic development for two basic reasons: First, it allowed him to bypass the more traditional bureaucracies, many of which were considered inefficient. Second, keeping in mind AD's suspicion of the local business community and its international allies, President Pérez saw state capitalism as an organizational form that would allow the entire nation a chance to make profits on its large investment and use those profits for the general welfare. Investments in state capitalism, however, proved more massive than initially anticipated, while their payoff was in the medium and long run. Consequently, even given sharply increased petroleum revenue, Pérez was forced to borrow on the international financial markets in order to carry on with many amitious development projects. Between 1974 and 1978 the Venezuelan state borrowed almost $10 billion overseas. Although this level of debt was manageable, total foreign indebtedness increased by almost $17 billion from 1979 to 1982, almost all of which was related to capital flight.[10]

At the beginning of the Pérez government there were great popular expectations. AD responded to them in the Fifth National Plan. It committed large sums to the creation and/or expansion of heavy industries, especially petrochemicals, steel, and shipbuilding. A plethora of state corporations, stimulating a dramatic increase of the so-called DPA (decentralized public administration)—swiftly grew up to meet such needs. In time, the list of projects assumed daunting proportions: expansion of the steel and aluminum industries in Guayana, exploitation of coal deposits in Zulia, a new steel complex in that same state, another construction phase to the Guri Dam for greater hydroelectric power and a fishery industry in the Paraguaná Peninsula, a national rail system, modernized port facilities—and more.

With the nationalization of iron in 1975 and of petroleum a year later, President Pérez implemented the nationalistic trade and investment policies long favored by both AD and COPEI. While nationalization of iron came at a time of excess global production capacity, petroleum nationalization occurred with market forces favoring the suppliers. Even though Venezuela paid out billions of dollars in compensation to the nationalized petroleum companies, attracting funds back into the country was not assigned a high priority. Decision 24 of the Andean Pact was rigorously enforced, while the government decreed in 1976 that major foreign manufacturers would be required to sell 80 percent of their stock to Venezuelans.[11] Although the FIV had initially been promised 50 percent of all revenues from petroleum, government obligations gradually forced it to reduce the share of income going to the fund. As indicated earlier, there was a deficit in the current account balance for the first time in five years.

Notwithstanding the predilection for ambitious works that would support extensive industrialization, the Pérez government was, at the same time, committed to creating a modern, capital-intensive agriculture sector. The policy assumptions that had linked agrarian reform with agricultural productivity during the preceding years had been brought into serious question.[12] The traditional peasant had not been transformed from sharecropper into modern agricultural producer. Working conditions remained much as they had been. Consequently, Carlos Andrés Pérez had pledged during his campaign that he would direct "priority attention to the needs of Venezuelan agriculture as the essential motor of economic development, as the generator of employment for the most numerous sector of our economically active population; as a primordial base for the nourishment of our growing population; and as the indispensable source of primary products."[13]

Shortly after taking office the new president proclaimed a five-year program of irrigation, dam construction, and an expansion of water resources and facilities. By April of 1975, Pérez officially claimed the achievement of an agricultural miracle; however, the facts were otherwise. Government programs, especially those devised by the Fifth National Plan, concentrated more on capital-intensive modernization and development than on landowner-ship. Productivity rather than social priorities was stressed. In practical terms, AD policies were favorable to agribusiness and to organized economic interests. A program of debt cancellation disproportionately benefited large farmers. Small producers received little. Nevertheless, even from the perspective of productivity alone, results were discouraging. Where Venezuela had imported 46 percent of its basic foodstuffs in 1971, by the close of the Pérez years it was approaching 70 percent. Imports included 27 percent of eggs, 43 percent of sugar, and 70 percent of *caraotas negras*, Venezuela's staple black bean.[14] On balance, the Pérez government had been unable to reverse the unfavorable trends of the previous 15 years for the agricultural sector.[15]

Pérez shared with his three predecessors an awareness of the distortions that extreme dependence on petroleum revenue introduced into the economy. However, his efforts to cope with this problem in the context of the post-1973 rise in petroleum income were less than successful. Given Pérez's commitment to move Venezuela into the ranks of the developed countries, the emphasis on gigantic projects proved irresistible. Also, Pérez's economic team saw no need to challenge the consensus that Venezuelan economic activity should be divided among local entrepreneurs, state corporations, traditional bureaucracies, and transnational corporations. It continued as an article of faith that capital-intensive projects divided among these entities would lead to sustained economic growth and development. In turn, prosperity would be extended to all sectors of society. While a definitive evaluation of the Pérez economic record remains to be made, there is no denying that expectations of government extravagance were further nourished. During the 1974–79 constitutional period, the government managed more funds than all of its predecessors since the coming of Venezuelan independence in 1830. The historic attitude of dependence on state economic initiatives became more deeply ingrained than ever. José Vicente Rangel, a left-leaning populist and presidential candidate, put it well:

> Powerful entrepreneurs have not even known how to propel a process of capitalistic development. Many of them have lived in the shadow of the State, despite criticizing it, and they work with a captive and protected market, benefiting in diverse ways from monopolistic foreign investment and from the dependent character of our society.[16]

With the closing of the Pérez years, it was apparent that notwithstanding a host of political accomplishments, Venezuelan democracy was still confronted with unresolved problems of economic development. As we wrote elsewhere,

> The system had not extended its economic largesse and natural resources on an equitable basis to large numbers of the population ... the social agenda remained unfulfilled. With the rise of new sectors, the continuing migration from rural to urban settings, and the rapid population increase, it remained to be proved that the political and economic progress that had taken place could be translated into benefits for the great mass of the citizenry.[17]

THE WAGES OF MISMANAGEMENT

Experimenting with Austerity

At the inaugural festivities of March 12, 1979, a new Social Christian president broke with tradition by facing his Social Democratic predecessor and angrily charging that Pérez had "mortgaged" the nation's future with his spending policies. This frontal attack worsened the COPEI-AD relationship; it also triggered a national debate.[18] Exchanges during the next several months produced a consensus over the need to stabilize and cool off the overheated economy. President Luis Herrera Campins rode the crest of these feelings when he promised an administration of austerity and fiscal discipline. His first minister of finance, Luis Ugueto, was a vocal advocate of the conservative Chicago school of economics. As a prime architect of COPEI's economic policy for nearly four years, Ugueto focused on four principal problems: control of spending and reduction of public sector expenditures, reduction and stabilization of the pace of export expansion, removal of price controls as a means of stimulating domestic production, and a diminution of import tariffs to encourage manufacturing competition and greater efficiency. Tight credit policies were to curb inflation while promoting economic growth and domestic production. As had the Pérez administration, President Herrera affirmed that agricultural development was critical to the nation. Overall, the COPEI government began by proclaiming its intention of cutting back state controls and allowing private enterprise to work its "developmental magic."

Luis Herrera Campins proceeded to remove price controls on some 175 consumer products during his first year in office. Only a few "essential" goods were exempted. Entrepreneurs applauded this apparent reversal of long-standing policy, and domestic production was expected to leap ahead. Before the year was out, however, the administration produced one of many later policy contradictions by yielding to demands for compensatory salary increases. Between August and October of 1979, prices had risen 9.4 percent. In all of 1978, prices had risen only 7.4 percent, and at the time COPEI had used this rate of increase with telling effect against the government party's presidential candidate, Luis Piñerúa Ordaz. The Venezuelan Labor Confederation, long a stronghold of AD support, brought irresistible pressure on the COPEI government during late 1979. In response, COPEI joined with AD in the national Congress to approve salary raises of 25 to 30 percent for low-paid workers. Soon afterward, in January 1980, subsidies on many imported foodstuffs were withdrawn. This further stimulated inflation. Where the long-standing application of controls had held the inflation rate to an annual average of 3 percent from 1930 to 1970—growing to as much as 8 percent under Carlos Andrés Pérez—the figure leapt upward soon after Herrera's inauguration. The cost of living index for metropolitan Caracas, which had risen 7.1 percent in 1978, grew by an additional 11.6 percent in 1979.

Ugueto's wavering application of Chicago school economics led to a marked slackening in the growth rate of economic activity. Thus, after having increased at an average rate of 7.5 percent in 1976 and 1977 and risen by 3 percent in 1978, the gross domestic product stagnated almost completely in 1979 and 1980; it actually went down in 1981. This sluggish movement of the GDP was the consequence of several important negative influences: reduction in petroleum activity, declines for the third year running in construction and commerce, and a drop in mining activity. The product of other economic activities increased by about 2 percent on average, although manufacturing production grew more slowly than during the 1970s.

There was also a marked reduction in the growth rate of the

value of exports of goods and services in 1981, and the value of imports went down only slightly. Nevertheless, petroleum revenue ensured that the trade balance generated a substantial surplus of more than $3.7 billion. Warning signals, however, were beginning to appear. After more than doubling in the previous two years, the value of petroleum exports rose by only 4 percent in 1981; nevertheless, it exceeded $19 billion for the first time. This increase was due entirely to the rise of about 12 percent in the sale price of petroleum, since the physical volume of crude production stagnated. That of petroleum products went down by more than 20 percent. On the other hand, sales of iron ore and aluminum totaled $580 million, registering increases of 14 percent and 4 percent, respectively. Imports of goods and services, for their part, came to $17.2 billion, 9.5 percent more than in 1980.[19]

While the unemployment rate approached 15 percent in 1981, the inflation rate came down. The latter had exceeded 20 percent in 1980, but by the end of 1981 it had fallen into the single-digit range. This was largely due to Herrera's modification of his Chicago school policies following his annual address to Congress in March. In this accounting he admitted that stimulation of the private sector had not proven sufficient. "Our decision to free prices has been a healthy and patriotic economic objective, but it cannot be left to the market to impose efficiency. The state will continue to stimulate competition, but can never renounce its regulatory function."[20]

The weather vane for COPEI's preferred economic policy was the Sixth National Development Plan. First scheduled for release on February 1, it was delayed and revised several times before its August 28, 1981 presentation to the Congress. Alterations responded both to strong criticisms from Acción Democrática and to an anticipated drop in the oil revenues on which expenditures would rely. The plan called for an annual growth rate of 3.5 percent and declared its preoccupation with social expenditures. Health, housing, and education would receive 23 percent of the total gross fixed investment. A reduction of poverty was promised, as was the creation of 1 million new jobs over the life of the plan. At the same time, the plan stressed industrial development. It envisioned growth in the capacity to produce steel and aluminum, in the efficiency of transportation and communications, and in the ability to generate electric power. Investments for industrial expansion also included $3.5 billion for the Carbozulia coal project and $1.2 billion for the petrochemical industry.

Investment in the petroleum industry was cut from $22.1 billion in the first draft of the plan to $18.4 billion in the version presented to the Congress. This included a reduction from $3.5 billion to $2.8 billion provided for development of the Faja Bituminosa (Orinoco Tar Belt) and its heavy crudes. Despite a weakening in the world petroleum market, the plan did not foresee any reduction in the enduring dependence on petroleum income for economic development. Inexplicably, it rested on the assumption that international prices would increase 12 percent by the close of 1982. By January 1982, however, Venezuelan heavy crudes were actually selling at some $5 per barrel less than they had 12 months earlier. Although the Herrera economic team continued to echo the president's assurance that the corner would be turned before the end of 1982, in point of fact the international petroleum market was becoming even softer, and Venezuela's economy was staggering.[21]

The unwillingness of President Herrera to come to grips with economic reality undermined confidence within the financial community. Capital flight, a problem since the 1979 inaugural statement about having inherited a mortgaged country, reached alarming proportions during 1982. For whatever reason, COPEI's economic team maintained the bolivar at an unrealistically high rate of exchange in relation to the U.S. dollar. Free convertibility continued. Consequently, between 1979 and 1982 more than $20 billion in private capital left the country. The government responded in late 1981 and early 1982 by increasing the money supply in an attempt to stimulate the economy and restore confidence. This effort was unsuccessful; the gross domestic product remained below the level of 1979. At the same time, moreover, the foreign debt was continuing to accumulate.

Borrowing had accelerated toward the close of the Pérez government as it was discovered that even the post-1973 revenue bonanza was insufficient to finance AD's massive development projects. Herrera also borrowed, but most of the funds he obtained were needed to compensate for capital flight.[22] As early as 1981 nearly $10 billion in short-term foreign debts had been acquired through the nation's numerous public sector agencies. The need to reduce short-term borrowing resulted in the drafting of a new public credit law. Adopted in August 1981, it led to a refinancing of nearly $1 billion at the medium term in the Euromarket. The law authorized efforts to refinance a total of $4.3 billion, while plugging existing loopholes that had permitted the state corporations (decentralized public administration) to negotiate international loans without government review or approval. Nevertheless, within a year the public debt had more than doubled, and the result was the emergence of a new economic issue of critical importance to the government and the nation.

As Herrera began his fourth year in office, his policies superficially reflected a commitment to the state capitalism that had been pioneered by his predecessor. Major economic activities remained largely in the hands of the state despite the government's repeated calls for greater private investment and production. Partially because of unfulfilled expectations, however, the private sector had become more sharply critical of Herrera's economic policies than it had been of those followed by his predecessor. Also, while Pérez was viewed unsympathetically, he was seen as competent in what he undertook. Now not only was Herrera viewed unsympathetically, his decisions were perceived as ill-informed and ineptly administered.[23] FEDECAMARAS, although itself unable to speak with a single voice, was barely communicating with Herrera's economic managers. Almost in isolation, cabinet officials continued to issue periodic complaints about private business's alleged lack of initiative. Individual entrepreneurs and their spokesmen, on the other hand, charged the administration with presiding over a condition of economic stagnation that was slipping into outright recession.

From Stagnation to Crisis

As the 1982 Christmas holidays approached, it was undeniable that the end of an era was at hand for Venezuela; the spending spree of the past decade was swiftly drawing to a close. The revenue from petroleum exports was 12.5 percent below estimated levels, the foreign debt had passed $30 billion, capital flight was accelerating, and gross domestic product was showing a decline of 1.5 percent. The first major domestic economic shock reflecting the new situation came on February 18, 1983. This was the date on which President Herrera allowed the bolivar to float against the dollar and implemented exchange controls. However, almost ten days of bitter debate within the cabinet passed before specifics of the new policy were announced. There was to be a 60-day price freeze and the exchange system would be three-tiered. The administration decided to retain the rate of 4.3 to 1 for "essential" imports, government purchases overseas, and the expenses of Venezuelan students living abroad. Nonessential imports were to be at an intermediate rate of 6 to the dollar, and luxury imports, foreign travel, and the remittance of money abroad would be at a floating rate. The floating rate began at 7.5 to 1, but by June it was in the neighborhood of 11 to 1.

Venezuela's capability to import immediately suffered a sharp decline, the increased cost of imported goods became an inflationary time bomb, and weekend trips to Miami by the middle class were no longer feasible. Almost at the same time a second shock wave shook the nation's economic foundations. At its February 1983 meeting, OPEC lowered production quotas for member nations. In the case of Venezuela, official figures for production were dropped to 2.02 million barrels, while projected exports of 1.79 million barrels per day were revised downward to 1.6 million. With petroleum at this juncture providing some 94 percent of Venezuelan export revenue and nearly three-quarters of government income, the Herrera administration had little choice but to tighten its belt even more. At the July bicentennial celebrations of the birth of the Liberator Simón Bolívar came government pleas for sacrifice and hard work in the name of historical legacy.

At least three problem areas confronted the government as of mid-1983: changes in the international petroleum picture that had been unanticipated or ignored in Caracas; misjudgment in the formulation and application of fiscal, monetary, and foreign exchange rate policies; and poor or nonexistent coordination and consensus among policymakers at the ministerial level. The first of these was linked to the lower price of some $27.50 per barrel of crude petroleum; this meant that annual income would be no more than $14 billion at best, while the Sixth National Plan had assumed $20 billion per year. The 1982 budget had been conceived under the plan's guidelines. Despite congressional adjustments as economic conditions worsened, the 1982 budget eventually produced a shortfall of $3.1 billion. This deficit was covered by further borrowing. The 1983 budget was even more austere. Because OPEC had lowered the price of market crude in February, after Great Britain, Norway, and Nigeria reduced the prices of their petroleum, Venezuela stood to lose approximately $2.8 billion in annual revenue over the depressed state of affairs in 1982.

1983 was also an election year, and the level of political debate was aggravated by the deterioration of the economy. At the beginning of the year Minister of Finance Luis Ugueto was flying back and forth to New York City and Western Europe in an effort to convert short-term loans into long-term credits. Conversion would allow the government maneuvering space in its efforts to inflate the economy and strengthen COPEI's political position. Ugueto was optimistic that Venezuela's $12 billion in foreign reserves would provide him with the leverage he needed for renegotiation. However, foreign reserves were more than offset by a public debt of $20.7 billion, a third of which was due in the short term. Ugueto's efforts came to naught when the February 1983 OPEC production cuts significantly reduced the government's income earning capability. He became President Herrera's sacrificial offering when someone had to shoulder the blame for economic mismanagement during 1981 and 1982.

Arturo Sosa, one of the private sector's most prestigious money managers, was appointed minister of finance because of the situation that resulted in the debacle of February 18, 1983. He quickly produced his own estimate of the foreign debt—$24.3 billion. This included $9 billion in short-term commitments.[24] Still another source to weigh in with its own figures reported in March 1983 that, based on data from the World Bank, Morgan Guaranty Trust, and other sources, the total debt at the start of 1983 was $28.5 billion, with some $15 billion in short-term commitments. [25]

Initially, it was expected that Arturo Sosa would be the dominant figure in Herrera's economic cabinet. This had been the position of Luis Ugueto between 1979 and 1981, when Herrera had reduced subsidies, removed price controls, and lowered trade barriers. Because these economic policies had not produced the intended results, Ugueto's star began to fade in 1981. When legislation was approved in September 1982 that increased the tariffs on more than 420 products, for example, it was over Ugueto's pronounced opposition. At the same time, Ugueto became involved in an unending battle with Central Bank president Leopoldo Díaz Bruzual. The latter, "*el Búfalo*" to friend and foe alike, prevailed over the finance minister to secure the bank's seizure of the international reserves of PDVSA (the Venezuelan Petroleum Company), as well as on other issues. Even before the economic disasters of February 1983, Ugueto increasingly was ignored by the president and constantly engaged in brouhahas with other ministerial officials, usually on the losing side. In contrast, Sosa's position was immeasurably stronger than that of Ugueto. Sosa, however, never enjoyed the total confidence of President Herrera, although the chief executive used him extensively in negotiations with the international financial community.

Arturo Sosa concentrated on convincing bankers in Western Europe, the United States, and Japan to reschedule Venezuela's debt. After he became unhappy with the signals he was receiving from them, he cancelled the scheduled March 4, 1983 meeting with the advisory committee representing some 300 creditor banks. On March 24, Sosa announced Venezuela's decision to call a moratorium on debt repayment until July 1.

In the meantime, differential treatment of government, private, and non-Venezuelan debts constituted elements of policy that at once were controversial and confusing. Such was the disarray of the government that it could debate over the definition of "essential" (in regard to which tier of the foreign exchange rate should be applied) as it pertained to imported whiskey. The rate to be applied to medical supplies also remained unresolved for many weeks. In time, the preferential rate of 4.3 was allowed for public sector debt, although service payments on the debts of Venezuelan-owned companies might qualify only if the debt payment could be stretched out. Firms controlled by foreigners would not be eligible for the preferential rate, a decision that aggravated relations with overseas creditors. The official reluctance to spell out its interpretation of "essential" imports added to the uncertainties of both foreign and national entrepreneurs. Controversy over the rules for repayment of the private debt especially fueled disagreements between Díaz Bruzual and Sosa over basic policy, typifying the growing befuddlement of the Herrera government. The official program that banned some imports and licensed others merely magnified the problem, for, as the *Wall Street Journal* remarked, "such an approach requires that the government efficiently process applications for foreign exchange and monitor (the) flow of goods across the nation's borders. These are requirements that exceed the government's competence."[26]

Díaz Bruzual became increasingly uncompromising in his opposition to Sosa's approach to the economic crisis. He openly and repeatedly denied Venezuelan bankers the Central Bank funds to which they believed themselves legally entitled in order to pay their foreign debts at the preferential rate. Given Sosa's links with the private financial sector, the running dispute between the two men became bitter. Certainly the interpretation of "essential" imports, coupled with the basis for application for preferential treatment, stood at the heart of the matter. Imports in 1982 had totaled roughly $13.4 billion; an estimated $8 billion of this would have qualified for the exchange rate of 4.3 to 1 if the most liberal interpretation of government regulations was applied. Because cheap dollars in this quantity simply could not be made available if the nation were to remain financially solvent, it was obvious that businessmen would never receive all of the cheap dollars to which they considered themselves entitled. In addition, by mid-1983, it was clear that a refinancing of the entire foreign debt, not just the $9 billion in short-term obligations that had been sought initially, would be ultimately necessary.

Herrera's initial application of the three-tiered exchange rate effectively doubled the foreign debt burden of the private companies. State corporations, in contrast, still enjoyed access to dollars at the cheap rate. Also, this approach allowed the government to profit by purchasing dollars at the 4.3 to 1 rate and selling them to the private sector at the 6 to 1 or still higher floating figure. The furor over this procedure led Herrera to promise in his March 9, 1983 address to the Congress that the preferential rate would soon be made available to the private sector. At this juncture, the internal disarray of the *herrerista* policymakers again surfaced. Díaz Bruzual announced that he had not been informed and, indeed, would not abide by the provision. Over the next few months, consequently, imports ground to a halt while all concerned waited for clarification on the terms of international financial transactions.

While these controversial, complicated, and debilitating issues provided daily melodrama, the Herrera government was still attempting to stimulate progress in both minerals and agriculture. The former effort centered largely on exploitation of the vast Guasare coal deposits in Zulia, where some 4 billion tons of high-quality, low-sulfur coal were being developed by CORPOZULIA, a regional development corporation. Zulia, after Caracas Venezuela's most populous region and the key to COPEI's effort to retain the presidency, continued to receive scarce investment funds after other regions saw their development projects placed on hold or cut back drastically. However, even Zulia was not exempt from reductions related to the economic crisis that loomed on the horizon as early as 1981. In anticipation of falling revenues, President Herrera had told the Zulian economic community of his final decision to scrap plans for a new steel complex in their state, as well as accompanying infrastructure improvements.

Powerful Zulian interests immediately began maneuvering to reverse this decision. After an extended lobbying campaign in which they exerted financial and political pressures, as well as making technical arguments linking return on investment in Guasare coal to construction of the steel plant, Herrera reversed himself. In September 1982 he signed a congressional bill authorizing some $2.2 billion for a steel mill and for supporting coal-mining activities. Addressing a Maracaibo audience, he promised that the recession was soon to end, aided locally by the previously rejected project's first developmental stages. The resurrected project included a coking mill, an open pit coal mine, a thermo-electric plant, and a connecting railroad of 115 kilometers. Its second stage was to begin in 1986, by which time massive production increases would be in evidence. Notwithstanding the political impact of these plans, the president soon was charged with advocating inappropriate and nonproductive expenditures by none other than Leopoldo Díaz Bruzual. The Central Bank president termed the project both unnecessary and costly. He also questioned the constitutionality of the enabling legislative proceedings. Just as in its international financial and petroleum policies, therefore, the regional industrialization decisions of the Herrera government were marked by expedience and a lack of leadership.

This same pattern carried over into agriculture. In his inaugural address Luis Herrera Campins had analyzed at great length the problem of farmers and livestock ranchers. He promised to give them preferential treatment. While agricultural production had risen slightly during the final Pérez years, as of 1980 it only accounted for 6 percent of gross domestic product. In 1981 a 40 percent increase in consumer demand forced Venezuela to import more than half of its food requirements. In an attempt to increase dramatically domestic production, the government extended higher subsidies and support prices through the Fondo de Crédito Agropecuario (Agriculture and Livestock Credit Fund—FCA). An allocation of $1.4 billion was also directed to an insurance program that might provide protection against crop and livestock losses through natural disasters. Even so, by early 1982 the agricultural sector was registering only modest increases—at that amount, barely half of the 6 percent called for in the Sixth National Plan.

Characteristic of endemic bureaucratic problems accompanying the formulation and implementation of agricultural policy was the plethora of agencies with overlapping jurisdiction, the low level of administrative competence, and outright corruption. A prime example illustrating these problems was the Corporación de Mercadeo Agrícola (Agricultural Marketing Corporation—CMA). Bureaucratic delays—not to mention the practice of placing funds allocated for the payment of commodities already delivered in 90-day, interest-bearing accounts—so backed up payments to small and medium-sized farmers that toward the end of the Herrera government they found themselves without the capital needed to purchase seeds and fertilizer. This led to a contraction of agricultural output and food imports continued at record levels.

A task force looking back on Venezuelan agricultural policy during the Herrera years emphasized shortcomings in marketing and storage. Its ultimate evaluation, a masterpiece of understatement, remarked that "the Government of Venezuela has implemented numerous programs designed to improve and expand agriculture, but the results have been disappointing."[27] For local observers the necessity of importing two-thirds of the nation's food as of mid-1983 was scandalous. Shortages, however, were becoming even more severe. As one critic declared, "When this began, we had seven weeks' worth of food within our borders, but we have taken three weeks arguing over economic measures, and in this time the country has been paralyzed—bureaucrats haven't known what to import and at what price, and we are eating commercial inventories and prime materials. If you consider that we import up to 70 percent of what we eat, that means we have only four more weeks of food left."[28]

By the conclusion of his constitutional term, Herrera had, at the very least, magnified the alleged "mortgaged" condition that he had attacked upon his inauguration. Carlos Rangel wrote of the Herrera and Pérez administrations, "There must be examples of worse fiscal mismanagement than of . . . the last eight or nine years, but I am not aware of them."[29] He went on to note that the *herreristas* had ignored their own warnings about the earlier quadrupling of public spending. When market conditions accompanying the Iranian revolution shot the price of oil to $34 per barrel, the Herrera government "blithely forgot all its own demonstrances . . . and went down its own path to an even greater quagmire."[30] In the process it succeeded in spending, during its first three years, more than Pérez had in five.

In all truth, the fiscal, monetary, and foreign exchange fiasco that was full-blown by 1983 had been long in the making. Even as early as the 1940s, petroleum revenue had provided Venezuelan public administration with extra resources that allowed for a greater margin of error than in other developing countries. The bonanza attitude fostered by the post-1973 petrodollar explosion was merely an intensification of careless habits that had been in place for decades. Given these habits, as well as the association of private enterprise with foreign domination and the seller's petroleum market of the 1970s, it was easy for politicians to assume that the answer to developmental problems was the expenditure of ever larger sums, and that the organizational mechanism should be state capitalism. If many undertakings and initiatives of the Pérez years had been overly ambitious, it is also a fact that by and large they were overdue responses to fundamental structural problems. However, these structural problems were such that five

TABLE 4.1. External Economic Indicators (in billions of U.S.$ unless otherwise noted)

	1980	1981	1982	1983	1984	1985
Trade Balance	8.1	7.9	2.7	7.9	8.4	6.7
Exports	19.0	20.0	16.3	14.7	15.9	15.1
Nonoil exports	0.8	1.0	0.8	1.0	1.2	1.4
Oil exports	18.2	19.0	15.5	13.7	14.7	13.7
($/bbl)	26.7	29.6	27.4	25.0	26.7	25.0
(mb/d)	1,864	1,760	1,550	1,500	1,502	1,500
Imports	10.9	12.1	13.6	6.8	7.5	8.4

Source: Banco Central de Venezuela, Inter-American Development Bank, and *Latin American and Caribbean Contemporary Record*, vols. 1–3.

or even ten years were insufficient for their resolution. In an ill-advised and sometimes demagogic effort to do what could not be done, the Herrera government's economic policymaking became a succession of unpredictable shifts and turns, responding in an expedient fashion to pressures from labor, business, the middle class, and internal bureaucratic struggles for power, wealth, and turf.

Whether or not a genuine and effective austerity program would have met Venezuela's economic and developmental needs at the close of the 1970s remains a moot point, for the Herrera government did not effectively or efficiently provide a test. It was left for Acción Democrática's Jaime Lusinchi to mount a renewed attack on economic problems when he entered office in 1984 (cf. economic data summarized in Tables 4.1–4.7).

TABLE 4.2. Gross Domestic Product, Total and Per Capita

Total (millions of 1980 dollars)				Per Capita (1980 dollars)			
1960	1970	1980	1982	1960	1970	1980	1982
13,605.9	24,633.6	36.935.2	37.286.5	1,779.5	2,295.6	2,649.0	2,537.7

Source: Inter-American Development Bank.

TABLE 4.3. Purchasing Power of Venezuelan Petroleum Exports and of the Average Price Paid for Petroleum

Year	Petroleum Exports, Current Prices (billions $)	Average Price Paid, Current Prices ($/barrel)	Index of Purchasing Power (1974 = 100)	Petroleum Exports, Constant Prices (billion $)	Average Price Paid, Constant Prices ($/barrel)
1960	2.149	2.19	54.56	3.938	4.01
1965	2.305	1.94	56.63	4.070	3.43
1970	2.380	1.85	64.63	3.701	2.88
1973	4.450	3.71	84.31	5.278	4.40
1974	10.762	10.53	100.00	10.762	10.53
1978	8.705	12.04	139.78	6.228	8.61
1979	13.673	17.69	154.57	8.846	11.44
1980	18.301	26.44	174.95	10.461	15.11
1981	19.094	29.71	180.57	10.574	16.45
1982	15.659	27.47	182.12	8.598	15.08
1983	13.780	25.31	175.92	7.833	14.39
1984	14.770	26.57	172.48	8.563	15.40
			Optimistic Scenario Projections		
1985	13.930	27.07	181.10	7.692	14.95
1986	14.190	27.07	190.16	7.462	14.25
1987	14.620	27.07	199.66	7.322	13.56

Note: Index for the cost of imports has been adjusted to the rate of exchange between the dollar and other currencies.
Source: Calculated by Luis Zambrano Sequin, Chi-Yi-Chen, Matías Riutort M., and Wilmer Pérez, in *Resumen* 46, no. 585 (March 1985): 36.

TABLE 4.4. External Public Debt (millions of dollars)

1960	1970	1975	1979	1980	1984 (est.)
363	924	1,393	10,239	11,144	33,500

Source: Inter-American Development Bank and International Bank for Reconstruction and Development.

THE QUEST FOR ECONOMIC REACTIVATION

On February 2, 1984, Jaime Lusinchi took office as Venezuela's sixth constitutional president during the continuing quarter-century cycle of democratic government. He assumed power amid an economic crisis of historic proportions. The combined public and private sector foreign debt of $34 billion to $35 billion was more than double that of 1978, more than $20 billion in private domestic capital had fled overseas, investment was semi-paralyzed by the complexity and arbitrary application of the three-tiered exchange rate, and, after three decades of stability, the bolivar had tumbled on foreign exchange markets. International creditors were demanding Venezuelan adherence to the International Monetary Fund's guidelines before rescheduling the debt, and gross domestic product had declined by more than 2 percent during 1983.

Economic malaise had festered throughout the final year of the outgoing administration. Upcoupling the bolivar from the dollar produced a floating bolivar that rose as high as 14 to 1. Unemployment was unofficially estimated at between 20 and 25 percent. Final figures concerning the impact of falling petroleum prices revealed a drop in Venezuela's revenues to $16.2 billion, more than $6 billion short of covering the 1983 budget. On the basis of Venezuela's production quota, each drop of $1 per barrel oil cost roughly $500 million in foreign exchange earnings. Thus, when crude hit $29 per barrel in March 1983 (given the earlier benchmark price of $34 per barrel), it produced a loss of some $2.7 billion for Venezuela. President Lusinchi merely stated the obvious in his inaugural address when he conceded the urgent need to take unpopular measures. Demanding austerity and a change from past enslavement to exaggerated consumption, the

TABLE 4.5. Structure of External Public Debt by Type of Creditor (in percent)

Official Multilateral			Official Bilateral			Suppliers			Private Banks			Other Creditors		
1960	1970	1981	1960	1970	1981	1960	1970	1981	1960	1970	1980	1960	1970	1980
—	35.1	1.6	14.3	13.8	1.6	25.1	15.0	2.1	60.6	32	65	—	4.1	9.7

Source: Inter-American Development Bank.

TABLE 4.6. Petroleum and Government (millions of bolivars)

	1960	1970	1980
Government income	4,967	9,498	62,697
Government income from petroleum	2,891	5,709	45,331
Petroleum as percentage of ordinary revenues	58.2	60.1	72.3
Average realized dollar price per barrel	2.08	1.84	26.44

Source: Various, as cited by Judith Ewell, *Venezuela: A Century of Change* (Stanford, Calif.: Stanford University Press, 1984), p. 229.

new president attacked the rapid growth of too-easy petroleum riches as having "unchained in our society radical changes, aggravating unhealthy tendencies to waste, squandering, and illicit profiteering."[31]

Renegotiation of the foreign debt was among the most immediate issues. Lusinchi pledged that "Venezuela will pay everything it owes, up to the last cent."[32] The final *herrerista*-declared moratorium had expired on January 31, 1984, and refinancing of some $18.4 billion was due by the close of 1984. The president-elect's economic advisers actually began meeting with foreign bank representatives soon after Lusinchi's election. Manuel Azpúrua, the incoming minister of finance, had joined Arturo Sosa in discussions with the 13-member Bank Debt Advisory Committee in Caracas. Both the outgoing and incoming

TABLE 4.7. Venezuelan Debt and Debt Service (millions of bolivars)

	1960	1970	1980
External	986	2931	41,516
Internal	1,186	2,560	19,237
Floating	406		
Total	2,578	5,491	60,753
Service on national debt	543	693	11,801

Sources: Various, as cited by Judith Ewell, *Venezuela, A Century of Change* (Stanford, Calif.: Stanford University Press, 1984), p. 231.

finance ministers had made their careers in the most powerful local financial circles. It was expected that they would persuade their international contacts of long standing to reprogram $18.4 billion for an 18- to 20-year period. This was to be accompanied by four additional years of grace.[33] At the same time, the new Social Democratic government was not inclined to mollify its 400-odd creditor banks by adopting the kind of drastic austerity program that the International Monetary Fund was imposing on Argentina and Brazil.

The Lusinchi administration was able to resist demands for an IMF austerity package because, with more than $11 billion in foreign reserves, Venezuela had no need for further bank loans. Acción Democrática's party platform, moreover, had promised "to refinance the public debt without provoking undesirable effects on the standard of living of the citizenry."[34] However, this did not mean that the new administration might not implement policies broadly similar to IMF thinking. Where the latter urged a unification of the three-tiered exchange system, for example, Lusinchi promised the same action, but phased in over time. Less than a month after taking office, Lusinchi addressed the nation to proclaim formal devaluation of the bolivar by 74 percent. The new parity was set at 7.5 to the dollar; the old rate of 4.30 to 1 would be retained for payment of the private external debt of some $8 billion and also for amortization of the public debt. In addition, the government would have authority to provide foreign currency, and if demand exceeded the supply, purchases would have to be made on the open market. Throughout 1984 and into the first half of 1985, the free-floating exchange rate between bolivar and dollar averaged 12.5 to 1.

President Lusinchi pledged to cushion the impact of recession and reactivate the economy. Devaluation was to be offset by compensatory measures for the poor, and efforts to combat unemployment were to be given the highest priority. Interest rates were to be reduced to 15 percent, from the prevailing 17.5 percent average, and preference extended to agriculture and housing construction. In the arena of symbolic politics, Lusinchi repeated his campaign pledge (discussed elsewhere in this volume) to combine the interests of individual groups into an aggregative *pacto social*. The national budget was to be brought under closer scrutiny, with public expenditures rigorously controlled. Finally, in a move unprecedented for a Social Democratic president, Lusinchi warned that many ineptly administered state corporations would have to be sold off to private enterprise. Studies were to be initiated to determine which should be retained and which transferred.

During March of 1984, the government announced that public hiring would be frozen and positions being vacated would not be filled. In language not dissimilar from that of the Herrera government in 1979, there were official promises to eliminate subsidies over time, allowing for a freeing of prices. A dramatic testimony to the seriousness of the Lusinchi government was the second hike in gasoline prices in three years. Low octane rose 0.28 to 0.80 bolivars. High octane rose from 1.00 to 1.20 bolivars per liter, and other fuels increased anywhere from 20 to 140 percent.[35]

An attack on unemployment also took shape in March 1984, when Juan José Delpino, president of the Venezuelan Workers' Confederation (CTV), outlined government plans for a so-called "Recovery of National Patrimony." Delpino proclaimed that 100,000 unemployed would be organized for the repair of streets and highways, the painting of public buildings, and similar tasks. The Lusinchi government would pay 30 bolivars daily, a bare subsistence wage, but still a symbolic source to preserve the self-esteem of the recipients with more than outright gifts. Delpino also indicated that all businesses would be required to hire an additional 10 percent, and that this would produce perhaps 300,000 new jobs. In reality, however, there was little likelihood that such a program could be implemented. What it did was to signal to the 800,000 jobless, 16 percent of the total work force, that the government recognized their plight and was committed to doing something about it. In the short run this took the form of a new food program. President Lusinchi offered a basket of 33 basic items that was to be distributed gratis to 970,000 indigent families.[36] Subsequently, however, the bureaucracy's inability to administer the program led to its abandonment.

The Lusinchi administration thus began by demonstrating a willingness to call for belt tightening and to adopt unpopular measures on a limited scale. Implementing policy, as it had been for so long, remained the Achilles' heel of Venezuelan public administration. By mid-1985, however, a pattern of activity and movement had been established on several fronts. The first 15 months had produced at least a modestly credible performance. The rate of decline in the gross domestic policy was held to 1.7 percent, foreign reserves rose to $12.4 billion, and the rate of capital flight had been reduced. During September 1984 Finance Minister Manuel Azpúrua and the foreign banking consortium holding Venezuelan debts reached a tentative agreement on rolling over most of what the public sector owed; payment on $21 billion, or 94 percent, was stretched out to mature between 1983 and 1988. The initial $750 million repayment was scheduled for the second quarter of 1985, and the IMF was excluded from matters.[37]

The agreement between Azpúrua and the foreign banks remained tentative because of difficulties relating to payment of the more than $8 billion private sector debt. Those holding this debt pressured the Venezuelan government to guarantee payment. They feared that if domestic private corporations were allowed to go bankrupt, foreign creditors would never recover their loans. In order to prevent multiple bankruptcies, the international banking community also proposed that RECADI, the Venezuelan government agency responsible for controlling foreign exchange, make dollars available at the old rate of 4.3 to 1 for the payment of both interest and principal on the foreign private debt.[38] The Lusinchi economic team initially resisted this position. Led by Luis Raúl Matos Azocar, the national planning minister, the government argued that private entrepreneurs should not receive the preferential rate of exchange to pay their debts, even though the debts had been contracted when the bolivar to dollar rate was 4.3 to 1, until they began to repatriate the capital they had sent abroad when that same rate prevailed.

In spite of his hard line on providing cheap dollars to the private sector, Matos was not implacably hostile to entrepreneurial activity. When CORDIPLAN released the first draft of the Seventh National Plan (1986–91), in December 1984, it recognized businessmen as a valuable resource for the creation of national wealth. Private risk taking was treated as an important means for reactivating the economy. After a quarter-century of veiled hostility toward free enterprise, the Venezuelan Social Democrats were shifting emphasis—at least in the language of the seventh plan. Reliance on state corporations and government bureau-cracies was to be reduced, and there was a frank admission that important economic activities might well be conducted without the direct involvement or supervision by the state. This turnabout reflected new economic reality. During the life of the seventh plan, annual petroleum revenues were projected at $14.8 billion, a far cry from the $20 billion on which the unrealistic Sixth National Plan had been based.

The Seventh National Plan came under attack from leftists, who accused Acción Democrática of selling out to capitalism. On the other hand, the private sector and its international allies strongly opposed Matos' position on the release of cheap dollars to Venezuela's private debtors. Also, Matos was involved in a struggle for bureaucratic power with more senior cabinet ministers, especially Development Minister Hector Hurtado. Having become a liability both inside and outside the government, Matos was asked to resign by President Lusinchi in January 1985. At the same time, RECADI approved the release of a large quantity of dollars to the Caracas Electric Company at the cheap rate of 4.3 to 1. These dollars were used to prevent a default that would have forced the state to take over the company. RECADI's release of the cheap dollars was a clear signal that the Lusinchi administration viewed private enterprise more favorably than did its predecessor. Whether or not this presaged a more enduring shift of Social Democratic attitudes toward developmental perspectives, at least the approach to economic policymaking had shifted for the moment.

This shift also surfaced in the Lusinchi administration's attitude toward foreign investment. Until the crisis of 1982 the nation had benefited from an overvalued exchange rate and protectionist trade policies. Foreign companies already in Vene-zuela were not treated badly, but the government had little interest in attracting new foreign investment. During the final year of the Herrera government, the Superintendency of Foreign Investment (SIEX) made some limited moves to attract foreign capital by promising to streamline procedures for project approval and profit repatriation. These efforts, headed by Alfredo González Amare, continued with the new government. For the third quarter of 1984 he could announce that foreign investment had risen 7.2 percent above the $947 million total at the close of 1983. However, the flow of fresh capital had not increased substantially, for the 1984 increase had been largely due to the sizable reinvestment of retained earnings accumulated by firms already operating in Venezuela.

Early in 1985, about the time of Matos' resignation, SIEX presented a series of proposals to reform the foreign investment code. While these consisted largely of procedural and regulatory simplifications, other government policymakers were seriously considering a more far-reaching revision of the Andean Pact's Decision 24. Behind this discussion lay the fact that Venezuelan businessmen were offering to return billions of dollars of the private capital they had taken out of the country if the Lusinchi government would treat the repatriated capital as protected foreign investment. However, under the Andean Pact's Decision 24 foreign capital could not control Venezuelan corporations. Businessmen, on the other hand, would only bring back the capital if they were permitted to control the enterprises in which they invested.[39] Facing an economic situation far more obdurate and ominous than Venezuela had known in more than a generation, President Lusinchi's best hope for obtaining needed foreign investment seemed to lie in responding affirmatively to the demands of his entrepreneurial countrymen. Therefore, as of mid-1985, it appeared probable that, despite nationalistic opposition, some means would be found to experiment with innovative and creative arrangements that would circumvent the original intent of Article 24. For the first time since the return of democracy, the government appeared determined to shrink the role of the state in the economy.

NOTES

1. Juan Pablo Pérez Alfonzo, *Petroleo: Jugo de la tierre* (Caracas: Editorial Arte, 1961), pp. 83–84.

2. James A. Hanson, "Cycles of Economic Growth and Structural Change Since 1950," in *Venezuela: The Democratic Experience*, ed. John D. Martz and David J. Myers, (New York: Praeger, 1977), p. 64.

3. José Antonio Gil, *The Challenge of Venezuelan Democracy*, tr. by Evelyn

Harrison I., Lolo Gil de Yanes, and Danielle Salti (New Brunswick, N.J.: Transaction Books, 1981), p. 173.

4. Rómulo Betancourt, *Dos años de gobierno democrático* (Caracas: Imprenta Nacional, 1961), p. 404.

5. Judith Ewell, *Venezuela: A Century of Change* (Stanford, Calif.: Stanford University Press, 1984), p. 138.

6. David E. Blank, *Venezuela: Politics in a Petroleum Republic* (New York: Praeger, 1984), p. 138.

7. Donald L. Herman, *Chistian Democracy in Venezuela* (Chapel Hill: University of North Carolina Press, 1980), pp. 55 ff.

8. José Antonio Gil, "Entrepreneurs and Regime Consolidation," in *Venezuela: The Democratic Experience*, ed. John D. Martz and David J. Myers (New York: Praeger, 1977), p. 154.

9. Ewell, *Century of Change*, p. 174.

10. M. Ignacio Purroy, "De los dolares a 4.30 a la inversión extranjera," *SIC* 48, no. 483 (March 1985): 100–03.

11. John R. Pate, as quoted in *Journal of Commerce*, December 13, 1984.

12. John D. Martz and Enrique A. Baloyra, *Electoral Mobilization and Public Opinion: The Venezuelan Campaign of 1973* (Chapel Hill: University of North Carolina Press, 1976), pp. 140, 150–51.

13. Carlos Andrés Pérez, *Acción de gobierno* (Caracas: n.p., 1973), p. 31.

14. *Financial Times*, October 25, 1978, p. 1.

15. For a further discussion, see John D. Martz, "The Frailties of Venezuelan Policymaking," in *Politics and Public Policy in Latin America*, ed. Steven W. Hughes and Kenneth J. Mijeski (Boulder, Colo.: Westview, 1984), pp. 101–17. Especially note pp. 108–16 on agriculture.

16. José Vicente Rangel, *Tiempo de verdades* (Caracas: Ediciones Centauro, 1973), p. 273.

17. John D. Martz, "The Evolution of Democratic Politics in Venezuela," in *Venezuela at the Polls: The National Elections of 1978*, ed. Howard R. Penniman (Washington, D.C.: American Enterprise Institute for Public Policy Research, 1980), p. 27.

18. David J. Myers, "The Elections and the Evolution of Venezuela's Party System," in *Venezuela at the Polls: The National Elections of 1978*, ed. Howard R. Penniman (Washington, D.C.: American Enterprise Institute for Public Policy Research, 1980), p. 224.

19. "Venezuela," in *Economic Survey of Latin America—1981* (Santiago, Chile: UN Economic Commission for Latin America, 1983), pp. 763–90.

20. *Latin American Weekly Report*, March 27, 1981, pp. 4–5.

21. For a discussion that stresses the impact of petroleum on policymaking, see John D. Martz, "Venezuela: Democratic Politics of Petroleum," in *Policies, and Economic Development in Latin America*, ed. Robert Wesson (Stanford, Calif.: Hoover Institution Press, 1984), pp. 161–88.

22. Purroy, "De los dolares."

23. *Financial Times* June 8, 1981, p. 1.

24. *Latin American Weekly Report*, February 11, 1983, p. 1.

25. *New York Times*, March 13, 1983, p. F-4.

26. *Wall Street Journal*, April 15, 1983, p. 5.

27. *New York Times*, March 27, 1983, p. 27.

28. *New York Times*, March 21, 1983, p. D-1.

29. Carlos Rangel, "How Venezuelans Twice Squandered Their Oil Wealth," *Miami Herald*, March 20, 1983, p. 7.

30. Ibid.

31. Lusinchi's inaugural address appeared in the Caracas press on February 3, 1984. Especially see *El Nacional, El Universal*, and *Diario de Caracas* for text and commentary.

32. Ibid.

33. *Informe Latinoamericano*, January 27, 1984, p. 43.

34. Jaime Lusinchi, *Un pacto para la democracia social* (Caracas: n. p., 1983).

35. *Hoy* (Quito, Peru), February 26, 1984, p. 4.

36. *El Nacional*, March 1, 1984, p. 1.

37. Miguel A. Rodríguez F. "Los mitos y readidades del endeudamiento externo venezolano," *Resumen* 46, no. 585 (March 1985): 46–52.

38. *Latin American Andean Report*, January 25, 1985, pp. 6–7.

39. Luis Zambrano Sequin, Chi-Yi-Chen, Matías Riutort M., and Wilmer Pérez, "Perspectivas de la balanza de pagos (1985–1987)," *Resumen* 46, no. 585 (March 1985): 33–45, and "Los empresarios y el estado: Informe especial," *Zeta*, May 2–13, 1985, pp. 30–31.

Part Two
Articulating and Aggregating Interests

5

The Venezuelan Party System: Regime Maintenance Under Stress

David J. Myers

Political party and party system performance, with the possible exception of developments in the international petroleum market, is the factor most directly affecting the viability of Venezuelan democracy. Political parties are of course central in all modern states; they mobilize their supporters, recruit individuals to fill government positions, broker the demands of competing interests, and create symbols that either strengthen or undermine regime support. Venezuelan party leaders demonstrated considerable skill and imagination during the 1960s and 1970s; they institutionalized a competitive two-party system that continues to be dominated by representatives of the democratic center, Democratic Action (AD) and the Social Christians (COPEI).[1] The former operates with a Social Democratic perspective, while the latter is an advocate of Christian Democracy.

In the 1980s serious challenges have emerged that could undermine the national consensus on which the political domination of AD and COPEI rests. The purpose of this chapter is to describe and analyze the behavior of political parties in democratic Venezuela and the consequences of that behavior. Description and analysis centers on three basic questions: How is the Venezuelan party system structured? How has it evolved? And why did the party system evolve as it did? Finally, some concluding remarks will speculate on how political party and party system behavior has affected the quality of political life. The intent of these closing comments is to prepare the ground for discussion in the final chapter of this volume concerning the performance of contemporary Venezuelan democracy.

PARTY SYSTEM: STRUCTURE

Venezuela's modern political party system took shape during the final years of the Juan Vicente Gómez dictatorship (1908–35). Gómez's cunning and barbarism enabled him to destroy the discredited nineteenth-century Liberal and Conservative political parties; their intractable hatred for each other had plagued the country with seven decades of violence.[2] Only after Gómez's iron peace were Venezuelans again willing to experiment with a more open system. Between 1935 and 1958, Venezuela experienced three distinct political regimes: "controlled" democracy (López/Medina, 1935–45, and Delgado/Suárez, 1948–53), open elections and radical socioeconomic democracy (Betancourt/Gallegos, 1945–48), and populist authoritarianism (Pérez Jiménez, 1953–58). The failure of these three convinced most Venezuelans in 1958 to opt for a fourth, the uniquely sui generis version of liberal democracy that continues as of this writing. Here political parties and the party system have acted successfully as a balance wheel in managing nonviolent conflict.

The political party configuration of the mid-1980s may be characterized as a dynamic "two-and-a-sixth-plus" system. The "two" are AD and COPEI. Together they command 80 percent of the total vote. While AD clearly is stronger, COPEI has elected two of the six post-1958 presidents; in 1978 COPEI even received a slightly larger national congressional vote than AD. The "one-sixth" of the party system is a collection of militantly leftist organizations that range from the personalistic Democratic Republican Union (URD) to the ideologically orthodox Venezuelan Communist Party (PCV). Finally, the party system's "plus" encompasses several rightist and personalistic movements, the most important of which is National Opinion (OPINA).[3]

Venezuela's political party system may also be described in terms of its four ideological families: the Social Democrats, the Christian Democrats, the militant left, and the personalistic right. During the early years of the post-1958 democratic era, only political parties espousing the Social Democratic and Christian Democratic ideologies were unequivocally committed to free and open multiparty democracy. Nevertheless, the system's unanticipated strength and resiliency eventually won over both militant leftists and personalistic rightists. It remains an open question, however, whether their public acceptance of liberal democracy

TABLE 5.1. Percent of Total Congressional Vote Received by Ideological Family and Important Political Party in the National Elections on December 4, 1983

Ideological Family and Component Political Parties	% of Total Congressional Vote, 1983	
	Political Family	Ideological Family
Social democracy:		50.0
Acción Democrátic (AD)	50.0	
Christian Democracy:		29.7
Social Christians (COPEI)	28.7	
Independents with Caldera (ICC)	1.0	
Militant left:		16.1
Movement Toward Socialism (MAS)	5.8	
People's Electoral Movement (MEP)	2.0	
Democratic Republican Union (URD)	1.9	
Communist Party of Venezuela (PCV)	1.8	
Movement of Revolutionary Left (MIR)	1.6	
New Alternative (NA)	1.1	
Others	1.9	
Rightist personalism:		3.2
National Opinion (OPINA)	2.0	
National Integration Movement (MIN)	0.8	
National Rescue (RN)	0.2	
Others	0.2	
Unclassified microparties and movements	1.0	1.0
Total	100.00	100.00

Source: Consejo Supremo Electoral, *Elecciones 1983*, Boletín 12.

constitutes a genuine change of heart from earlier authoritarian preferences, or whether it is a tactic of expediency.

Table 5.1 portrays the "two-and-a-sixth-plus" party system as it appeared following the elections of December 4, 1983. The remainder of this section describes its most important components.

Venezuelan Political Parties

Of the four ideological families represented among Venezuelan political parties, the Social Democratic and Christian Democratic possess the most coherent and internally consistent belief systems. In contrast, militantly leftist political parties advocate doctrines as diverse as Marxism, Marxism-Leninism, Eurocommunism, and left wing populism. They are, however, united by their portrayal of themselves as more egalitarian and more committed to comprehensive socioeconomic change than either AD or COPEI. Rightist personalist political parties also constitute a diverse group. In general, they seek to modify or reverse what their leaders portray as the statism and party sectarianism of the post-1958 democratic regime.

Social Democracy

AD, the Social Democrats, emerged as Venezuela's strongest political organization during the post-Gómez liberalization. In October 1945 Rómulo Betancourt, the party's founder and maximum leader, joined with youthful military officers in a revolt against General Isaías Medina. During the following three years, while presiding over rapid social, economic, and political modernization, AD became sufficiently powerful and well organized to win free and open presidential elections; in 1947 the party received more than 70 percent of the total vote. AD interpreted this victory as a mandate to increase the pace of social change. However, AD's arrogant demeanor alienated other democratic political parties and provided authoritarian traditionalists with significant support when, in November 1948, they ousted the AD government of President Rómulo Gallegos. AD spent the following decade in the underground; it became the rallying point for resistance against the increasingly brutal but inept efforts by traditionalists to consolidate their authoritarian populist political order. Following the January 23, 1958, overthrow of General Marcos Pérez Jiménez, the strongman who oversaw that effort, AD received a new opportunity when it elected Rómulo Betancourt to the presidency.

The immediate post–Pérez Jiménez period presented AD with three great challenges: to develop and implement tactics that would enable the party to enact key elements of its social program, while at the same time not so antagonizing traditionalists that they would turn on the fledgling democracy; to craft ideological symbols capable of unifying the party and legitimating both intraparty decision-making procedures and their policy outputs; and to manage personalistic rivalries within the party so that they did not undermine its ability to complete electorally. These challenges have reappeared over and over; they remain as central for AD in the 1980s as they were during the 1960s.[4]

Following the triumph of Rómulo Betancourt in the December 1958 elections, AD leaders decided that before continuing with the programs they initiated between 1945 and 1948 they would concentrate on "educating" traditionalists and militant leftists to support democratic norms and procedures. AD thus reserved positions in the Betancourt administration for the two strongest opposition political parties, URD and COPEI. The second AD government of Raúl Leoni followed a similar policy in this regard, although COPEI was replaced with a newly important conservative grouping, the National Democratic Front (FND). While this strategy of forming a broad-based coalition calmed traditionalists' fears, it led many of AD's more militant leftists to argue that in order to consolidate democracy the leadership had sold out AD's nationalistic and anticapitalist heritage. Conflict over this matter played a significant role in the divisions of 1961 and 1967.[5] In the latter division the party's influential left wing broke away; AD subsequently united behind those who preferred compromise and incrementalism as a strategy to bring about social change.

In the early 1980s debate over the costs and benefits of consensus building with the loyal opposition broke out anew. This time disagreement was less over the rapidity and comprehensiveness with which the state should implement change than over the economic consequences of alternating party governments every five years. Shifts in the development priorities of new administrations during 1969 (AD–COPEI), 1974 (COPEI–AD), and 1979 (AD–COPEI) led to many government projects being abandoned or poorly completed when the opposition came to power. Lack of continuity was blamed for the slow pace of economic development. Late in 1982, when it looked as if AD's Jaime Lusinchi would win the 1983 presidential election, party leaders began discussing whether they should provide COPEI with the patronage that democratic Venezuelan government traditionally reserved for the principal opposition political party. It became popular to argue that economic growth considerations demanded that COPEI should not be given resources that might assist its 1988 presidential campaign. At that time, AD leaders were extremely angry over what they perceived as COPEI efforts to deprive them of their ability to compete effectively for presidential power following Luis Herrera's triumph in the presidential election of December 1978. During the first year of the Lusinchi administration, therefore, AD has provided less patronage to the loyal opposition than during any of its previous governments.[6]

The challenges of articulating a unifying ideology and securing support for internal policymaking procedures are ongoing. During AD's early years many preferred militant socialism to Betancourt's Social Democratic approach. They were disillusioned by his second administration's (1959–64) failure to curb the private sector and by his close cooperation on international matters with the United States. In 1961 the most radical of these critics broke with AD to form the Movement of Revolutionary Left (MIR)—a split that cost AD an entire generation of young leaders.

Conflict between AD's militant socialists and Social Democrats again bubbled to the surface during the final years of the Leoni administration (1964–69). The politics of presidential succession became the arena in which the two groups struggled for control of AD. Militants preferred Luis B. Prieto, the party president; moderates backed Gonzalo Barrios, the secretary-general. When the former's victory in the disputed 1967 national primary elections was not respected by the Barrios majority in the National Executive Committee, Prieto and his followers formed their own political party, the People's Electoral Movement (MEP).

For the first time since the founding of AD, in 1942, its Social Democratic faction completely dominated the party's functional and areal infrastructure.[7]

Since the 1967 division, one of AD's major ideological challenges has been to articulate a Venezuelan variant of Social Democratic ideology that would both hold the party together and enable it to attract new members, especially the young. Here AD received important assistance from West Germany's Social Democratic party. Ironically, contact with West Germany's Social Democrats has sharpened ideological debate within AD. Conflicts between their West German patron's moderate and militant factions were reproduced within AD on more than one occasion. However, these disagreements have lacked the intensity of the internal disputes that divided the party during the 1960s.

Finally, personalistic rivalries present a challenge with the potential to weaken AD and open the way for COPEI's return to power. On the eve of the 1983 election, personalistic rivalry between AD's founding generation (the "old guard") and younger leaders (the *arsistas*) divided the party. The 1967 division discussed earlier, while primarily ideological, also involved personalistic rivalry. In both 1963 and 1967 other factors, especially the geographical separation of the party leaders during the resistance and conflict between socialist and Social Democratic policies, reinforced the divisive potential of personalistic rivalries. These reinforcing elements are absent or less intense at present.

Some important rivalries do remain. The mid-1980s have become a time for competition between factions associated with President Jaime Lusinchi and former President Carlos Andres Pérez. Each seeks the party's presidential nomination for one of its own. In 1977 and 1978 competition for the presidential nomination generated so much bitterness that many party loyalists did not vote. This contributed to the narrow loss of the presidency by AD's Luis Piñerúa to COPEI's Luis Herrera Campins.[8] The memory of this defeat still exerts a moderating influence on both Lusinchi and Pérez partisans. While each covets the 1988 presidential nomination, both share the goal of keeping AD dominant.

Christian Democracy

The Social Christian party (COPEI) speaks for Christian Democracy in Venezuela. While younger than AD, COPEI is also a product of the rapid changes that followed the passing of General Juan Vicente Gómez. In contrast to AD, COPEI's founding generation came from elite Catholic high schools in the cities. COPEI supported the October 1945 revolution, and the party's most important leader, Rafael Caldera, served briefly in Rómulo Betancourt's first government (1945–48). However, Caldera soon found himself in opposition to AD's Marxist ideology and partisan style of governing. He resigned from the government and embarked on an effort to make COPEI electorally competitive. He achieved limited success; COPEI placed a weak second to AD in the elections of 1946, 1947, and 1948.[9]

COPEI protested, although halfheartedly, against the November 1948 coup; after the fraudulent 1952 elections, however, COPEI joined with AD in the underground to fight against General Marcos Pérez Jiménez. COPEI thus began the post-1958 democratic era with increased prestige and ties to AD that had been lacking earlier. Following a shaky start, COPEI took advantage of divisions within the militant left and became the only viable challenger to AD's control over the presidency. Along the way COPEI has faced three major challenges: expanding out of its initially restricted base of support among Andeans, professionals, and pro-clericals; reconciling its revolutionary Christian Democratic ideology with the conservatism and privileged economic status of much of its clientele; and managing personalistic rivalries, especially that between party founder Rafael Caldera and Luis Herrera, the most prestigious spokesman for the Christian left. While the immediacy of these challenges has fluctuated since 1958, they have proved surprisingly persistent.

To the dismay of COPEI, its share of the total presidential and congressional vote in 1958 was less than it had been before the 1948 coup. COPEI began the post-1958 era as Venezuela's third electoral force, behind AD and URD. However, a pre-electoral agreement by these three to share power during the 1959–64 constitutional period gave COPEI access to patronage for the first time. On the other hand, COPEI's presence in the coalition strengthened Betancourt and AD. COPEI enjoyed the confidence of clericals, entrepreneurs, and merchants, traditional interests whose support the government needed as it came under increasing attack from Marxist guerrillas and terrorists trained by Fidel

Castro. Deteriorating relations between Betancourt and Castro eventually led to the withdrawal of URD from the official coalition. COPEI remained, and its presence became even more important for the maintenance of political stability.

COPEI used patronage to increase its support among peasants and workers and in regions that had proven difficult for party organizers. COPEI expanded its following even further in 1967 and 1968, when divisions within AD opened the way for Rafael Caldera to become Venezuela's first Christian Democratic president. COPEI stored away enough resources while in power to continue these efforts during its five years as the first party of the loyal opposition (1974–79). They bore fruit in the presidential and congressional elections of December 1978 and in the municipal elections of May 1979. In the former, COPEI's total congressional vote surpassed that of AD for the first time, and Luis Herrera Campins became Venezuela's second popularly elected Christian Democratic chief executive.[10] In the latter, COPEI crushed AD and took control of all but a few of the country's 205 district councils. Christian Democracy appeared to have surpassed Social Democracy as the first political force.

During Herrera's years in office, in contrast with Caldera's tenure as president, COPEI failed to grow. Economic difficulties diminished Herrera's ability to wield patronage. Also, hostility intensified between supporters of the two leaders. In concert with growing doubts about Herrera's capabilities, party factionalism and economic difficulties led to electoral debacles in December 1983 and May 1984. These elections reversed a 20-year trend of uninterrupted COPEI growth. Rebuilding party morale and infrastructure looms in the mid- and late 1980s as a challenge equal in magnitude to that of expanding beyond a regionally narrow electoral base in the 1960s.[11]

For Venezuela's Christian Democrats, in contrast to the Social Democrats and militant Marxists, ideology has served as a rallying point and strengthened party unity. The ideology of COPEI closely identifies with the social thought of the Roman Catholic church as expressed in the encyclicals of *Rerum Novarum* (1891), *Quadragesimo Anno* (1931), *Mater et Magistra*, (1959) and *Pacem en Terris* (1960). Such modern European writers as Jacques Maritain, Luigi Sturzo, and Emmanual Mounier also had a great impact on

COPEI's founding generation. Finally, Padre Miguel Aguirre Elorriaza, the Spanish Jesuit who spent most of his career at the San Ignacio High School in Caracas, directly influenced Rafael Caldera. Caldera's interpretation of Catholic social thought provided the early doctrinal basis for COPEI.

Caldera's interpretation stressed three general areas. First, he emphasized implementation of the church's teaching on social justice. Second, because he concluded that liberal democracy provided the political environment most conducive to realizing social action, Caldera came to stress obedience to the law, constitutionalism, and strong opposition to dictatorship. Finally, he placed a strong emphasis on dealing as quickly as possible with certain social problems, such as breaking the cycle of poverty and achieving a more equitable distribution of wealth within Venezuela and among nations. To a remarkable extent, Caldera's interpretation of Roman Catholic social thought has guided Venezuelan Christian Democracy from the mid-1930s to the present.[12]

COPEI always has attracted support from advocates of policies to the right of its Christian Democratic doctrine and ideology. Initially, traditionalists saw in COPEI a confessional party that offered a Christian alternative to prevailing Marxist ideology. Also, traditionalists perceived COPEI as the only vehicle capable of challenging AD for power, and AD's defeat was for many years their highest priority. Some traditionalists did break with COPEI after it became clear that conservative traditionalism would always be a minority position within the party;[13] however, most remained loyal and influential until well into the Caldera administration. As president, Rafael Caldera disappointed the traditionalists. His implementation of social justice closely resembled the policies of AD.

Traditionalists, especially the former COPEI leader Germán Borregales, attempted to take advantage of Caldera's progressive presidency to gain support for a more conservative political party, the National Action Movement (MAN). However, the overwhelming defeat of all conservative political parties in 1973 suggested that support for rightist policies had diminished significantly. MAN subsequently disappeared. The outcome of the 1973 election also helped leftist Luis Herrera take control of

COPEI's party organization. Herrera long had argued that COPEI would gain more support than it would lose if the party became an advocate of speeding up the pace of social transformation. Subsequently, while serving as president, he championed policies intended to create a more egalitarian society and reduce private sector influence.

Herrera's manipulation of Christian Democratic doctrine was an important factor in the ascendancy that COPEI achieved briefly over AD during the late 1970s. However, Venezuela's economic difficulties in the early 1980s discredited Herrera as a leader and COPEI as a political party. Christian Democratic social justice doctrine rang hollow as unemployment rose and inflation skyrocketed. Making this doctrine credible is a major challenge facing COPEI as the party prepares for the 1988 elections.[14]

For many years COPEI appeared more able to manage internal personalistic rivalries than other political parties. In the wake of the 1983 and 1984 electoral debacles, however, the clash between Rafael Caldera and Luis Herrera Campins threatens to divide the party. Herrera never has forgiven Caldera for blocking his nomination as COPEI's presidential candidate in 1973. On the other hand, Caldera believes that Herrera deliberately pursued policies during the 1983 presidential campaign that sealed Caldera's defeat. Both enjoy support inside COPEI, and each commands important financial resources that they are committing in the struggle for control. Even if these two are able to cooperate and rebuild COPEI's shattered infrastructure, the road back to parity with AD will be long and difficult. COPEI stands on the threshold of losing its capability to challenge effectively for the presidency.

Militant Leftists

Political parties belonging to this family never have lived up to expectations of their leaders or of supporting intellectuals. The Venezuelan Communist party (PCV), as indicated earlier, is the country's oldest existing political party. As with AD, COPEI, and URD, the return of democracy in 1958 gave the PCV new life; it squandered its opportunity when the party joined with Castroite guerrillas in their ill-fated attempt to re-create the Cuban revolution. An equally devastating blow came soon after PCV reincorporation into the legal political spectrum for a second time, in 1968. This was also the year of the Soviet invasion of Czechoslovakia. Many PCV leaders openly criticized the Soviets' use of force. When the party's Central Committee supported Moscow, critics split from the PCV to form a nationalistic Communist organization, the Movement Toward Socialism (MAS). In subsequent elections, support for the weakened PCV has stabilized at roughly 2 percent of the total.

National elections in 1973 made MAS the most influential of the militant leftist political parties. MAS attracted intellectuals and demonstrated significant electoral strength in Caracas, Maracaibo, and other large cities.[15] The MAS leadership, while not abandoning its commitment to socialism, has been relatively successful in associating the party with such popular themes as nationalism, democracy, and political toleration. MAS placed a third in the elections of 1973, 1978, and 1983. However, MAS has been unable either to eliminate or absorb its small militant leftist rivals.

MAS itself has suffered increasingly from internal party factionalism. One dimension of factionalism involves personalistic rivalry between its two most important leaders, Pompeyo Márquez and Teodoro Petkoff. Another is ideological. On the party's left is a faction advocating Marxism-Leninism while rejecting Soviet imperialism. MAS's right is composed of individuals whose ideology is almost indistinguishable from that of AD. In the center sits a group that seeks to synthesize Marxism-Leninism and Social Democracy. Infighting among the three factions largely explains why MAS barely held its own in the national elections of 1983.[16] Whether these factions will be able to paper over their differences and resume building MAS into a viable contender for power remains an open question as Jaime Lusinchi completes his first year in office.

Other political parties on the militant left are small and in decline. URD, once the second political force, supported AD in the 1983 presidential elections. Even with financial backing from AD, URD polled just under 2 percent of the total congressional vote. Over the past 25 years its personalistic leader, Jóvito Villalba, has expelled all who disagreed with him. What little remains of URD likely will be absorbed by AD or MAS when Villalba passes from the scene. The Movement of the Revolutionary Left (MIR), once the backbone of militant leftist insurgency against Presidents Betancourt and Leoni, accepted legalization in time to participate in the 1973 balloting. Never a significant electoral force, MIR split in 1982 because of rivalry between its two most important leaders, Moisés Moleiro and Américo Martín. The People's Electoral Movement (MEP), what remains of the AD faction that supported the presidential candidacy of Luis Prieto in 1968, clings to political life by a slender thread. Unable to compete with AD for the Social Democratic vote, MEP has also failed to attract a large following among militant leftists. Finally, José Vicente Rangel, the perpetual presidential candidate of the militant left, established his own political party, Nueva Alternativa (New Alternative), in anticipation of the 1983 elections. Nueva Alternativa received 1 percent of the total congressional vote and added yet another fragment to an already highly divided militant left.

Personalistic Right

Between 1948 and 1958, traditionalists struggled to articulate a rightist doctrine with mass appeal. The corruption and degeneracy of General Pérez Jiménez, however, discredited personalistic rightism as a political force. Throughout the post-1958 democratic era personalistic rightists generally have been viewed as pariahs by other political leaders. Nevertheless, on several occasions it appeared that a political party of the personalistic right might take root; those with the greatest potential, however, managed to discredit themselves in a surprisingly short time.

The National Democratic Front (FND), the only personalistic rightist party to have participated in government during the current democratic era, was part of President Raúl Leoni's "broad-based" coalition. FND contributed to legitimating democracy with traditionalists who planned or supported the 1948 military coup. However, FND broke with Leoni over tax legislation. Once in the opposition, FND no longer enjoyed access to the patronage with which its leaders had intended to build a national organizational infrastructure; at the same time, many of FND's most ardent supporters were alienated because the party had helped to stabilize a political system dominated by "leftists." Election returns in 1968 confirmed that FND had lost its popular appeal; nevertheless, its moribund cadaver lingered on for five more years. In addition, the 1968 election gave birth to the Nationalist Civic Crusade (CCN), a party that appealed to nostalgia for the Pérez Jiménez dictatorship. However, the inept performance of CCN leaders between 1969 and 1973 reminded Venezuelans that the ousted dictator had been corrupt and incompetent. When AD and COPEI combined to pass a constitutional amendment that barred Pérez Jiménez from the presidency, the CCN collapsed.[17]

OPINA (National Opinion) is the personalistic rightist movement of most significance on the contemporary political scene. It appeared during the 1973 election campaign to advance the presidential candidacy of Miguel Angel Burelli Rivas. OPINA presently serves as a political vehicle for Jorge Olavarría, the colorful and controversial editor of the weekly newsmagazine *Resumen*. OPINA received 2 percent of the total congressional vote in 1983 and elected several members to the Chamber of Deputies.

PARTY SYSTEM: EVOLUTION AND OPERATIONAL CHARACTERISTICS

The Venezuelan political party system has taken two distinct incarnations since the overthrow of General Pérez Jiménez. The first began with preparations for the December 1958 balloting. In that election AD secured half of the total popular vote; together the militantly leftist URD and PCV spoke for about one-third of the electorate; and COPEI, the third force, obtained support from one in seven voters. Between 1958 and 1968, the party system fragmented. AD divided three times and the militant left experienced even greater traumas. Its political parties splintered, and some even mounted an insurgency against the government. COPEI, however, remained united and continued to support liberal democracy.

A new configuration of forces began to coalesce following Rafael Caldera's inauguration as president, in March 1969. In this second phase, which continues at present, AD remains the strongest political party. COPEI commands loyalty and resources sufficient to oust AD from the presidency with help from independents and militant leftists. Another characteristic of this second incarnation is that all but a few radicals on the militant left have abandoned the guerrilla struggle; militant leftists compete for votes inside legalized political parties. Finally, although personalistic rightist political movements have ballooned on several occasions, the overall strength of this grouping has stabilized at about 4 percent of the total electorate.

Figure 5.1 profiles the electoral strength of Venezuela's four ideological families in national elections since 1958. It also reveals the strength of each tendency in the two national elections that immediately preceded the November 1948 military coup.

From Fragmentation to Consolidation, 1958–73

When AD emerged from the underground, it faced substantial organizational difficulties. Many local party cadres had been liquidated by Pérez Jiménez's dreaded security police, the Seguridad Nacional. Others had endured torture while in prison, served as guerrilla fighters, or contributed from their enforced exiles abroad. Not only was it necessary to choose new leaders but the survivors had to be reintegrated into a disciplined hierarchy. This was especially difficult because elements of AD had operated for long periods with minimal centralized control. In addition, AD leaders had to forge new linkages with the party rank and file. Given the complexities of these tasks, AD's success in capturing half the total presidential vote in the 1958 election, especially in light of the provisional government's hostility, was an impressive achievement.

COPEI returned to the electoral wars weaker than anticipated. During his decade in power, Pérez Jiménez had blocked COPEI efforts to penetrate into the great urban centers of Caracas, Valencia, and Maracaibo. Throughout eastern Venezuela the party had run up against AD's powerful underground organization. Nevertheless, COPEI boasted a skillful and charismatic political leader in Rafael Caldera. The party also possessed a highly trained cadre of middle-level leaders who were the products of Venezuela's most prestigious Catholic high schools. Caldera and his leader-

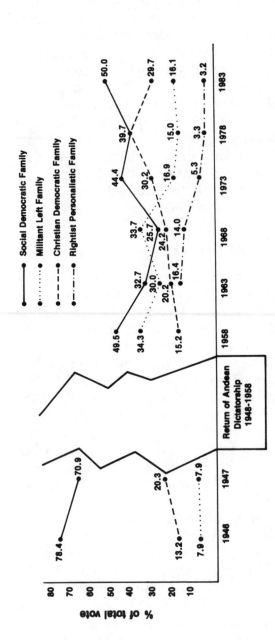

FIGURE 5.1. Party Families and Congressional Voting in Democratic Venezuela, 1946–83

Note: The political parties comprising the ideological families are as follows: *Social Democratic family*: Acción Democrática; *Christian Democratic family*: COPEI; *Militant left family*: Democratic Republican Union (all elections), Communist Party of Venezuela (1958, 1973, 1978, 1983), Popular Democratic Force (1963, 1968, 1973, 1978), People's Electoral Movement (1968, 1973, 1978, 1983), National Revolutionary Party (1963, 1968), Socialist League (all elections), Revolutionary Action Group (1978, 1983), New Alternative (1983), Movement of Revolutionary Left (1978, 1983), Movement Toward Socialism (1973, 1978, 1983), Advancement Union (1968), and "R" Cause (1983); and *Rightist personalistic family*: National Democratic Front (1963, 1968, 1973), National Civic Crusade (1968, 1973, 1978), National Action Movement (1968, 1973, 1978), National Opinion (1973, 1978, 1983), Developmentist Movement (1973), Common Cause (1978), National Union Force (1973, 1978, 1983), National Integration Movement (1978, 1983), and National Rescue (1983).

The totals for the above elections do not add to 100 percent because of rounding and the presence of numbers of microparties and movements.

Source: Compiled from official statistics of Venezuela's Consejo Supremo Electoral.

ship cadre (the *calderistas*) provided the ideology and organizational skills that resulted in COPEI winning out over militant leftists in the competition to become Venezuela's second political force.

The PCV and URD spoke for the militant left in 1958. Basking in prestige derived from bravery exhibited while fighting in the underground, the PCV received 6.2 percent of the total congressional vote. This marked the high point of its electoral appeal. Of the four political parties that received significant electoral support in 1958, however, the PCV was the least enthusiastic about pluralistic democracy and the most hostile to AD. When the Movement of the Revolutionary Left began its insurgency against Rómulo Betancourt's popularly elected government, the PCV also opted for violence. Its behavior while engaging in guerrilla activities cost the party important popular support.

In 1958 two factions competed for control of URD. The former, led by Jóvito Villalba, perceived itself as to the left of AD. The second was composed of opportunistic progressives from the traditional elite who had created a short-lived populist political party to support President/General Isaías Medina (1941–45). These progressives clustered about Medina's former minister of the interior, Arturo Uslar Pietri. Opposition to AD was the only important bond shared by URD's Villalba and Uslar factions. In the 1958 election, the charismatic appeal of URD's presidential candidate, Admiral Wolfgang Larrazábal, enabled the party to hide its divisions from the general public. After the popular admiral's defeat, however, he withdrew from active politics and accepted appointment as ambassador to Chile. Larrazábal's departure left Villalba in control of URD. During 1960 and 1961 Villalba nudged the party farther to the left. Arturo Uslar and his traditionalists responded by establishing their own movement, the Independent Electoral Front (IPFN). It evolved into FND.

Events within URD during the early 1960s suggest that the political party system remained highly fluid until the realigning election of 1973. For example, between 1963 and 1974, AD sustained two major divisions, saw its share of the national congressional vote shrink to roughly one-quarter of the total, lost control of the presidency, and then regained its position as Venezuela's first electoral force. AD also opted to coexist with

Venezuelan capitalism, continued to support the United States against the Soviet Union, and drew close ideologically to West Germany's Social Democrats. Finally, whereas in the early 1960s AD had substantial difficulties in unifying and disciplining its leadership cadre, in anticipation of the 1973 elections the party experienced greater unity than at any time since its formation.

Betancourt was largely responsible for the course of events inside AD between 1963 and 1974. He began this decade as Venezuela's president. He finished it by attending the inauguration of Carlos Andrés Pérez, his closest confidante, as Venezuela's fourth consecutively elected constitutional president. During the intervening years Betancourt purged the AD leadership of those opposed to him and his policies; he also attracted back into the party most of their followers. Betancourt thus placed AD in a position from which it could continue as Venezuela's most important political party for a very long time. Nevertheless, the former president did not believe that it was desirable, either for AD or Venezuela, that AD should preside over a single-party state. Consequently, he frequently cooperated with COPEI and Rafael Caldera so as to strengthen and legitimate their status as an acceptable alternative for governing.

Militant leftist parties, in contrast, were never perceived as legitimate governing options by most of the political elite. Many militant leftists had been insurgents during the 1960s. When they finally did accept amnesty and enter the loyal opposition, they were soon fighting as much among themselves as against AD and COPEI. Personalistic and institutional rivalries were two important causes of this internecine warfare. Another involved previously analyzed feelings about Soviet behavior toward Eastern Europe, especially the 1968 decision to invade Czechoslovakia. These developments discredited and weakened the militant left.

Political parties of the personalistic right fared worst of all between the early 1960s and mid-1970s. For one brief moment, when IPFN received more than 15 percent of the total presidential and congressional vote in the 1963 elections, it looked as if Venezuelan conservatives might succeed in forming a genuinely popular political party. These hopes were dashed when its leaders fell to fighting among themselves over coalition politics and ideology. The second personalistic rightist movement of consequence, the Nationalist Civic Crusade (CCN), polled almost 10 percent of the total congressional vote in 1968. It was, however, highly dependent on expectations that General Pérez Jiménez would return to Venezuela and actively participate in democratic politics. When AD and COPEI united to prevent this, support for the CCN collapsed. A third rightist political party, the Movement of National Action (MAN), never attracted significant support; this was also true for the pro-business Development Movement (Movimiento Desarrollista). In the realigning 1973 election all personalist rightist parties together attracted only slightly more than 5 percent of the total congressional vote.[18]

OPERATIONAL CHARACTERISTICS OF THE CONTEMPORARY PARTY SYSTEM

The post-1973 political party system displays four central operational characteristics. They concern its structure, its locus of competition, its evolving patterns of accountability, and its linkages with the international environment.[19] The events of Jaime Lusinchi's first year in office confirmed that these characteristics have been only marginally affected by economic difficulties during the early 1980s.

The Dynamic "Two-and-a-Sixth-Plus" Party System

Not only did the 1973 election returns restore AD dominance, they also reshaped Venezuela's party system. Voting in 1978, 1979, 1983, and 1984 confirmed the new configuration as a "two-and-a-sixth-plus" party system. Within this system COPEI and AD constitute the two; each is capable of winning the presidency. The sixth belongs to parties of the militant left, especially MAS. While militant left political parties together receive between 12 and 19 percent of the total vote, no single party breaks the 10 percent barrier. The personalistic right comprises the system's "plus"; its political parties speak for about 4 percent of the electorate.

The basic structural dynamic of the "two-and-a-sixth plus" party system is that each of the two major actors attempts marginally to strengthen the militant leftist parties. Rightist parties are perceived as pariahs. The intention of AD and COPEI is to diminish the other by bleeding off some of its support. The weakened major actor is not to be eliminated, merely rendered incapable of capturing the presidency. Decades of cooperation and controlled competition between AD and COPEI have made each more comfortable with the other than with any militantly leftist organization. Neither wants the other to be replaced as the second political force. The desired state of affairs is what AD achieved in the December 1983 congressional elections; AD captured the presidency, received roughly half of the total congressional vote, and limited COPEI to just under 30 percent. Militant leftists divided most of the rest, although several personalistic rightist political parties persisted as gadflys.

The "two-and-a-sixth-plus" party system forces the militant leftists to play a waiting game. Their hope is that some cataclysmic event will destroy one or both of the major political parties and leave them to pick up the pieces. Barring such an eventuality, militant leftists must content themselves with marginal increments in their support facilitated by dissatisfaction with the big two and continued impotence on the part of the personalistic right.

Competition to Occupy the Left Center

Venezuelans expect the state to be heavily involved in economic activity; this includes such commonly accepted responsibilities as the development of transportation infrastructure, rural electrification, and mail delivery. In addition, Venezuela relies on government corporations to produce steel, extract minerals, refine petroleum, and operate fishing fleets. Businessmen sometimes participate in these activities, but only in construction, ranching, commerce, and assorted light industries does the private sector dominate. Few Latin American countries delegate more of their total economic activity to the public sector than Venezuela.

One explanation for this reluctance to entrust economic development to private enterprise derives from the early history of Venezuelan capitalism. Until recently, most important businesses were controlled from abroad; government was a mechanism Venezuelans used to prevent foreigners from exploiting the economy for the benefits of multinational capitalism. Another source of hostility to private enterprise is the feudal communalism that structured colonial society and dominated Venezuelan political thinking until Marxism became the new orthodoxy. Feudal communalism is a spiritual precursor of the community property ideology so prevalent within Venezuelan Christian Democracy.

For COPEI, as well as for AD, private enterprise exists only because it serves the interests of the collectivity as determined by the state. The burden of proof is on entrepreneurs to convince government that they should not be regulated or taken over directly. AD and COPEI often compete for votes by accusing each other of being too favorably disposed toward private interests. In attempting to monopolize political space on the democratic left, however, the two major parties do take care not to appear radical. Being too far to the left is associated with communism, and public opinion is strongly anti-communist. Part of this aversion to communism derives from the PCV's long history of subservience to the Soviet Union. Another element is its previously discussed involvement in the unpopular guerrilla movement of the 1960s. So deeply rooted is this aversion to communism that other militant leftist political parties have discovered that because of similarities between their ideology and that of the PCV their appeal has been greatly limited.[20]

Increasing Accountability for Performance While Governing

During the first decade of post-1958 democracy, the prevailing mythology in Venezuela held that AD voters were the majority and that they were unswervingly loyal to the party. Events in 1967–68 cast doubt on these assumptions. AD members divided their votes between Gonzalo Barrios and Luis Prieto. This division, as indicated earlier, allowed COPEI's Rafael Caldera to capture the presidency. However, the overwhelming victory of Carlos Andrés Pérez in 1973 suggested that AD was unbeatable as long as it remained united. Many observers speculated that, having learned the lessons of 1967 and 1973, AD would govern until the turn of the century.

In this context Herrera's victory in 1978 was highly significant. He defeated a unified AD that controlled the presidency and enjoyed unprecedented resources with which to dispense patronage. Herrera's party, in turn, was defeated five years later by AD's Jaime Lusinchi. These shifts in electoral support argue that neither major political party can count on voters' automatically renewing its mandate. Indeed, the 1983 balloting was the fourth consecutive election in which the opposition won.

AD and COPEI strategists presently assume a large floating vote that supports the democratic system but is not irrevocably committed to either major political party. They believe that these voters made the difference in 1978 and 1983. After Herrera's inauguration, COPEI mounted an unsuccessful attempt to convert floating voters. President Jaime Lusinchi now presides over a similar effort. In the short run Lusinchi intends to convince independents that their interests are best served by an AD government. While COPEI hopes to create the opposite impression, it is experiencing great difficulties because of persisting perceptions that the Herrera government was economically inept and corrupt. The point here is that the leaders of each of the major political parties act as if they believe that their hard-core supporters alone are not sufficiently numerous to win elections. Past voting behavior suggests to them that victory belongs to the party that better demonstrates its responsiveness to an independent and pragmatic electorate.

Technological and Programmatic Dependence on the North Atlantic Democracies

Recent studies of Venezuelan election campaigns have profiled the influence on political parties of campaign technology, organizational methods, and programmatic appeals developed in Western Europe and North America. The likelihood that this will change any time soon is remote. Preoccupied with the economic consequences of falling petroleum prices, Venezuelan political parties lack the financial and human resources to invest in developing an indigenous electoral technology that would be more effective than methods imported and adapted from the industrial democracies.

COPEI's experience with David Garth, and to a lesser extent that of AD with Joe Napolitan, suggest that, in the short run, important technology can provide a winning advantage. Like most democratic political parties, AD, COPEI, and MAS are pre-occupied with winning elections. In the long run, however, winning will require party leaders to blend foreign technology with appeals that are uniquely Venezuelan.

DETERMINANTS OF PARTY SYSTEM EVOLUTION

The most significant factor influencing party and party system evolution since 1958 has been the extraordinary leadership skills of those who created and sustained the mass-based political parties.[21] They demonstrated that liberal democratic institutions and procedures could produce positive results. In turn, this reinforced underlying beliefs and attitudes that legitimated institutions and procedures that embodied liberal democracy, especially political party competition and free elections. Party system change also responded to socioeconomic trends and conditions—for example, urbanization and level of urbanity, modernization and level of modernity, and economic growth and societal level of wealth. Finally, the behavioral characteristics of political institutions also shaped the contemporary political party system. Each of these factors merits further examination.

Leadership, Organization, and Patronage

After the overthrow of Pérez Jiménez, democratic political party leaders displayed exceptional talents. Not only did they craft and manage a functioning democracy, they successfully defended it against great odds. They also increased respect for minority opinion and majority rule. In the process these leaders altered the distribution of political, economic, and social power. President Jaime Lusinchi belongs to this remarkable group; so do most high-ranking officials in AD and COPEI. The group's prestige is such that even the leadership of MAS claims to be in its tradition. Nevertheless, because of their role in the 1960s insurgency, MAS leaders remain suspect. The same is true for most other militant leftist politicians, as well as for personalistic rightist leaders. While the latter pay lip service to democratic pluralism, past collaboration with and manipulation by dictators cause other politicians to view them either as pariahs or gadflys. Also, personalistic rightists' inability to create and use the kinds of resources managed by AD, COPEI, and to a lesser extent MAS, suggests that their leadership skills do not measure up to those of Rómulo Betancourt, Rafael Caldera, or Teodoro Petkoff.

Party organization has been a key to AD and COPEI's domination of politics. Both are centrally controlled and penetrate all sectors of urban and rural life. Their skills in mass mobilization ended centuries of elite political domination. For AD and COPEI, as well as for the MAS, the national party convention is the maximum authority; on a daily basis, however, each is controlled by its secretary-general and national organization secretariat. A national executive committee meets weekly. The national executive committee's most influential members usually are the party's secretary-general, the secretary of organization, and assorted luminaries, such as former presidents and others who once held high office in either the government or the party. Finally, the national executive committees include the national secretaries of their party's societal organizations, for example, labor, peasants, educators, and women.[22]

The national executive committee sets the party position in relation to ongoing political developments and exercises control over the party's areal organizations. For example, the leader of each party's congressional delegation coordinates with his party's national executive committee when introducing legislation or when instructing the delegation on how to vote in the congress. The national executive committee also has the final word when a party member has been elected president and must engage in forming a multiparty coalition in order to pass legislation through the Congress. However, no power allows the national leadership to exercise greater control over state and local organizations than that to intervene, remove dissident leaders, and replace them with individuals of their choosing. All national party leaders have exercised this prerogative at one time or another. The most important limitation in exercising this prerogative is that intervention usually weakens the state party organization experiencing the intervention.

The state and local organizations of Venezuelan political parties re-create their national counterparts on a smaller scale.

There are between 20 and 25 state or regional secretary-generals, secretaries of organization, and executive committees.[23] Functional secretariats, such as labor, peasants, and professionals, are present in each state organization and in the most important local organizations. Both are linked to party headquarters in Caracas by a dualistic command structure.

For simplicity, only the national to state command structure will be discussed. Within any state the entire party organization is subject to the authority of the state secretary-general. In turn, he reports directly to the national secretary-general. State secretaries of the functional organizations also report to their national counterpart, as well as to the state secretary-general. The state secretary of organization, for example, reports to the national secretary of organization, as well as to the state secretary-general. The party thus maintains two channels through which to enforce its commands and gather information about the needs and desires of the general populace. These channels also enable party leaders to detect threats and take remedial actions before situations get out of control.

The patronage capabilities of the centralized political parties described above are obvious. Here the prerogative of the national organization to determine the composition of the party's list in each state for the Congress and state legislative office deserves special mention. It allows national leaders to short-circuit the careers of popular but independent-minded state leaders. Only individuals who have demonstrated their acceptance of party discipline are placed on these lists. If an elected official displays unexpected independence after taking office, his career will be terminated by denying him a place on the party's lists for the next election. National leaders are empowered to deny renomination to any individual of whom they disapprove, regardless of the wishes of a state executive committee. Also, the national leadership can force the state organizations to add names to the party's list of congressional candidates, even if those being imposed reside in different states. An important reason for this extreme centralization is that nineteenth-century state leaders used their autonomy for seven decades to wage bloody civil war. Surpressing this potential for violence retains high priority with present-day party leaders.

Economic incentives add immensely to the patronage powers

of the political parties.[24] They can reward those who do their bidding and ignore those who refuse. Being treated as a nonperson by party leaders carries a very stiff penalty. It eliminates the possibility of public sector employment. Also, there are only a limited number of jobs in the private sector, and entrepreneurs are fearful of antagonizing the politically powerful. Firms that the government views favorably receive lucrative contracts. When a contract has been let, recipients who desire fortune to smile on them a second time are expected to express their gratitude; also, even relatively minor public officials return a portion of their salaries to the government party. Contributions from public sector employees and contractors, of course, add to the ability of the government party to dispense patronage.

Beliefs and Attitudes

The impact of public opinion on regime support between 1973 and 1983 is explored at great length in the chapter by Enrique Baloyra; his analysis will not be repeated here.[25] Nevertheless, several patterns of influence are of particular interest from the perspective of how political beliefs and attitudes influenced party system evolution. In the first place, surveys over the past decade have confirmed the strong preference of Venezuelans for democracy. Since personalistic rightist parties emerged as critics of post-1958 democracy, and in the case of CCN as a vehicle to advance the ambitions of its archenemy, broad societal support for democracy goes far in explaining why personalistic rightist parties have demonstrated little appeal. Similarly the antidemocratic image of the PCV has rubbed off on other militant left parties such as MAS and MEP; their electoral appeal is largely confined to a small core of true believers.

In addition to preferring democracy, Venezuelans are optimistic that it can be made to work. AD and COPEI remain the political parties most overtly committed to sustaining the democratic system. Consequently, when the electorate has become dissatisfied with how either major party has performed while in office, they have turned to the other, rather than to parties on the militant left or right.[26] Also, survey research confirms that more than six in ten Venezuelans have some faith in either AD or

COPEI as political institutions. In summary, prevailing beliefs and attitudes reinforce perceptions relating to democracy; their cumulative effect has contributed to the continuing domination of the two major political parties.

Social and Economic Change

Far-reaching changes have taken place since 1935. Where once Venezuela was a predominantly rural country of 3 million inhabitants, it is now a nation of cities. Its population has grown more than fivefold. In place of one of the lowest standards of living in the Caribbean, Venezuela has substituted the highest per capita income in Latin America. Nevertheless, income distribution remains highly skewed toward the most affluent fifth of the population.[27] The greatest concentrations of have-nots reside in the slums of Caracas, Maracaibo, and other large cities. Peasants, while better off than in 1935, remain poor. However, they now comprise a dramatically reduced proportion of the total population. Regional loyalties, also historically a driving sociopolitical force, have diminished since 1935. People now think of themselves more as Venezuelans than as "Andeans," "Plainsmen," "Easterners," or "Zulians." Finally, soaring birth rates have made Venezuela more than ever a country of the young. Each of these changes has affected the political parties.

AD and COPEI became Venezuela's most important political parties during the 1940s because peasants, except in the Andean region, overwhelmingly supported the former; Andean peasants backed the latter. The PCV displayed strength in the urban areas, but at the time cities accounted for a comparatively small proportion of the population. In the post-1958 period, COPEI's ability to establish itself in the rapidly expanding cities limited the growth potential of the militant left and enabled Rafael Caldera to challenge successfully for the presidency within a decade. Also, the charismatic appeal of Carlos Andrés Pérez among the urban poor in 1973 allowed AD to reestablish itself as the preeminent political party.[28] Toward the end of the Pérez government, and during the 1982–83 recession, economic difficulties were felt most intensely in the urban areas. City dwellers as a group voted against the government party in the elections of 1978 and 1983, and their vote was decisive. This suggests that cities have become the most important geopolitical arenas of political party competition; they are likely to remain so for the foreseeable future.

Since independence the central region, "Caracas," has dominated for substantial periods; so has the Andes. At the beginning of the ongoing democratic regime, COPEI received disproportionate support in the Andes. The central region voted for URD in 1958, for FND in 1963, and for the Burelli Rivas presidential candidacy in 1968. It was the eastern, plains, and western states, however, that provided AD with the overwhelming support on which its initial domination of national politics rested. Between 1958 and 1968, COPEI cut into AD's western base. This step in COPEI's journey toward becoming a truly national political party foreshadowed the decline of regionalism's importance as a factor in party voting. Nevertheless, AD continues stronger in the east and COPEI retains disproportionate strength in the western states of Zulia and Lara and in the Andean state of Mérida. The electoral position of MAS and the personalistic right remains marginally stronger in the cities of the Center.[29]

Class is important for explaining differences in voter preference for the two major political parties. In the 1947 election campaign, Venezuela's first free presidential election, COPEI received support from those who ruled between 1899 and 1945; it remains the favorite of upper- and upper-middle-class voters. In contrast, those who founded AD came disproportionately from the middle classes of the interior and the peasantry. AD continues to portray itself as the "party of the people."

Throughout the 1940s Rómulo Betancourt and AD outorganized Rafael Caldera and COPEI, except in the Andes. Peasant villages and small market towns predominated at that time. After the fall of Pérez Jiménez, AD experienced great difficulties in attracting support among the slum dwellers who had migrated to the cities between 1948 and 1958. Consequently, the party mounted a decade-long effort that, culminating with the 1973 election campaign, consolidated its position as spokesman for the urban poor. In contrast, neither AD nor COPEI achieved domination over the urban middle and lower-middle classes. Depending on which electoral issues proved most salient, and on the relative appeal of their presidential candidates, both at one time or another have received majority support from urban middle- and lower-middle-class voters.

Additional complexities cloud relationships between class and voting for the two major parties. COPEI counts on support from a significant minority of the poor and elements within the traditional elite help to finance AD's presidential campaigns. This cross-class appeal of the two major parties is reflected in their ideology. Each declares itself opposed to class warfare and aspires to aggregate the interests of all.[30]

Class also influences support for the minor political parties. MAS and the PCV draw heavily from urban lower-middle-class voters and intellectuals.[31] While personalistic rightists also appeal to the urban middle class, the intellectuals reject them. On occasion, personalistic rightist movements have been embraced by the urban poor. A personalistic leftist movement, the FDP, also received substantial support from slum dwellers in 1963 and 1968. However, as noted above, the 1973 presidential campaign of Carlos Andrés Pérez enticed the urban poor away from personalistic movements of both the right and the left.

High birth rates make Venezuela a country of the very young. Just under 30 percent of the electorate is between 17 and 24 years of age. Youthful voters are especially concerned with finding jobs so they can marry, obtain housing, and raise a family. Even during the 1970s, a decade of sharply increasing petroleum revenues, the government experienced great difficulties in fulfilling these expectations; even fewer opportunities for their realization exist in the depressed economy of the 1980s. Consequently, in the elections of 1973, 1978, and 1983, youthful voters—far more than other cohorts—expressed their dissatisfaction by voting for the opposition. This is a major reason why neither AD nor COPEI has made much headway in establishing a single-party-dominated state. Nevertheless, President Herrera's bad economic luck, ineptitude, and clash with Rafael Caldera weakened COPEI dramatically; in the 1988 presidential election, AD stands a good chance of breaking the four-election trend in which government is turned out of office.

Behavioral Characteristics of Political Institutions

Finally, party and party system evolution has responded to the behavioral characteristics of political institutions. Four of these characteristics merit special attention: centralized control exercised from Caracas, dominance by executive committee, cultivation of and reward for personalistic loyalty, and lack of attention to the technical demands of policy implementation. The impact of these characteristics has been complex and multidimensional.

The ever-growing domination of Caracas is analyzed at length in John Lombardi's overview chapter. He points out that since Bourbon Spain centralized Venezuela's government during the late eighteenth century, political decisions have been perceived as legitimate for the entire country only after they were ratified by the institutions of government located in Caracas. All who subsequently aspired to political power and influence, regardless of their origin, focused on Caracas. Important elements of each region's political elite took up permanent residence in the capital city. They understood that to get what they wanted for their region or state it was necessary to reside close to the national political decision makers. In Caracas, residents from other regions, known collectively as the "interior," cluster in colonies—for example, the Zulian colony, the Eastern colony, and the Andean colony.

Those who shaped the present-day political parties created mechanisms and procedures that enabled them to exercise control from Caracas. Consequently, it is almost impossible for dissidents in the states to seize power in a national party organization. The 1967 division of AD illustrates their predicament. Betancourt and his allies lost control in a majority of AD's state and local organizations. However, the Betancourt faction retained control over the Caracas-based national organization; this enabled followers of Betancourt to intervene, reinstate their supporters, and expel the dissidents. Similarly, after partisans of Caldera gained control of COPEI's Caracas-based national organization, in 1979, they were able to intervene and replace state party leaders loyal to Luis Herrera Campins, even while Herrera was serving as president. Analogous interventions have occurred in all other political parties. This gives rise to intense competition among ambitious politicians in the region to curry favor with national leaders and for positions that would enable them to become players in the Byzantine politics of the capital city.

Executive dominance, a traditional pattern of Iberian political behavior, is no stranger to Venezuela. Lynn Kelley's discussion of national political institutions profiles the broad scope of executive dominance in spite of the checks and balances inserted into the constitution of 1961. Political party statutes contain no such checks and balances. However, in the case of the political parties, no single individual enjoys power and authority analogous to that of the Venezuelan president. Within each political party the secretary-general is first among equals. Final authority inside the party rests with the Caracas-based national executive committee. Even such dominating figures as Rómulo Betancourt and Rafael Caldera have not always been able to impose their will on the national executive committee of their respective political parties. Control by executive committee also predominates within the state and district party organizations. At these lower levels, however, decisions can be appealed to the party's national executive committee.

Except when the party's national convention is in session, decisions by the national executive committees are without appeal. Not surprisingly, there is fierce jockeying for the few favored positions on the national executive committee and at the state level for membership on the state executive committees. Costly and elaborate campaigns have been conducted for the office of national secretary within the functional subdivisions of the parties, for example, the youth secretariat and the professionals and technicians secretariat. These national secretaries sit on the party's national executive committee. Other offices that carry with them membership on the national executive committees, expecially the national secretary-general and secretary of organization, are contested throughout the entire party. Which factions coalesce behind the winners and the losers reveals the basic alignment of forces within a political party. Control of the secretary-general and the organization secretariat usually guarantees domination of the all-important process for nominating the party's presidential and other candidates.

The politics of reaching a political party's national executive body draws attention to a third behavioral characteristic of Venezuelan political parties: the cultivation of and reward for personal loyalty. While ideological and regional differences contribute to the shaping of party factions, factions are most often identified with individuals. AD has its *carlosandresistas* (followers of Carlos Andrés Pérez), COPEI its *calderistas* (followers of Rafael Caldera), and MAS its *teodoristas* (followers of Teodoro Petkoff).

Career politicians in the political parties quickly become identified with a leader and his faction. Advancement depends both upon how the individual is perceived by the leader of the faction and upon that leader's success in the national party organization.

When a national leader loses influence, those whose political star was hitched to his group may bargain for incorporation into a rival faction. If these maneuvers prove unsuccessful, attempts may be made to restructure the fallen leader's faction. Would-be new leaders will attempt to mobilize the faction and sound out new supporters; their goal remains to force their way into the party's governing elite. Much about this elite circulation process remains unclear. It continues to be complicated by a behind-the-scenes presence of individuals who played an important role in founding these parties; they are able to veto admission of "undesirable" decision makers to the inner circle.

Finally, party and party system evolution has been influenced by lack of attention to the technical demands of policy implementation. Cultural norms incline Venezuelans to search for the dramatic; politicians tend to rely on rhetorical brilliance and grandiose plans to attract attention. There is a tendency to assume that issuing a directive or verbalizing a policy somehow leads to modifications in behavior. The importance of overseeing policy implementation is acknowledged in theory; however, in practice few care to immerse themselves in the nuts and bolts of making a plan work. Rómulo Betancourt and Rafael Caldera are exceptions. Their attention to organizational detail was an important reason why AD and COPEI became the two most important political parties. In contrast, Jóvito Villalba's failure to oversee efforts to create URD's party infrastructure in the early 1960s precipitated its decline from the country's second political force to a position of dramatic insignificance.

Lack of attention to policy implementation continued to influence party system evolution in the 1970s and 1980s. Following the triumph of Carlos Andrés Pérez in the 1973 election, AD denuded its national and state party organizations in order to staff the government. Little thought was given to the political consequences of this action; the skeletal AD infrastructure was unable to nurture or strengthen state and local party organizations. At the beginning of the 1978 election campaign, consequently, many AD organizations existed only on paper. This was an important factor in AD's defeat by COPEI and Luis Herrera Campins. After Herrera's inauguration as president, his faction promptly lost control of COPEI. He had failed to oversee replacement within the party of those he selected to staff his administration. Consequently, individuals loyal to Rafael Caldera moved into influential positions throughout the COPEI party organization.

Also during 1979 and 1980, COPEI held numerous conferences in which the party planned how to consolidate its newfound positions as the first political force. A closely related objective was to weaken AD to where that party would be unable to challenge effectively for control of the presidency. One important program for doing this centered around the creation of neighborhood councils in the urban slums. These councils were to dispense patronage so as to bind slum dwellers to COPEI. The councils, however, never lived up to expectations. COPEI gave little thought to who should organize the councils, or to how they might coordinate party and government activities so that their dispensing of patronage would have the desired result. In a number of instances the councils came under the control of MAS and actually blocked COPEI efforts to organize among the urban poor.[32] Also, by the midpoint of Herrera's term, effective cooperation between his government and the Caldera-controlled party had ceased. Although this sealed COPEI's fate in the 1983 elections, the party's failure to draw up implementation guidelines dealing with how to create and manage the neighborhood councils made it unlikely in any case that COPEI could have reached the goals of its 1979 and 1980 plans.

CONCLUDING COMMENTS

Venezuelan political parties, as we have seen, dominate political life. They mobilize public opinion, assemble coalitions of interests, and communicate demands to the government. Political parties also control recruitment to internal leadership positions, governmental office, and the bureaucracy. Finally, they articulate to their followers the concept and meaning of the broader community. In so doing, Venezuelan political parties demonstrate the considerable skills that enabled them to gain widespread acceptance for liberal democracy. Also, political parties mold the quality of democratic life. Here three dimensions are especially relevant: the quality of procedural democracy, of participatory democracy, and of socioeconomic democracy. The conclusion of this discussion will focus briefly on the impact of political parties on these qualitative dimensions.

Venezuelan political authorities seldom have provided meaningful procedural protections for their citizens. Barbarism surfaced often during the nineteenth century, and as recently as during the dictatorship of General Pérez Jiménez, human rights violations were commonplace. Those who led the political parties in the immediate post-1958 years had experienced personally the cruelty of dictatorial power. Due process and human rights for them were central pillars of democratic life. Soon after taking power, however, these democratic leaders found themselves, and the system they were seeking to create, under attack from the authoritarian right and the radical left. In order to conduct a defense, given the absence of a tradition that respected due process and individual rights, they were sometimes forced to take actions that they would have preferred to avoid.

The radical leftists' initiation of an insurgency against the Betancourt government, as well as their ongoing flirtation with violence, has prevented AD and COPEI from fully implementing the kinds of procedural guarantees that are accepted as basic to Western European and North American democratic life. For example, survival dictated that Betancourt neutralize the power of radical judges who were releasing insurgents from prison almost before authorities had an opportunity to complete their processing. Neutralization gave rise to domination of the judicial system by AD and, to a lesser extent, COPEI. Judges at all levels remain closely linked to leaders in the two major parties. Not only are minor favors for party leaders commonplace, this linkage makes it extremely difficult to use the courts in matters involving corruption and the behavior of law enforcement institutions.

The democratic political parties' accomplishments in the area of procedural democracy should not be judged only in terms of prevailing standards in the more established liberal democracies.

It is important to take into account where Venezuela stands in such matters from the perspective of where the country stood prior to the 1958 revolution. Using this as a measure, the democratic party leaders have made great strides. It is especially significant that AD and COPEI have legitimated the idea of a loyal opposition and of respect for the right of that opposition to organize and present its point of view. In addition, support for free and open elections as a mechanism for choosing national leaders is widespread. In the long run institutionalizing party competition may correct many of the persisting procedural problems, especially in regard to policy implementation. If the government party perceives that there is a chance of voters turning it out of office, and that once in power the opposition will search out and punish the abuses of its predecessor, concern that this may happen acts as a deterrent to reduce the abuse of rights and procedures intended to protect the individual.

In no area can party leaders boast of greater successes than in the strengthening of participatory democracy. They transformed the elitist political ethos and practices of four centuries into the mass-based liberal democracy of the present. AD and COPEI penetrate sociey both spatially and functionally, and as survey research documents, the overwhelming majority of Venezuelans hold a positive view of these two major actors. With a membership of close to 1 million, each has continued to recruit aggressively. That most new voters over the past decade have opted for either AD or COPEI is proof of their continuing vitality. Since 1973, of course, MAS has given the two major political parties important competition.

Participation is not unlimited. Obviously, AD and COPEI rule out violence as an acceptable mode of participation. Equally important, especially given opponents' failure to prevent the consolidation of liberal democracy, is the democratic political parties' success in channeling most political participation through their respective party organizations. For example, as early as in the seventh grade, aspirants for student offices run as COPEI, AD, or MAS candidates. In organizations as diverse as the professional engineering association and labor unions, adults also run for office as candidates on slates presented by the political parties. Furthermore, all manner of government jobs are allocated on the basis of approval by party leaders. The enormous impact of this becomes fully evident only when one takes into account that the public sector controls most economic activity.

Socioeconomic democracy, the final dimension, is one about which an increasing number of questions are being raised; at issue are the consequences of policies followed by the political parties since 1958. AD owes much of its early strength to promises that it would implement a more equitable distribution of wealth. COPEI's continuing commitment to Christian Social justice carries a similar promise. While these two have controlled the executive and legislative branches of government for almost three decades, the promised economic democracy seems as far away as ever. A UN study in the mid-1970s found that the top 20 percent of Venezuelans earned 65 percent of total income; the poorest 40 percent of income-earning Venezuelans accounted for only 8 percent.[33] Little suggests that this situation will change.

A basic decision made by the leaders of AD, COPEI, and URD in 1958 accounts most directly for this disparity between promise and performance. At the time the three political parties' leaders had spent more than a decade either fighting in the underground or as exiles. They were tired and impoverished. Many of their friends and companions had been murdered in the struggle to topple General Pérez Jiménez. They desperately wanted an opportunity to exercise power. However, Venezuela had experienced less than one year of constitutional democratic government in its entire history. Those who led AD, COPEI, and URD decided that if they were to have any chance of institutionalizing a liberal democratic regime they would have to give priority to cultivating societal acceptance for the norms of procedural and participatory democracy. They calculated that once these norms were internalized, their acceptance, along with the parties' domination over a similarly legitimated participatory process, would enable them to restructure the economy and redistribute wealth. In addition, the leaders of AD, COPEI, and URD assumed that increased Social Democracy would be the product of economic democratization.

The political and economic dynamics of post-1958 Venezuela have never been such that the democratic political parties were willing to initiate far-reaching socioeconomic democratization.

URD quickly disintegrated. AD and COPEI established close ties with the upper and upper-middle classes while institutionalizing procedural and participatory norms. Many hard political choices could be avoided because petroleum revenue provided the state, independent from any necessity to tax, with massive resources. Rising petroleum prices during most of the 1960s and 1970s thus enabled AD and COPEI to distribute to the poor without taking from the more fortunate. Given the contracting international petroleum market, this is no longer possible. The inability of COPEI to recognize and deal with the new situation undid two decades of organizational efforts that saw it surpass AD as the first political force. AD and the Lusinchi administration face a similar challenge. How they respond will go far in shaping Venezuela's political party system for the remainder of this century.

NOTES

1. COPEI is an acronym for Comité de Organización Política Electoral Independiente, its initial label four decades ago.

2. Laureano Vallenilla Lanz, *Cesarismo Democrático* (Caracas: Tipografía Garrido, 1964), especially "Los partidos históricos," pp. 185-209.

3. For a comprehensive analysis of the December 1983 election, see Donald L. Herman and David J. Myers,"The Venezuelan Election," in *American Enterprise Institute Election Yearbook—1983*, ed. Howard Penniman (Durham: Duke University Press, 1985).

4. John D. Martz, *Acción Democrática: The Evolution of a Modern Political Party in Venezuela* (Princeton, N.J.: Princeton Unversity Press, 1966).

5. David J. Myers, *Democratic Campaigning in Venezuela: Caldera's Victory* (Caracas: Editorial Natura, 1973).

6. Interview with a high-ranking official of CORDIPLAN, November 7, 1984.

7. Myers, *Democratic Campaigning in Venezuela*, pp. 79-83.

8. David J. Myers, "TheAcción Democrática Campaign," in *Venezuela at the Polls: The National Elections of 1978*, ed. Howard R. Penniman (Washington, D.C.: American Enterprise Institute, 1980), pp. 91-132, and Andrés Stambouli, "La Campaña Electoral de 1978," *Politeia* 9 (November 1981): 53-132.

9. The best single work on COPEI is Donald L. Herman, *Christian Democracy in Venezuela* (Chapel Hill: University of North Carolina Press, 1980).

10. Donald L. Herman, "The Christian Democratic Party," in Penniman, *Venezuela at the Polls*, pp. 133-152.

11. Herman and Myers, "The Venezuelan Election."

12. Rafael Caldera, *Especifidad de la democracia cristiana* (Barcelona: Editorial Nova Terra, 1973).

13. Germán Borregales, *COPEI hoy una Negación* (Caracas: Editorial Garrido, 1968).

14. John D. Martz, "The Crisis of Venezuelan Democracy," *Current History*, February 1984, pp. 77, 89.

15. David J. Myers, "Venezuela's MAS," *Problems of Communism* 29 (September-October 1980): 16-27.

16. Herman and Myers, "The Venezuelan Elections."

17. John D. Martz and Enrique A. Baloyra, *Electoral Mobilization and Public Opinion: The Venezuelan Campaign of 1973* (Chapel Hill: University of North Carolina Press, 1976), pp. 75-82.

18. Ibid.

19. Cf. David J. Myers,"The Elections and the Evolution of Venezuela's Party System," in Penniman, *Venezuela at the Polls*, ed., pp. 247-52.

20. Robert E. O'Connor, "The Electorate," in Penniman, ed., *Venezuela at the Polls*, ed., pp. 56-90. Polling by the author in 1983, in the eastern state of Monagas, confirmed the electorate's continuing anticommunism.

21. Robert J. Alexander, *Rómulo Betancourt and the Transformation of Venezuela* (New Brunswick, N.J.: Transaction Books, 1982).

22. Herman, *Christian Democracy in Venezuela*, and Martz, *Acción Democrática*.

23. Not all subnational party organizations have the same boundaries as the states. For example, in the state of Sucre, AD maintains two equal and autonomous "regional" party organizations.

24. "Acceso: Bases institucionales para el ejercicio de la influencia en el proceso de formación de políticas," in *El Reto de Las Elites*, by José Antonio Gill Yepes (Madrid: Editorial Técnos, 1978), pp. 138-71.

25. See also Enrique A. Baloyra,"Criticism, Cynicism, and Political Evaluation: A Venezuelan Example," *American Political Science Review* 73, no. 4 (December 1979): 987-1002.

26. David J. Myers and Robert O'Connor, "The Undecided Respondent in Mandatory Voting Settings: A Venzuelan Exploration" *Western Political Quarterly* 36, no. 3 (September 1983): 420-33.

27. Judith Ewell, *Venezuela: A Century of Change* (Stanford, Calif.: Stanford University Press, 1984), pp. 182.

28. Enrique A. Baloyra and John D. Martz, *Political Attitudes in Venezuela: Societal Cleavages and Political Opinion* (Austin: University of Texas Press, 1979), pp. 46-78.

29. Daniel Bloom, "El desarrollo de los partidos polítics en Venezuela: Crecimiento electoral del partido social cristiano (1963-73) y observaciones sobre la elección presidencial de 1978," *Politeia* 9 (1980): 287-309, and David J. Myers, "Urban Voting, Structural Cleavages and Party System Evolution: The Case of Venezuela," *Comparative Politics* 8 (October 1975): 119-151.

30. This was reflected in the government programs of AD and COPEI as recently as during the 1983 presidential election campaign.

31. Steven Ellner, "The Venezuelan Left on the Eve of the Popular Front 1936–1945," *Journal of Latin American Studies* 2, p. 1 (May 1979): 169–85, and Myers, "Venezuela's MAS."

32. Personal observation by the author during visits to Venezuela during the Herrera government.

33. Allen Loring *Venezuelan Economic Development: A Politico-Economic Analysis* (Greenwich, Conn.: JAI press, 1977), pp. 183–84.

6

Political Articulation of the Military Sector in Venezuelan Democracy

José Antonio Gil Yepes

In this chapter we describe the model of the Venezuelan state as "organic statism." This definition is necessary in order to understand the political articulation of the diverse sectors of national life, most notably the military. We will argue that the concept of interest articulation is reformulated by adaptation to a model of the state different from that of classical liberalism for which it was originally formulated. This results in the concept of political linkage, which is relevant for all sectors of national life— business, political parties, unions, and the like. The concept is applied to the military sector, employing examples taken from the experiences of civil-military relations and intersectoral negotiations. In concluding, we will sketch two possible scenarios for the furture of military participation within the Venezuelan political context.

MODELING THE VENEZUELAN STATE

Contemporary states fall into three models: classical liberal, socialist, and organic statist, as summarized in Table 6.1. The classical liberal state posits the individual as its central value, with the principle of individual liberties the basis for the organization of society. This depends in turn upon individual and group interactions and mutual collaboration. Interactions are regulated in the economic sphere by the invisible hand of the free play of

TABLE 6.1. Models of the State

Characteristics	Liberal	Organic Statist	Socialist
Central Value	Individual	Individual as part of community; corporate sectors	Collectivity
Principal Role of the State	Subsidiary	To order and direct	To order, rule, and achieve
Relation with Social Groups	Dependent variable of group action	Independent variable of group action	Tends to minimize its autonomy
Mechanisms of Economic Interchange	Invisible hand, free competition	Mixed economy, regulated freedom, state capitalism	Central state planning
Mechanisms of Political Interchange	Competition among pressure groups and public powers	Competition between groups ordered, directed, and controlled by the state	Single party controls group competition and minimized pressure on public powers
Predominant Defects	Individuals and/or groups that unbalance competition; the military-industrial complex	State exaggerates decisive role; one group penetrates state, distorts its role to its own benefit; parties and military	State exaggerates; statism; parasitic bureaucracy; single-party rule; the new class

supply and demand and in the political realm by competition among groups. Under this model the state is a variable that relies on the actions of individuals toward the public powers. The state must only act on its own initiative infrequently, undertaking activities that are unattractive to the private sector while keeping order and defending the nation. Its intervention in the regulation of group relations is not desirable, or at least must be limited. The structural defect of this model is the fact that some groups in society can organize themselves and gain greater power than others, thereby producing unbalanced competition.[1]

The socialist model is organized under a doctrine contrary to the liberal, with value given to the collectivity while conferring autonomy of action on the state in order to guide society. This is the case with the dictatorship of the proletariat, a transition stage during which the state, personified by single-party representatives of the proletariat, eliminates in a coercive fashion the elements that encourage social class differences: the bourgeoisie and private property. Thus the socialist state is converted into the principal actor in society. This state also has a structural defect: the tendency toward excessive coercion on the part of the state and the development of what its very leadership has termed the parasitic bureaucracy and party "new class."

Given the defects of these two opposing models, multiple alternatives between individualism and collectivism have emerged. Organic statism is perhaps the term that can group this great diversity of intermediate positions that includes models of Social Democracy, Christian Democracy, and corporatism.[2] These models are differentiated among themselves by the greater or lesser weight given to components employed in the organization of society and its relation to the state. The central idea of organic statism incorporates a double meaning. The worth of the indivudal is recognized; he is valued as a member of a society in which he participates actively, both contributing and receiving. This idea comes as much from Aristotelian, Augustinian, and Thomistic traditions as it does from utopian socialism. Another major facet of the model holds that the state achieves an organic integration that balances diverse social components. Under this formula, individualism as an expression of personal interests has little value.

The structural defect of organic statism is dual: The strong role of the state is necessary at certain moments in order to organize and mobilize pluralistic groups, but such initiative can be self-perpetuating as a consequence of the power and controls established between the state and interest group. The participatory role of groups can also reach extremes when the interests of one gains an extra quota of power and acts to the detriment of the autonomy and rights of the others. The extreme case was the Nazi regime, while Latin American military dictatorships also fall into this category. The recent Brazilian military regime was a more moderate version, as have been party regimes in Latin America that, although more moderate than the military, may also apply group exclusivity to the detriment of others.

THE CONCEPT OF POLITICAL LINKAGE

The concept of political linkage comes from the notion of interest articulation, which, according to Gabriel Almond and Bingham Powell, is the process by which individuals and groups make demands on those who make public policy decisions.[3] Insofar as group behavior and resources condition social interests under the pluralism characterized by the classical liberal model, the concept of interest articulation would be sufficient to explain group relationships with one another. The probability of success in their external actions as related to the exercise of influence is also noteworthy. However, in the organic statist model of Venezuelan social organization, there are no true interest groups but, rather, elites with their own subdivisions. The notion of interest articulation is insufficient to explain the interrelationships of these interests. The model of Venezuelan society does not respond to the liberal depiction of interest groups but rather to an organic statist model of elites that is characterized by the several elements that operate against free political competition.

First, the controlling role of the state in this model is exercised by the military during so-called dictatorships and by the political parties during so-called democracies. Second, the only interest groups that are internally articulated, autonomous, and with unlimited access to the formulation of public policy in Venezuela are the military or the political parties, whichever controls the government. Third, public officials, policies, programs, and budgets are influenced principally by the military or the political parties during their respective governments. Fourth, both military and party governments rely on politicization of interest groups and monopolistic control of the channels of public and private communication in order to enjoy an extra quota of power over other social groups.

There is obviously an enormous difference in the degree of politicization exercised by party and by military regimes. The latter tend to be increasingly exclusivist and repressive against groups that might try to influence their governments. In contrast, the governments of parties are more subtle in exercising their hegemony and in fact permit sectoral interests to be reflected in public policies and in political opposition. Nevertheless, the democratic game is not truly liberal or effective pluralism but limited pluralism instead. In the case of developing countries, it is fully understood that political models can never be effectively pluralistic and that there will be limits on pluralism. This is owing to the fact that such countries require models in which the state is sustained above interest groups in order to control competition of the more against the less powerful and in order to accelerate the processes of social and economic mobilization.

The limitation on pluralism, however, is exaggerated even in the democratic regimes of developing countries. To begin with, there is a need to stabilize democracy, while mechanisms for the concentration of power are implanted by the parties to stabilize these regimes. These tend to be unnecessarily perpetuated because interests continue to enjoy the benefits of power while there is intersectoral lack of confidence. This latter reflects the belief that any institutional change means the delivery of a quota of power that is dangerous for the stability of the regime. We believe that this preoccupation is not justified in the Venezuelan case, for democracy is deeply rooted among business and military elites, as well as in public opinion.[4] But, for reasons to be explained later, the central motivation of the parties is to maintain or increase their quotas of power rather than to achieve social or economic objectives for the populace. This drive for power distorts the analysis of reality and tends to perpetuate the institutional forms

TABLE 6.2. Typology of Political Linkages

Linkage of autonomous sectors:

Political Parties

Linkage of autonomous sectors with limited access:

Military
Commercial
Industrial
Church

Political linkage of captive sectors with limited autonomy:

Labor
Bureaucracy
State enterprises and public services
Small and medium-sized industry
Professional trade unions, peasantry, students, etc.

Political linkage of nonarticulated sectors:

Marginal

of state organization and decision making—centralism, presidentialism, and partyism—although these prejudice the efficiency of the nation and the very legitimacy of the parties.

Partyism, or the process through which the parties limit but do not exclude the capacity for political influence of other groups, generates the categories of articulation or political linkage set forth in Table 6.2. This has several implications. In the first place, the only autonomous sector with free access in the Venezuelan democratic system is that of the parties. In addition, government parties exercise full control over public posts and only slightly less over the national budget. The guiding role in the organic statist model is absorbed by the parties. They reserve for themselves the right to organize society and to determine the degree of group access to the centers of governmental decision making. In addition, the access of autonomous groups to the decision-making process concerning matters that affect their interests is restricted by the attitudes of the parties toward such sectors as the military, business, and the church. Furthermore, political autonomy is limited for those captive groups organized and promoted by the parties themselves. Among these are the labor, student, professional, peasant, and bureaucratic sectors.

With communication channels between these groups and public powers enhanced by the personification of political parties to which they are captive, these interests can secure responses should they be viewed favorably by the party that controls them. In this sense it must be understood that captive groups will have ties dependent upon the parties that organized and promoted them. This relationship can be either functional or positive, as the groups' interests will be favored by the parties that can form a bridge to public powers. At other moments it may be dysfunctional, with groups utilized for political purposes in supporting or opposing the government. Thus the institutional objectives of groups may be lost or distorted. The forms whereby marginal groups in the process of political formation gain access are peculiar for a developing country where the interests of non-organized sectors are represented openly and freely by the bureaucracy and political parties. The latter, in fact, conceive of themselves as defenders of mass interests. Such peculiarities in the form by which groups attempt to articulate their interests under organic statism make it necessary to reformulate the concept of articulation. This leads us to propose the concept of political linkage.

The linkage of a sector is the process by which each sector is located in its "political place" in society, from which it makes demands on public policy decision makers in order to secure its interests. The key difference between the concepts of articulation and of linkage is that the first, as part of a classical liberal model with effective pluralism, reflects the direct access of any group to those who make public decisions, with the potential for influence determined principally by economic, organizational, and legal resources that can be employed. In contrast, the concept of linkage presumes that the groups are ascribed to a "place" or location that is politically predetermined. This placement conditions those matters about which the groups may be able to exercise pressure; the channels of communication that can be employed to articulate their interests; and the potential for influence, not only via available economic, organizational, and legal resources but also by the relations that each interest group establishes with other groups, most notably the political parties. This link with the parties is especially powerful because the latter exercise a monopoly in communications between public powers and all interest groups.[5]

The political linkage of each sector is determined by the following factors: the ideological definition of the empowered group with which each interest group operates, the organization and resources available to the group the level of intersectoral access between the government and the interest group in question, and the relations that each group may have with other groups in society. Let us further trace each of these components of the concept of political linkage.

Ideological Definition

The dominant group in the state, which in Venezuelan democracy are the political parties, is empowered with the prerogative to order society and its groups in accord with the place that its ideology assigns to each group. The differences between industry and commerce are illustrative of this process. The industrial sector has been seen by the parties as presumably more important for development and for employment than the commercial sector. The latter has been defined as more speculative. Such attitudes produce very different policies for each of the sectors. Industry enjoys tariff protection, soft credits, pro-industrialization policies, permanent mediatory mechanisms with the national executive (mixed commissions), and, to a certain point, relations with the parties and the labor unions. In contrast, the commercial sector does not receive defined policies or special treatment by the state. The decisions of the executive are not sufficiently normalized in a code of laws or regulations, so the commercial sector is administered instead in a relatively arbitrary and unpredictable manner. The mechanisms of permanent communication between commerce and the executive are relatively sparse, while those from this sector to the parties and labor unions are limited and occasionally produce hostility.

In the case of military governments, the role of the dominant group as the determinant of the place of the other interest groups is much more profound. Albert Hirschman observes that the military generally intervenes in response to social agitation that tends to occur when democratic governments cannot meet popular expectations because of the impossibility of fulfilling or continuing their policies.[6] Facing these conditions, the military has acted as much to put in order and to limit the populism of party-based regimes as to establish new governments to restrict the budgetary voracity of the parties and entrepreneurs protected by the state. Military intervention places the parties at a great protected by the state. Military intervention places the parties at a great political distance, including their proscription and persecution, while also limiting the capacity for influence on the part of those economic groups seen as possible allies of the politicians in a civil revolt. In the Venezuelan case, the placement or political linkage that the military has assigned to all interest groups has been that of "not mixing in politics," this with the justification of "avoiding disorder."

Concerning the ideological conceptual location of groups, it is important to recall the postulates of Emile Durkheim on the types of social solidarity generation in traditional and in developed societies.[7] In the former, solidarity was a mechanical type, which is to say the relation between components of society demonstrates an equalization of their functions. Durkheim emphasized that the cohesion of this kind of organization is limited, for the social division of labor is quite low. Other characteristics of mechanical solidarity are these groups' high sense of identification between themselves and their lack of confidence or antagonism toward external groups. This attitudinal element plays an important role in relations among Venezuelan groups. All sectors, therefore, without exception behave as monopolistic compartments or divided elites,[8] in an effort to maintain high intragroup solidarity and to protect even its most corrupt members against the attacks of other groups. At the same time, a climate of frank lack of confidence and even antagonism between the diverse sections of national life is maintained.

These kinds of relations correspond more fully to societies organized under clusters of primordial or traditional loyalties— race, family clans, region, or religion—as was the case for Venezuela during the nineteenth and the beginning of the twentieth centuries. But Venezuela adopted a social division of labor and modern organization based on the functions of production, politics, defense, and voluntary organizations that do not emerge, as would be expected, with a sense of organic solidarity among its social sectors.

Organic solidarity is generated in the sense that the social division of labor produces groups dedicated to achieving different institutional functions and that are complementary in the satisfaction of needs and the realization of the objectives of each society. The sense of complementarity is Venezuela is subject to ambivalence because all sectors of national life reorganize the pluralistic nature of the system, with relations among modern sectors mediated by the sense of lack of confidence and even antagonism. Military versus political persuasions—or the political purges of the military sector—have played an important role in spreading this lack of confidence. The survival of the business sector under both military and party regimes generates suspicions from the former.

It is our interpretation that, if Venezuelan society has developed forms of institutional organization to function as modern promoters of defense, production, and politics, motivation at the same time has endured among groups corresponding to primitive society, where there is a high degree of internal solidarity and a pronounced lack of confidence in relation to alien groups. We will subsequently observe that the politicoideological "place" in which the most powerful group locates other sectors is influenced by internal organization and by channels of communications. In short, ideological definition is the most important of all the variables that determine the political linkage of a group.

Organization and Resources

The classic theory of interest group politics[9] assumes that the principal resources for developing group potential for influence are material and human, along with a capacity for coordinated action. This vision of the determinants of interest groups' influence originates from the complementary vision of a society in which free political competition is prevalent. In situations of limited pluralism, such as Venezuela, where the political game is not fully competitive, the vision is inadequate. In addition to internal organizational factors, other external forces intervene that generally carry greater weight.

In some cases these external factors, such as ties with political parties, determine the most important traits of their internal organization. This occurs with groups that are captives of the parties, such as the majority of unions, professional societies, students, peasants, small and medium-sized industrial organizations, and even the governmental bureaucracy. The internal organization of these groups is penetrated by the parties, and such groups tend to function in accord with the interests of groups and even divide the organizations, less in terms of strategies to achieve their interests than in terms of subgroups organized around partisan preferences. These divisions limit the possibilities for coordinated control of groups, which thereby experience a reduction in their potential for influence.

There are other autonomous groups, such as business, the church, and the military, whose organizations are much less influenced by the parties. In these cases groups can control their resources and mobilize their organizations in a much freer fashion than groups captive to the parties. The role played by partisanship in these groups is one of aggregating interests that will pressure governments significantly. This constitutes a functional role that stabilizes democracy at the outset but that is also a mechanism playing a dysfunctional role because it distorts the institutional ends of the captive groups. In military regimes one does not find this phenomenon of group penetration by the dominant sector, because military governments do not permit the exercise of pressure by interest groups. Nevertheless, there have been peculiar cases, such as the utilization of the "black" Communists by the 1948-52 military junta in order to penetrate unions controlled by Acción Democrática.[10]

Channels of Public-Private Communication

The establishment of channels of communication between the government and interest groups is the key to political participation in the decision-making processes that affect the group. This is the essence of democracy, and each time that this participation has been systematically restricted in Venezuela for the major interest groups, the regime has been overthrown.[11] In military governments, channels of communication are very restricted and fill sporadic and protocol functions, with pressure rarely being productive.

In party regimes pressure is accepted and permanent channels of communications are developed, such as so-called mixed commissions, consultative councils, and the like. But the monopoly of the parties is maintained through diverse mechanisms. In most cases the public representative who directs the office in contact with the interested group has been appointed by the government party, and decision making is determined by a clientelist-party ethic. This functionary does not respond to an autonomous bureaucracy that represents the interests of the state and acts through an ethic of civil service but, instead, represents partisan interests and acts under a clientelistic ethic of sharing positions and budgets to pay for political and electoral favors. In cases of captive groups, moreover, the party itself virtually constitutes the channel of communication. The parties are also represented in some of the mixed commissions that serve as communications channels. Lastly, the context within which decision makers measure the effect of their policies is defined principally by party and by public opinion. It is scarcely strange that diverse authors argue that Venezuelan parties enjoy a monopoly over political communication.[12]

Other relationships that form a net of secondary or horizontal linkages are those that can be established between businessmen and labor, between the military and industrialists, between entrepreneurs and educational sectors, and so on. Our hypotheses on the development of networks of interrelationships in countries with organic statism are several. First, the networks that develop will be vertical or public-private. As we has seen, these linkages will assume the characteristics set by the most powerful sector— either the state or, in its absence, the parties or the military. In addition, the networks of private or secondary interrelationships will present only minimal links with statism, whether military- or party-based, for the majority of problems and the meeting of group interests will be resolved by the state. Private ties, such as those that develop between the military and the private industrial sector, will not be promoted by either military governments—which tend to statize strategic industries, such as steel—or by party governments. Both types of governments would tend to view such links with suspicion.[13]

Horizontal private relations will be directly influenced by both institutional factors and group ideologies, as seen in cases lacking ties, such as business and labor or business and the educational sector. With the latter example, the lack of linkage is incomprehensible unless we include the ideological factor according to which partisan student or labor organizations are mobilized by their leaders against capitalism. In the case of military governments there tends to be a better link between business and the student sector, while the expression of antagonisms between business and the labor sector is not permitted. Where there is a lack of confidence in intersectoral relations and a relative absence of direct links between interest groups, the parties themselves may not be tied to the state.[14] Secondary intersectoral relationships are almost nonexistent, resources are squandered, and the entire system is weakened.

The concept of political linkage can be summarized by noting that interest groups under the organic statist model are not free to act and to compete in the political arena, but must do so through a political location that predetermines for each group its possibilities for action and therefore preconditions its potential for influence. Political linkage depends upon the ideologies of each sector, particularly the group ideology that predominates within the organic state organization, the internal group organization, and the establishment of relations with the other sectors.

THE MILITARY SECTOR'S POLITICAL LINKAGE

The major alignments of the political linkage of the military sector emanate from one very basic point. This sector has been, along with the political parties, one of the two groups that have gained power in the Venezuelan organic state and as such have dominated society, establishing control mechanisms over all other sectors. In addition, its departure from power was by means of violence in a confrontation with civilians, including a lengthy process full of uncertainty for civilians that occupied government positions during early 1958[15] and included *golpista* outbursts during the second government of Rómulo Betancourt (1959–64).

Another key point in determining the political location of the military sector is that, despite being an institutional interest group that is a part of the bureaucracy,[16] the military also operates as an autonomous interest group with a private character. This duality is understood in the following fashion: The military sector is an institutional interest group when, as in 1958, it acts as guardian of national sovereignty and the democratic order. This clearly implies that the military sector has been drawn out of itself, removing *golpista* elements that seek the direct control of power. Nevertheless, despite the fact that this process of institutional purification has been very effective, the military sector continues to demonstrate traits as an autonomous interest group owing to its own separate identity, which it shares in systemic terms with national elites divided into parties, business, the military, and even labor groups. The division of national elites is due to their cultural and socioeconomic origins, and therefore the ideologies of each elite are different.[17] Visions of society and its different components are not only different but are filled with a strong sentiment of solidarity toward the group itself and with antagonisms toward the other groups.

Venezuela entered 1958 with this general configuration. It was a time for the establishment of a government that would be statist but less organic, less coercive, and more pluralist. This implied the coexistence of all sectors, with each meeting its institutional duties in society and minimizing any possible hegemonic role. The same division of the elites played a functional role in introducing a balance of power among all sectors. In this configuration, *lack of confidence was the key to interaction among all the sectors.* This lack of confidence in 1958 was also functional in representing the synthesis between a thesis of pluralist coexistence among different sectors and an antithesis of hostility among them.

In 1958 and thereafter, the system had to produce a series of mechanisms that permitted the participation of all sectors in the making of public decisions but that simultaneously preserved the hegemonic pretensions of each. From that point forward, Venezuelan pluralism was fated to be limited. What is the linkage or political placement of the military sector in its institutional reaccommodation of 1958, which was necessarily realized under conditions of lack of confidence? What are the costs and benefits as regards security and defense for political linkages granted to the military? Once the system eliminated guerrilla and *golpista* elements, was the political linkage of sectors under this lack of confidence still justified?

Ideological Definition

The most important principle in the reestablishment of democracy was the change of the military group role, as it became a bureaucratic exercise of power with the responsibility for the security of democratic institutions and the defense of the country. From 1900 until 1958, there had been civilian government by direct vote only for a few months in 1948 (with Rómulo Gallegos). Thus the factors that produced the change of role for the armed forces had to exercise considerable impact. Among these were the popular rejection of military rule; internal divisions among the military; the duration and prestige of the Betancourt government; definition of new rules of the democratic game (pluralism and participation, party monopoly as the channel of public-private communications, and the right to opposition while eradicating violence); the threat of militarism, which helped to reorient the military mission;[18] internal economic crisis during the last year of dictatorship; and international support for the new democracy.

In the process of redefining the military role, a very important part was played by the determination of matters with particular significance for the military sector. These included security and defense against the insurrection; the budget and military training; professionalization and the socioeconomic situation of military personnel; and the linkage of the security and defense function with foreign policy and with the nation's developmental policies as set forth by the constitution. Furthermore, there were diverse areas in which the military sector had a reduced or merely ritualistic participation, although the themes were related to the strategic situation: production and maintenance of military equipment (with high dependency on foreigners), local production of food-stuffs and other essential consumer products (also dependent upon foreign interests), border policy, foreign policy, and the situation of basic industries.

At one end of the hypothetical continuum that runs from high participation to total marginalization, we find that the greatest level of military action was in its active and highly successful role as a veto group toward the government. This antisubversive struggle not only motivated the military to redefine its institutional position but gave the sector the opportunity to demonstrate the sincerity of its democratic commitment and its willingness to sacrifice life itself in defense of the system.

In other respects the military sector has had a less significant impact. Generally, the partial or total exclusion of the military from public policy formulation in matters of great importance for the strategic situation of the country makes manifest the lack of confidence that serves as an important element in the post-1958 reorganization of Venezuela. In this instance the lack of confidence was demonstrated principally by the exclusion of the sector from matters related to developmental policy. This contrasted to the experience of the Escola Superior de Guerra in Brazil, where the themes of security and defense were tightly linked to development policy as justified by geopolitical considerations. From this school sprang the militarist movement that has guided Brazil for more than two decades, beginning in 1964.

Despite these ambivalences, the Instituto de Altos Estudios de la Defensa Nacional (IAEDEN) was created in 1972, and in 1976 was followed by the Consejo Nacional de Seguridad y Defensa (CONASEDE) and its permanent secretariat (SECONASEDE), an advisory board to the presidency of the republic. In both cases we find instruments that are designed to broaden the concept of security and defense by including ties with questions of development, arguing that these cannot be separated. Nevertheless, the Venezuelan version of this linkage is unlike that of the Southern Cone. That is, it is not contained within an expansionist geopolitical concept but it is inspired by the preamble of the constitution according to which war, conquest, and economic domination are repudiated as instruments of international politics. This leads to the unfolding of Venezuela's defensive policy, which its responsive capacity limited to the subregional zone.

Despite the conceptual coherence of the Venezuelan linkage of security to development, contradictions are observable in implementation. The policy of military armaments is contrary to constitutional precepts because Venezuelan armaments have traditionally kept the country in the vanguard of warmaking capability in the subregion, with its forces principally offensive. This was a continuation of the policy of Marcos Pérez Jiménez. Besides, the tie between security and development policies is at best weak because there is no instrument that works in practical terms for such a linkage. Despite the existence of SECONASEDE, military programs and policies are not tied to the development policies formulated by CORDIPLAN, the office of the presidency of the republic with responsibility for planning and national coordination.[19] The activities of IAEDEN focus on the broad concept of security related to development and incorporation of both civilians and military personnel into its courses. However, these are not translated into concrete programs or even into recommendations to any institution that relates security plans to those for development. In the case of participation in border affairs, one notes that the Dirección de Fronteras del Ministerio de Relaciones Exteriores (Frontier Office for Foreign Relations) generally is directed by an officer on active duty.

Nevertheless, the role of this leadership is not important in major negotiations over territorial problems, which are customarily conducted at a political level by the minister and commissions or working groups that are named on such occasions. In this fashion one can explain that a matter as important as the draft border treaty with Colombia was aborted by protest from the military. That was occasioned when senior officers were not informed of the course of negotiations; when the minister of foreign relations, in 1982, presented the definitive draft agreement to a large group of officials meeting in the auditorium of the Military Academy, he was thunderously drowned out by an officialdom that found the draft highly disadvantageous for Venezuela. Conversations with Colombia had reached the point at which the nonparticipation of the armed forces in direct negotiations had become crucial.

Another achievement for the military in border matters was promulgation of the Organic Law of Security and Defense, which, in response to a military request, identifies a stretch of territory subject to supervision and special programs under the armed forces. This was intended to ensure Venezuelan sovereignty, although the law has not been fully implemented both because of a lack of political will and limited budetary support. The control and colonization of the border strip by the armed forces had previously revolved about the construction of highways in order to serve as routes of penetration in combatting guerrillas. The present concern has the newer objectives of serving to penetrate for greater colonization of the frontier zone. However, the national government has not fulfilled its commitments to the defense ministry concerning construction expenses, which would ordinarily be met through public credit. This has forced the ministry to restrict such activity, which if pursued would provide a key to the linkage between security and development.

The absence of a tie between defense and foreign policy is evident.[20] Nevertheless, according to Samuel P. Huntington, this seems normal in pluralistic societies where military policy is not the result of a national pronouncement but rather the product of competition between individuals and groups for the recognition of values at national and international levels.[21] In the management of military budgets one can observe great discretion for the acquisition of goods and services considered military secrets. Thus we find total discretion in the management of funds from the national budget; approval at the ministerial level of public credit without discussion in the Congress; lack of fiscal itemization by the comptroller-general for military expenses;[22] and the fact that the military has its own comptroller who reports to the president of the republic rather than the Congress.[23] Besides the discretion granted to the military in such matters, we also find that the commanding generals of each branch have substantial freedom in the formulation of their own budgets, in their management, and, ultimately, in decisions concerning arms.

The preceding is due to the fact that no plan of military investments that orients the acquisition of weapons and materials under a sense of mutual support among the three branches has ever existed. The navy, air force, and army have thus been permitted to purchase arms in response to the pressures of each commander upon the national government, sometimes bypassing the judgment of the minister of defense,[24] who is always a military man.

Organization and Resources of the Military Sector

The organization of the military sector is necessarily pyramidal, which at the very outset means a high capacity to coordinate human, financial, and material resources and consequently to control the potential for substantial organizational influence. The base for the organization of the military sector rests upon the constitution, the Organic Law of Centralized Administration, and the Organic Law of the Armed Forces, which are structured pyramidally for hierarchial authority and absolute discipline. In accordance with the constitution, furthermore, the military sector is an apolitical, obedient, and nondeliberative institution,[25] one that should avoid partisan factionalism. The military sector is the only one in which all members have a clear identity as such, an organizational position to occupy, and a clear definition of functions that should be fulfilled. All these factors give the sector a capacity for coordinated and disciplined control beyond that of any other sector. Nevertheless, the coherence of the sector presents certain disarticulations, both at the institutional level of organization and at that of the individual. These diminish the capacity for coordinated management and therefore the potential for influence.

Organization experienced an important change after the fall of the dictatorship. The pyramidal structure of the four forces had been centralized and coordinated by the Estado Mayor General (General Staff). With the departure of Pérez Jiménez, this situation was modified, and the Estado Mayor Conjunto (Joint Staff) was created, which became an advisory rather than centralizing organ, one which no longer coordinated policies and defense budgets as before.[26] Two factors played an important role in this change: For the party regime it is preferable to keep the four services under control, and to negotiate decisions with four actions rather than only one; if a high degree of coordination were allowed, this would have a greater potential for influence. But within the military sector, there also exists a factor that bears upon this reorganization.

The status of "first among equals," the power of the army over the other three forces, was exercised largely through the Estado Mayor General. In Venezuela, as in all Latin America, the army was the strongest and most politically inclined of all services. The air force did not have great importance in Latin America until World War II. The navy, less politically inclined than the army, presented cadres of officers with the highest socioeconomic status, ones who spent long periods of time in study abroad or on the high seas.[27] Given these patterns, it is scarcely surprising that in Venezuela the army retains command as the major military institution. The other forces are in effect subordinated to the army, and the officers of the latter even take decisions concerning the promotion of officers in the other services.[28]

The problem of interservice relations is so transcendent that it was decisive in the uprising of January 1, 1958 on the part of navy and air force officers. This first attempted *golpe* was purely military. Then civilian forces received the support of these services plus some army officers, thus organizing the decisive *golpe* of January 23. The primacy of the army was a factor that not only threatened the party regime but frustrated the aspirations of the naval air force and of the national guard. This was evident in Decree 288 of June 27, 1958 where there was a repudiation of powers outside of command, organization, administration, and instruction. This included formulation of individual budgets, something that the minister had previously controlled by means of his own allocations to all the military forces.

This liberality for the four service commands has an important limitation in the case of financial operations based on public credit, by means of which the majority of large arms purchases and the development of border areas are financed. These decisions are shared at the sectoral level as well as that of the executive and legislative branches. The commanders of each service must justify requests for public credit before the following organs: the estado mayor conjunto, the junta superior of the armed forces, the minister of defense, the Senate Defense Committee, the Senate Finance Committee, the minister of treasury, the congress, and the president of the republic. The liberality with which each commanding officer acts concerning the management of his budget is converted into competition between and among them:[30]

> The decision to heed separately the needs of the forces, to recognize each component in an individual fashion, so that their needs are adequately met by the national government, at the same time weakened the internal cohesion of the military sector and the capacity of the institution to negotiate with other sectors of national life, thereby reinforcing the predominant role of the political parties in the reality of the Venezuelan state.[31]

Professionalization and the management of socioeconomic conditions for military personnel are important, as are the internal coherence of the sector and its adherence to the government. Among the factors that originated with military participation in the 1945 *golpe* was the discontent of troop personnel and of junior officers, who received income less than the salaries paid to specialized workers in oil fields and in other industrialized areas of the country.[32] In addition, one might cite the collaboration of the navy and the air force in the 1958 military *golpe*, manifesting not only the democratic vocation of many *golpista* officers but also the primacy of the army among the military forces and its domination of promotions in the others. Another indication of the extreme importance of the management of military personnel is the fact that each *golpe* has been followed by an increase in military pay.[33]

The professionalization and systematization of the management of socioeconomic conditions for military personnel began with the coming to power of the *andinos* (Castro and Gómez) in 1899. The first step was to achieve for the army of irregulars its conversion into the only standing army of Venezuela.[34] Previously, each state had its own army, and each revolution created its own proliferation of officers—often illiterate—who succeeded to power. The second step in the professionalization of the armed forces was the reduction of the army, which, under Castro, had 12,000 members, to a mere 5,000 men. This process, hastened by budgetary limitations, meant that belonging to the army was not only to be an *andino* but also to progress as soliders and officers.[35]

In 1910, General Gómez reinaugurated the Academia Militar de Venezuela, which operated under two important premises: highly selective admissions and a requirement of studies for subsequent promotion. The prerequisites to enter the schools of the different branches became ever more demanding, significantly increased by the number of aspirants seeking entry. One could also note that the number graduating from the schools that trained officers was reduced, indicating every greater rigor in the selection process.[36] Also based on the autonomization of the four services was the decision to substitute the Escuela Básica for the training of officers in the four respective service academies that had been founded progressively in the initial years of the democratic regime.

The system of military education has been increasingly diversified through creation of militarized schools at the bachelor's degree level, with the Instituto Universitario Politécnico de las Fuerzas Armadas (IUPFAN), with the courses of military specialization, the courses of the Estado Mayor, and the creation of the IAEDAN.[37] Officers have also been permitted to earn university degrees in civil institutions and, during a period beginning in 1974, were granted degrees in diverse specialties from the officer training schools. However, this practice has been suspended because it was seen as distracting the officer from military affairs; thus obtaining university degrees has not been fully accepted. Those officers who receive such degrees can be seen unfavorably by "pure" military officers. Nevertheless, we believe personally that the dedicaton to earning university degrees and, in general, the emphasis on linking professionalization to formal education have played a very important part in the change of the sector's organizational mission, its exercise of power in the achievement of democratic stability, and the connection of security to development. Professionalization changes the way of viewing society and gives the individual a technical form of participation in order to achieve concrete advances instead of focusing interest solely on the exercise of power.

Recently, the new Law of Conscription and Military Recruitment broadened the social bases of those eligible for recruitment. Traditionally, the upper and middle classes have claimed exemptions and have been automatically excluded. Nevertheless, the new law has not changed the basic situation significantly, one in which recruitment is directed primarily at youths from the rural and marginal sectors—socially unintegrated and representing a force that might promote the actual division of the elites. Parallel to this process of professionalization is the development of military participation in the management of a series of decentralized state organisms that deal with the socioeconomic condition of military personnel and that, like the military academies, are managed directly by officers. Among these organisms are the Instituto de Previsión Social de las Fuerzas Armadas (IPSFA); Almacenes Militares (ALMIL); Horizonte, C. A. de Seguros;

Inversiones FAMIL, C. A. Viajes y Turismos FAMIL, C. A.; and OFIDIRE, the office empowered with responsiblity for the socioeconomic status of retired officers.

From the presidency of Rómulo Betancourt to the present, the party system has been attentive to the needs of military personnel in order to deflect their discontent, assuring that pay for officers and enlisted men is maintained more or less at the equivalent level of professionals and of military pay in the United States.[38] Another element that the parties have handled with delicacy is military promotion and questions about military conduct. There are those who believe that military personnel are untouchable and that they exercise a veto over certain aspects of national life.[39] Nevertheless, there is much to indicate that not even promotions, pay, weapons purchases, military expenditures, and charges of military corruption are untouchable.[40] These themes have been discussed publicly in the Congress (purchase of frigates and of F-16s), the courts (cases of three former defense ministers accused in 1984 of administrative corruption), and the communications media (charges of corruption made by General Oscar Alvarez Beria in early 1985).[41]

Another limitation on the internal cohesion of the sector and its potential for influence is suggested by the moderate tendency of officers to be identified with the principle parties. This in turn is related to promotions and the distribution of administrative posts. In the handling of promotions, a rigorous institutional regime is observed. Up to the rank of lieutenant colonel these are handled exclusively by the military. But in promotions to colonel and general the Congress formally intervenes, recognizing a certain partisanship in the selection of those to be promoted, although this almost always is done without violating military norms. The impact of party ties is more open and evident in the distribution of administrative posts. There have been cases in which the president names a minister, service chief, or similar official who has less seniority or ability than others. This phenomenon generally is tied to party sympathies.

Finally, it should be mentioned that since the 1958 *golpe* retirement has been mandatory with 30 years of service. When first instituted, this was welcomed by both politicians and by junior officers. The former saw it as cleansing the military of those with *perezjimenista* ties, and the latter gained through the creation of vacancies at higher levels. Today the practice is perceived as functional, as a mechanism that permits many officers the opportunity to exercise command. Nevertheless, the norm has two important dysfunctional effects. On a personal level, it means retirement in one's fifties, at an officer's optimal point of individual potential. This means that in the last two years of service many officers may be tempted toward corruption or, at the least, are stimulated to resentment and personal frustration. At the organizational level, this norm contributes to instability in higher positions, which are only reached by those with 27, 28, or 29 years' seniority. For example, the majority of defense ministers and service commanders in the last ten years have spent about one year in their position. This rotation affects the quality of institutional management, creating discontinuity in policies and a lack of experience in decisions, while also avoiding the development of strong leaders within the armed forces.

Channels of Communication

In this area the armed forces enjoy a relatively privileged situation through the defense ministry as a specialized institution that has direct representation. That is, all important positions in this bureaucratic apparatus are held by officers. This is a concession from democracy because in previous regimes, including that of Juan Vicente Gómez, there were instances of notable civilians in charge of the ministry.

The management of channels of communication with the rest of the public sector tends to be pyramidal in structure. According the Organic Law of the Armed Forces, the minister of defense is the only authorized spokesman for the military. Nevertheless, just as the pyramidal structure presents some inconsistencies, this can also be seen at the level of communication channels, such as the role of the president and of the four service commanders as regards arms purchases. In this sense the military organization tends to present the same problem as the decentralized public administration entities; their presidents report to the appropriate minister, but the majority have been named by the president and not the ministers. Similarly, the service commanders enjoy an informal but effective link with the president, while ministers tend to be ignored.[42]

Channels of communications between the military sector and the remainder of the public are highly developed in such matters as the handling of subdivision, with the Ministry of Interior Relations; military equipment, with the Ministry of Treasury, the Congress, and the presidency; promotions, with the presidency and the Congress; and border affairs where they have direct representation in the Ministry of Foreign Relations. But in matters of foreign policy and those that touch on security and development, although there have been proposals to create ties with civilian authorities, it remains true that there are no channels between SECONASEDE and CORDIPLAN or between IAEDEN and other institutions; participation in the Border Directorate regarding frontier negotiations, in the meantime, is not significant.

What can be said to constitute linkages in matters of security and development is the establishment of industries with a military orientation: CAVIM, producer of munitions and light arms, and VENEMAICA, an enterprise whose objective is the eventual development of the aeronautical industry. These two undertakings are under the tutelage or direction of military officers. In addition, the naval industry is being developed by DIANCA, which is directed by civilians. To be sure, it must be remembered that these enterprises cover a very reduced portion of broad military supplies. Even more important, the tie that existed during the dictatorship of Pérez Jiménez between such basic state industries as steel and petrochemicals, and the programs of the military sector, have disappeared during the democratic period.

Relations with Other Sectors

Linkage between security and development is not merely defined by the military policy of the state; it is a central theme expressed in the preamble to the constitution. This declares that the Venezuelan state must strengthen the concept of "collective security" of the international community through the notion of "national security." National security, of course, presumes the development of a policy that had its roots in *perezjimenista* authoritarianism. In contrast, the commitment to a defense of democracy should follow a strategy of general resistence to authoritarianism such as that exercised by Switzerland and Yugoslavia.[43] This presupposes that the military sector and its policies should be tied to public and private sectors in order to implement the strategy of "general resistance." But, as we will see, no such linkage exists.

We have already indicated that military procurement policy has never been adapted to the postulates of the constitutional preamble because, according to the latter, armaments should be of a defensive character. Yet the purchases are more often of an offensive character and, in any case, attempt to maintain a favorable strategic balance.[44] Another contradiction in this sense is seen in the fact that the offensive potential has not been used, with the exception of the 1978 mobilization provoked by the threat of Nicaraguan reprisals against Costa Rica, when the latter provided a base for the *sandinista* movement against the Somoza regime. This perhaps explains why the military budget has dropped as a portion of the national budget from 9 to 12 percent (from 1936 until 1974) to merely 5 to 7 percent (since 1974).[45]

It should also be understood that all equipment, including rations and uniforms, is acquired abroad. The maintenance of equipment is also dependent on foreign technology, which results in a contradictory posture as concerns the strategy of general resistance or even of national offense. In either case, the national interest is shackled by high dependence on foreign military material and know-how and by the notorious absence of ties between national industry and research centers and the development with military requirements. Curiously, this lack of utilization of national factors is not protested by the organized labor movement or by the business sector, although it could mean thousands of jobs. In short, a horizontal relationship of the military in Venezuelan society—that is, with private sectors—is virtually nonexistent. This carries the extremely high cost of absolute dependence on foreign sources plus a waste of internal institutional resources. The explanation of this situation forms a part of the political linkages of the sector that must now be summarized.

CONCLUSIONS

In the dominant partisan political sector there has been little hostility toward the military sector, although the latter traditionally persecuted and sought the elimination of parties when it was in power. There were exceptions, such as the institutionalist governments of Generals Eleazar López Contreras and Isaías Medina Angarita during the years when the present party system began to coalesce (1936–45). Democratic sectors, led by the parties, relied on the collaboration of the democratically inclined military officers in redefining the role of the armed forces, uprooting the orientation toward the exercise of power, and implanting the missions of guaranteeing security and national defense.

If there was no hostility toward the military sector, the political context also included a sense of lack of confidence, as was amply justified by events under the first administrations of the democratic regime. This lack of confidence was manifested in a curious configuration of ambivalences toward the participation of the military sector. Nevertheless, the level of participation and of ambivalence varied widely. In order to illuminate this variability, we must place matters of high military priority on a scale that runs from high penetration, capacity for decision and veto power opposite other governmental sectors, to cases of obvious marginality. In the intermediate positions we place those cases in which there is politicized or partisan participation as well as ritualistic participation. These latter are cases in which certain formalities are observed but there are no measures adequate to achieve proposed objectives (Table 6.3).

Where there are matters in which the military sector has a high potential for influence—budget, promotions, and equipment—we find that the internal organization of the sector is partially disarticulated. In the case of budgetary management there is a division of interests among the four services. Concerning professionalization, the peak of the pyramid for promotions is relatively politicized. Individual appetites for power within the sector motivate individuals to play the game from outside, which weakens the internal cohesion of the group and its potential for influence on other sectors.

In addition, in those matters over which the sector has no real

TABLE 6.3. Military Resources and Objectives

High Penetration	Politicization	Ritualism	Marginalization
Armaments, equipment		Border policy	Foreign policy
Antisubversive combat			Management of basic industries
Budget	Formulation		Autonomy of food supply
	Management		
	Professionalization		
Promotions	Promotions (colonel and general)	Linkage of security and defense policies with development policies	
		Autonomy in production and maintenance of military equipment	

potential for influence, an absence of resources and of channels of communication is evident. Another contradiction is also present. Despite the fact that political parties are central to the conduct of national affairs, constitute the predominant sector in the exercise of authority, and accept the institutional forms of military participation as a means of assuring quotas in the sharing of power, they nonetheless have permitted and promulgated laws and institutional developments that tend to modify and to narrow military participation in national development. Unfortunately, these changes have been distorted or diminished by a combination of advances and retreats, such as the promulgation of the frontier zone without including regulations, programs, and budgets; creation of IAEDEN without permitting the institute to make recommendations on public policy; and the founding of SECONASEDE without linkages for the planning of security and of development.

At the level of sectoral organization, there has developed a series of characteristics appropriate for a pyramidal, disciplined, and political organization that thereby gains great capacity for coordinated mobilization. But there are other organizational factors, such as the absence of a service General Staff and the autonomy of the four services which, if understandably necessary in 1958, with the overthrow of the *golpista* menace and army domination, now display dysfunctional elements through a lack of coordination in budgetary management and in military arms purchases. The process of service professionalization has been a determinant of cohesion in the sector, especially considering that at the beginning of the century any local caudillo could organize an army and launch an assault on the central power. It has also been crucial in obtaining the support of the military for democracy. But in this process of democratization of the military, the partisan penetration of its ranks has also been imposed, and these sympathies distort both promotions and assignments. Mandatory retirement after 30 years of service adds to the other factors, further nurturing negative consequences for the quality of military leadership.

Personnel recruitment and the entrance of officer candidates into service schools, unlike business, labor, and party sectors, continue to be dominated by those of rural and small-town origins, which also encourages maintenance of sociocultural differences and a consequent lack of confidence among sectors. Channels of communication between the military and the rest of the public sector continue to respond to the definition of areas in which the military may not actually participate. The armed forces enjoy close ties to the government on matters tightly linked to military management but lack channels of communication that permit participation in management of foreign policy and programs of security and development, excepting the military firms CAVIM and VENEMAICA.

The dependence on foreign sources for military goods and the total lack of ties with business, labor, and research groups in the country operates to undermine the policy of collective security set forth in the constitution and against national security and military domination for Venezuela within the Carribean and Andean subregions as well. In addition, this scarcity of national ties imposes a high cost on the security and the economy of the country. These costs have not been protested by either the business or the labor sector. In summary, the political linkage of the military throughout the Venezuelan system would have been very marginal were it not for the guerrillas. This situation, however, gave the military an opportunity to revindicate itself with democracy, to exercise its potential for influence, and to offer its quota of sacrifice. The political linkage achieved in the decade of the 1960s was one that we could term "active participation and revindication."

Once the country was pacified, however it seemed that new institutional forms had to be created in order to increase military participation and to channel the enormous human and organizational resources that were in place. This, however, was undertaken with a lack of confidence, while new mechanisms of participation were not fully adequate. What followed was a gradual increase of resources for the military, but ones that had no linkage to foreign policy and, furthermore, were not managed in a coordinated fashion. The military, then, has become a sector whose policies are defined more by criteria of distributions of quotas of power at the domestic level than by considerations of internal security and external defense. The military in this sense is a sector wrapped up in itself more than oriented toward the system.

This status began to take shape in 1972, and can be characterized as "golden marginality." The date of 1972 is apt because that is the year of the creation of IADEN, the first key instrument, although underutilized, for promoting the linkage of security policies with those of development. The linking of these policies could serve to overcome the lack of confidence syndrome among Venezuela's divided elites by highlighting the mutual need to face common problems.

POSSIBLE SCENARIOS

Several scenarios for future political linkages of the military sector to the Venezuelan system can be delineated. Contrary to what the reader might expect—accustomed to seeing a Latin America torn between dictatorships and democracies—we will not speculate in that sense because Venezuela does not face military subversion, and any revolutionary subversion by civilians of either right or left that might spring forth would be very isolated. The scenarios, then, are defined within the democratic context: that of limited pluralism with continuation of the present political role of the military and another of effective pluralism with a deepening of institutional participation.

Scenario of Limited Pluralism

Continuation of the present scenario is explained by the interests created about it. These in turn clarify the contradictions found in various areas of the military political linkage that has just been termed "golden marginality." One instrument that will serve to consolidate the "golden marginality" linkage would give the vote to the military sector. On being converted into a deliberate sector, instead of making it the most powerful participant in discussions of public policy that concern it, the result would be a deepening of partisanship and therefore a division of the military sector.

The institutional consequences of maintaining the linkage of "golden marginality" could produce an eventual failure of the armed forces against a potential adversary because of inadequate internal coherence or of incompatibility in its armaments, or the progressive loss of sector image and legitimacy in the eyes of the public, with the consequent effects that this latter could have on budgetary decisions. These would tend to be reduced, owing to the scant increases of Venezuela's financial resources.

In terms of military behavior, a sense of futility would result. This would be accompanied by a tendency to view the rest of the system as improper; by frustration over systemic errors, in which collaboration to resolve them would be impossible; by a tendency to consumerism instead of participation; and self-realization by the military of its flawed position within the social context. In grave situations this could produce serious administrative corruption, despite the high moral, patriotic, and religious training that all military personnel receive; the lack of mechanisms for adequate social expression would also worsen the situation. Meanwhile, other sectors would gradually lose the image of respect, security, and the role as ultimate guarantor of the institutional order that the military now enjoys. The probability of this scenario is greater than the following. The velocity with which its traits and consequences can be accentuated or diminished may well vary widely.

Scenario of Effective Pluralism

The probability for this scenario is less than that of the preceding. In the first place, it is very difficult to change institutional arrangements, especially if this implies a redistribution of the quotas of power. Nevertheless, we can depict three facts that might produce a political relocation of the sector: economic crisis, resurgence of subversion, or external conflict. Mechanisms by means of which the last two causes could operate would appear similar to the role played during the antiguerrilla struggle in the decade of the 1960s.

Economic crisis places the system in a difficult situation whereby the government cannot continue to share with all sectors the quantities of resources previously distributed. From an economic point of view, the game is lost if we are thinking of extending the same politicoeconomic pattern with which the country has been managed in recent years. Granted the creative capacity of politicians to change the rules of the game and to incorporate not only the military sector but also industry, commerce, labor, communications, the church, neighborhoods, and municipal councils and governments, a new set of political regulations permitting greater benefit from Venezuela's enormous resources would emerge.

For each of the sectors previously identified it would be necessary to produce political liberalization in order to secure freedom from controls imposed by a lack of confidence. With liberalization of the military sector, the political system has already defined the mechanisms that might encourage incremental participation. These tie security to development programs, located in IAEDEN and SECONASEDE. What is still necessary is to endow them with instrumental ties and institutional resources that might meet this function. In addition, there should be linkages of industrial, labor, and academic, and research sectors with the military in order to reduce external dependency on military material and to take advantage of the great opportunities that are presently being lost. Quite evidently, it is today senseless to think that ties and linkages could produce pretensions of power on the part of such crucial sectors. The parties are and will continue to be the major foci for concentration of power in the country, even in the state; they need to succeed in resolving sectoral frustrations if liberalization of the political game in Venezuela were to follow the path toward effective pluralism.

NOTES

1. Alfred Stepan, *The State and Society: Peru in Comparative Perspective* (Princeton, N.J.: Princeton University Press, 1978), p. 22.

2. Ibid., pp. 28–29.

3. Gabriel A. Almond and Bingham Powell, *Comparative Politics: A Developmental Approach* (Boston: Little, Brown, 1966), chap. 3.

4. Encuesta DATOS, *Pulso Nacional* (Caracas, 1970–85), mimeo.

5. Juan Carlos Rey, "El sistema de partidos venezolanos," *Politeia* 1 (1972): 203.

6. Albert Hirschman, "The Turn to Authoritarianism in Latin America and the Search for Its Economic Determinants," in *The New Authoritarianism in Latin America*, ed. David Collier (Princeton, N.J.: Princeton University Press, 1979), pp. 61–99.

7. Emile Durkheim *The Division of Labor in Society* (New York: Free Press, 1966).

8. José Antonio Gil Yepes, *El reto de los élites* (Madrid: Editorial Tecnos, 1978), chap. 1.

9. Harry Eckstein, "The Departments of Pressure Groups Politics," in *Comparative Politics* ed., Harry Eckstein and David Apter (New York: Free Press, 1963). See also David Truman, *The Governmental Process* (New York: Knopf, 1951).

10. Gil Yepes, *El reto*, chap. 5.

11. Robert J. Alexander, *The Communist Party of Venezuela* (Stanford, Calif.: Hoover Institution Press, 1969), p. 38.

12. Rey, "El sistema."

13. Gil Yepes, *El reto*, pp. 61–66.

14. Or to the military sector, should it be in control of the state.

15. Philip B. Taylor, Jr., *The Venezuelan Golpe de Estado of 1958: The Fall of Marco Pérez Jiménez* (Washington, D.C.: Institute for the Comparative Study of Political Systems, 1968).

16. Almond and Powell, *Comparative Politics*, chap. 11.

17. Gil Yepes, *El reto*, chap. 1.

18. Gene E. Bigler, "Professional Soldiers and Restrained Politics in Venezuela," in *New Military Politics in Latin America* ed., Robert Wesson (Stanford, Calif.: Hoover Institution Press, 1984).

19. The recent termination of the rail line from Puerto Cabello to Barquisimeto provides evidence that the military had not been consulted on its characteristics; the AMX tanks cannot pass through the tunnels on the route.

20. Albert Muller, *"Políticas públicas: El equipamiento military en Venezuela,* M.A. thesis Simón Bolívar University, 1982, p. 64.

21. Samuel P. Huntington, *The Common Defense: Strategic Programs in National Politics* (New York: Columbia University Press, 1969), p. 2.

22. Rule in the Organic Law of the Comptroller General of the Republic, Article 8.

23. República de Venezuela, *Gaceta Oficial No. 3.256, Extraordinario del 26 de septiembre de 1983*, "Ley de Reforma Parcial de la Ley Orgánica de las Fuerzas Armadas Nacionales," Article 321.

24. Case of the purchase of F-16 planes.

25. Article 132 of the National Constitution.

26. Beatriz Anselmi and Rita Elena Estrada, *Análisis Socio-político del sector militar,* paper in Public-Private Interrelationships (Caracas: Instituto de Estudios Superiores de Administración, 1982), p. 7.

27. Juan Linz and Alfred Stepan, *The Breakdown of Democratic Regimes in Latin America* (Baltimore: John Hopkins University Press, 1978).

28. Anselmi and Estrada, *Análisis*, p. 8.

29. República de Venezuela, *Gaceta Oficial*, Decreto de la Presidencia de la República No. 288 del 27 de junio de 1958.

30. Muller, *Políticas*, pp. 63-64.

31. Ibid., p. 67.

32. Rómulo Betancourt, *Venezuela, Política y petróleo* (Caracas: Editorial Senderos, 1969), p. 551.

33. Bigler, "Professional Soldiers," p. 181.

34. Angel Ziems, *El gomecismo y la formación del ejército nacional* (Caracas: Editorial Ateneo, 1979).

35. Bigler, "Professional Soldiers," p. 179.

36. Ibid., pp. 179-80.

37. Ibid., p. 180.

38. Ibid., p. 181.

39. David E. Blank, *Politics in Venezuela* (Boston: Little, Brown, 1973).

40. Bigler, "Professional Soldiers;" p. 177.

41. *El Nacional* (Caracas), June 7, 1982, P.D-12.

42. José Antonio Gil Yepes, *El estado blando y las empresas públicas en Venezuela* (forthcoming).

43. Muller, *Políticas*, p. 62.

44. Ibid.

45. Bigler, "Professional Soldiers;" p. 177.

7

State Enterprises and the Decentralized Public Administration

Gene E. Bigler and Enrique Viloria V.

The vast network of state enterprises, autonomous institutes, foundations, and other quasi-public entities that have mushroomed on the periphery of the Venezuelan state has been a subject of increasing controversy as Venezuela's democracy begins to mature. In the mid-1970s the hydra of the uncontrolled, wasteful, gigantistic, antiprivate enterprise, state capitalizing government suddenly appeared. In truth, however, the Pérez and Herrera administrations were simply using a familiar tool of Venezuelan public policy in much the same way their predecessors had, albeit some of the results were poorer and the visibility was certainly higher. Reform of the decentralized public administration has been a repetitive goal of democratic governments, and even the privatization of state enterprises became a hackneyed promise during the election campaigns of 1978 and 1983. Yet the urgency for reform has increased with the economic adjustment program of the new Lusinchi administration, and because of the key role of these organizations in policymaking and in the operation of Venezuela's mixed economy, it is clear that the need for substantial achievement in this arena is one of the major development challenges confronting Venezuela's democracy today.

CONTROVERSIES AND CRISES

Public enterprises almost escaped public attention during the late 1960s and the first half of the 1970s. Public concern naturally focused on more dramatic issues, such as guerrilla pacification and oil industry confrontation. Of course, some sectors of the government were considerably more attentive, but rather than concentrate on problems among existing state corporations, efforts usually emphasized the formulation of new policies, the creation of new entities, and the satisfaction of different constituencies as COPEI and AD rotated in office. Even with Caldera's reform program, the first systematic analysis and reform package for the decentralized public administration were lost sight of in juxtaposition with regionalization, sectoral development, civil service reform, and other proposals.[1] Scandals came to light over waste and unproductivity in the Centro Simón Bolivar (CSB), the Venezuelan Petrochemical Institute (IVP), and elsewhere, but the creation of a huge new IVP petrochemical complex at El Tablazo and the building of the Parque Central complex by the CSB were really at the center of debate. Similarly, the rush to create a series of new regional development corporations and to control foreign investment and technology transfer almost completely obscured the old policy of industrialization based on the Guayana heavy industry regional pole for development. And as the flow of petrodollars increased after the first success at reference price setting in 1971, few had time to worry about the relative virtues of public enterprises and other decentralized entities. Everyone's evergy had to be devoted to the creation of new state corporations to spend the money because all seemed to agree that the ossified old public administration just could not handle the job.

An average of only about eight new state enterprises and other entities of all types were created yearly during the leaner period from 1968 to 1970, but the number increases to eleven in 1971, sixteen in 1972, fourteen in 1973, seventeen in 1974, and then, incredibly, forty-nine in 1975. Mauricio Garcia Araujo, a prominent banker and business consultant, was one of the first to notice the dimensions of change and to decry the growth of the state's role in the economy. He pointed out in articles for *Resumen* and numerous lectures that the central, state, and local governments were not doing a lot more, but consolidated public spending—the total achieved after expenditures by public enterprises, administrative entities, and financial intermediaries are added—had suddenly leaped from less than a fifth of the gross domestic product to almost half. In his view the mixed economic system that supported the primacy of private enterprise was being suddenly converted into a statist political economy. Yet the tide did not change, and 46 new decentralized organizations were established in 1976.

By this time the nature of the changes also became a matter of increasing concern to the political left. In their view the nationalization of oil and of iron mining and the creation of so many new public enterprises had just substituted one pattern of bourgeois domination for another. The new pattern of state capitalism simply maintained a system of associated dependent development in which the international capitalist centers in the United States and Europe still controlled markets, capital and technology flows, and prices. The transfer of ownership to the state was seen merely as capitalistic adjustment to nationalistic pressures and compensation for the inadequacy of domestic entrepreneurship. The lucrative service contracts signed by the new public oil enterprises with former multinational owners of the industry, the participation of Venezuelan businessmen in the management of many state corporations, the profitability of contracts with private firms for service and construction, and the increasing co-optation of labor through public enterprise employment were proof that international capitalism had developed new mechanisms to perpetuate the domination of the ruling class.[2]

Gradually, other criticisms and controversies arose as economic growth declined, the balance of payments deteriorated, and inflation mounted in the 1977-79 period. The new critical catchword for state projects became pharaonic because of the gigantic dimensions of the public works involved. New scandals arose repeatedly over huge deficits in the IVP, financial rescue operations for the Agricultural Marketing Corporation (CORPOMERCADEO), sudden losses in VIASA airlines after years of profitable operations, and the failure of one decentralized entity after another to meet their financial obligations to entitled beneficiaries, suppliers, and contractors.

All the major candidates in the 1978 campaign promised reform, privatization of inefficient enterprises, and greater efficiency in the rest. The Herrera platform went further and pledged a more liberal economic policy—price liberalization, reduction of subsidies and tariffs—to go along with a return to a private sector-centered economic development program. The state would become a "promoter" of private entrepreneurship and less entrepreneurial itself. However, when a second windfall of petrodollars began to enter the Treasury just a semester after Herrera took office, nearly all such plans were forgotten. The new government proved less entreprenurial in the industrial arena than its predecessor, but rapidly launched a series of new foundations, centers, and institutes; the decentralized public administration continued to grow.

The clamor briefly abated but, as the economic situation worsened in the second half of 1981, the bloated dimensions of the state and its multitude of wasteful and inefficient decentralized entities again became the center of attention. And as the economic crisis continued and new scandals arose, the cry for reform and destatization also returned to the center of platform appeals in the 1983 election campaign. What is more, the role of state enterprises in precipitating the payments crisis of 1982 and the devaluation of 1983 gradually became fairly widespread knowledge. The repeated failure of the CVF to make payments on foreign loans had forced the issue in the fall of 1982. Then it was revealed by the comptroller-general and other authorities that close to 40 percent of the country's foreign debt was made up of short-term obligations at very high interest rates that had been incurred by CORPOMERCADEO, CVF, BIV, SIDOR, and other state entities. Furthermore, the proportion of the total debt that was accounted for by all decentralized entities was estimated at 70 to 85 percent of the total owed by the nation. It was not the ministries, the municipalities, or even the Congress that had mortgaged the nation, but this huge, amorphous complex of seemingly unaccountable and uncontrolled organizations at the margins of the state.

THE DECENTRALIZED PUBLIC ADMINISTRATION

The phenomenon of decentralized growth of the state and sudden eruption of controversy is a familiar pattern among developing and even industrialized countries. As elsewhere, it is also the subject of a great deal of misinformation in Venezuela. Such terms as the decentralized public administration (DPA) or the third sector or the off-budget sector are increasingly used to designate the complex of all public enterprises and other entities as though they were some fairly uniform, coherent whole, but quite the contrary is true. The decentralized organizations of even a single country are extremely diverse as to type, legal status, linkage to the state, structure, autonomy, personnel systems, financing, operations, size, control mechanisms, and so on. There is also little agreement about generic names for the organizations. More general designations include parastatal organization, decentralized or autonomous entity, and the British term QUANGO (quasi-autonomous non-governmental organization). Other nomenclatures, such as public/state corporation enterprise or state-owned enterprise (SOE), statutory organization, autonomous institute, and public authority are used to refer to more specific types of entities.[3]

The complexity and diversity within the structure of the DPA in Venezuela may be represented in several ways (see Table 7.1).[4] For instance, nearly all decentralized entities are ascribed to some ministry, but often the connections are quite indirect. A few shares in one company may be owned by another company, which is partially owned by an autonomous institute, which is in turn ascribed to a ministry. For instance, before the 1982 intervention by public authorities in the Workers' Bank (BTV), of which about 45 percent of the stock was owned by the Treasury with adscription to the Ministry of Labor, only three to five subsidiaries of the BTV were listed on public records. After the intervention, the BTV was found to have major share interests (usually through wholly owned subsidiaries) in 80 other enterprises. Furthermore, there is a practical question about when a state interest occurs and the extent to which competence to exercise oversight or control actually takes place. This is complicated further by overlapping ministerial jurisdictions, especially when the presidents of entities (such as the FIV and CVG in recent years) are given ministerial rank, or when a minister simply decides to exert control, as Public Works Minister Leopoldo Sucre Figarella did with respect to the Centro Simón Bolívar during the mid-1960s even though it was ascribed to the Ministry of Finance.

TABLE 7.1. Illustrative Structures of the Decentralized Public Administration

I. Ministerial Organization	II. Organizational Clusters	III. Sectoral Organization
A. Min. Sec. of Presidency B. Min. of Development	A. The Corporación Venezolana de Guayana (presided over by a minister of state)	A. Agriculture and livestock development
1. Autonomous Institutes n = 6 includes FIV and regional finance companies n = 23 includes BIV and 22 other banks/finance companies	1. The CVG is an autonomous institute that exercises stockholder authority for the state, although a majority of the stock may be owned by the FIV, CVF, or shared with private partners.	—Peasant enterprise and coop subsector 32 joint ventures, including some with municipal government participation —Agroindustrial subsector 12 canneries and processors, mostly CVF or regional corporation subsidiaries
3. SOEs (including mixed and public interest)	2. SOEs include SIDOR (steel), EDELCA (electricity), INTERALUMINA, BAUXIVEN (bauxite mining), Ferrominera del Orinoco (iron mining), ALCASA (aluminum), VENALUM (aluminum), MINORCA (iron reduction), Pulpa Guayana, and Tubopetrol.	—Dairy products subsector 5 dairy products and milk processing companies —Sugar industry subsector all 15 firms are under Ministry of Development —Financial subsector 2 autonomous institutes and 6 other special funds
n = 60 includes 6 shipyards/ports 8 mining companies 8 urban or industrial zone developers air and naval industry holding companies Guayana heavy industry complex n = 80 includes 15 firms in sugar industry 13 hotels & tourist C.A.S. 11 industrial zones Others are small manufacturers, large cement plants, AVENSA airlines, and so on.	3. Mixed ownership enterprises include Fior de Venezuela, Cementos Guayana, Metalmeg, and Fesilven. Some closely related firms, such as Ferralca and	B. Wood, pulp, and paper sector 8 firms are involved, but they are

4. Other Entities

$n = 3$ includes regional development associated foundations

$n = 2$ Fondo de Crédito Industrial and CIEPE

(The same diversity is found for each of the 15 current cabinet departments. These two have the most entities and were chosen to illustrate.)

Proacero, are excluded because they are subsidiaries of other entities.

4. Other nonindustrial enterprises: CVG International (marketing); and PRODURGA (urban development firm).

B. The example of another organizational cluster and exemplary model of a public holding company, PDVSA, is found in Chapter 9 on the petroleum industry.

(A very large number of clusters of varying size exist. These are again for illustration purposes only.)

under 5 different ministries and all but one are subsidiaries of firms not included in the sector

C. Mining sector
13 entities are included but only 2 are ascribed to the Ministry of Energy and Mines

Other sectors with varying organizations are (in alphabetical order):

D. chemical and petrochemical
E. development
F. electricity
G. industry
H. naval and maritime
I. petroleum and gas
J. public service
K. real estate
L. transportation
M. tourism

An alternative representation of the structure of the DPA is based on the patterns of practical, coordinating or controlling (and not just proprietary) interest that is actually exercised by any public entity over a group of decentralized entities. Under this system, it would be immaterial to expect any more than a formal relationship between many ministries and their parastatals. The emphasis in this alternative pattern is instead on true organizational clusters. The PDVSA holding company system is an ideal example of this type of arrangement. The CVG, now that its president holds ministerial rank and special authority, approximates the ideal, but many CVG entities are still "owned" by the FIV or "ascribed" to some other ministry. A third example is the National Council of Universities and its Office of Planning for the University Sector that tie together the whole network of national universities and link them for budgetary, research, and educational policy coordination purposes to the Ministry of Education; however, some of the universities are legally autonomous, and others are actually administered through the ministry. The problem with organizational representation of DPA structure is that there is a very large number of clusters, many lack a uniform focus, and they complicate policy coordination. For example, until recently, the FIV tried to exercise control, in holding company fashion, over its majority-owned enterprises, including some in cement, aluminum, shipbuilding, steel, electricity, and so on. By doing so, the FIV interfered with or complicated regional development policy, electricity sector coordination, metal-mechanics industry development, and other government programs.

The third structural pattern divides the Venezuelan government into sectoral groupings of ministries and substantively related entities in order to reduce the fragmentation of programs and policies that arises naturally because of the large number of ministries, often 15 to more than 20, and the lack of policy focus that may plague the organizational groupings. Thus all entities formally ascribed only to the Ministry of Energy and Mines would be grouped in the mining or petroleum or petrochemical or electricity sectors and other relevant ministries, and just their appropriate decentralized entities would be involved in each sectoral coordination. However, the problem of practical ties is even more complicated than in the first case because some subsidiary enterprises are included in one sector or another but not their proprietary or controlling enterprises. Besides, many entities as well as ministries pertain to several sectoral cabinets because their activities are quite diverse. Thus the burdens of coordination escalate dramatically. It appears now, however, that the success of the PDVSA holding company arrangement with its linking to the appropriate sectoral subcabinet has created a consensus among many of the leading analysts as to the utility and greater efficiency of such a combined arrangement, and efforts are being made to restructure the whole DPA in this fashion.

Another area of uncertainty about the basic nature of the DPA relates to its role in the economy. The DPA is very large and diverse, but its size and intrusiveness are often still exaggerated. In some sectors, such as petroleum and telecommunications, the SOEs (state-owned enterprises) monopolize the field, and private firms are generally their suppliers, consultants, and subcontractors. In sectors such as transportation, state corporations dominate among national producers in certain subsectors (rail, maritime, and air transport), but they play a minor role in the truck, auto, and collective (bus) subsectors. The same is true in mining where private enterprise prevails in minor areas (diamonds and other minerals), but the state firms dominate iron, coal, bauxite, and gold extraction and processing. In chemicals, petrochemicals and electricity private producers are still quite important and to a degree autonomous, but the decentralized entities have been at the hub of highly interrelated activities. The IVP (and now PEQUIVEN) has controlled the flow (production and importing) of raw materials for petrochemicals, and state electric enterprises regulate the interconnected national network, while the private Luz Eléctrica de Venezuela conglomerate still supplies the Caracas metroplitan area. In finance and tourism, to a lesser degree, there is considerable direct competition, and market shares are fairly equal in some segments, but autonomous institutes, such as the BCV, BANAP, and CORPOTURISMO, also partially supervise the behavior of both private and state corporations.

The industrial sector is the most varied with respect to the private public division. Large SOEs, such as SIDOR, VENALUM, and ALCASA, dominate in basic metals production, and they have operational control over imports in product lines related to their manufacturing. Some subsectors, such as cement, textiles, sugar milling, and food processing, may include many and large state corporations with a considerable share of production and major roles in industry organizations, but the performance records of the state companies tend to be very poor in comparison with those of private firms. The multiple other divisions of the industrial sector have a few SOEs, and these tend to be small and frequently unsuccessful.

In sectors of the economy—agriculture, commerce, construction, and services (real estate, insurance, recreation, professional, mass media)—other than health and education, SOEs contribute very little to value added in production, but decentralized entities of many types may still be major purchasers, financers, regulators, or intermediaries. This discrepancy is, in fact, one of the main sources of confusion about the state's role. For instance, state enterprises directly contribute some 9 or 10 percent of the value of gross domestic production (GDP) in the nonpetroleum economy but more than one-third of total GDP with the addition of the state-owned petroleum industry. Yet the amount of the combined expenditures of decentralized entities is about a third of the value of nonpetroleum GDP, and these expenditures have for over a decade been the source of a third to more than half of domestic investment. Thus there may be little construction by SOEs, but INAVI, FONDUR, the CSB, and other DPAs may dominate the purchase of houses, buildings, and other projects. SOEs produce few agricultural commodities, but CORPOMERCADEO, MERSIFRICA, and other SOEs have been intermediaries in a large share of all commodities transactions since the early 1970s. The state owns only one radio station, one television station, and one publishing company (besides university and government presses), but the purchases of publicity by DPAs account for close to one-eighth of the advertising revenue of the mass media—this is apart from another one-eighth to one-fifth share that is bought directly by the government.

Clearly, the confusion over the role of the DPA in the economy will be difficult to resolve because experience with DPAs is so varied, subjective, and sometimes not distinguished from that of the government itself—hence the superintendent of banks or foreign investment or the office of consumer protection may be incorrectly considered to be decentralized entities. However, recent strides in record keeping and reporting and more elaborate national account data are beginning to help. Meanwhile, fairly detailed breakdowns along the lines provided above can supply a descriptive overview of some of the relevant dimensions.

Another reason for the uncertainty over the scope of the DPA in the economy is the disagreement over just how many decentralized entities there are, and in what organizational categories they should be grouped. The first systematic listing of entities was by the Comisión de Administración Pública in the early 1970s. The list included only 84 entities and grouped them by juridical categories.[5] In the mid-1970s several inventories were conducted by CORDIPLAN, but these identified from 70 to 120 fewer entities than the 345 Bigler (1981) found record of in 1978. One 1984 study (Kelly de Escobar and Villalba) counted 354 entities but excluded the autonomous national universities and subsidiaries of mixed enterprises (30 to 50 percent public ownership), while another project (Gil Yepes and Brizuela, 1984) at about the same time concluded that both universities and other collegiate institutes and mixed enterprise subsidiaries should be added, so that total would be 449.

The problem of counting and categorizing DPA entities has many explanations: poor records, degree of decentralization, whether the entity exists on paper or actually operates, and so on. There is also a great deal of discussion about what a state-owned enterprise is and of differences between entities. The BCV divides the DPA into administrative authorities, financial intermediaries, and state enterprises. CORDIPLAN uses juridical/adminstrative categories. Other analysts emphasize proprietary (ownership) or behavioral characteristics (whether revenue is produced commercially, if there is statutory administrative authority, type of operations). Table 7.2 provides a rough estimate of current number of decentralized entities in the CORDIPLAN categories for classification. Some autonomous institutes, such as CORPO-MERCADEO, are practically the same as SOEs but are not counted as such. Regional banks and finance companies, which the BCV would not consider state enterprises, are incorporated under private law and thus included with other SOEs in the CORDI-PLAN system. Other financial entities, such as the Institute for

TABLE 7.2. Estimated Number of Entities in the Decentralized Public Administration by Juridical/Proprietary Categories

	No.	Examples
Public Law		
Autonomous institutes* (including 6 universities)	60	Institute for Water and Sewage Works (INOS) Institute for Vocational Education (INCE) Tourism Corporation (CORPOTURISMO) Venezuelan Development Corporation (CVF)
Public corporations*	3	Central Bank (BCV) Agriculture and Livestock Development Bank (Bandagro)
Autonomous patrimonies and others (not including collegiate institutes)	39	Fund for Export Financing (FINEXPO) National Endowment for Elderly (PANAI)
Private Law		
Foundations	42	Ayacucho Scholarship Foundation Industrial Experiment Center for Exports (CIEPE) National Library
Civil associations	11	Fund for Development of Sunflower Production Institute for Petroleum and Petrochemical Administration (INAPET)
SOEs (those with greater than 50% public ownership)	206	C.A. Metro de Caracas (subway) Venorca (gold mining) Cenazuca (sugar mill holding company) CAVIM (military industries)

Mixed enterprises (with 30% to 50% public ownership)	35	Monomeros Colombo-Venezolano (chemicals) Hilanderias Venezolanas (textiles) CANPROLAC (milk products) Fior de Venezuela (steel alloys)
Public interest enterprises (corporations with less than 30% public ownership)	38	CAVENDES (finance company) Cementos Caribe Centro Higuerote (beach club) Acelecar (specialty steel)
Total	434	

*The legal distinction between these categories is intricate and may not have any practical consequences since both are created and governed by individual legal statutes, but the corporations have or have had share ownership structures.

Source: Updating of the 1978 Bigler inventory based on reviews of the Gil-Brizuela, Kelly-Villalba, and CORDIPLAN inventories.

Agricultural and Livestock Credit (ICAP, formerly BAP), have public law status and are counted as autonomous institutes or in some other subcategory under public law.

The final general area of misunderstanding that merits consideration here relates to similarities and differences between decentralized and private entities. It is not widely enough recognized in government or the private sector that the structure of objectives in SOEs is much more complex than the profit-centered motivation of a private business. Furthermore, the value of standard business practices, such as secrecy, financial and operational autonomy, flexibility in personnel and marketing practices, and so on, tends to be neglected in some SOEs, while they are still expected to operate as efficiently and profitably as the best private enterprise in the field. Perhaps even more troublesome is the fact that expectations about financial solvency may be totally unrealistic if the SOE is required to subsidize clients, if publicly subscribed capital is not paid but the same production goals are maintained, if the obligations owed by other government entities cannot be collected, if labor practices and other input costs are imposed arbitrarily, and so on.[6]

The basis for more realistic attitudes toward the DPA in Venezuela is now being created by the convergence of several trends. First, a clearer understanding of how and why decentralized entities have been created is laying the groundwork. Second, reflection on repeated unsuccessful reform experiences is improving the quality, reducing the scope, and raising the practicality of reform efforts. This trend is abetted by the visibility of the success of PDVSA within the parastatal sector and a growing acceptance of some new premises about the nature of the mixed economy that are being forged by the democratic system. Finally, the harsh adjustments that are being enforced on society by the ongoing economic crisis may be sufficient to alter permanently the business climate and management culture of both the DPA and the private sector and their relationship to the state.

THE GROWTH OF THE DECENTRALIZED PUBLIC ADMINISTRATION

Recent studies have shown three contexts in which the creation of individual parastatals and the growth of the whole sector must be understood. First, Viloria and Brewer-Carías have outlined the objectives and functions that the evolution of the Venezuelan state and juridical-administrative policy and practices have imposed on the decentralized public administration.[7] Second, Gil Yepes (1981) has evaluated the policymaking framework related to the choice of decentralization for meeting government objectives. Third, Bigler (1981) has identified the political-economic conditions that have created patterns of underlying continuity and growth in the DPA since the 1920s.

Viloria's studies place the creation of decentralized entities in juxtaposition with the evolution of the productive goals of the state. These have changed from primary product exporting, to production for final consumption, to capital goods production. By demonstrating that the state's policies to achieve such goals are distinguishable as regulatory, infrastructure creating (accumulative) or financially supportive in emphasis, he is able to outline a taxonomy of the functions that parastatal creation has actually served: supplying public services, supporting private initiative, controlling key economic sectors, implementing specific economic policies, substituting for the absence of private initiative, alteration of social and economic structures, assertion of sovereignty, and enhancement of public income.

The juridical-administrative framework of the decentralized public administration was Brewer-Carías's first concern, and he remains the foremost authority on the subject. His later studies of political change and reform of the state broaden and elaborate on Viloria's evolutionary categories and clarify the overall alterations of the state itself: from bourgeois-liberal, to welfare, to democratic social justice state. Thus Brewer-Carías differentiates goals such as the creation of basic public services, general industrialization, regional development, and international economic independence that overlap with the productivity goals outlined by Viloria. By adding a comparative dimension to their analyses, the two individually or jointly delineate the context in which specific juridical-administrative designs, such as the public holding company, may be utilized to serve specific functions or evolutionary goals of the system.

The emphasis in studies by Gil Yepes is more sociopolitical, and his analyses accordingly grapple more with the external demands and internal constraints that shape decisions made by the state to create decentralized entities. He is especially concerned with how this particular policy instrument responds to the state's needs. He has found that an SOE or other autonomous entity generally can serve five requirements that the general bureaucracy or other policy devices cannot meet as well:

1. Parastatals provide much more administrative flexibility; that is, government regulations on finances, personnel, hierarchical control, physical location, and other restraints can all be maintained or relaxed as needed.
2. Funds may be transferred from the central government to the entity as a lump sum without the detailed accounting, potential for controversy, and limitations on their use that accompany normal appropriations.
3. Decentralized entities may generate some of their own funds to help achieve the government's policy goals without the automatic opposition that arises with respect to government revenue proposals.
4. The actual operation of the decentralized entity is freer from oversight and formal controls and is less publicly visible, if desired, than government offices.
5. Parastatals may incur contractual obligations, including debt, personnel privileges, program responsibilities, and so on, without directly depleting the resources of the state, so they are understood to add to the total resources applied to the achievement of the state's goals.

The historical record, 1928–78, of creation and dissolution of 430 decentralized entities provided the empirical base for Bigler's analysis. His study reaches four major sets of conclusions about the phenomena. First, two other constraints may be added to Gil's list of policymaking circumstances. The first is that decision makers presume the inadequacy of existing government arrangements for accomplishing new or more complicated purposes. Such perceptions are due to beliefs that existing government agencies are corrupt, unqualified technically, partisan, too cumbersome, already overburdened, and so on. The consequence is the conclusion that the administration would not get the desired job done if it did not create a new instrumentality for it. The second is that specific new socioeconomic or political groups or increased effectiveness in demand making by existing groups are associated with the creation of new entities. Thus the patterns of political mobilization of different segments of society, that is, industrialists, university students, workers, peasants, the urban middle class, modern agriculture, and so on, spur the formation of new parastatals.

The second finding from Biglar's studies is that the decisions to create new entities are patterned. The actual number of entities created (and dissolved) varies cyclically over time. A plot of the number of entities created by year thus has a sine curve appearance, although the peaks and valleys occur more abruptly. These cycles do not relate to whether early or late in a particular administration, and they may overlap administrations. In each of the five different cycles, there is also considerable similarity among the types of entities created throughout the cycle.

In the first cycle, between 1928 and 1945, a large number of autonomous institutes and a few state enterprises were started to provide a basic infrastructure for development in such areas as finance, higher education, transportation, and water supplies, or to manage businesses confiscated from the estate of the defunct dictator. The second cycle, 1946–53, was characterized by the populist nature of many entities, such as cafeterias, educational and health facilities, and worker and peasant cooperatives. In the third or basic industry cycle, SOEs in electricity, steel, petrochemicals, petroleum, aluminum, and so on, were set up between 1954 and 1963. The next decade witnessed the proliferation of a large number of subsidiaries, which responded to all the objectives associated with earlier cycles, under older parastatals, and relatively few totally independent new organizations. The final cycle, since 1974, added the management of interdependence through oil and iron nationalization as a policy goal of many new entities, but the cycle was also overwhelmed by the influence of the ebb and flow of two huge petrodollar bonanzas that allowed for continued proliferation of subsidiaries. Again, a major new objective was added, but the previous commitments to infrastructure, popular services, and basic industry were retained as raison d'êtres for the creation of new entities.

The identification of patterns in the intensity of DPA activity suggested the operation of a few determining variables. To evaluate this hypothesis, a systematic sociopolitical analysis of the type designed by Gil Yepes was combined with a study of structural economic and budgetary factors. The result was the discovery of a five-variable model that explains between 40 and 80 percent of the variance (depending on both the Y variable selected and the years included) in the total number of new entities and the number of important entities created per year over the 1928–77 period. The five variables are the tendency of price and demand for oil, the ability of the government to increase its income, the nature of programmatic government commitments, the relationship of the government to political mobilization activity, and the political strategy of the regime. The single most powerful of the five variables in most of the experiments was the fiscal success of the government, but it nearly disappeared from the equation if different periods of only very low revenue increases were grouped together—that is, 1930–35, 1941–44, 1948–50, 1960–64, 1968–70.

The finding of cyclical growth in the DPA helps clarify the reasons for the tremendous spurt in growth in the 1974–76 period and then again, but to a much lesser extent, in 1978–81. These two oil bonanzas had the same kind of impact as those of 1936–37, 1946–47, and 1954–56, except that of the OPEC bonanza of the mid-1970s was the biggest by far. In the 1930s and 1950s examples, government revenue increased by just over 50 percent per year. During the 1940s bonanza the government got a 161 percent average increase, but in the mid-1970s the Pérez government collected 212 percent more per year.

The other four growth influencing variables under the Pérez government were also at or near maximum values: (1) OPEC took temporary charge of the world oil market; (2) the Pérez commitment to "democracy with energy" subsumed a programmatic pledge to nearly all the unfulfilled promises of previous democratic governments; (3) the landslide AD electoral victory of 1973 mobilized more of the population behind the government than at any time since 1948; and (4) the political strategy of urgency (since it was the "last chance" for democracy), emergency decree legislation powers for the presidency, and the drive to overcome and not just manage dependency drove the Pérez government to an unprecedented rhythm of activity.

The last of Bigler's findings is that there has been a surprising degree of underlying continuity in decentralization policy. The same juridical-administrative structures that were originally developed between 1928 and 1938 have been used repeatedly, albeit a few innovations have been introduced. The policymaking framework elaborated by Gil Yepes has also proven relevant time after time, and the evolutionary development of the state and gradual accretion of functions to the decentralized part of government that were found by Brewer-Carías and Viloria support the notion of continuity. There is added evidence in the coherence of formal government development plans from López Contreras' plan of 1938 through the Fifth and Sixth National Plans under Pérez and Herrera Campins. Baloyra's discovery of incrementalism in the budgetary process and the confirmation by other studies of the pervasiveness of gradual budgetary evolution in spite of radical revenues swings also show continuity.[8] The idea is further supported by patterns of subsidiary growth, organizational redundancy, and the additive nature of the goal structures found in the successive growth cycles.

The only noteworthy exceptions to continuity are the abrupt swings in the number of entities actually created at any given time. This single exception is especially important because it helps reveal the meaning of the growth pattern. The record seems to show that when circumstances combine unusual resources availability with the right sociopolitical conditions, then the extreme bursts of governmental development activities that marked the López Contreras government in the 1930s, the *trienio* in the 1940s, the New National Ideal Program in the 1950s, and the Pérez government in the 1970s will be focused and implemented primarily through the decentralized public administration. With more modest resources and less favorable conditions, every other Venezuelan government since 1928 has tried to follow this pattern but has been able to add far fewer enterprises over shorter time spans. The implication of these findings about the growth of the DPA is that Venezuelan governments have consistantly reverted to the use of decentralized public administration to spearhead the country's continuing drive for development.[9]

THE REFORMIST ECHO

The DPA may have been the habitual spearhead of bursts of development activity, but the results have repeatedly failed to measure up to expectations. Venezuela has sustained a record of economic growth since the 1920s that has propelled it almost from last place in Latin America to near the top in every development category, from per capita income to quality of life measures. Yet the perception remains that the country's economy has not become sufficiently autonomous, that income distribution is still unfair, too many still live in misery, the opportunity through education and employment is still too restricted, and the country remains sadly underdeveloped.[10]

The issues underlying misunderstandings and controversies, especially the notion of statization of the economy, build on the frustration felt with respect to development performance. What is worse, the more decentralized entities there are, the poorer seems to be their performance (or the perception of it). Governments are dissatisfied with the responsiveness to new directives (and new direction). The public becomes more frustrated with the "deterioration" of public services. Businessmen chafe at the mounting delays in payments, inconsistency in supplies of materials for their factories, or ubiquity in the administration of loans, granting of contracts, delivery of services, or application of regulations. The comptroller-general and the private watchdogs of the public purse rail against mounting deficits, and everyone worries about corruption, incompetence, patronage, and collusion with the capitalist or foreigners.

The immediate consequence of these perceptions has been the repeated efforts to reform the decentralized public administration. Improvement drives have taken diverse forms. In the late 1930s, early 1960s, and late 1970s, and again at present, there has been considerable emphasis on privatization. During the latter half of the *trienio*, again under President Leoni, and during the Herrera administration, improvement was sought through the expansion of labor participation or the development of worker co-management systems. Finally, more rational organization schemes were proposed and at least partially implemented during the early 1950s by the civil-military junta, the Betancourt government from 1958 to 1961, under Caldera and the CAP in the early 1970s, through Pérez's Commission for Integral Reform of the Public Administration (CRIAP) in the mid-1970s, by congressional committees during the last government, and now again through CORDIPLAN. All of the above are in addition to the countless and repeated attempts to improve virtually every individual decentralized public entity that ever existed.

The repetitiveness of reform efforts and the continual hue and cry about DPA shortcomings give the impression that the results of reform have been very meager. And clearly they have been in the view of those who demand more reform. An objective review of the reform record is clearly beyond the scope of this chapter. Rather, a modest and tentative review of the reform processes and the potential for institutional learning will be attempted.

The outlook for privatization is fairly good in the short term, although mixed with respect to significance and continuity. The consensus in recent years that SOEs are legitimate in strategic sectors of the economy (such as oil and natural resources exploitation) and in basic services and industries (those which initially process natural resources or provide a product or service input, such as steel, petrochemicals, electricity, transportation, or port facilities for other productive activities) reduces the scope of the privatization debate and adds force to it. Attention can be drawn to the many enterprises, especially hotels, sugar mills, small manufacturing firms, and banks, which operate poorly or at a loss as SOEs in contrast to more successful private enterprises in the same economic sectors.

The alternative to privatization for the least legitimate entities in the DPA is obviously refinancing and reforms within the public sector. Yet this alternative is complicated by the fragmented structure of the DPA discussed earlier. Furthermore, the holding companies or supervisory institutes for the enterprises—those that would be responsible for alternative reform measures, such as the CVF, CORPOTURISMO, CENAZUCA, and the BIV—are themselves now more discredited than ever because of the magnitude of their own losses, confusion of operations, and role in the debt crisis. Instances of highly publicized failures at rescue operations in some of these subsectors of the economy, especially the scandal over the public intervention board operation of the Banco Nacional de Descuento (BND) in the wake of the scandalous collapse of the BTV, reduces confidence that could be placed in public sector reformers. Finally, there just is not any money to recapitalize firms as has been done in the past with hotels, banks, small mines, and textile firms.

The likelihood is thus a much greater likelihood that the

Lusinchi administration will actually hive off or dissolve a fairly substantial number of parastatals of the types mentioned above. The continued stringency of his economy adjustment program contrasts greatly with the boom in public revenue that reversed the commitment of the Herrera Campins administration to similar policies before it had been in office for a year. However, the privatization of all the SOEs and even a few of the major autonomous institutes of the types mentioned would not greatly reduce the size of the DPA except in the number of entities. It would reduce current operating losses to some degree, but many major deficitory enterprises, such as SIDOR, INOS, INAVI, ICAP, and Aeropostal would remain public property, and the large debt load incurred by the disappeared entities would still have to be borne by the government.

Experience also shows that some hived off enterprises do not stay private and that with time more enterprises from a given subsector of the economy may end up under public control. This has been the case in the past with sugar mills, textile firms, dairy products companies, banks, and hotels (among others) and should continue in the future as long as there is any regional development corporation, public financial intermediary, or state holding company with the potential to respond to appeals from some interest group. Of course, that is what it means to have a mixed economy. The rescue of jobs, production, consumer, and capital interests or partnership with private enterprise to spur development are all legitimate functions of the state in a mixed economy, even if less so than is the operation of basic and strategic industries.

Substantial reorganization of the DPA under the Lusinchi administration is also quite likely and holds promise for some substantial gains because of advances in institutional learning. First, it is common today to find bureaucrats, cabinet members, congressmen, outside consultants, party specialists, and public critics who are familiar with past reform efforts, but this has rarely been the case in the past because of abrupt regime changes, alternation of party governments, and the less specialized or less advanced educations among those concerned. Second, previous reform efforts are being studied systematically, and at times by the same people who may have been involved in a different way in the past, so that a data base and some "tested" knowledge can be added to the experimental base. Third, some successful models for holding company operations or administrative and financial control or ministerial adscription have occurred in Venezuela and more attention is being paid to them. PDVSA works quite well, so it has been carefully scrutinized to delineate the process for the creation of workable holding company arrangements elsewhere. And fourth, the designs for reform have become more specialized and less intricate than earlier schemes. The consequences of this latter achievement may be the greatest. It should facilitate improvements in the responsiveness to policy, financial account-ability, or efficiency of operations in one segment of the DPA at a time.

The latter instance of institutional learning is also extremely significant with respect to prospects for the reform of individual entities. Horror stories notwithstanding, there have been many cases of both successful operations and successful reform of decentralized entities in the past. The favorite example of the *cognoscenti* is now PEQUIVEN. This enterprise, which as the IVP for 20 years was the champion all-time net loser on operations and resister of countless reform efforts, was turned around after it was made a subsidiary of PDVSA in 1978. It showed a modest profit for the first time in 1983 and has still brighter prospects for the future. AVENSA Airlines, run under contract by a private group in the fashion of what was once lauded as the VIASA model, has remained successful despite its public takeover. Other cases could be cited, and although they do not abound, conditions are ripe to produce more.

These propitious conditions can be summarized succinctly. First, management technology and managers capable of em-ploying it are now more abundant in Venezuela. The first case studies of SOE management by Venezuelans and readily available to others were carried out less than a decade ago. Now entire courses can be based on such case study material. Less than two decades ago, there were probably only a dozen Venezuelans with MBA/MPA degrees, and undergraduate management science programs were just starting in Venezuelan universities. As recent as a decade ago, when 40 to 50 decentralized entities were created each year, fewer Venezuelans than that received MBA/MPA degrees. Today the picture has changed dramatically. The Ayacucho Scholarship holders have returned or are continuing to return home or have graduated from significant new degree programs at Venezuelan universities, such as IESA, and they are beginning to occupy increasing numbers of jobs and more significant positions in the DPA.

Second, the commitment to reform and significant support for it within the Lusinchi administration seem quite high. During his first months in office, Lusinchi took a number of actions that affirm such dedication. For instance, he replaced a partisan executive with a respected technocrat at PDVSA; he restored other previously successful technocratic managers to offices they once held at VENALUM; he acted to liquidate the BND, CVF, and a few other entities after repeated reform failures; and he appointed and then supported new managers in VIASA, IAN, and other entities in spite of the hundreds of jobs they eliminated.

Third, the current economic crisis is enforcing more market discipline on the DPA than ever before in its history. Thus, to continue operations, structural adjustments are being imposed on many SOEs and other types of entities. Some programs are being eliminated or reduced; new markets are being developed; excess personnel, cost-inefficient technology, and many perquisites are being shelved; new systems for adjusting finances to operational revenues are being implemented to head off cash flow problems; and subsidies to clients, other government entities, and subsidiaries are being pared down or removed. The austerity of economic adjustment in Venezuela since 1981, and the likelihood that it may continue through 1985 or 1986, have been hard indeed after the petrodollar bonanzas of the 1970s. Yet the real achievements by PDVSA in altering its market strategy to squeeze out more revenue from less production, the increasing exports from SIDOR and the aluminum companies, the reduced losses at VIASA, and many other developments show that the DPA is responding positively. Moreover, given the human, natural resource, and democratic endowments that Venezuela has, it may only need to learn to manage with a scarcity criterion in order to fulfill developmental expectations that it has so far failed to meet by creating organizations that do only half the job.[11]

THE DEMOCRATIC DIFFERENCE

A common supposition about the relationship between the degree of state intervention and type of regime is that military regimes are allied with the business elite, so they minimize the role of the state in the economy. In contrast, democracies are more interventionist and would therefore foster development of the parastatal sector at the expense of the market economy. Venezuela is nearly an ideal case to test this hypothesis because of its rotation from military to democratic regimes. However, the record shows almost no support for the hypothesis, and knowing about the continuity within the cyclical growth pattern discussed above, this is what should have been expected.

Several aspects of the record may, indeed, be interpreted to the contrary of the standard hypothesis. That is, Venezuelan military governments have actually interfered more with the scope for the private market than have civilian regimes, especially if the role allowed for foreign investment is treated separately. For instance, the first private sector mobilization in opposition to the formation of state corporations was in protest against the formation of the Central Bank, the expansion of the BIV, and other measures in the late 1930s and early 1940s. At about the same time businessmen were also pressuring the López Contreras government to privatize a larger share of the business holdings that had been confiscated from the estate of ex-dictator Gómez. Under the juntas and Pérez Jiménez from 1948 to 1958, the state took control of numerous private electric companies, investing heavily in hotels, sugar mills, commercial banks, and other businesses that competed directly with private business. More significantly, it was the dictatorship that developed the doctrine that basic industries should be reserved to the state. Pérez Jiménez thereby also justified his dissolution of a private consortium that had been formed in the early 1950s to create Venezuela's first steel plant.

The democratic regimes did not reverse economic roles in the economy that had been established by their military predecessors. They have modified the rules with respect even to basic industries to permit a private sector presence, including privately owned steel mills, and have been somewhat less prone to establish public corporations in economic sectors well served by private initiative. Of course, this has not prevented rescues and other mixed economy justifications for entry into such sectors on a piecemeal basis, and there has certainly been more regulatory intervention in the economy directly by the government under democracy.[12]

The treatment of foreign investment is more confused. Both

types of regime have been relatively nationalistic. Democratic governments have been much more restrictive, eventually nationalizing the oil and iron ore industries, while allowing foreigners to participate in several very important joint ventures in other areas of the economy. Foreign ownership participation in SOEs was never permitted by any military government, and they also nationalized railroads, telephones, and some electrical and mining operations of minor importance. On the other hand, the military regimes did give foreigners private investment, colonization, and contracting advantages, and they treated foreign oil companies much more leniently. Pérez Jiménez was again the extreme case when he granted new concessions to the multinationals in the mid-1950s after a consensus against them had been established over a decade earlier under General Medina.

Another difference between military and civilian regimes in their roles in the economy is that a far larger proportion of the autonomous entities established by the democratic regimes has had the promotion of private business activity as a principal objective. The CVF, founded by AD, was the first state corporation of this type, and all the regional development corporations have had this as a major goal, except the CVG where it was given very minor importance. CORPOINDUSTRIA was created to promote small and medium-sized business development. ICAP and IAN and several agricultural funds have promoted peasant enterprises. The IVP reversed the militarily decreed exclusiveness for the petrochemical industry and encouraged joint ventures with both private and foreign interests there. Numerous financial ventures, such as CAVENDES, FONCREI, Central Hipotecaría, FIVCA, FONEXPO, COFITECA, and others, have underwritten private activities in construction, industry, the mortgage market, commerce, petroleum industry services, exporting, and so on. However, a major failing of both democratic and military regimes has been in the promotion of backward and forward linkages—input suppliers and output utilizers—between basic and strategic industries and the private sector in order to increase value added in domestic production.

Democratic regimes have also been explicitly more supportive of regional development, although military governments had as good a record in the actual regional dispersion of the decentralized entities they established. The only precedent for the first CVF regional development effort had been some colonization schemes for foreign immigrants under López and Medina, but the CVF laid the groundwork for Guayana development and regional activities elsewhere through a system of mixed ownership banks in major cities around the country. The Pérez Jiménez dictatorship carried on these initiatives, but the focus was altered substantially. For instance, the regional bank for Barquisimeto (BANFOCOVE) was organized by the CVF with a large number of small private stockholders who together had a majority interest, but when later regional banks were started by the BIV (a CVF subsidiary) during the dictatorship, they had relatively few private investors and their stock purchases were to a large extent actually financed by the BIV or CVF. This pattern was also followed in the CVF takeover of municipal, state, and a few foreign electricity companies during the 1950s.

With the return of democracy in 1958, a network of regional development corporations, industrial, and other enterprise zones, such as fishing and crafts, regional universities, municipal enterprises, and other entities, was spread gradually across the country. The headquarters of a few major national autonomous institutes were even relocated. In short, the military governments carried out activities in the regions but with a great degree of centralized control. Democracy, in contrast, promoted more explicitly regionally focused and geographical deconcentration activities, and there was a greater degree of local participation and somewhat more local control.

In general, the encouragement of broader participation in entrepreneurial activities, called the democratization of capital when applied to stock ownership regulations in Venezuela, has been a hallmark of the DPA under democracy.[13] The vehicles have been extremely diverse, as has been suggested above. One additional important mechanism has been worker participation. This actually commenced with miner and agricultural ventures and cooperatives under the CVF and other institutes during the *trienio*. Some of these also had financing or joint ownership by Nelson Rockefeller's Basic Economy Corporation. Later, the Leoni administration gave organized labor representation on the boards of directors of all SOEs, enterprises with 50 percent or more public ownership, and autonomous institutes. His government also established the Workers' Bank (BTV) and financed the acquisition of majority ownership by the CTV and its union affiliates. By the late 1970s, organized labor had begun to push for worker co-management. Alternative co-management schemes were in fact under study in 1982, when the BTV intervention and corruption scandals and the revelation of a vast network of CTV-union controls paralyzed any further progress in this direction.

The trend, however, is clear. Democratic governments will continue to involve new and diverse segments of the population in the ownership and control of decentralized entities and establish ever more specialized entities to serve the needs of sometimes very restricted segments of the population. This pattern of expansion in popular participation in modern economic activities is the principal impact of the growth of the decentralized public administration on the Venezuelan political economy under democracy. It has provided myriad avenues for distributing the oil wealth controlled by the regime to ever broader segments of the population. In doing so, it has remarkably broadened access to both benefits and decision making in a very short period of time since 1958. Moreover, the jobs, the higher education and much of the housing, health, public, and financial services of the decentralized public administration have become the pillars of the Venezuelan middle class.

THE DPA AND THE CONSOLIDATION OF DEMOCRACY

Yet the pillars referred to are more than a bit shaky and are perhaps the basis of as much trouble as support for the regime today. That is, there are a number of aspects of the DPA that may weaken the Venezuelan democracy. These weaknesses derive chiefly from administrative underdevelopment in the central government, the continued importance of ascriptive values, and the inadequacy of accountability mechanisms. Of course, there are some ways that the DPA invigorates the democracy as well, but these will be considered later.

In the previous discussion of reform efforts related to the DPA, the absence of a role for the central government should have been glaringly apparent. This has in fact been a common characteristic of most reform proposals. With the exception of the juridical-administrative issues, such as ascription, statutory procedures, sectoral grouping, and holding company creation, the operational relationships between the central government and decentralized entities and the capacity of the former to exercise any oversight, achieve coordination, provide support, and not prejudice the activities of the latter have been ignored. Not surprisingly, state enterprise managers report the same bottlenecks, *permisología* (requirements to get permits or clearances), information gaps, dysfunctional regulations, and improvisations as do private businessmen. There are, however, two important differences in the consequences. SOEs are more likely to be able to cut red tape than are private firms, and when they do so they provide evidence of arbitrariness, discredit the public administration, and provide more reason to demand privatization. Second, the methods used by SOEs to resolve their problems with the bureaucracy rarely contribute to, and may short-circuit the development of institutions for demand making and demand aggregation. Thus the underdevelopment of government relations with the DPA may actually inhibit the articulation of democracy.

Ascriptive values and practices—patronage, arbitrary authority, group privilege or prejudice, and personalism—that are abetted by the decentralized public administration are also commonplace elsewhere in Venezuela. The significance of the role of these values with respect to the DPA is, first, that the exceptional juridical-administrative status of DPA entities may allow them to elude changes that are taking place elsewhere, that is, the implementation of merit reforms in the civil service. The record in this regard is actually mixed. There are, after all, only islands of rationalistic meritocracy among decentralized entities. But this is where the second problem occurs, because more is actually expected of the DPA. No president would hesitate to name a partisan figure to any cabinet post, but the same behavior is intolerable in appointments to PDVSA. Personalism, factionalism and cronyism are expected in the parties, the Congress, and ministries but are reviled when CANTV telephone service deteriorates or INOS fails to supply water.

Decentralized entities have in the past been especially important dispensers of both group (IAN to peasants, BTV to labor leaders, INAVI to urbanites) and individual patronage, and that was expected of them. But under democracy Venezuela has gone from a country in which less than 2 percent of the population (1957) received any higher education to one in which more than 30 percent now receive at least one year. These more educated people form a new, vastly larger and relatively modern middle class, and the DPA is increasingly their realm. Thus their anticipation of finding the prevalence of their new values in the DPA may be higher than for any other segment of society, and their assessment of the performance of democracy must accordingly take careful stock of how the DPA works.

The inadequate accountability of the decentralized public administration may weaken the Venezuelan democracy the most, but some variation of this problem bedevils nearly every country where there is any significant decentralization.[14] In the Venezuelan case the most serious aspect of the accountability problem takes the basic form represented by a 1978 COPEI campaign taunt of AD: "¿Dónde están los reales?" (Where is the money?). The tragedy is that in the 1983 campaign after the COPEI government experienced nearly as great a petrodollar bonanza as had the AD government five years earlier, the same taunt could be repeated by the adecos. For both governments the answer would have to be the same because during both more money was spent by the DPA than state, local, and national governments combined: The money went down the decentralized sink hole.

This answer oversimplifies the fate of the billions of bolivars that passed through CORPOMERCADEO as subsidies, paid interest on short-term debt, poured cement for the Metro, Guri Dam, Parque Central, and countless other structures, provided tuition for an extra 200,000 university students (including more than 10,000 abroad), and purchased an endless array of imports, among other things. It also reflects the concern Venezuelans have shown for the investment of their petrodollar wealth in productive activities since the national development slogan (sembrar el petróleo) was first voiced nearly a half century ago, and so returns to the earlier discussion of the reform process, efforts to achieve efficiency, and related topics. But it is not entirely the same. The approach to accountability here is in the context of democratic performance and that makes the issue systematic. Along these lines of thought, some authors have suggested that the wastefulness of the development through the decentralized model that Venezuela has followed may eventually doom its democracy.[15] Unquestionably, it weakens it.

The appropriate question is whether the decentralized public administration provides any or enough support to compensate for its weakening of democracy. The answer requires a very complicated balancing of very different factors. We will leave the outcome in abeyance and just identify some key ways in which the DPA may help underpin and build democracy in the meantime. These are policy versatility, increased participation, consensus and compromise building, and crisis responsiveness.

The policy versatility of the DPA subsumes the traits of the DPA that Gil Yepes and Bigler found in their policymaking studies. The creation and, to a lesser degree, transformation (in contrast to reformation) of decentralized entities are relatively straightforward processes, with low initial costs, reduced potential for interference or opposition, and potentially great effectiveness for meeting the needs of specific groups or carrying out specific tasks. It is also a familiar tool to policymakers who have witnessed its use in a wide variety of contexts, so its adaptability to new circumstances is quite great. The policy versatility of the decentralized public administration supports the potential of the government to respond to specific demands.

Democracy is often associated with pluralism. The amount and diversity of participation in the political economy that has been achieved through the decentralized public administration, as discussed earlier, should foster such pluralism in Venezuela, but many would challenge this view. Instead, it has been alleged that the DPA, especially during the Pérez administration, merely became a conduit for private enrichment and the perpetuation of elite domination of society.[16] Moreover, given the at times admitted partisan manipulation of benefits through decentralized entities, the visible participation of major family groups (such as the Boultons, Brillembourgs, and Neumans, in mixed enterprises), the regular circulation of key managers back and forth between parastatals and other key business groups, and the apparent co-optation of the labor aristocracy, a very plausible case can be made for an elitist interpretation of participation in this field. If this were exclusively the case, then such participation would of course add weight to the weakening of democracy already attributed to the operation of ascriptive values.

The weight of evidence related to the actual achievement of elitist control appears, however, to provide more support for the idea of increasing pluralism even if it may be very effective, as Gil Yepes (1981) has noted. The most compelling evidence relates to such facts as the failures of incumbents to maintain control of the government, the economic losses that some very powerful elites have suffered in mixed enterprises or due to SOE actions, the political independence and even extremism of labor in many parastatals, the commonness in decentralized entities of managers and technicians who have experienced great upward mobility without elite ties, and finally just the diversity and number of beneficiaries—tens of thousands of scholarship and small business and agricultural loan recipients and hundreds of thousands of employees, land reform participants, occupants of subsidized homes, and so on.

The decentralized public administration has contributed to the formation of some of the key consequences underlying the Venezuelan political economic system today, and it is or has the potential to forge others in areas of troublesome conflict.[17] For instance, the fringes of public economic intervention, that is, requiring employment increases or setting wages by decree, may be disputed, but the productive role of the state in basic industries or its promotive activities in the small business and agricultural areas are today legitimate after heated controversy over earlier decades. This is possible because decentralized activity may be increased incrementally, more limited agreements are ususally enough for something to be accomplished, and the unusual juridical-administrative flexibility of a decentralized entity abets compromise. Thus even in areas where no consensus may yet exist, the development of the activity within the DPA may provide grounds to minimize conflict while action is taken and thus provide a framework that will eventually yield fuller agreement.

The last of the traits associated with the DPA that may strengthen democracy relates to the ability it provides the system to respond to crises. The policy versatility, participatory nature, and consensus/compromise–creating capacities that have been associated with decentralized policymaking all converge in the crisis management situation. This can be clarified by distinguishing the use of crisis here from the more common notion of a situation of danger that requires instant action. Rather, the idea here is related more to usages that denote difficult choices between courses of action, or societal crisis, as in crisis of democracy or legitimacy crisis.

The value of the decentralized public administration in this regard may be understood most clearly by making reference to the repeated use of parastatals by Betancourt at the outset of Venezuela's democracy. His many actions included the bestowal of autonomy on Venezuela's universities to deflect their radicalism away from the center of the political system; the creation of the CVG to provide a coherent focus for and to relegitimize the state development of Guayana's natural resources; the development of the Corporación Venezolana de Petróleos to reverse the dictator's oil industry policies and begin the nationalization of the industry; the joint venture with Reynolds Aluminum to form ALCASA and demonstrate both the country's receptivity to foreign capital and that there would be restraints upon it; and finally, the creation of FUNDACOMUN, the Central de Crédito Hipotecarío, CAVENDES, and others. These and other actions enabled Betancourt to show that the new democracy would try to decentralize power by promoting local development, befriend and enter into partnerships with business, and benefit the middle class.

Over a decade later when President Pérez confronted the first OPEC petrodollar bonanza amidst the galloping expectations of his countrymen, a situation that he thought was the last chance for democracy, it is not at all surprising that he too turned so dramatically (and repeatedly) to the decentralized public administration to respond in the crisis. And while many other instances before and since these two governments could be cited, it is important to recognize that the parallels between the situation that confronted Betancourt and the one today are much greater. In doing so, it also helps to recall that Betancourt did use the DPA policy instrument exclusively to create new entities. Indeed, his transformations of earlier establishments into EDELCA and SIDOR and their coupling with the CVG, his selling off of some enterprises, closing of others and reorganizing elsewhere may be the most significant of his acts for the situation that exists today.

The answer to our earlier question should now be clear. If Betancourt's path sets the precedent, and if the initial achievements of the Lusinchi administration in cutting back, rationalizing, and improving parastatals indicate commitment to the course, then the decentralized public administration will continue to strengthen the Venezuelan democracy in the future.

NOTES

1. Comisión de Administración Pública, *Informe sobre la reforma de la administración pública nacional*, 2 vols. (Caracas, 1972). Within the 1,252 pages of this comprehensive work, only 99 are devoted to the decentralized public administration.

2. See Petras and Morley (1983) in the bibliography. References in the text that include only the author's surname and publication date also refer to works listed in the bibliography.

3. Bigler and Saulniers (1984) places the Venezuelan decentralized public administration in the context of similar developments throughout Latin America. Key works on the phenomenon elsewhere include Ira Sharkansky, *Whither the State?* (Chatham, N.J.: Chatham House, 1979); Michael E. McGill and Leland Wooten, "Management in the Third Sector," *Public Administration Review* 35, no. 5 (September/October 1975); Thomas T. Bennett and Thomas J. DiLorenzo, *Underground Government: The Off-Budget Public Sector* (Washington, D.C.: Cato Institute, 1983); and Leroy P. Jones, ed., *Public Enterprises in Developing Countries* (New York: Cambridge University Press, 1982).

4. Table 7.1 is based primarily on work by Gil Yepes and Brizuela (forthcoming), Brewer-Carías and Viloria (1984), and unpublished or earlier works by Viloria, especially *El estado empresario: Ensayos sobre la empresa pública*, which is scheduled to be published by Editorial Jurídica Venezuela. His *Estado, dessarrollo y empresa pública en Venezuela* (Caracas: Escuela Nacional de Administración Pública 1974,) and *El proceso de nacionalización de la industria del hierro* (mimeo.), also provided background.

5. See note 1, pp. 307–37.

6. Unedited essays by Janet Kelly de Escobar, "Las empresas del estado en Venezuela," and Julián Villalba, "El estado de la gerencia en la empresa del estado," and several works presented at the November 1983 International Conference on State Enterprise Management Problems held at IESA (and which will be published by that institute) deal competently with these problems.

7. In addition to works mentioned in note 4, other essential studies by

Brewer-Carías on the subject include *El estado: Crisis y reforma* (Caracas: Biblioteca de la Academia de Ciencias Políticas y Sociales, 1982), *Regimen jurídico de las empresas pública en Venezuela* (Caracas: Centro Latinoamericano de Administración para el Desarrollo, 1980), and especially *Cambio político y reforma del estado en Venezuela* (Madrid: Editorial Tecnos, 1975).

8. Enrique A. Baloyra, "Oil Policies and Budgets in Venezuela, 1938-68," *Latin American Research Review* 9 (Summer 1974), and Gene E. Bigler, "Congress, Parties and Regimes in Venezuelan Budgetary Politics," International Conference on National Styles of Policymaking, IESA, March 1976.

9. Gene E. Bigler and Franklin Tugwell advance a pulse theory of the Venezuelan Development process in an essay recently prepared for the World Resources Institute: "Oil, Economic Crisis, Democracy and the Entrepreneurial State in Venezuela" (Washington, D.C., September 1984).

10. These views are expressed in myriad forms in the collection of articles by 39 prominent Venezuelans; *1984: ¿A dónde va Venezuela?* (Caracas: Editorial Planeta, 1984).

11. The idea and nature of management with a scarcity criterion in contrast to the prevailing management culture in Venezuela is analyzed by Moisés Naim, "La empresa privada en Venezuela o qué pasa cuando se crece en medio de la riqueza y confusión," in Moisés Naim et al. (1985).

12. Gil Yepes (1982), especially chap. 5 and 6.

13. The ousted CORDIPLAN director, Luis Raúl Matos Azocar, has proposed extending this concept to current privatization efforts by vesting control of nonstrategic, deficitory public enterprises in groups or associations of young professionals.

14. In addition to the studies mentioned in note 3, see Bruce L. R. Smith and L. C. Hague, eds., *The Dilemma of Accountability in Modern Government* (London: Macmillan, 1971). The recent concern for the autonomy of the state from control by civil society cannot be analyzed here, but it is the central issue in Gil Yepes' (1981) contrast of effective to limited pluralism. The subject is developed theoretically in Eric A. Nordlinger, *On the Autonomy of the Democratic State* (Cambridge, Mass.: Harvard University Press, 1981).

15. Robert D. Bond, "Where Democracy Lives," *Wilson Quarterly* 8 (Autumn 1984): 60-62. A frequently voiced scenario for the Venezuelan future holds that the country may follow the path of the once prosperous Southern Cone democracies and gradually exhaust both the sources of wealth and the democracy.

16. Terry Karl, "Petroleum and Political Pacts: The Transition to Democracy in Venezuela," Latin America Working Paper Number 107 (Washington, D.C.: Woodrow Wilson Center, 1981), and Petras and Morley (1983), among other works, develop the elitist model.

17. Conflict and consensus building in the Venezuelan democracy have been analyzed in several works by Daniel H. Levine, see especially "Venezuela Since 1958: The Consolidation of Democratic Politics," in *The Breakdown of Democratic Regimes: Latin America*, ed. Juan Linz and Alfred Stepan (Baltimore: Johns Hopkins University Press, 1978).

8

Public Administration

William S. Stewart

Venezuelan public administration before 1958 did not employ a great number of people and was accountable primarily to dictators and the wealthy, insofar as it was accountable at all. Given the conditions under which they worked, it is hard to fault the bureaucrats of those times, but in terms of their contributions to the welfare of the people, it is equally difficult to be very enthusiastic. Before the development of the oil industry, Venezuela was not wealthy, and the resources available to the bureaucracy were correspondingly small. During the Gómez era (1908–35) only the military and public communications were well funded and efficient. When oil revenues increased during World War II and greater emphasis was put on "development," the bureaucracy was expanded , its roles diversified, and the money channeled through it greatly increased. Especially during the Pérez Jiménez period, there was a great deal of money, most of it in dollars. This meant that it was spent primarily in the United States. While some remained there in the form of Florida and New York real estate and investment portfolios, most returned to Venezuela in the form of imports. It is hardly surprising that many bureaucrats did not resist the opportunity to acquire some of it for themselves.

It is this era that is primarily responsible for the reputation of the Venezuelan bureaucracy as inefficient and corrupt. Not all of the bureaucracy was corrupt, of course, and although there are still some problems today, it is not a principal concern for the country. Far more important is the nature of Venezuelan wealth. As

218

Lombardi has pointed out, wealth since the Spanish conquest has been a product of exports. Whether cacao, coffee, or oil, the result has been foreign exchange to be spent on overseas goods. When these are imported the results can be catastrophic for national industry. The governmental strategy since 1945 has been to import capital goods, using the infrastructure developed with these goods to produce the consumer items that might raise the standard of living. This program is complicated by two major factors.

First, this was, and is, to be accomplished within the general framework of a free market economy based on profit. The efficiency of state enterprises is judged by profit and loss statements rather than in meeting program goals. Second, the population is expanding rapidly. A healthier but still very poor majority continues to grow. Moreover, illegal immigration, primarily from Columbia, adds from 6 to 30 percent of the population, almost all of them poor.[1] The combination of factors is difficult for any government. If internal production is to grow, the importation of consumer goods must be kept low. On the other hand, the poor in Venezuela represent very little demand in a free market. Their needs are great but they have little or no money. The only wealth available to the government has been foreign money, a situation that dictates massive importation of consumer goods, a contradiction of the basic policy of import substitution.

The response of the Pérez Jiménez government was to minimize services, allow free importation by the private sector, build up basic infrastructure, and accumulate personal assets overseas. The 1958 institution of democratic governments has made things more complex. Legitimacy derives from honest elections based upon universal suffrage. Governmental power depends upon the popular vote, which over the years has become a function of party organization. Given the electoral power of the poor, they cannot be ignored. Their needs are simple and physical, and the democratic government must respond. The strategy for doing so has been to provide for them primarily through an administrative apparatus split into three parts: services, production, and security. All offer an immediate solution to the problems of the poor. Employment in any of these sectors is perhaps the most direct means of alleviating poverty and, if political organization is maintained, of retaining the vote of the people involved.

ADMINISTRATIVE SECTORS

Security

The military and police forces are very much a part of the public administration but for historic reasons are treated very differently from the rest. The military since 1958 has excluded itself from political and economic dynamics, for which it has been rewarded. There are some safeguards, such as appointing all service chiefs and the defense minister for a single year, after which they are retired. Primarily, however, the military stays out of politics because of satisfaction with its status and, presumably, with government policies. It has been called out of the barracks to combat rural-based guerrillas and to patrol the borders. In the first few years of democracy it also had to deal with internal splits in the form of barracks revolts. This has not recurred since that time.

The police have been maintained apart from the armed forces, and care has been taken to concentrate their efforts on crime and services. They have not been used to sop up unemployment and, especially in metropolitan Caracas, there have been efforts to professionalize them while limiting their scope. Everyone in Venezuela who lived through the pre-1958 years is painfully aware of the problems of corruption and unaccountability when police forces are given power to determine political crimes, and few have any desire to return to such a situation.

That such things remain possible is illustrated by reports in the spring of 1984 of possible army collusion, if not sponsorship, in growing and exporting marijuana, along with reports of corruption in the Treasury and metropolitan police.[2] Whatever the truth of these reports, they reinforce government desires to keep them out of politics. Since what broadly allowed the military to win the armed struggle with the guerrillas was the support of the vast majority of the population for the democratic system, this also reinforces official service policies.

Services

The traditional elements of the Venezuelan administrative apparatus are either service agencies or supervisory agencies of "independent" state enterprises. While there is some overlap, the general division is between those that produce things and those that do not. Those that provide services are generally under the direct control of the government, draw all their funds from the central Treasury, and should follow policies that are set solely by the national government. They spend money on things; they do not make money or produce tangible wealth. Because of this, they cannot be judged by whether or not they make a profit. In short, they are the agencies that are traditionally known as "public administration."

Production

Given the Spanish heritage, the role of the state as a major actor in the economy is unquestioned. The older, corporatist assumptions of the Spanish state are combined with the democratic socialist assumptions of AD. The result is a set of state-owned productive corporations that are independent of the fiscal and administrative authority of the traditional bureaucracy. At first under direct presidential authority, they are now generally under ministers or the Venezuelan Investment Plan (FIV). The fund is separate from the Development Ministry because its roots are in the radical liberalism of *copeyanos* rather than the corporatist roots of the older agency. The *copeyanos* believe that government should regulate the economy, primarily through financial measures, but that the free market should be the basic dynamic of the economy. Thus, it is reasonable to use government funds for investment in the economy while leaving control of the corporations to the private businessmen involved.

At the same time, the older autonomous government enterprises coexist with the newer system. In this area it is difficult to say whether or not the employees are part of the public administration. If we are speaking of an enterprise in which the state holds minority interest, they are not; but if the state enjoys a permanent and active majority, then they are. At the same time, their employees come under general laws governing employer/employee relations rather than the personnel laws for more traditional government employees. This is further complicated by the fact that while theoretically all traditional government employees are covered by these laws, most have not been classified and are therefore not as yet subject to the personnel office's jurisdiction.[3]

CONTEMPORARY PUBLIC ADMINISTRATION

Alternating governments with overlapping but different assumptions about the role of the government in the economy have resulted in the creation and maintenance of everything from traditional governmental service agencies to minority interests in essentially profit-making private companies. Underlying all of this are the labor unions, to which both public and private employees belong. Since the unions are strongholds of Acción Democrática, employees not only have the power of the party system but can also strike, demonstrate, and otherwise bargain. Public employees are not without resources in their struggles for more security and a higher standard of living, and these resources are hardly limited to reliance upon the professionalism of the bureaucracy.

The establishiment of democracy radically altered the nature of public employment, but the traditional structure has changed slowly, if at all. Administrative structures have been and are centralized, authoritarian, and open to political influence. Autonomy is desired by agency heads, and can often be achieved by those with direct ties to the executive. Political influence is the straightforward use of party membership to affect the implementation of national law. The route is through local party leaders to the national party heads, from there to the presidency or the ministry, and back to the local branch of the agency. This system works because of the centralization of power in Caracas.

The amount of such influence possessed by an agency is directly related to the degree of its involvement with people and the degree of consensus within the nation of the policy being implemented. For example, the oil agency (PDVSA) has been relatively free from the type of influence described above. (See extended discussion of the issue of politicization in chapter 9.) The Ministry of Education, on the other hand, is so involved with political influence that this factor can never be discounted. The raison d'être for public education since 1958 has been marked by significant lack of consensus. Prior to 1958 it was generally held that education was an attribute of social and economic status. Since that time all the parties have agreed on the need for more education, but its exact nature has been a matter of dispute.

Most national leaders have agreed that education should equip people with skills required by the technological economy they are attempting to build. A deeper understanding is the older notion of education as an attribute of class. Students and their families often believe that a degree is an assurance of status. When teachers share this conviction, as many of them do, the consequences for technical proficiency are enormous. A related factor comes from the 1958 decision to more than double the student population, with the only requirement for entrace the successful exit from the lower level of education. It is easier and quicker to build schools than to train teachers, and the result was a massively underqualified teacher corps.

Although the ministry systematically upgraded teachers through in-service training, the consequences for students and the systems itself were and are enormous. Unqualified teachers produce unqualified students, but these latter have legitimate aspirations and, given the circumstances, can hardly be blamed for their scholastic inadequacy. On the other hand, the educational bureaucracy can scarcely be said to be doing its job if large numbers of technically unqualified students are graduated. The problem is complicated by the deep ambiguity with which many Venezuelans view a technologically oriented career. There is a strong tendency to see the question as humanism versus technology in a culture that clearly prefers the former. That the educational bureaucracy is as involved in this cultural transition as the students is not surprising, particularly in view of the rapid expansion of the teacher corps.

The point is that the schools are intimately involved in a "people" problem, whereas an entity such as PDVSA is not. It is obvious that the Ministry of Education will be the object of intense and continuous pressure, which will be channeled through the political parties. The lack of consensus on what an education is for, and the simultaneous consensus that as many people as possible must be educated, result in a high degree of political influence in the schools. Such influence on the bureaucracy in democratic Venezuela is not constant for all agencies, but varies directly with the degree to which it is involved with people rather than with matters more narrowly defined as technical. A strategy for an agency desiring freedom from political pressures would be to define its work wherever possible as "technical." The schools have little chance of carrying this off successfully.

AUTHORITY AND IMPLEMENTATION

Centralization

Centralization is much more uniform throughout the bureaucracy than political pressure. National agencies have their headquarters in Caracas, where decisions of any consequence, as well as relatively minor ones, are normally made. Since Venezuela is the approximate size of Texas and Oklahoma combined, and communications are generally good, this is unsurprising. The physical and cultural disparities between Caracas and the rest of the country are great, however, and have a negative effect upon national administration. Given the cosmopolitan life in the capital, it is not unusual for administrations to lose their perspective and to view "the interior" as a rather alien and backward area, qualitatively different from their own world. Cultural assumptions of this sort tend to hinder communications.

State governments reinforce rather than counteract this attitude, for, although the legislatures are elected, they have little control over the governor or state finance, both of which are allocated by the center. The role of the former is to represent the national government, with funds disbursed almost entirely through national agencies. The governor's power is that of a high party official and is exercised through the party. An important recent development was the spring 1984 decision by President Lusinchi not to appoint state AD leaders as governors. This was understandable in terms of internal party struggles, but also will reinforce the power of Caracas bureaucrats. In addition, the regionalization begun in the 1960s by administrative reform and enacted in the 1970s overlaid the twenty-one states and two territories with eight development regions. This further lessened the importance of the state governments, but not the primacy of Caracas bureaucrats.

Local governments have historically been the holders of residual powers. Given the pervasive nature of the formal Spanish state, these were minimal. They have been exercised mostly when the central government has broken down. Since 1962 there has been a government-sponsored effort to establish local governments as major political and bureaucratic forces, but the issue remains in doubt, primarily because municipal revenue still comes from the national government.

Patterns of Authority

Effective state and local governments and the delegation of authority to regional centers would all run counter to the well-established pattern of authoritarianism that exists in most Venezuelan agencies. Centralization is partly structural, with governmental agencies run from Caracas, but it is basically a centralization of authority. Traditionally, leadership is a prerogative exercised only by the head of the agency, and all effective lines of communication to and from this leader are personal. A preoccupation with personal ties and loyalties is high, and other considerations are often slighted. The classic form is that of the *caudillo*, with the usual leader/follower or patron to client relationship. The immediate circle around the leader is the *rosca*, the personal group that has grown about the leader, often going back to university days. Forming a stable and identifiable entity, it moves through the bureaucracy with the leader and shares his fortunes.

The main problem with authoritarian leadership patterns in the bureaucracy is that binding decisions are reserved to the leader and that formal communications are decidedly secondary in effectiveness to those reaching the leader through his personal contacts. The effect is to paralyze the agency for any but the most routine actions when the leader is elsewhere. Any meaningful decision must become a crisis before it can compete for the leader's attention. Once his time had been captured, the crisis (if not too complex) can be solved in short order, since the leader has both the authority and staff to deal with it. Given a minimum number of crises and a capable leader, this style can be very effective.

One of the main requirements for limited crises, however, is a stable culture and a national policy of maintaining that culture.

Venezuela's economy and culture are changing daily, and the advantages of authoritarian bureaucratic leadership are outweighed by its disadvantages. The time and effort expended in gaining the leader's attention are so large that bureaucratic executives outside Caracas find it expedient to visit the city whenever an important decision is needed. Within Caracas the same routine is followed, although the advantages of a messenger over the mail service are obvious and less is lost in traveling. By the same token, the drain upon subordinates' time and efficiency can only be negative, while the leader's time is also finite. Higher executives are typically conscientious and overworked, but are also typically behind in meeting the crises that are continually piling up before them. Add to this the time in dealing with political pressures, and the picture is complete.

Control of Implementation

A serious consequence is the difficulty for agency heads in maintaining control over policy implementation. The greater the centralization of authority, the more difficulty there is in implementation. With economics and culture in Venezuela changing, agency regulations are inadequate and often ill-suited for the situations in which the agencies find themselves. Decisions on changing regulations take even longer than decisions on individual cases, and thus emphasis tends to be placed on the latter. There is also a temptation for line personnel to short-circuit the whole process by informally solving the problem through the falsification of forms and reports. "Corruption" in the sense of payment for services rendered need not be a primary motive, or even be present. The problems lie in the difficulties and in applying static regulation to fluid situations in getting authoritative decisions.

A logical response to falsification is to increase the supervision of subordinates and to further curtail the area of their authority. This sets off a vicious circle. Carried to its logical extreme such "corruption" is necessary if the system is to work at all, but it has the regrettable effect of vitiating adherence to regulations while providing strong motives for the increased production of these same formal regulations in order to increase the occasions for payoffs. The political influence tends to work against this, at least for the local members of influential political parties. Moreover, the wealth of the government throughout the 1960s and 1970s permitted fairly good salaries for public officials, although the recent fall in oil income is affecting this. Even so, political participation through membership in the two major parties and, when possible in the unions, remains the most effective way for ordinary people to get positive results in their dealings with the bureaucracy. Given the role of *adeco* unions in swinging the last presidential candidate to Lusinchi, this is not likely to change under his administration.

Without this rather roundabout system of accountability it is unlikely that the service-oriented sectors of the bureaucracy would function as well as they do. While direct service to the people is a formal goal of such ministries as Health and Education, all organizations have functions that are quite distinct from the implementation of overt policy goals. Continued employment, distribution of wealth, support for the government, symbolic importance, party patronage, and the simple provision of welfare through government employment are all latent functions of most bureaucracies everywhere. In Venezuela they are all important, especially since the distribution of wealth is very unequal. The Pérez Jiménez government was primarily accountable to the producers of wealth, and the bureaucracy showed it. The great achievement of democratic Venezuela has been to provide a system of accountability that does not depend upon the bureaucracy itself for information and the generation of policy. Without it the general tendency would undoubtedly be for latent goals to overcome manifest goals, and the main functions of public administration would simply be its own perpetuation.

POLITICS AND STRATEGIES

Parties, Patrons, and Patronage

In Venezuela the basic relation between party leaders and the rank and file is that of patron to client. In return for votes and support within the local community the patron uses his influence to see that the client benefits at least enough to keep him from changing patrons. That the relationship is inherently unequal, with the weight of power and influence clearly on the side of the patron, is an inherent danger of this system.[4] It is always possible that the party hierarchy will find it more comfortable to engage in elite rather than mass politics. Then the direct and personal nature of the system would be lost.

Given the importance of personal contacts at all levels in Venezuela and the consequent conviction that only through personal ties can benefits be expected, the loss of the personal element in party life would most probably result in a great diminution of political activity by the mass of the people. The effect of the bureaucracy would be to remove one of the greatest pressures to implement policy effectively in the nation: the political pressures from the parties generated by their need to deliver benefits to their members. This method of ensuring bureaucratic performance results in unequal and biased implementation. "Nonpolitical" Venezuelans are not very likely to gain the benefits of law passed on a formally universalistic basis. The arrangement is hardly perfect, but in recent years has benefited the mass of Venezuelans more than any of the previous systems.

It is often argued that the bureaucracy is used more for its symbolic value than for actual development. Certainly the explosive expansion of the school system was undertaken for reasons as much symbolic as they were educational. The ministry and the party elite were perfectly aware that the quality of education would be very poor for a relatively long time. Still, the expansion was clearly desired by most citizens. It is problematic whether or not a more elitist and gradual expansion of education would have resulted in a more positive outcome, since it might never have occurred. The present situation is one that results in continuous and strong pressure on the parties to provide better education to the children of their members. Because something has been delivered, there is increased pressure for more.

A second symbolic effort was land reform (see discussion in chapter 12). The program has benefited local party leaders and their clients, while the goal of many small, family owned and operated farms has not been reached. That is, the program has been responsive to particularistic party pressures rather than to the universalistic, humanistic goals written into the law. On the other hand, the program has resulted in a more widespread distribution of wealth and land than would have been the case without it. There is no compelling reason to believe that without party pressures and the necessity to deliver on the patron/client relation that the reform would have been effective at all. This mixture of symbolic and real policy implementation, then, is present in any governmental action. In Venezuela the bureaucratic implementation of law would be far more symbolic than it is were it not for the political pressure of the parties to benefit their members.

Patronage, endemic in the system, is a natural result of the patron/client nature of the parties. Surely the most direct and easiest way to benefit a client is to get him a government job. This requires no great change of social or economic culture and brings immediate benefits to the client. If the clients are unqualified, this can only have negative effects on bureaucratic efficiency. A system of attainment has developed, however, that combines achievement and party status. Under this system employees are chosen on the basis of party membership and professional qualifications. Unskilled laborers are generally chosen solely on the basis of party qualifications. On the whole, the highest and lowest levels of bureaucracy are most vulnerable to patronage pressures. Middle-level staff are generally retained, although titles may change. They provide the continuity and knowledge upon which bureaucratic effectiveness is based. The gradual extension of job classification and civil service rights by the Central Personnel Office has tended to professionalize the bureaucracy and weaken patron/client ties, but it has not yet been extended to the majority of government workers. Given the stability of both national goals and methods since 1958, this reform is probably positive, but it does not tend to lessen the power local parties can exert over local bureaucrats.

Bureaucratic Strategies

The object of most bureaucratic strategies is agency autonomy. Among other things, bureaucratic independence cuts to a minimum the patronage that must be met, isolates the agency from the daily supervision of the parties, permits the agency better control of information, removes competing patron/client networks from management, and generally makes the internal management problems less complex. One great advantage in external relations is that a nonpartisan image can reinforce the idea that the agency is fundamentally "national" rather than "political" in focus. On the negative side, agency autonomy removes much of the need to produce, tends to focus attention upon latent goals, makes the national coordination of policy more difficult, and renders comprehensive reform impossible. Moreover, the scope for bad leadership as well as for good is amplified, along with the increased possibility that the *rosca* system will degenerate into simple internal patronage.

The positive aspects of autonomy have been obvious to bureaucrats in every administrative system, but the colonial heritage made them especially possible in Venezuela. The parallel and overlapping organizations of the Spanish administration depended upon relative autonomy for their continued existence. The practice has continued in Venezuela to such an extent that Mark Hanson could find exact counterparts for colonial officials in the Ministry of Education.[5] In particular, the use of inspectors attached directly to the minister with the authority to jump the entire hierarchy is of interest. Such a system combines checks and balances with the personal basis of authority.

On a national scale the independence of each agency is limited in part by the practice of requiring multiple checkoffs with other agencies. Thus, if Education wishes to build a school it must gain the agreement of Public Works, along with the national planning agency (CORDIPLAN). One effect is that any substantial disagreement will be referred to the president for his decision. This process enhances the authority of ministers close to the president, and makes the CORDIPLAN director a key element in bureaucratic politics, since he is in a position to force issues into the presidential office.

The Technology Strategy

For agencies in a position to employ it, the appeal to technological necessities is highly rewarding. In essence this strategy dictates a proven effectiveness in a technological field, a national consensus that the work of the agency is very important, and an ability to avoid becoming closely involved with programs directly involving large numbers of people. This last is necessary if political pressures generated by the needs of these people are to be avoided. The foremost practitioner of this strategy has been the Venezuelan Guayana Corporation (CVG), which came from a commission set up in 1953 to study the hydroelectric potential of the Caroní River. An office to develop an iron and steel mill was also established in the same area, and set a remarkable record for peculation and failure to implement its goals. The hydroelectric commission had meanwhile proven itself technologically proficient, and in 1960 it was called in to pick up the pieces. The result was a combination of excellent leadership and impressive results.

Since its inception the CVG has followed a pattern of avoiding involvement in policies requiring interaction with large numbers of needy people. The factors that enable the CVG to pursue such a policy, however, emphasize the difficulties facing other agencies attempting to employ it. First, the area was and is relative uninhabited; hence, the CVG was free of the need to respond to political pressures generated by the unemployed and the needy. Also, the types of industries it was creating did not exist in Venezuela, so the agency did not suffer from political pressures generated by competing businesses. That more people have not come to the Guayana has been a combination of CVG policies and the checks and balances system of agency responsibility.

The charter of the CVG was written very broadly, providing authority and responsibility for all the people of the Guayana. At the same time the more traditional ministries and agencies involved with social policy were also responsible. Not surprisingly, they left the sparsely settled region to the CVG; hard-pressed to respond to demands in heavily populated areas, they were not eager to make major investments where another agency had equally good jurisdiction. The result has been to delimit an area in which industrial and infrastructural development has been separated from short-range social responsibilities. Venezuelan workers are acutely aware that while skilled work is available in the Guayana, support for those unable to get jobs is small or nonexistent, while it is available elsewhere. If the other agencies of government were not concentrating on the traditionally settled areas of the country the CVG strategy would probably not work.

From the administrative point of view, this strategy also depends upon technological proficiency and the ability to deliver upon the promises of production. The division that the CVG successfully made was that of the production and distribution functions. By stressing technological productive competence and exploiting their physical location, it was possible to retain formal independence. While location has been a factor, the basic appeal to technical proficiency has also been used with some success. Another example is CADAFE, the national agency responsible for generating and distributing electrical power. In contrast, INOS, the water and sanitation agency, is frequently embroiled in controversy over sewers but less so over water, a less expensive and technically simpler matter. Public Works is even more exposed, being responsible for most public construction in the country while employing large numbers of people. Health and Welfare probably receives more criticism than any agency except Education. Self-fulfilling prophecies operate against it, as in the case of hospitals. The poor rarely go there until seriously ill, and often die. That the hospitals are generally crowded and the staff overworked does not help.

Even so, all agencies appeal to "technical" norms. This is, of course, an appeal to the professional standards and achievement norms dear to the heart of any administrative reformer. It tends to be successful in direct relation to the degree in which the agency disassociates itself from people. This is why Education can scarcely expect its appeals to academic standards to lessen materially the political pressure brought to bear upon it. The ministry can hardly dissociate itself from either its actual or its potential students, just as Health and Welfare cannot dissociate itsel from those who die in its hospitals.[6]

The appeal to the "uncultured" or "uneducated" nature of the clientele is itself a bureaucratic ploy, although much less successful than the appeal to technology. It is not likely to be very effective in warding off criticism and outside "interference" in the agencies' affairs when those same agencies are responsible for improving the culture and education of the populace. Generally speaking it is a dangerous tactic capable of boomeranging on the agency, and is consequently used very sparingly. A third strategy is that of concealment. This is also limited by the amount of contact the agency has with people, and has the drawback of reducing the agency's likelihood of increased funding. Potential success depends upon ties with powerful officials willing to defend the agency in private. It was fairly common under Pérez Jiménez but rare during the period of wealth and expansion that followed, and is doubtless becoming common again during the present fiscal crisis.

Finally, the appeal to national need is obvious. Most effective when combined with a reputation for competence, it is nevertheless used by almost all agencies. It has its strongest political appeal in precisely those areas in which bureaucratic action is most difficult, that of "people" problems. Of all these strategies, however, that most frequently used remains the appeal to technology. With the multiplication of autonomous agencies—going from two in the 1950s to more than four hundred by 1984—the appeal to a technical strategy seems more likely to be successful than its alternatives.

REFORMS

Administrative Reform

Criticizing the administrative agencies of the state is almost a national occupation in Venezuela, and there has been much to criticize. The blatant corruption of the Pérez Jiménez years was responsible for the creation of the Public Administration Commission (CAP) and its placement in the presidency. From the outset, it was clear that two quite different aspects of public administration required change. First was the problem of agency inefficiency and corruption. This was difficult, especially given *adeco* policies for development, which required a greatly expanded number of administrators at the same time it had to benefit large numbers of AD supporters (clients). A great push to tighten efficiency and accountability would cut across the political need to hire as many people as possible as soon as possible.

Faced with this reality, a gradual approach to the internal reform of public agencies was adopted. A second need created by the *perezjimenista* years was clearly structural. The dictatorship had spread the money around through many new organizations, which by 1959 were unsupervised, overlapping, and uncoordinated. The development strategy in use had been that of adopting North American practices and trying to re-create them in Venezuela. This problem was both more urgent and easier to attack than was the first. The key was the creation of an office of coordination and planning attached to the presidency (CORDIPLAN), which would provide a framework for allocating resources within the government and in the nation as a whole.

As with most planning agencies, CORDIPLAN was, and is, only one of the elements that the president must consider. Worked into the law, however, was an important procedural requirement: All agencies had to submit their projects to CORDIPLAN and could not legally proceed without its clearance. This not ony gave the CORDIPLAN director power but also provided the president leverage in dealing with the ministries, independent agencies, and the Congress. While CORDIPLAN is hardly all-powerful, depending to a great degree upon a presidential propensity to use it, the agency has proven a force for order and clear thinking.

COPEI governments have given national planning, and therefore CORDIPLAN, far less emphasis than the *adecos*. They have emphasized resource allocation through the National Investment Fund (FIV) and through the eight regions defined by CORDIPLAN. AD governments, employing economic management to a greater degree, have given more importance to controlling the bureaucracy and have used CORDIPLAN to do so. For all governments, the four- and five-year plans developed by CORDIPLAN have served as outlines of their goals and policies. While these plans have been unable to predict accurately either oil income or the speed of policy implementation, they are well reasoned and thoughtful attempts to do so. They have proved to be very important elements in governing Venezuela.

Internal Reform of the Bureaucracy

The Public Administration Committee set up in 1958 quickly contracted with UN and U.S. experts to review the state of public administration and to make recommendations as to reforms. The experts found it unorganized and unprofessional, recommending

Weberian internal reforms to remedy these faults. Jobs within the bureaucracy were to be defined, pay scales refined and generalized, a civil service beyond the reach of "politics" instituted, and the bureaucracy itself made into an impersonal implementing organization prepared to carry out the orders of the political leaders of government.

Such advice was wildly out of touch with the times. This was recognized by the reformers themselves as well as the government. Decreeing civil service protection would have tenured in most of the *perezjimenista* bureaucrats, while breaking the political client/patron ties of of those hired by the new government. The Weberian model tacitly assumes either a stable culture with fundamental agreement upon procedures, or strong coercive forces and other bureaucratic elements unconditionally loyal to the government. Venezuela in the 1960s had neither of these.[7]

Generally speaking the commission spent the 1960s introducing concepts of regular personnel procedures and civil service tenure, providing low-level skill training to those agencies willing to work with them, and serving as a symbol of the government's commitment to efficiency and honesty in government. During the Caldera government the Central Office of Personnel was spun off from the commission, having developed a fairly widespread acceptance throughout the bureaucracy as a useful and positive sort of activity. With the growing trust between COPEI and AD, the public bureaucracy experienced increased stability, even though both parties had large numbers of their supporters in government service.

The change to a COPEI administration with Rafael Caldera brought a new head and *rosca* to the CAP, but did not result in large-scale firings of *adeco* supporters throughout the bureaucracy. The two parties had agreed to live and let live as far as the public services were concerned. This provided for continued patron/client political relationships and for an increase in the personnel office's activities. The bureaucracy was gradually becoming more "professional" but the political element was hardly lost. The commission proceeded in two directions. The new director opted for internal reforms through cooperation with existing government agencies, offering expert advice to those who were interested. Each agency instituted an office of reform (ORCA), but the agency head decided how much it would be used. The second approach was to formulate a reorganization of the entire bureaucracy at the ministerial level and its dispersal to the development regions at the agency level.[8] As might be expected this was not immediately acted upon.

The Pérez government set up a separate reform commission to deal with the state enterprises, which had greatly multiplied under COPEI. It was widely perceived as the tool of private interests and faded into the background, while the original reform commission became a subsection of CORDIPLAN in 1977. Both the ministerial and regional reorganization plans were enacted into law, but the effects upon the administrative apparatus were minimal. The Herrera administration again emphasized state enterprises and the gradual extension of those covered by the career law, although by this time the model had been changed from rank-in-the-job to rank-in-the-man. This was not inconsistent with job classifications and was far more compatible with the reshuffling that occurred with government changes. It is probable that the Lusinchi administration will continue to support both the personnel policies and the planning elements of reform, but there is no indication that drastic reforms within the bureaucracy are either contemplated or any more necessary than for the last 20 years.

CONCLUSIONS

Public administration in Venezuela confronts three broad problems: relations among organizations and with the office of the president; the authority structures and relations within organizations; and the accountability of the bureaucracy. All three can be profitably approached through an examination of the concepts of authority and control. This relation is central to an understanding of bureaucracy, and especially to bureaucracy in a changing society.[9]

When authority is concentrated in one or a few offices, effective control of the actual implementation of policy becomes very difficult. The usual response is to tighten up on regulations and fiscal accountability in order to retain control. Such an effort restricts discretion at the middle and lower levels of the administration and can best be seen as an effort to impose the classical

Weberian model even more strictly upon the bureaucracy. The result, unfortunately, is an even greater concentration of authority and greater lack of real control. This is largely caused by multiple norms held by administrators. While they may believe in the legitimacy of regulations and Weberian norms, bureaucrats also believe in other norms that may contradict their bureaucratic values. The classic example for Latin America is the "*obedezco pero no cumplo*" doctrine of colonial years, an explicit recognition of the legitimacy of the king's authority and his simultaneous lack of actual control.

The concept of span of control is also relevant. It focuses upon the inability of any single executive to control more than a relatively small number of direct subordinates. The reasoning is that as direct subordinates multiply and the executive's time remains finite, he becomes increasingly unable to assimilate the information needed to make correct decisions. In a crisis such a system is capable of generating intense energy and highly successful implementation of specific goals in specific instances. It does so by concentrating the attention of national and organizational executives upon particular projects. The number of critical projects in a nation undergoing the rapid changes that Venezuela is experiencing, however, practically ensures that concentration of attention upon specific projects will occur only under crisis conditions. A crisis mentality will develop, and crisis management become the order of the day.

Such a situation leads to delay and stagnation on the operational level. The retention of authority at the upper levels of the bureaucracy has as its purpose and consequence the absence of authority or operational personnel to deal with situations not foreseen by regulations. On the other hand, the information necessary to adapt the regulations to the changed conditions creates a bottleneck when sent to the top because of the mass of specific detail it contains. Only a few top executives are engaged in making decisions on bureaucratic problems and consequently find themselves immersed in details important to specific cases but not to overall policy. The middle- and lower-level bureaucrats who are aware of this information are denied the authority to decide these small questions of policy as they arise.

In a society with a slower rate of change than Venezuela, the problem would be less acute, for the regulations promulgated at higher levels would be more capable of meeting a situation, and the bottleneck at the top would not be so badly clogged. However, it is unlikely that the pace of development in Venezuela will slow in the near future. Seen in historical perspective, its bureaucracy is confronting problems of rapid development with methods and authority patterns that evolved over hundreds of years in administrations designed for a stable and unchanging culture. They served the Spanish Empire very well but have not functioned in the interests of an independent Venezuela. This has been especially true since the 1930s, when the government explicitly accepted the task of guiding and creating a new Venezuela.

Because of oil revenues the nation has been able to survive and to learn from costly mistakes in implementation that a poorer country could not have afforded. Attempts at structural reorganization have had mixed results. The reshuffling of agencies among the ministries has helped some and hurt others but has not materially changed the basic situation. Regionalization has had a greater impact, not so much in decentralizing bureaucratic authority as in planning and investment. With the increasing congestion, smog, and other urban blights in Caracas, it is possible that resistance to the idea of life in the interior will drop, especially as other cities in Venezuela develop more of the contemporary amenities of life and as television tends to even out the cultural differences. In this case the dispersal of offices from Caracas will be easier to achieve. Such a dispersal is unlikely until the government grows more concerned with maintaining a prosperous society than with creating one. That day continues to recede into the future with the continuing contradiction between a desire for economic self-sufficiency and an oil-exporting source of wealth.

Some Venezuelan governmental organizations are well run and efficiently meet their overt goals. Excellence within the system is possible. On the other hand, Venezuela can ill afford a system of public administration in which only a few agencies are able to deliver effectively the substance of governmental policy. Given the cultural and historical background, it is unlikely that thoroughgoing internal changes will be accomplished any time soon, or that they would be extremely beneficial if they were. The record indicates that motivation for performance is crucial, and that accountability is for most people the primary factor in motivation. Historically, Venezuelan governments have held the bureaucracy more accountable for their latent functions than for overt goals. The result has been inefficiency in achieving overt goals and crisis leadership.

The major effect of the democratic regimes beginning in 1958 has been to render the bureaucracy accountable to at least part of the masses for the implementation of their overt goals. It can be argued that this has been a major motivating force even for the agencies with success in avoiding it, such as the CVG. Their method has been to emphasize their accountability to the norms of technical professionalism, and the resulting achievements have been a major benefit to the nation. If the pressure for performance from the masses was to recede or be rendered ineffective by a more elite political focus, the bureaucracy would in large measure cease to achieve overt goals. It might be argued that pressures from the business community would be sufficient to ensure an adequate degree of implementation, but the weight of history is against it.

A functioning democracy of the sort now existing in Venezuela is the best insurance of continuing improvement in the public administration. While all of the reforms initiated by the government and entrusted to the bureaucracy for implementation are worthy of support and have at least some hope of success, pressure from outside the government is most important. A mass-based democracy based upon the patron/client relationship and a consequent particularistic focus is in many ways inconsistent with universalistic conceptions of justice. In Venezuela, the gap between the real and the ideal has always been large, and the bureaucracy is in the middle. In a time of continuing change the present political system is consistent with both Venezuelan culture and democratic ideals. As such, it is workable, and the public bureaucracy is being positively affected by it.

In the long run the welfare of the Venezuelan people will depend upon how well the contradiction between external dependency and internal welfare is met. Venezuela in 1984 is clearly possessed of more and better infrastructure and industries than in 1958, and the standard of living, public health, education, and other aspects of life for the common people are also very much better. The democratic government of Venezuela has reached these achievements largely through the bureaucracy. It is more practical and useful to measure achievements by what has been accomplished than by what might or should have occurred. By these measures the bureaucracy of Venezuela has been a success, in no small measure precisely because its politicization by the two major parties has provided much of the support needed to maintain a democratic system.

NOTES

1. There is a long report on this problem in *Latin America Regional Reports: Andean Group RA-80-05*, June 20, 1980. These are published by Latin America Newsletters, Ltd., Boundary House, 91-93 Charterhouse Street, London BEC1M6LN, England. Subsequent reports indicate the problem persists despite attempts to control immigration. The regional reports and the *Latin America Weekly Report* are the best English-language sources of ongoing news of Venezuela.

2. *Latin American Weekly Report*, WR 84-06.

3. Linn A. Hammergren, *Development and the Politics of Administrative Reform* (Boulder, Colo.: Westview, 1983), p. 117.

4. The best work on this remains John Duncan Powell's *Political Mobilization of the Venezuelan Peasant* (Cambridge; Mass.: Harvard University Press, 1971).

5. Mark Hanson, "Organization Bureaucracy in Latin America and the Legacy of Spanish Colonialism", *Journal of Inter-American Studies and World Affairs* 16, no. 2 (May 1974): 167.

6. *Latin American Weekly Report*, WR 82-05.

7. *Venezuela: Evaluación de la estrategia para la reforma administrativa del gobierno central* (Washington, D.C.: Departmento de Asuntos Economicos, OAS, 1970). Also see Roderick T. Groves, "Administrative Reform and the Politics of Reform," *Public Administration Review* 12, no. 4 (December 1967): 436-46.

8. Allan-Randolph Brewer-Carías, *Introducción al estudio de la organización administrativa venezolana* (Caracas: Editorial Juridica Venezolana, 1978). Brewer-Carías was head of CAP under Caldera.

9. Bill Stewart, *Change and Bureaucracy: Public Administration in Venezuela*, James Sprunt Studies in History and Political Science (Chapel Hill: University of North Carolina Press, 1978).

Part Three
Policy and Performance

9

Petroleum: The National and International Perspectives

John D. Martz

"At home, Venezuela faces a severe test in the management of the petroleum industry . . . the challenge remains: in the conduct of the oil business, Venezuelan society cannot tolerate inefficiency, corruption, or incompetence. First and foremost, this is a political challenge, a formidable one indeed, for an emerging democratic society."[1] With these words, written shortly after the 1976 nationalization of petroleum, Franklin Tugwell concluded his analysis in the first edition of this volume. During the intervening years, the nationalization model proved capable of providing the industry with administrative skill and technological expertise. However, it was also subjected to increasing politicization. The spirit of selfless nonpartisanship that surrounded the installation and implementation of national control was gradually eroded by the pressures of narrow political interests. When the deep economic reversals of the early 1980s further magnified Venezuelan dependence on petroleum income, the temptation to interfere in the industry proved irresistible.

Certainly the challenge, as Tugwell wrote, is highly political. If the production of oil has provided the wherewithal to fund the reformist programs of post-1958 Venezuelan democracy, it has been deeply affected by the interplay of politics epitomized by democratic pluralism. The dependence of the nation on petroleum has become equally profound and enduring. Since 1917, some 40 billion barrels of oil have been produced, of which 90 percent has been exported. Petroleum stands as the most basic fact of national destiny. And notwithstanding the consensual view of Venezuelan leaders for the past four decades to "sow the petroleum"—*sembrar el petróleo*—the inability to diversify and transform the economy has remained. As the intellectual and essayist Arturo Uslar Pietri has put it, petroleum "presents to Venezuela today the most serious national problems that the nation has known in its history. It is like the minotaur of ancient myths, in the depths of his labyrinth, ravenous and threatening. . . . Petroleum and nothing else is the theme of Venezuela's contemporary history."[2]

FROM CONCESSIONS TO NATIONALIZATION

Origins and Evolution

The principle of state ownership of hydrocarbons originates in the Spanish legal tradition and can be traced back at least to the sixteenth century. When the first Venezuelan petroleum concession was awarded in 1878, the concept of sovereign control was already widely accepted. This continued during the next century while the desire for total authority slowly but inexorably mounted. The institutionalization of a concessionary system proceeded during the 1908–35 dictatorship of Juan Vicente Gómez. Exploration and exploitation increased, with competition between Standard Oil and Shell intensifying in the years after World War I. In 1922 the fabled blowout at the well Los Barrosos-2 began producing some 100,000 barrels per day, and foreign participation was stimulated. Before the close of the decade Venezuela had become the world's leading exporter of petroleum. Six times the hydrocarbons legislation was rewritten, resulting in a liberal approach to petroleum policy. When Gómez died, production was running at some 400,000 barrels per day, with oil generating 25 percent of government income.

During the next decade government administrative control increased while the industry was consolidated, and Venezuela became dependent on petroleum. In 1942 the first income tax incorporated a progressive lien on the profits of oil corporations. The next year a new hydrocarbons law increased taxes, subjected existing concessions to more stringent conditions, and introduced the notion of a 50/50 division of profits between government and industry. Concessions were also converted into new titles running for another 40 years. The 1943 law was an important watermark; it also produced strong criticism, most notably from Acción Democrática and its spokesman Juan Pablo Pérez Alfonzo. When the government was overthrown in October 1945 and AD came to power, a tax of $27 million was decreed to give meaning to the 50/50 formula. While nationalization was explicitly rejected, the government sought to strengthen the control of the state while integrating petroleum policies into national development plans. National dependence on oil continued to grow, approaching 60 percent of the budget by the time the armed forces seized power for themselves in 1948.

During the *perezjimenista* years, the dictator squandered huge sums while accumulating his own personal fortune. New concessions negotiated in 1956 and 1957 brought in an estimated $675 million, and the nation became what AD's Rómulo Betancourt labeled a "petroleum factory." Government income from oil multiplied while the share of the budget approached 70 percent. When democracy was reestablished and Betancourt took office in 1959, Pérez Alfonzo was again the major oil policymaker. He had written during his exile years:

> Venezuela has a great resource in its petroleum, but it is also faced with great responsibility. It must not impede use of this resource to satisfy the needs of other peoples but, in protecting its national interest, it must never let the industry become dilapidated.... Venezuela needs to maintain and even to increase the income it receives from petroleum. With a policy of just participation, the exploitation of present concessions is enough.... [3]

Once in office, the Betancourt government declared its policy to be that of Pérez Alfonzo's "Petroleum Pentagon," which consisted of five basic principles: (1) no more concessions to foreign companies, (2) uncompromising defense of prices, (3) a quest for preferential treatment from the United States, (4) creation of a national oil company, and (5) promotion of an organization of petroleum-exporting countries.[4]

The views of Acción Democrática were shared by COPEI, which agreed that the state was responsible for national development and that petroleum was basic for distributive justice. As junior member of the Betancourt coalition, it supported Pérez Alfonzo in the 1960 creation of a state oil company, the Corporación Venezolana del Petróleo (CVP). The party also favored the founding of the Organization of Petroleum Exporting Countries (OPEC), of which Pérez Alfonzo became the principal architect. More broadly, there was strong domestic agreement over the need to reduce dependence upon petroleum. As President Betancourt put it in 1961:

> We must dispel the happy theory that the oil derricks are producing an inexhaustible quantity of dollars and *bolivares*. The truth is that we are spending the proceeds of unrenewable, perishable wealth, and that we must spend it well, taking advantage of the extraordinary current situation of Venezuela to establish solid and durable bases for the Venezuelan nation.[5]

A similar orientation prevailed during the subsequent administration of Raúl Leoni. When Rafael Caldera and COPEI won the December 1968 elections, the new government soon moved to strengthen further its control of the industry.

The Politics of Nationalization

Rising nationalism was suggested by an August 1971 law that officially nationalized natural gas. Even more significant was the Hydrocarbons Reversion Law. Also adopted in 1971, it stated that all assets belonging to the concessionaires would revert to Venezuela without compensation upon expiration of the contract. Companies were also required to post a bond of some 10 percent of the value of their properties, thus guaranteeing that assets would be maintained in good working condition. National supervision of the industry was further strengthened by adoption of Decree 832, which mandated the regular submission of highly detailed reports to the Ministry of Mines and Hydrocarbons by the oil companies. All of these measures taken under the Caldera government, with strong bipartisan support, meant that by 1972 the petroleum industry was under almost total control of the nation. Both the political climate and economic realities were moving more swiftly toward eventual nationalization of petroleum.

During the 1973 electoral campaign, AD and COPEI candidates treated oil questions prudently. Following his landslide victory, Carlos Andrés Pérez pledged careful studies in preparation for advancing the date of reversion. In his March 12, 1974 inaugural address, Pérez stressed the importance of a broad political consensus:

> It will be the National Congress which says the final word, but not by exercise of a simple parliamentary majority; rather, by decision of the entire nation. . . .
>
> I will proceed to name a broad commission, composed of persons representative of national life, who will advise the Government in the study of alternatives to be examined prior to submission to the consideration of this Sovereign Congress. In this fashion I hope to obtain effectively the cooperation of all Venezuelans in the search for that great national consensus that must be possible for transcendental decisions which we are to adopt.[6]

That consensus over nationalization was already taking shape, spurred on by OPEC pricing and production decisions as well as by the 1983 expiration date for most concessions. Thus it remained for political elites to negotiate the details.[7]

The public debate over the shape of nationalization occupied the nation throughout 1974 and 1975. In addition to rival bills introduced by COPEI and the Movimiento Electoral del Pueblo (MEP) in Congress, there were official pronouncements by such groups as FEDECAMARAS and by Pro-Venezuela for the business community. The newly organized Agrupación de Orientación Petrolera (AGROPET) produced a forum for the expressions of oil industry employees, while public declarations came from other organizations such as the national engineering society. The official report of the Nationalization Commission was delivered to Pérez on December 23, 1974, and provided the base for the government bill that was subsequently forwarded to the legislature in March 1975. The major point of contention centered on Article 5, which foresaw the possibility of operational agreements between the state-owned corporation and private enterprises. The controversial provision read, in part:

> In special cases and when it suits the public interest, the National Executive or the above state entities may, in the exercise of such activities, enter into agreements of association with private entities, but with participation such as will guarantee State control, and for a

limited duration. Such agreements will require prior authorization of Congress meeting in joint session to fix conditions of the contract after having been duly informed by the National Executive as to all pertinent circumstances.[8]

COPEI was among the sharpest critics, arguing that such a provision contradicted Venezuela's nationalist conscience. The MEP and Marxist parties also attacked Article 5, as did the retired Pérez Alfonzo. It was contended basically that the door was being opened to foreign participation and a resultant wave of multi-national interference. The Pérez administration retorted that there were areas in which the industry would need external advice and assistance. Furthermore, no agreements of association or service contracts could be initiated without explicit congressional approval and, in all cases, would be limited to no more than 15 years. The president himself took personal responsibility for inclusion of the article, and resisted opposition efforts to remove it from draft legislation. After some months of argumentation and debate inside the Congress and in other forums, it became evident that legislative consensus would not be possible. Pérez thus brought to bear the Acción Democrática majority in order to secure adoption.

The congressional scenario was drawn to a close by the speeches of the nation's three most prominent statesmen—ex-presidents Betancourt and Caldera, along with AD party president Gonzalo Barrios. Rafael Caldera outlined the accomplishments of his own administration, criticized his successor, and closed with an eloquent call for national unity. Gonzalo Barrios in turn spoke out against partisanship over petroleum policy, minimized the significance of association agreements, and urged prompt passage. Rómulo Betancourt also supported Article 5, contending that agreements would be infrequent, modest in scope, and unfailingly under Venezuelan direction. His final peroration effectively ended the national debate:

> ... All we Venezuelans, including those who in the exercise of their democratic rights now dissent from specific aspects of the Law about to be approved, will lend their efforts to administrative success for the country with its basic source of wealth.
> We are at the point of taking an historic and transcendental step but, as in all other opportunities which have been given to us in

Venezuela, we men and women of this land must act with a high sense of responsibility.[9]

Final congressional approval was voted on August 21, 1975, and Carlos Andrés Pérez signed the Petroleum Industry Nationalization Law four days later.

The major provisions included the formulation of indemnification to concessionaires on the basis of the net book value. In addition, a guaranty fund was to be established, with the companies depositing the usual 10 percent of investments as a means of assuring proper maintenance of assets. A national holding company would be established—Petróleos de Venezuela (PDVSA)—which would provide the umbrella under which the numerous individual companies and subsidiary units would operate. All of this, as President Pérez repeatedly stated, was to be undertaken with a guarantee that the industry would be totally free of political interference. It was to be this pledge which, supported by all political leaders, assured the operational independence of the nationalized industry that was officially proclaimed on New Year's Day of 1976. It was to be the gradual erosion of commitment to nonpoliticization that helped produce the problems of the 1980s.

At the moment of nationalization, however, national consensus and nonpartisan support for the moderate path chosen by the government were evident. Moreover, the national debate had stimulated the bargaining and negotiation that had become a hallmark of Venezuelan post-1958 pluralism. As a Venezuelan oil executive later remarked, the decision to nationalize was far more than a mere pact among political elites. Rather, it stemmed from a participatory process that incorporated labor, business, the middle class, intellectuals, professionals, and the leaders of the petroleum industry itself. It was this national exercise in discussion and dialogue that would ultimately explain "the freedom from criticisms enjoyed by the national oil companies for some years after nationalization and the low degree of partisan politics coming into play when dealing with oil industry issues."[10]

The nationalization model provided that PDVSA, as the national holding company, would own all shares of the 14 operating companies. This included the responsibility for planning, coordination, and supervision of the subsidiaries' activities.

The relationship was the equivalent of that which had existed between former concessionaires and their own foreign-based holding companies. The underlying managerial philosophy was committed to an uninterrupted flow of operations, with organizations held intact, professional management retained, and self-financing assured. This last point, intended further to insulate PDVSA from the political system, was based on retention of 10 percent of the net value of industry exports and offset operating profits. With its founding in January 1976, PDVSA instantly became the eleventh largest non-U.S. corporation in the world, with assets including 12 refineries, 14 tankers, and some 6,000 miles of pipeline.

Beyond the most immediate short-term objective of avoiding any interruption in the industry's operations, PDVSA needed to pursue extensive modernization of equipment and facilities. They had become partially obsolete and required prompt attention. A third pressing need was that of generating new reserves, for the years of policy denying exploration had led to an inevitable decline of proven reserves. All of these were to be sought within the basic context of "democratic management," which constituted the commitment of the political sector to the industry's administrative discretion, technocratic operation, and financial self-sufficiency.[11] By 1976 petroleum continued to account for two-thirds of government revenue, more than 90 percent of export earnings, and at a minimum, one-quarter of gross national product. With Pérez's naming of retired General Rafael Alfonzo Ravard as first PDVSA president, the initial independence of the organization was underlined.

As head of the Corporación Venezolana de Guyana (CVG) for many years, Alfonzo Ravard had built a reputation for administrative professionalism that extended beyond Venezuela. He accepted the appointment with Pérez's commitment to PDVSA independence. Alfonzo Ravard was therefore able to declare at the very outset that PDVSA "has been structured and operates as a commercial company ... which seeks to obtain maximum economic benefit for its sole shareholder, the Venezuelan State."[12] It was this ideal that would be challenged increasingly by political events in the years ahead. First under Carlos Andrés Pérez, and then under the *copeyano* government of Luis Herrera Campins with a vengence, politics and partisanship intruded into the functioning of the state-operated petroleum industry.

PERFORMANCE AND POLITICIZATION

The Pérez Years

The immediate priorities for PDVSA were sufficiently clear at the outset. Exploration was undertaken to increase the 18.5 billion barrels of proven reserves. Refining capacity was gradually expanded and the condition of equipment was improved. Technological skills were regarded as inadequate and, aided by the Instituto Venezolano de Petróleo y Tecnología Petroquímico (INTEVEP), programs were instituted to improve training and educational opportunity. While the role of PDVSA President Alfonzo Ravard was buttressed by a nine-person board of directors, which included technocratic and political appointees, even more crucial was the relationship between PDVSA and the Ministry of Mines and Hydrocarbons. Given the extent to which the latter had become a dominant force in the early 1970s— especially after Decree 832 came into effect—it was evident that a bureaucratic struggle over turf was a potential danger for the industry.

For the Venezuelan managers and technicians who were directing the PDVSA, they viewed their proper responsibility as that of directing and supervising the activities of the nationalized industry. For ministry officials, however, there was a mistrust based on the experience of earlier years; there was a prevalent suspicion that PDVSA held back information and was secretive in its policy deliberations. From the moment of nationalization, then, the relationship was at issue. Minister Valentín Hernández Acosta had early misgivings over the authority that he saw as having devolved upon the industry. In March 1976 he remarked that the ministry must retain responsibility over major policy decisions. Speaking of tax reference values for petroleum, he maintained that "we cannot let Petróleos de Venezuela treat the subject from the purely commercial point of view, without taking into account national policy on prices as well as the commitments Venezuela has accepted in international organizations like OPEC."[13]

An important area that reflected the innate tensions was the development of the Orinoco Tar Belt deposits. Not only were there technical disagreements over ways of developing this vast reservoir of heavy oil; jurisdictional issues were also deeply felt. PDVSA believed itself to possess the knowledge and resources necessary to conduct efficient operations, while the technical staff of the ministry wanted control for itself. Hernández himself believed that PDVSA would be more appropriate, but was understandably pressed by his own staff. The debate reached the pages of the daily press, while partisan spokesmen entered the fray and President Pérez was deluged with mail, memoranda, and policy recommendations. The president ultimately decided the struggle in behalf of PDVSA, and the Orinoco project staffers within the ministry were transferred to the industry. Such an outcome was not always the result of PDVSA-ministry struggles, however.

Throughout the remainder of the Pérez administration, the competition continued, with personal relationships often strained and bureaucratic interactions guarded at best. Valentín Hernández Acosta himself resisted pressures to exert undue authority over PDVSA, largely persuaded of the resources and skills that it could bring to bear. He was also profoundly aware of the dangers of politicization, and wished his government to enjoy unfettered economic benefits from an efficient operation. If his attitude toward Alfonzo Ravard was decidedly less than warm, Hernández was supportive of the industry even when ministerial advisers disagreed. The extent to which PDVSA depended upon the understanding and goodwill of the industry, however, hinted at the organizational and bureaucratic problems that lay close to the surface. In addition, PDVSA was favored by the monthly meetings of Alfonzo Ravard with Carlos Andrés Pérez, at which the minister was not present. This further implied an institutional vulnerability that might emerge under another president and a different minister. This would come to pass in 1979.

Operationally, PDVSA during this period was also engaged in a reorganizational effort that reduced from fourteeen to four the operating companies in Venezuela: LAGOVEN, MARAVEN, MENEVEN, and LLANOVEN. Following a carefully drawn blueprint, the process was set in motion in January 1977. Within two years, the rationalization of the industry had been largely accomplished, and without any operational interruptions. Administrative procedures were systematized, as were financial and personnel measures. This important task had responded to the technocratic and professional skills of the industry. The same was true in the case of the Petrochemical Institute, which for years had been notorious for corruption and mismanagement. First created by Pérez Jiménez in 1954 and located on the property of a close friend, this became a symbol of dictatorial graft and waste.

However, this Moron "complex" fared little better under the democratic system. A former head of the institute later wrote that practices and plans were dominated by political considerations. For example, "We wanted the investments rapidly improved because any delay would mean ... the partial failure of our government program. We had 5 years to prove we were capable, so as to be able to win the next elections."[14] By 1977, losses had reached approximately 4 billion bolivars, and the government turned over control to PDVSA in March 1978. The rechristened PEQUIVEN, rather than contaminating PDVSA, itself benefited from industry control. By the beginning of the next decade, the level of losses had been reduced tenfold, and there were finally prospects for an ultimately productive petrochemical enterprise.

These first years of existence for the nationalized industry were both demanding and exciting. There was a pressing demand for rapid operational expansion in a number of areas, including exploration, refining, and marketing. Goals were raised, which deepened the immediacy of PDVSA responsibilities. The expansion that occurred from 1976 to 1979 was substantial, and its comparative success reflected both administrative skill and organizational discipline on the part of the industry. The long overdue expansion was initiated and carried forward with considerable skill. Total investment in the industry increased from Bs 1,113 million in 1976 to Bs 5,840 million in 1979, while basic operational expenditures for exploration were increased from Bs 132 million to Bs 658 million during the same period. Proven reserves were increased modestly (from 18,288 million to 18,515 million barrels).

The financial performance was generally positive, favored in part by world market conditions. The nation's political leadership continued to rely on the wealth of petroleum for developmental purposes. Government revenue per barrel of exported oil rose from $2.29 in 1973 to $9.45 in early 1975. The Fifth National Plan (1976–80) represented an enormously ambitious effort to move toward balanced modernization. Among its many weaknesses was an unduly optimistic projection of oil income. Mismanagement and poor planning also plagued the Pérez administration, as it had those of his predecessors. While it ultimately spent more funds in its five years than the republic during its entire 143 years of independence, the Pérez administration closed with growth and development more distorted than ever before. Despite the best *carlosandresista* intentions, "The system had not yet extended its economic largesse and natural resources on an equitable basis to large numbers of the population ... the social agenda remained unfulfilled."[15]

The government, originally embarked on huge investments in developmental projects, soon found itself faced with a growing national debt, inflation of some 25 percent, declining productivity, a deterioration of public services, and greater corruption. The drift toward financial chaos was recognized, and the Pérez policy-makers from 1977 sought to cool the overheated economy, to little effect. When COPEI's Luis Herrera Campins was inaugurated president in March 1979, he excoriated his predecessor for having mortgaged the nation. Herrera promised Venezuelans a government of austerity and financial discipline. He undertook a policy of reduced public spending and a series of conservative fiscal and monetary policies. While the outcome remained to be proven, the economic deterioration increased the possibility of greater politicization. At the outset, however, *herrerista* assurances were no less firm than those of earlier ministers and politicians.

The Process of Politicization

When Luis Herrera Campins was elected president, his choice as minister of energy and mines was Humberto Calderón Berti, at age 38 a dynamic professional geologist who had worked in the ministry since January 1973. There was initial approval of his selection as a confidante of Herrera, whose own past career suggested understanding of the industry and of PDVSA ties with the political sector. That the question of interference remained alive could be suggested by AGROPET's public insistence that the administration continue to honor the nonpolitical independence of the industry. The new minister-elect pledged in January 1979 that it would "be kept free of political pressures.... The industry should be managed as a private concern."[16] By midyear, however, the process to select a new PDVSA board of directors provided harbingers of future trouble.

Contrary to earlier practice, Calderón Berti kept secret the names of the new members until the final hours. The choices, which numbered several partisans of COPEI, were nonetheless reasonable in terms of background and experience. More questionable was the change in bylaws that reduced board members' tenure from four years to two. This effectively increased the authority of the minister. At the same time, General Alfonzo Ravard was reappointed. The choice was received with mixed feelings by operational authorities of PDVSA, but suggested continuity. Notwithstanding the institutional stress between the offices of minister and PDVSA president, there were also grounds for mutual accommodation. It came at the time when not only the politically ambitious Calderón Berti but more generally the political sector were casting ever more covetous glances in the direction of the industry.

In addition to predictable complaints from Marxist spokesmen, such figures as Caldera's former minister of energy and mines spoke out in criticism of the nationalized industry. The veritable four-year honeymoon enjoyed by PDVSA was coming to an end as political interests intruded into petroleum. Not only was Calderón Berti seeking a level of personal and institutional control that his predecessor Hernández had eschewed, but party leaders were also becoming more directly concerned. This was dramatically demonstrated in April 1981, when the respected AD president Gonzalo Barrios raised the question of PDVSA extravagances and inefficiencies. His understated concern triggered a wave of partisan statements, most of which were at least implicitly critical of the industry. Among the more vocal critics were influential figures from Acción Democrática, including Pérez's former interior minister, Octavio Lepage, who spurred a drive for congressional hearings.

A congressional inquiry and subsequent debate took place in

May and June 1981. While AD persistently raised questions and doubts, pro-government *copeyanos* displayed hypocrisy in calling for greater ministerial supervision. Herrera issued executive decrees calling for greater PDVSA emphasis on the promotion of socially oriented programs. Calderón Berti himself initially spoke out in defense of the industry, and continued to appear as a champion of PDVSA prerogatives. By the time the furor had run its course, however, the minister could be seen as moving toward politicization. As the public sector—including both the government and its major opposition—displayed growing intentions of exercising its authority, the response of the industry further intensified the debate. The politically deft Alfonzo Ravard had little to say publicly during this particular flurry, but other industry spokesmen were less restrained. The executive vice-president of MENEVEN would write that the industry was unwilling to heed "the warnings of petty politicians, but invited the dialogue or the controversy with the better members of the political world. . . . We believe in our mission. We are well paid, and pilfering is not our business. We are never absent from work, as is often the case with our critics."[17] As he himself conceded, such opinions were scarcely endearing to the political leadership.

In August 1981 there was another manifestation of ministerial ambition. With rumors circulating about the new PDVSA board to be named that month, a major administrative judgment was unexpectedly revealed with the government's decision to relocate MENEVEN and its Caracas offices in Puerto La Cruz in the east. It was a momentous decision and, whatever the merits and drawbacks, had received little serious study by any responsible authorities, including those of MENEVEN. A preeminently political decision that met *herrerista* commitments to party leaders in the *oriente*, this provoked the resignation of prominent company executives while setting the stage for a new wave of politicization with the appointment of the next PDVSA board. The interests of the Herrera administration, along with Calderón Berti's own ambitions, were evident.

When Herrera subsequently announced the names of the new PDVSA board members in September, it was apparent that political elements were anything but dormant. In the first place, General Rafael Alfonzo Ravard was reappointed as president for the 1981–83 years, a move favorable to Calderón Berti's long-term interests. The general was already past retirement age and, many speculated, the naming of the next board in 1983 would then permit outgoing President Herrera to name Calderón Berti himself to PDVSA leadership. In the process, the highest ranking oil executives were being shoved aside; promotion from inside the industry to the presidency would be effectively barred. On the new board, there were reappointments of highly qualified and representative figures, such as the pro-AD Julio César Arreaza and the former *copeyano* cabinet minister Antonio Casas González (under Rafael Caldera). New members, however, were less qualified than their predecessors, while the second vice-president was clearly Calderón Berti's man.

The debate over the issue of politicization was predictably revived. Calderón Berti declared that the Herrera announcement had produced a board that blended experience with new blood. Alfonzo Ravard, whose survival had been at the price of his earlier authority and independence, praised the maintenance of "the objective of keeping the oil industry from being politicized." Among the doubters were the respected journalists Kim Faud and Gerardo Inchausti, the influential pro-COPEI writer Abelardo Raidi, the popular newsweeklies *Zeta* and *Resumen*, and the prominent economic analyst Roberto Bottomo. Such experienced industry executives as MARAVEN president Albert Quirós Corradi and the ousted MENEVEN officer Gustavo Coronel were also publicly disapproving. An analysis in the *Wall Street Journal* summarized the criticisms:

> Petróleos de Venezuela's achievements in the country's highly charged atmosphere have apparently only increased its attractiveness as a political plum to be plucked. So, forgetting the original vow to keep hands off, President Luis Herrera's government has launched a full-scale intervention in the company's affairs. . . .
>
> Mr. Calderón Berti further jolted Petróleos de Venezuela management by naming members of the firm's board of directors who were personally loyal to him. Company insiders say the new members couldn't have met the usual criteria of merit and experience that usually govern who goes on the board. They express fears that Mr. Calderón Berti's action threatens the company's carefully nurtured system of promoting on merit rather than on political credentials.[18]

The threat of yet further politicization also confronted the oil industry fund. From the moment of nationalization, the necessity for self-financing had been buttressed by the provision that PDVSA receive 10 percent of the net value of petroleum exports. By the close of 1981 the fund had grown to nearly $8 billion and offered a tempting source of income for a government increasingly besieged by economic recession. Early the next year Calderón Berti conceded to ranking Acción Democrática figures that financial reserves had declined, but insisted that the administration had no intention of tapping into PDVSA funds. In June, however, Finance Minister Luis Ugueto proposed to AD that petroleum-related investment funds might be employed for the payment of non-oil–related debts. Gonzalo Barrios rejected the proposal, stating that his party believed it would be "highly dangerous for the country to utilize financial resources of the oil industry to cover the waste and inefficiency of government entities in debt."[19] FEDECAMARAS echoed the same sentiment on behalf of the business community.

As the international petroleum market gradually softened during the course of 1982, however, the administration continued to eye the PDVSA fund. Faced by Venezuela's deepest economic crisis in a quarter-century, it was inevitable that Herrera and his advisers would weaken their resolve against politicization of petroleum. It later became known that since March 1982 the cabinet had been seriously contemplating intervening in the petroleum industry reserves. Moreover, both fiscal and personal concerns were motivating the *herrerista* Leopoldo Díaz Bruzual, who had recently moved from the Fondo de Inversiones Venezolanas (FIV) to the presidency of the Banco Central de Venezuela (BCV). His annual report for 1981 had directly charged PDVSA with producing more new employees than new wells. He was also on record publicly as declaring for the petroleum industry that "when employment increases in 50 percent... and salaries are doubled, there is no doubt that the industry is being poorly managed."[20] Such charges received greater attention than the PDVSA rebuttals that followed.

By this time the PDVSA reserve fund was estimated at more than $9 billion. Planning Minister Ricardo Martínez confessed to interest in the possibility of employing PDVSA monies to service the foreign debt. With international reserves having dropped by at least $3 billion and capital continuing to flee the country, the pressures grew. Despite objections from numerous public figures, including Carlos Andrés Pérez, the administration, on September 28, 1982, authorized the BCV to take control of the PDVSA investment fund. The measure was in every sense legal, but in a practical sense violated the understanding between political and petroleum sectors at the time of nationalization. It also marked a personal triumph for Díaz Bruzual—known in the political vernacular as "El Búfalo"—over the politically astute Alfonzo Ravard.

The latter, a veteran of bureaucratic wars, was not totally defeated. He secured that the petroleum industry would retain a fund exclusively for the financing of capital projects. In November 1982 it became known that PDVSA would exercise authority over collections and receivables, as well as free use of income earned through domestic sales. PDVSA was also authorized to acquire foreign exchange for imports or for external obligations otherwise contracted. Even so, the intrusion of the political sector into petroleum management was unmistakable. Alfonzo Ravard conceded in congressional testimony that PDVSA had basically lost control of its investment funds. By this time, the relative health of the Venezuelan oil industry at the close of 1981 had been weakened by a crisis of OPEC unity, the impact of a mild winter in the industrialized nations, and a domestic economic crisis suggested by the rise of the public debt to more than $20 billion. Official reserves of nearly $20 billion at the end of 1981 had dropped in a year to half that amount; oil export prices had fallen from about $29.50 to $25 per barrel at the close of 1982.

This growing political intervention had come at a time when the industry, with traditional fields declining, had turned to development of the Orinoco Tar Belt. In early 1982 PDVSA had estimated that the nation's proven reserves of some 19.6 billion barrels could be increased by another 12 billion, which at existing production rates would meet national needs for nearly 25 years. Refining and marketing strategies also centered increasingly on heavy oil, so that a premature depletion of supplies of light might be avoided. However, the placement of $4.51 billion in PDVSA reserves under BCV control had been damaging to industry plans, especially with the assertive Díaz Bruzual seeking a voice in petroleum industry investment decisions. Among the victims of politicization and of national recession were the industry's plans for growth and expansion.

PDVSA had programmed at a cost of $37 billion from 1983 to 1988 in order to augment refineries, exploration, and existing facilities. By the close of 1982, however, it was announced that the year's $3.5 billion in investments would remain; the retreat was at the level of a $20 billion reduction over five years. The scaling down of earlier plans strongly emphasized the Orinoco deposits; the commitment of about $7 billion for 1983–88 was withdrawn. At the same time, 1982 oil exports dropped by 13 percent. Government targets of 2.2 million barrels produced per day and 1.79 million for export were cut back to 1.6 million for daily export and 2.02 million in total output of crude. In time, even these figures proved unduly optimistic. All of this came at a time when it was estimated that each dollar reduction in the price of a barrel would cost $500 million (2 percent of the national budget), while a 100,000 barrel per day reduction in exports from 1.6 million would cost Venezuela a flat $1 billion.

When Alfonzo Ravard admitted in February 1983 that PDVSA was reviewing the possibility of foreign financing for its investment programs—a total of $4.4 billion that could not otherwise be undertaken—the loss of technical control was evident. This was also apparent as the naming of a new PDVSA board for August 1983 loomed in the foreground. Informed observers had long anticipated the replacement of General Alfonzo by Minister of Energy and Mines Humberto Calderón Berti. Such was the announcement August 31, 1983 by President Herrera Campins. Politicization was rampant. To be sure, it was important to note that the technical abilities of the minister were not in question. However, the politicization of the choice was sufficiently blatant as to be attacked not only by Acción Democrática but also by COPEI's Rafael Caldera, who was seeking a second presidency. In addition, although the new board included such highly competent figures as Antonio Casas González, its composition was such that three-fourths had been named in partisan fashion by an unpopular chief executive would who be leaving office within months. In the meantime, Herrera Campins was engaged in a struggle to cope with an economic recession without parallel during the democratic era; this would further impinge upon the operations of the petroleum industry.

PETROLEUM AND THE ECONOMY

The Broadening Economic Crisis

Luis Herrera Campins had initially received praise for his pledge to cool the overheated economy. Conservative fiscal and monetary policies were adopted, prices were deregulated, and subsidies for consumer goods were largely eliminated. The cost of living swiftly rose, however, and the administration bent before the pressure to decree a general wage increase. Having been elected largely on a platform of administrative order, the president had raised expectations that there would be tangible benefits from petroleum wealth. In the wake of the waste and mismanagement that had grown under Pérez, Herrera was faced with the necessity of delivering on promises of true and equitable modernization. The performance of his government proved unequal to the challenge.

When initial efforts to restructure the economy were frustrated by policy inconsistencies and wrangling among *herrerista* economic advisers, the recession began to set in. The proclamation of the Sixth National Plan (1981–85) was presented to the Congress in August 1981, accompanied by the promise that economic expansion was close at hand. However, the domestic product actually declined by 1.5 percent in 1980. Inflation was 21.6 percent and the debt problem was worsening. By early 1981 some $10 billion in short-term loans had been contracted. Meanwhile, when the Iranian revolution led to dramatic new price increases, the Herrera government forgot its own remonstrances. Within three years he had spent what it took Carlos Andrés Pérez five years to commit. As one Venezuelan commentator declared, "There must be examples of worse fiscal mismanagement than that of Venezuela in the last eight or nine years, but I am not aware of them."[21]

By 1982 the fortunes of the international petroleum economy

had been drastically altered. With an oversupply of oil and a resultant drop of prices, the Venezuelan economy was further buffeted. Although the crisis was deepening, Humberto Calderón Berti insisted hopefully that "by the second half of 1982, we can and we shall see an increase in demand, with an immediate beneficial effect on prices."[22] However, petroleum income had already dropped some 20 percent during the first half of the year. With elections scheduled for 1983, the administration drafted proposed budgets that unrealistically assumed the export level of 1.7 million could be maintained with no decline in price. This ran contrary to mounting evidence that government expenditures could easily outrun the earnings of the industry. Venezuela could not control the course of international petroleum—perhaps only Saudi Arabia enjoyed this capability—and the administration reluctantly faced that fact. This further stimulated the prevailing mood that favored official intervention as a means of propping up the economy.

Industry exploration had increased tenfold over that of prenationalization years; capital investments were nearly $2.8 billion; PDVSA had further projected annual expenditures of $5 billion by the year 2000. Extensive plans for exploitation of the Orinoco Tar Belt had been developed, for these resources con- stituted a crucial element in long-range thinking about Vene- zuelan economic growth and necessary sources of income. Following the government raid on PDVSA reserves in 1982, however, the industry's capacity to finance fully its developmental requirements was thrown into question. Alfonzo Ravard bravely insisted that PDVSA possessed sufficient funds "to invest in our petroleum and to continue making substantial contributions to the country."[23] However, by the close of 1982 the reality, as noted above, was quite different.

Popular support for the government continued to sag. Stag- nating growth rates contrasted sharply to the previous two decades, when the expansion ran from 4 to 8 percent. In July 1982 the president conceded the existence of economic problems by slashing his budget 10 percent. Meanwhile, internal disputes among official economic policymakers encouraged prevailing inconsistencies, with Herrera choosing not to arbitrate the dis- putes. When the price of oil had fallen to $27.50 per barrel, this meant reduced earnings at some $14 billion, while the national plan continued to be based on annual expenditures of $20 billion. Many developmental targets had been predicated on a daily production of 2.2 million barrels; yet official figures had to be progressively revised downward. Petroleum continued to account for more than 90 percent of export earnings. If anything, government dependence on these revenues had increased under Herrera, for 1979 oil had provided 72.2 percent of ordinary revenues and by 1981 the figure had risen to 76 percent. Meanwhile, the foreign debt was nearing $34 billion, more than double the amount inherited from the Pérez government. Since 1980, each year had seen a further deterioration of the nation's economic situation, with 1983 easily the worst.

In addition to the disastrous foreign debt and the fall of the gross domestic product, foreign reserves were in decline. Investment was at a halt, unemployment increased, while the petroleum sector had been increasingly politicized. Luis Herrera Campins experienced few successes on the economic front during his administration. The public perception of his record contributed to extraordinary unpopularity in the opinion polls. Substantial damage was also done to the Caldera campaign in 1983, for AD predictably charged that *herrerista* failures would simply be extended should COPEI retain control of the government. To be sure, grave problems had been a part of the legacy from the previous government. In some senses, the problems were both structural and historic in character.

Judith Ewell is perceptive in her analysis, and merits quotation here. As she views it, both Herrera and Pérez were victims of history:

> They reaped the harvest from the accumulated problems which previous administrators had not been able or willing to solve. Ironically, great wealth strained the system's weak links more than the average revenues of earlier years. . . . Herrera and Pérez had learned to deal with political and ideological dilemmas. Their experience had not prepared them to be efficient managers of complex modern businesses lodged within a complex modern state.[24]

At the same time, it was undeniable that the economic deterioration had come despite income beyond that enjoyed by the preceding administration. Furthermore, the politicization of the petroleum industry, while representative of a broad postnationalization trend, had been basically the handiwork of the Herrera government.

Lusinchi and the Challenge to Democracy

On February 2, 1984, Jaime Lusinchi was sworn in as Venezuela's sixth constitutional president of the democratic era. Having led Acción Democrática to a decisive electoral victory in December, he took office with the nation mired in crisis. Calling for austerity in place of the "Saudi-like avalanche" of wealth and consumerism, he sought to restore confidence and reactivate the national economy. Venezuela, he declared, had suffered from the growth of too easy petroleum riches that had "unchained in our society radical changes, aggravating unhealthy tendencies of waste, squandering, and illicit profiteering." The new chief of state promised to reorder the economy, although not at the price of crippling the drive for development:

> Today's Venezuela is at once the creation and the victim of a well-known phenomenon—the sudden explosion of easy riches. In addition, with the petroleum crisis in world markets, our main income was reduced to such an extreme that it generated a chronic deficit.
>
> Venezuela will pay . . . to the very last cent, but in no way would we accept conditions that would impede the reasonable progress of the country and threaten the people's capacity to resist.[25]

As the new administration took charge, petroleum problems were an obvious source of concern. For Acción Democrática, under whose rule nationalization had been realized, there was a determination to restore adequate independence of action. This in turn would be intended as encouraging more rapid technification and expansion of PDVSA capabilities. The new minister of energy and mines was Arturo Hernández Grisanti, a ranking *adeco* leader and longtime party authority on petroleum. It was further decided that the PDVSA leadership required depoliticization. Barely one week after taking power, Lusinchi replaced the directorate named the previous August by Luis Herrera Campins. The major target was of course Humberto Calderón Berti, whose appointment as president had been bitterly criticized on all sides. Lusinchi replaced him with the president of LAGOVEN, Brígido Natera. A geologist with more than three decades of experience in the Venezuelan industry, Natera was a popular choice with PDVSA officials.

Five other members of the existing board were removed; their replacements came from the industry, with the exception of former FEDECAMARAS president Carlos Vogeler Rincones. This was the first time that such a prominent representative of the empresarial sector joined the directorate. In addition, Natera was replaced as president of the industry's largest operating company by Alberto Quirós Corradi, another longtime veteran of the industry. In balance, the reconstituted board was viewed as highly qualified. Most of those removed by Lusinchi were relocated in other branches of the industry. It was hoped that the drastic measure would strengthen industry leadership while arresting the trend toward politicization.

The action was sharply questioned by the ousted Calderón Berti, who attempted to argue that his removal was in fact the first example of industry politicization. His reaction included a public denunciation in the PDVSA lobby on the day of the action, which was soon followed by a personal attack on one of the new appointees. He questioned the legality of the action, a complaint that COPEI officially if unenthusiastically supported. Hernández Grisanti retorted for the government that PDVSA's legal character as an "anonymous society" permitted the action. It was contended that the politicization had begun under Herrera and was climaxed by the designation of the former minister. On February 1984 the new directors were sworn in by Lusinchi. The *Journal of Commerce* reported that most industry officials—whose professional careers had been largely as employees of the major multinationals prior to 1976—were in agreement with the government perception of the situation. Even more basic, however, was the concern that the recourse to political intervention might be too far advanced to be derailed.[26]

Partisan debate was also provoked by the AD-initiated investigation of Venezuela's joint participation with West Germany's largest industrial corporation. Under the prodding of then-minister Calderón Berti, PDVSA had paid $165 million to the Veba Group for 50 percent control of a Ruhr refinery. It was to refine and market 100,000 bpd of Venezuelan heavy crude; this was expected to produce yearly sales of some $1 billion. The contract was regarded by Calderón Berti as providing Venezuela with a major West European market in which to place its heavy crude. It also constituted a means of acquiring technical assistance through commercial agreements. Critics charged that influence peddling had been involved, questioning the true merit of the terms negotiated. Calderón Berti retorted that the negotiations had originated in 1978 under the Pérez administration. The partisan character of the controversy, whatever the precise details, provided a further indication that politics and petroleum remained tightly intertwined.

When Lusinchi, on February 24, presented his economic recovery program to the nation, it included sharp increases in the domestic price of petroleum derivatives. In addition, the exchange rate at which PDVSA sold its dollars to the Banco Central was devalued from 4.3 to 6 bolivars. It was anticipated that some 9 billion would thereby ameliorate the industry's cash flow problem. The president cheered PDVSA officials in pledging his commitment to a restoration of financial self-sufficiency. The industry's health, he stated, was "a matter of national importance that we should never hesitate to consider an important element of our own security as a state."[27] Within two months, the continuing world preoccupation with the Iranian-Iraqi war had permitted a price rise of some $0.63 per barrel, which would produce an additional $110 million. Some 180,000 daily barrels were to be affected. While Hernández Grisanti shared the view of opposition spokesmen that the impact of the increase on the economy would be limited, it seemed a modestly encouraging development. Before the close of 1984, however, the perspective had again worsened.

Falling prices on the world market, precipitated by the reductions of Britain, Norway, and OPEC member Nigeria, produced a new round of readjustments. At the close of October, in an effort to maintain prices, OPEC lowered production quotas by some 8.5 percent. Venezuela, which had been producing 1.67 million bpd, agreed to cut its output by 120,000 barrels, to 1.55 million. At the $26.74 per barrel price of light crude, this meant a loss of about $200 million. Coming at a time when the debt renegotiations were fragile and Lusinchi's belt-tightening measures were producing resentment, the action was less than welcome. The government sought to remain guardedly positive, however. Finance Minister Manuel Azpúrua assured the country that "we can say with absolute certainty that our oil industry is strong and has the necessary funds to carry out adequately its development."[28]

By early 1985, the Lusinchi administration projected total daily production of crude at 1,840,000 barrels (from a maximum capacity of 2.5 million bpd). It sought an average of $27.04 per barrel of exported oil, which was expected to earn about $14.5 billion for the year.[29] This level of performance was necessary, given the prevailing pattern whereby 97 percent of export earnings and more than 70 percent of government spending were provided by petroleum. PDVSA was beginning to revive a number of small-scale undertakings, including an electricity generating plant and completion of a lubricants plant in Zulia. Development of the Orinoco Tar Belt was also scheduled for new attention, especially as concerns research. In the longer range, by 1988 LAGOVEN was to be producing 30,000 bdp and MENEVEN 100,000 bpd from the Orinoco.[30]

As Venezuela faces the second half of the decade, its economy of course remains linked to petroleum. For better or worse, oil continues to provide the base on which development and modernization rest. Certainly the earnings from black gold provide a necessary if not sufficient element in the progressive solidification of Venezuelan democratic pluralism. Oil has fueled economic change and provided the resources for social reforms, however distorted or inadequate. The state of dependency was and is profound. If democracy has been well served by petroleum, it is uncertain that the obverse can be argued. Certainly the direction of the industry has been professionally and technically sound; the most important progress has been achieved during the democratic years.

Institutional and personal tensions are likely to reassert themselves periodically. In 1985 Brígida Natera will be stepping down from PDVSA leadership while Alberto Quirós Corradi has asked for early retirement from the LAGOVEN presidency. As Jaime Lusinchi seeks further to solidify AD party rule, it cannot be assumed that partisanship will be irrelevant. Meanwhile, the customary awkwardness of the relationship to the ministry itself will remain. While Hernández Grisanti is a veteran politician who has long specialized in petroleum affairs, he is viewed by some industry leaders as unduly sensitive to traditional patterns, to OPEC decisions, and to long-range contracts rather than spot market sales. While these are oversimplifications, they serve to underline once more the inherent problems of control, policy-making, and the sheer struggle for bureaucratic turf.

For those who in recent years have criticized the performance of Venezuela's petroleum industry, the analysis has been flawed. Current economic problems, for instance, are far less the responsibility of PDVSA than of political and economic leaders who have interfered in the industry while mismanaging its earnings. A well-informed observer of Venezuelan affairs has stated eloquently that "oil may have gone to Venezuelan heads, like an addictive drug, but it has also made Venezuela a modern, educated, healthy democratic country—the very qualities and advantages that are needed to face the present crisis."[31] It has doubtless become unrealistic to expect that the industry can operate in pristine isolation from national political reality—and perhaps undesirable as well. At the same time, it is evident that interference for transitory partisan advantage can only hamstring PDVSA, to the detriment of all Venezuelans.

NOTES

1. Franklin Tugwell, "Petroleum Policy and the Political Process," in *Venezuela: The Democratic Experience*, ed. John D. Martz and David J. Myers (New York: Praeger, 1977) pp. 253–54.

2. Arturo Uslar Pietri, *De una a otra Venezuela* (Caracas: Monte Avila, 1972), p. 18.

3. Juan Pablo Pérez Alfonzo, *Petróleo: Jugo de la tierra* (Caracas: Editorial Arte, 1961), pp. 83–84.

4. As cited in Gustavo Coronel, *The Nationalization of the Venezuelan Oil Industry: From Technocratic Success to Political Failure* (Lexington, Mass.: Lexington Books, 1983), p. 26.

5. Rómulo Betancourt, *Dos años de gobierno democrático* (Caracas: Imprenta Nacional, 1961), p. 404.

6. Carlos Andrés Pérez, *Mensaje del presidente* (Caracas: Imprenta Nacional, 1974), unpaginated.

7. For a detailed account of the entire process, see John D. Martz, "Policy-Making and the Quest for Consensus: Nationalizing Venezuelan Petroleum,"

Journal of Interamerican Studies and World Affairs 19, no. 4 (November 1977): 483–509.

8. República de Venezuela, Congreso Nacional, *Proyecto de ley de nacionalización* (Caracas: Imprenta Nacional, 1975), unpaginated.

9. Rómulo Betancourt, *Dueño de petróleo* (Caracas: Centauro Editores, 1976), p. 28.

10. Coronel, *Venezuelan Oil Industry*, p. 73.

11. The phrase is employed by David E. Blank, *Venezuela: Politics in a Petroleum Republic* (Stanford, Calif.: Hoover Institution Press, 1984).

12. As quoted in ibid., chap. 8.

13. *Resumen* (Caracas) March 28, 1976, p. 20.

14. Eduardo Acosta Hermoso, *Petroquímica, desastre o realidad?* (Caracas: n. p., 1977), p. 126.

15. John D. Martz, "The Evolution of Democratic Politics in Venezuela," in *Venezuela at the Polls: The National Elections of 1978* (Washington, D.C.: American Enterprise Institute, 1980), p. 27.

16. "Lo de Hoy," January 31, 1979, cited by Coronel, *Venezuelan Oil Industry*, p. 195.

17. *El Universal*, April 19, 1981.

18. *Wall Street Journal*, February 16, 1982.

19. *El Nacional*, June 15, 1982.

20. *Resumen*, January 3, 1982, p. 17.

21. Carlos Rangel, "How Venezuelans Twice Squandered Their Oil Wealth," *Miami Herald*, March 20, 1983.

22. *El Universal*, February 26, 1982.

23. *Latin American Times*, November 1982, p. 13.

24. Judith Ewell, *Venezuela: A Century of Change* (Stanford, Calif.: Stanford University Press, 1984), p. 219.

25. The inaugural address appeared in the Caracas press on February 3, 1984. Also see the review of recent and current national developments in John D. Martz, "The Crisis of Venezuelan Democracy," Current History (February 1984): 73–78, 89.

26. *Journal of Commerce*, February 22, 1984.

27. The text appeared in the Caracas press on February 25, 1984.

28. *Latin American Weekly Report*, November 9, 1984, p. 5.

29. *Journal of Commerce*, November 13, 1984.

30. *Latin America Andean Report*, Decemer 14, 1984, p. 3.

31. Rangel, "How Venezuelans Twice Squandered Their Oil Wealth." For an earlier treatment that stresses Venezuelan policymaking patterns and traditions, see John D. Martz, "Development and Democracy in Venezuela: Politics and the Management of Petroleum," in *Politics, Policies and Economic Development in Latin America*, ed. Robert Wesson (Stanford, Calif.: Hoover Institution Press, 1985), pp. 161–88. A comparison of agriculture with petroleum is John D. Martz, "The Frailties of Venezuela Policymaking," in *Politics and Public Policy in Latin America*, ed. Steven W. Hughes and Kenneth J. Mijeski (Boulder, Colo.: Westview Press, 1984), pp. 100–17.

10

Petroleum: The Community and Regional Perspectives

David E. Blank

Venezuela's management of its vital petroleum industry since the nationalization of 1976 has been an exception to the general trend of politicization and ineptitude in the planning and implementation of state corporate activity. The basic reason for the success of Venezuela's evolving democratic management of oil has been simply that, with oil responsible for 70 percent of government revenue and more than 90 percent of the nation's foreign exchange earnings, there has been no room for error and failure.

At first glance, the oil industry appears much too big for Venezuela to handle, especially if we are talking about democratic oversight. Yet a nation that has experienced difficulties in collecting garbage in its cities, educating its young, and caring properly for its sick has successfully managed its nationalized oil industry. This chapter examines the territorial dimensions of oil management in democratic Venezuela; it emphasizes the region-alization of the operating subsidiaries of Petroleos de Venezuela S.A. (PDVSA) and efforts to integrate their operations into local community life.

Given the unprofitability of most of Venezuela's public corporations, and the political leadership's awareness of Mexico's inability to manage its consolidated, state-owned oil company, PEMEX, Venezuelans wisely opted to maintain their oil industry as fragmented and competitive operations.[1] The 14 separate foreign-owned companies, however, proved too fragmented for efficient production. Building upon the three existing major foreign affiliates and a small national oil company, these 14 nationalized companies were merged into the "Four Sisters" in 1978.[2] Their structure can be seen in Figure 10.1.

The persistence of four competitive "sisters" as the operational subsidiaries of PDVSA has been a critical operational characteristic of democracy's control over oil. John Martz's chapter analyzes the national and international dimensions of democratic management; in contrast, this chapter focuses on the impact of the oil industry within the local community. By way of introducing the key actors in the regionalization and integration into the local community of petroleum associated activities, attention focuses initially on the four sisters:

LAGOVEN: The "big American" sister, which was essentially Exxon's Creole Petroleum subsidiary; it accounted for 40 percent of national production in 1976. LAGOVEN's first president (1976–83), Guillermo Rodríguez Eraso, had been with Creole Petroleum since 1945. Alberto Quiros Corradi became LAGOVEN's president in 1983.

MARAVEN: The "European" or "British" sister was essentially Shell of Venezuela. MARAVEN's president in the 1976–83 period was Alberto Quiros Corradi, the youngest Shell subsidiary president prior to nationalization. Quiros Corradi remained with MARAVEN despite attractive offers from Shell International. In 1983, Carlos E. Castillo became MARAVEN's president.

MENEVEN: Although the product of a merger between four former foreign companies, MENEVEN's primary historical legacy was that of the former Gulf Oil's Venezuelan subsidiary, Mene Grande Oil. Its president between 1979 and 1983 was Juan Chacin Guzmán, a close relative of Jaime Lusinchi. As Gulf's Mene Grande, MENEVEN had earned a reputation for "trying harder" and as the "other American sister."

CORPOVEN: Six second-order former foreign firms were combined with the small state company, Venezuelan Oil Corporation (CVP), to form CORPOVEN. The president of the former Mobil operations in Venezuela, Frank Alcock, has served as CORPOVEN president. CORPOVEN initially had to craft a mature identity; it continues as the "kid sister." CORPOVEN has become the advocate of investing in light rather than heavy oil production.

FIGURE 10.1. The Structure of Petroleos de Venezuela and its Affiliates

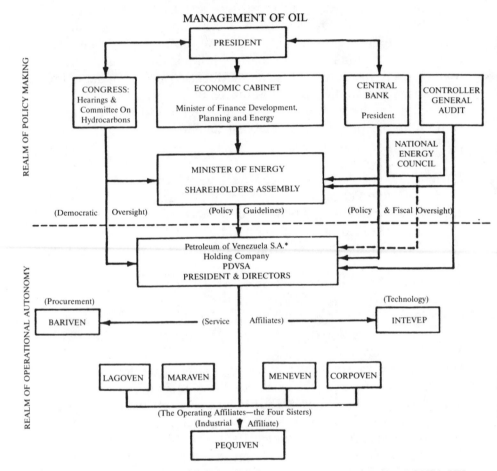

SCHEMATIC CHART OF DEMOCRATIC

MANAGEMENT OF OIL

*The international affiliates—POVSA-USA (New York), POVSA-UK (London), and BARIVEN-USA (Houston)—are not included in the schematic chart. There is also PETROLATIN created in 1982 by POVSA, Mexico's PEMEX, and Brazil's PETROBRAS.

Source: Prepared by author.

There are two principal regional settings for the territorial and community integration politics of oil. Only one of the two has a convenient acronym—the new Orinoco heavy oil belt, the Faja Petrolífera del Orinoco (FAPO). The original territorial definition of FAPO encompassed three states in eastern Venezuela: Guárico, Anzoátegui, and Monagas; all told, it covered 55,000 square kilometers. While mature light oil fields have existed along the northern perimeter of FAPO (Anzoátegui and Monagas), most of the FAPO area is virgin territory and represents a potential heavy oil venture for PDVSA (see Map 10.1).

The territorial actors interacting with FAPO are the states of Anzoátegui and Monagas and the State Regional Development Corporation for the Northeast, CORPORIENTE, which covers both Monagas and Anzoátegui, as well as the "oil-poor" state of Sucre. Also located in eastern Venezuela, immediately south of the FAPO area and the Orinoco River, is an area under the jurisdiction of the Venezuelan Guayana Corporation (CVG). The CVG is Venezuela's first and most important regional development corporation, dating back to 1960,[3] and it has definite territorial and economic stakes in FAPO.

The Lake Maracaibo region, first tapped in 1914, remains Venezuela's principal oil-producing area, accounting for approximately 75 percent of total national production. The Lake Maracaibo oil fields are located entirely within the state of Zulia, which boasted more than 11 percent of the nation's population in 1981. The indigenous "lake people" who dwelt on protected platforms in the shallow waters of Lake Maracaibo gave Venezuela ("little Venice") its name.

The state of Zulia is a powerful regional actor. In response to the above-mentioned creation of the CVG, Zulia demanded and in 1969 secured legislation creating CORPOZULIA (Zulia Development Corporation). The Zulia bloc in the Congress joined with that from the Andes region to push through CORPOZULIA and CORPOANDES (Andean Development Corporation). While Venezuela has been blanketed since 1969 with regional development corporations, CORPOZULIA has focused its attention on the increasingly unrealistic project of a second major steel complex (the first being in Guayana) on the western shore of Lake Maracaibo.

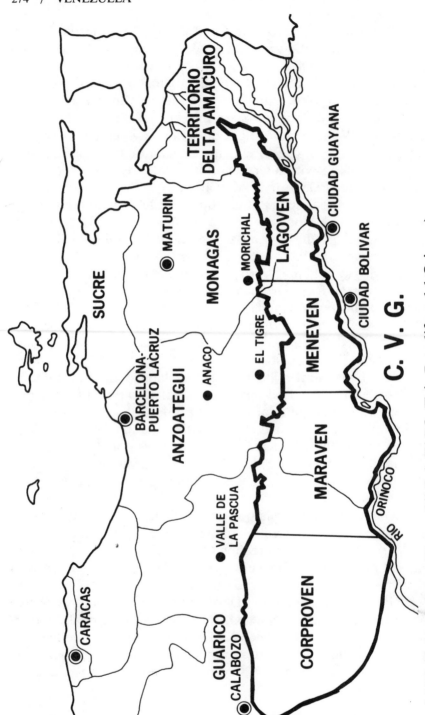

MAP 10.1. Orinoco Heavy Oil Belt FAPO (Faja Petrolífera del Orinoco)

Most of Lake Maracaibo's oil has been extracted from fields on the eastern shore of the lake (see Map 10.2). Even the construction of a major bridge crossing Lake Maracaibo in the 1960s has not tied together the competing cultures on the two shores of the lake. East coast communities seem as resentful of the city of Maracaibo on the western shore of the lake as they are of Caracas. Residents of these communities express their sense of frustration in the remark: "As soon as one makes a few cents, one moves from the east coast of the City of Maracaibo; as soon as one makes a few dollars, one moves from Maracaibo to Caracas."

In 1980, east coast residents acted to overcome both the benign neglect of CORPOZULIA and the accompanying fear and fury that they were about to be totally overlooked by the rest of Venezuela as momentum shifted eastward to develop the Orinoco's heavy oil (FAPO). East coast residents organized to push Caracas for the creation of their own regional corporation. In response, a new actor entered regional politics, COLM (East Coast of Lake Maracaibo Communities).

By definition, a key political actor on the regional stage would need strong ties to some component of the populist-style electoral system. Elsewhere I have written of the regional fault line separating the two pillars of Venezuela's political establishment, AD and COPEI.[4] The electoral base and the home turf of the leadership of the latter is western. Historically, COPEI has been protective of Zulia and the Lake Maracaibo oil fields. Thus, when David Myers analyzed the 1967–68 COPEI electoral strategy in Zulia, he pointed out that the Maracaibo-Lagunillas-Cabimas urban complex "provided President Caldera's margin of victory"; subsequently, COPEI invested disproportionately in greater Maracaibo.[5]

Taking advantage of the 1967 electoral division of AD into two parties, the Caldera administration developed a city and industrial activity for the east coast of Lake Maracaibo (COLM), the Alta Gracia or El Tablazo project.[6] When the El Tablazo petrochemical plant became infamous for its mismanagement, the accompanying urban redevelopment project never got off the ground.

The creation of CORPOZULIA in 1969 must also be seen as part of COPEI's "western electoral strategy." COPEI leaders, such as Rafael Caldera, Luis Herrera Campins, and Hilarión Cardozo,

MAP 10.2. East Coast Lake Maracaibo COLM (Sub-Region Costa Oriental del Largo)

are western born and sympathetic to the region's development. Cardozo served as governor of Zulia under Caldera; his state party organization was credited with Hererra Campins's smashing 1978 electoral victory. CORPOZULIA's longtime president, Fernando Chumaceiro (1969–84), was also identified with COPEI.

AD leaders, on the other hand, have an eastern predisposition. One contemporary expression of historical regionalism in Venezuela came with the 1960 decision to push the development of the southeastern frontier, the resource-rich Guayana region. The mechanism created for this purpose was the CVG. That in the 1960s the sparsely populated Guayana region received 10 percent of total government investment and a planned new city, Ciudad Guayana, stirred resentment in the western states. Nevertheless, when in power AD has continued to favor the east. Given the eastern origin of the party's leadership this is hardly surprising. Leopoldo Sucre Figarella, now president of the CVG, former president Raúl Leoni, and Luis Piñerua Ordaz, AD's 1978 presidential candidate, all came from eastern states. The incumbent Jaime Lusinchi was himself born in oil-rich Anzoátegui.

It is accurate to suggest as did Myers that COPEI administrations have lessened public investment in the Guayana region and emphasized projects in Zulia and the Andean region. The administration of Luis Herrera Campins did hope that the "boom" associated with its 1980 decision to push the MENEVEN and LAGOVEN pilot projects in Anzoátegui and Monagas states would help COPEI's 1983 electoral chances in the east. This proved to be an illusion. Also, declining oil prices caused the Orinoco (FAPO) oil boom to collapse early 1983; COPEI received fewer votes in the region than it had in 1978.

An ideological cleavage along a left-right continuum was reflected in the plans and policies of the major institutional actors. By the term left, the writer mean an ideological position that

1. Attacks an alleged overindependence on foreign transnational oil corporations and their technology in exploiting FAPO or in redeveloping the Lake Maracaibo field; it favors using home-generated or co-generated technology.

2. Attacks the concept of individual and self-contained oil development, especially when implemented in the form of megaprojects with their "megabucks" import requirements, and favors imposing an integrated and comprehensive regional development on PDVSA and its subsidiaries, which seeks social change as well as growth.
3. Attacks the "technocratic" style of planning in which the engineer managers of PDVSA decide public policy by calculating costs and benefits of resource development; leftists favor a style of planning in which those with both functional interests and territorial stakes are encouraged to participate in planning their future.

The Center for the Study of Development (CENDES) of the Central University of Venezuela, an important leftist think tank, has played a critical but episodic role in the politics of regionalizing oil. The orienting ideology at CENDES originated with Luis Lander, a former AD planning minister who split from AD with MEP in 1967. Younger scholars directing CENDES include José Agustín Silva Michelena and Heinz Sontag, who are identified with the Eurocommunist MAS. There is also a group of nonacademic oil experts who are often lumped together as left wing critics of PDVSA. In public statements on the oil industry they identify themselves as members of the consultative National Energy Council (CEN). The CEN has yet to meet as a formal body, but association with it gives one's pronouncements a sense of legitimacy within the left.

Aníbal Martínez, a political independent, is a prime example.[7] He has been an outspoken opponent of "rushing" to develop FAPO. Martínez argues that Venezuela would more efficiently expand its proven oil reserves by introducing enhanced recovery techniques in the traditional Lake Maracaibo fields. Other important leftist critics include Radames Larrazábal of the minuscule Venezuelan Communist party (PCV), Francisco Mieres of MAS, and Alvaro Silva Calderón of MEP.

BLENDING OIL AND NATION

The unfolding of the politics of regionalizing oil has occurred on three levels. The first is the national debate over whether

Venezuela should rush ahead at full throttle to develop Orinoco heavy oil (FAPO) and over the prospective administrative decentralization of the four sisters. The second level is the struggle for dominance among the PDVSA subsidiaries for oil reserves. At the third level is the integration of the former oil camps into their host communities.

Lake Maracaibo Recovery versus Orinoco Heavy Oil Development

In 1976, when the oil industry was formally nationalized, President Carlos Andrés Pérez made two basic decisions: to go at "full throttle" in developing the Orinoco heavy oil belt (FAPO) and to give the newly created PDVSA rather than the Ministry of Mines operational control over the project.[8] The reason for the first decision was the fact that behind the bravado of having successfully nationalized its oil industry was a fear that without heavy Orinoco crude the nation would exhaust its proven oil reserves in as little as 15 years. Venezuela was also acutely aware that the industrial plant it had inherited from 14 separate oil companies had run down and increasingly was obsolete. Between 1959 and 1975, the response of foreign oil companies to increasing Venezuelan pressures for additional petroleum revenues and control over the industry had been to disinvest and to minimize preventive maintenance in their local plants.

Venezuela wisely opted to secure a "friendly nationalization," supposedly with all winners and no losers. This was intended to secure a continuing flow of technological innovations and of marketing assistance from petroleum's former owners, the transnationals; the Venezuelan government also offered lucrative service contracts and favorable technology transfer agreements. Speeding development of the exotic extra heavy crudes of the Orinoco, especially given the established price tag of approximately $25 billion, appeared one means of securing the future friendly cooperation of the key transnationals—Exxon, Gulf, and Shell. In 1976, most experts mistakenly predicted that the oil deficit would continue indefinitely, and therefore saw the Orinoco as a secure and critical western hemisphere alternative to the volatile Middle East.

A key strategy for guaranteeing the success of Venezuela's nationalized oil industry was to secure maximum operational autonomy for PDVSA in running the industry, along with financial autonomy regarding its prospective investments. Consequently, the highly prestigious retired General Rafael Alfonzo Ravard, Venezuela's leading technocrat, was named as PDVSA's first president.

Alfonzo Ravard came from one of Venezuela's wealthiest and most distinguished families. He earned graduate engineering degrees from the Massachusetts Institute of Technology and for over a generation managed regional development in Guayana. He was the moving force behind President Betancourt's decision to create the CVG, and served as its president from 1960 to 1975. In this capacity he earned the reputation as being a tough, no-nonsense administrator who insisted that partisan politics be kept out of personnel decisions and policymaking. He was charged by President Pérez to run PDVSA in a similar manner.

General Alfonzo Ravard was not universally admired. Ministry of Mines senior staff, joined by leftist oil experts associated with the National Energy Council (CEN), insisted in early 1976 that the ministry, and not PDVSA, should be made responsible for planning and overseeing the development of heavy crude projects in the Orinoco. The issue principally dividing the "political" ministry from the more "technocratic" PDVSA was whether or not the technology inputs and financial costs in developing FAPO required high participation by multinationals or whether it could be done without foreign participation.[9] The left and the Ministry of Mines staff argued "that giving control of the Orinoco project to PDVSA was tantamount to handing it over to the multinationals."[10]

Alfonzo Ravard and PDVSA, with considerable support from the indigenous business sector, argued that FAPO was simply one more project within the (oil) sector. They pointed out that MENEVEN and LAGOVEN already had operations nearby in Anzoátegui (MENEVEN at San Tomé and El Tigre) and in Monagas (LAGOVEN at Morichal and Jobo).[11] Given that the nature of PDVSA's relationship with the operating companies (LAGOVEN, MENEVEN, and CORPOVEN) was yet to be determined, and since the primary concern of Venezuela was to ensure the efficient and profitable management of the industry in the aftermath of nationalization, President Pérez's choice to go with the technocrats appears almost preordained. In this context it is important to note that the four sisters acted in the 1976–78 period as autonomous affiliates rather than submissive subsidiaries. The implication was that the two "American sisters," LAGOVEN and MENEVEN, were to be in charge of the Orinoco; only loose PDVSA coordination would oversee their decisions.

MENEVEN, which as Gulf's Mene Grande had operated in the east since the 1930s, had active light crude operations in the Anaco and El Tigre areas of Anzoátegui State and a refinery in the port city of Puerto La Cruz. MENEVEN was assigned a pilot project to blend its existing light oil with heavy crude from the neighboring Orinoco belt. This project was to use onboard and proven technology. Designated as GUANIPA 100+, it sought to produce approximately 100,000 barrels per day of blended oil by the turn of the century.

LAGOVEN, which as Exxon's CREOLE managed producing fields in Monagas State, won the megaproject pilot assignment. The 1980 budget estimated expenditures of U.S. \$7 billion for the five-year LAGOVEN effort, which would produce a truly synthetic oil from the extra heavy Orinoco Crude. This gigantic undertaking, called DSMA (Development of South Monagas and Anzoátegui), projected construction of a high-technology upgrading facility and a new planned city to house an estimated 18,000 workers and their families. True to its tradition as the "big American sister," LAGOVEN turned to the Bechtel Engineer Group and allied U.S. firms to manage the DSMA project.

MARAVEN, the "British" sister was both apprehensive and furious at the prospect of being frozen out of FAPO. MARAVEN feared that, if confined to its traditional Lake Maracaibo fields, it might exhaust its proven reserves in ten years and become extinct. It was furious because, as Shell's Venezuelan subsidiary, it had the most extensive experience with heavy oil; its M-6 continuous stream injection project in Lagunillas (COLM) was already proving more feasible than initially anticipated.[12]

The president of MARAVEN (1976-83), Alberto Quiros Corradi, unlike the other operating company presidents, opted not to practice the policy of a low public profile and of maintaining all PDVSA disputes as quiet in-house rivalries. Quiros Corradi devised a two-pronged MARAVEN strategy. It built on

MARAVEN's already strong position in both Zulia and the Falcon state oil refineries and had as its primary goal to make MARAVEN the dominant "western" sister. By identifying itself with the west and the redevelopment of Lake Maracaibo oil production, MARAVEN sought to block MENEVEN and LAGOVEN from using their FAPO projects to gain control of PETROVEN. MARAVEN's second strategy was to orchestrate mass and elite opinion to gain a FAPO project. Therefore, winning over the hearts and minds of Zulia was the first step. The second involved gaining support for a concession in the ZUATA assignment of FAPO.

MARAVEN's Quiros Corradi and Venezuela's articulate left found themselves in an alliance of convenience to challenge the initial dominance of LAGOVEN in the anticipated development of Orinoco heavy oil. Francisco Mieres of MAS protrayed the LAGOVEN-FAPO megaproject as a prime example of what he labeled the "denationalization" or "transnationalization" of Venezuela's oil; in other words, while Venezuela would own the problems and risks, Exxon and the CIA would control the oil.[13] Mieres, however, emphasized that the MARAVEN-left coalition was only circumstantial, for Quiros Corradi was "orchestrating presentation of the Shell-MARAVEN plan merely to exploit its assigned area of the Orinoco Belt"(FAPO) in competition with Exxon and Gulf. In contrast, the left alone was presumably championing a "go-slow" nationalist policy.[14]

MARAVEN opted to go public in its orchestrated effort to gain a pilot project in FAPO because it correctly concluded that it stood little chance of winning a private in-house dispute with LAGOVEN. General Alfonzo Ravard was not an experienced oil man, and with one exception he had not personally known the top managers of the "four sisters." He had confidence in the objectivity only of Guillermo Rodriguez Eraso, a longtime friend and member of his social circle. In particular, the general seemed to have problems with the outspoken and extroverted Alberto Quiros of MARAVEN.[15] Alfonzo Ravard was sufficiently autocratic and private to have a low level of tolerance for the aggressive, sometimes abrasive, manner of Quiros. MARAVEN clearly needed public allies to win.

LAGOVEN followed the general PDVSA policy of focusing

on resource problems and resolving them by rational calculations. It was uncomfortable with people problems and their complex political entanglements. Therefore LAGOVEN was willing to cede dominance to its smaller sister in dealing with the complicated urban redevelopment issues on the east coast of Lake Maracaibo.

MARAVEN and Lake Maracaibo

The three interrelated components of the policy of prolonging the life of the Lake Maracaibo area oil fields were (1) the introduction of advanced recovery techniques that presented real and present dangers to adjacent residential areas and their ecology; (2) the redevelopment of existing COLM communities, including the relocation of a sizable population from cities located directly above recoverable oil reserves; and (3) the ecological restoration of the waters of Lake Maracaibo. The magnitude of associated people problems was far greater in the west than in the east. Whereas the entire 55,000 square kilometers of FAPO may have contained at most 35,000 people in 1980, the total population of COLM's communities exceeded 500,000.

LAGOVEN, because of its technocratic orientation, gladly conceded to MARAVEN coordinating responsibility of COLM; this included planning for the possible relocation of 50,000 people and the construction of a new city, El Menito. As the "big sister," however, LAGOVEN insisted on preserving an operational Western Division, even though its Lake Maracaibo production fields were reduced to one, Tía Juana. LAGOVEN has also retained its separate representation, along with MARAVEN, on the Inter-Enterprise Committee for the Conservation of Lake Maracaibo (COIC). LAGOVEN executives apparently see cleaning up lake pollution and preventing new contamination as a resource question, not one that is people-intensive.

The urban redevelopment plans of the COLM ran into problems associated with partisan politics. The 1978 elections in Zulia proved disastrous for AD; COPEI's Luis Herrera defeated AD's presidential candidate Luis Piñerúa Ordaz 52.1 to 40.0 percent. In the legislative ballot AD's vote was reduced to 37.2

percent, while that of MEP (the group that split from AD in 1967) was 4.5 percent. In the key east coast district of Bolívar, which before 1978 included both the cities of Cabimas and Lagunillas, MEP's legislative vote was 14.7 percent.[16] In the local political infighting that followed district council elections in 1979, the dynamic self-proclaimed MEP leader, José Bauza González, became president of the Municipal Council of Bolívar District. Thus, a politician not belonging to one of the two establishment parties exercised authority in a district that traditionally produced about half of Venezuela's wealth.

Rather than deal for five years (the term of office of a district council) with a politician they could not control, AD and COPEI agree to divide the Bolívar District; they hoped to diffuse opposition by playing to the rivalry between the communities of Lagunillas and Cabimas. The truncated Bolívar District remained the most important of the three petroleum-rich COLM districts; the other two were Baralt (the city of Bachaquero) and Lagunillas. In spite of the division of Bolívar, its political style remained truculent. This, along with the refusal of LAGOVEN to deal with human resource problems, resulted in a breakdown in communications between LAGOVEN and the Bolivar District Council government. Consequently, trapped inside its own sterile technocratic planning group, LAGOVEN ploughed ahead with plans for the territory and recovery of oil around Lake Maracaibo. These centered around the use of advanced steam injection techniques, and would have caused real but avoidable pain in terms of family and business dislocations.

Taking up the banner of western urban-community redevelopment coordination allowed MARAVEN to play the role of the sister most interested in people problems. Under this banner MARAVEN forged its community relations and regional coalition-building strategies. These were employed in its effort to gain an ORINOCO (FAPO) pilot project. MARAVEN began by agreeing to cooperate with the Bolívar District council; that council boasted one of Venezuela's most professional urban planning offices (OMPUs). Together MARAVEN and the council prepared a joint district council-public enterprise "Plan of Territorial Organization" for the east coast of Lake Maracaibo in

1979.[17] This plan solicited inputs from all eastern district councils, especially Bolívar, Baralt, and Lagunillas; the local labor unions, especially FEDEPETROL locals (AD-controlled Federation of Petroleum Workers); and two grass-roots business groups, the Chamber of Industry and Commerce of the Bolívar District (CAICOB) and the Association of Commerce and Industry of Lagunillas (CACIL). The resultant plan was presented as the product of an ample "democratic dialogue." It established and delimited urban areas that either would have been subject to excessive flooding or adversely affected by advanced oil recovery techniques that used alternating or continuous steam injection. The implication of this plan was that the public sector had responsibilities to individuals and firms in the affected areas, responsibilities that only MARAVEN was prepared to assume.

Even with the plan's analysis of the consequences of steam injection, the merchants and small industrialists of ACIL were convinced only with great difficulty that the move to a new planned city, El Menito, would be necessary. Efforts to gain their acquiescence stressed that this was the only way to extend the productive life of the east coast of Lake Maracaibo oil fields. However, in 1984, with OPEC production reduced to nearly half of what it had been in 1980, fewer inhabitants in the east coast districts of Lake Maracaibo were marked for relocation. This was partly because less steam injection would be needed to recover smaller quantities of petroleum over the coming years. Also, while dangers persist, new advances in safety controls have made the tertiary recovery of oil more compatible with urban living.

On the basis of lobbying from both CAICOB and ACIL, those residents of the Bolívar and Lagunillas districts who will have to move will be relocated to safer parts of existing communities, and not in a new town some 20 kilometers away. In order to make the relocation areas livable, MARAVEN joined with all the COLM communities in 1983 to create PRODUZCA (Promotion of Zulian Urban Development). PRODUZCA is charged with building adequate sewer systems, street pavement, parks (in the endangered areas), and schools. It brings new hope for a better quality of life in an area that has given Venezuela 75 percent of its export wealth over the past half-century.[18]

MARAVEN versus MENEVEN in Anzoátegui

In 1982 the Ministry of Energy decided to move MENEVEN's headquarters to Puerto La Cruz. This followed a three-way swap of MENEVEN's Lagunillas oil fields to MARAVEN for the ANACO oil fields formerly assigned to CORPOVEN. When these exchanges were completed, early in 1983, MENEVEN settled down to become the oil company of the east. The economic austerity of the 1983-85 years had little impact on MENEVEN. Its project to blend heavy and light oils, Guanipa 100+, was allowed to proceed without significant cutbacks.

MARAVEN's new president, Carlos E. Castillo, remained resolute in his drive to secure a FAPO pilot project. His key economic argument rested on MARAVEN's exploratory work in its assigned Zuate area. Zuate appears to contain the best quality and quantity of FAPO's reserves, and the M-6 continuous steam injection technology used by MARAVEN in Zuate also seems suitable to securing a profitable recovery of Anzoátegui heavy oil. However, MARAVEN's exploratory operations in the Orinoco, at least by MENEVEN, were perceived as temporary. MARAVEN's original field operations were housed in a "quest" arrangement in the El Tigre-San Tomé MENEVEN camp; what oil MARAVEN produced was to be stored or pumped in MENEVEN facilities. MARAVEN sources insist that, from the beginning, MENEVEN both spied on it and undercut its FAPO legitimacy. Consequently, MARAVEN quietly negotiated the removal of its field headquarters to Pariaguan, a community of approximately 10,000 inhabitants, some 80 kilometers from El Tigre, MENEVEN's FAPO field base.

As a newcomer to FAPO, MARAVEN was unencumbered by past mistakes. While MENEVEN was saddled with the difficult task of liquidating its closed oil camps and integrating their inhabitants into existing communities, MARAVEN was free to reinforce the growth already underway in Pariaguan. MARAVEN built an open suburb, separated from the existing community only by a park and school, both of which MARAVEN financed.

MARAVEN also moved to ingratiate itself with the economically strained and declining agriculture and livestock interests in the area. Burdened by competition from cheap imported food and by the boom caused by the original flurry of construction associated with the first push to FAPO, many people had abandoned farming for the well-paid oil industry jobs. The boom came to a halt in 1983, and many began to consider returning to agriculture. MARAVEN, through the Foundation for Serving the Farmer (FUSAGRI), opted to provide credit and technical assistance for returning small farmers. One experimental program still in operation seeks to utilize the rich soil of the Orinoco floodplain to restore the area's self-sufficiency in foodstuffs. MARAVEN, drawing upon its ties to the worldwide experience of Shell, also has introduced an Australian system that uses the roofs of public buildings to collect clean rainwater in arid areas.

San Diego de Cabrutica is a small rural community of 2,000, located amidst one of the world's largest heavy oil reserves. It is the site of a MARAVEN experiment that seeks to integrate the community into some dimensions of corporate decision making. The Chicago-based Institute of Cultural Affairs (ICA), with 30 years' experience in participatory problem solving and community development, was contracted in 1984 by MARAVEN to initiate the cooperative consciousness raising of San Diego.[19] This writer attended one all-night session and came away impressed with the growing ability of the local population to make focused criticism of MARAVEN and its operations. The company may yet decide to slow the pace of consciousness raising of its area's residents; however, its strategy is gaining grass-roots support for MARAVEN.

Mapire is another small community in MARAVEN's zone of operations. It is also a small port and market town along the Orinoco River. MARAVEN's community development division has funded improved docks and roadway construction in the Mapire area. It also plans to assist with the reintroduction of cotton cultivation. Again, MARAVEN appears as the "sister" most interested in people problems.

Pariaguan, San Diego de Cabrutica, and Mapire are examples of MARAVEN's attempts to forge a strong grass-roots coalition favoring its continued presence in the east. In order to gain national attention for its community development programs, Alberto Quiros approached CENDES. His initial overture came in 1979, prior to the formal FAPO concessionary assignments. Quiros

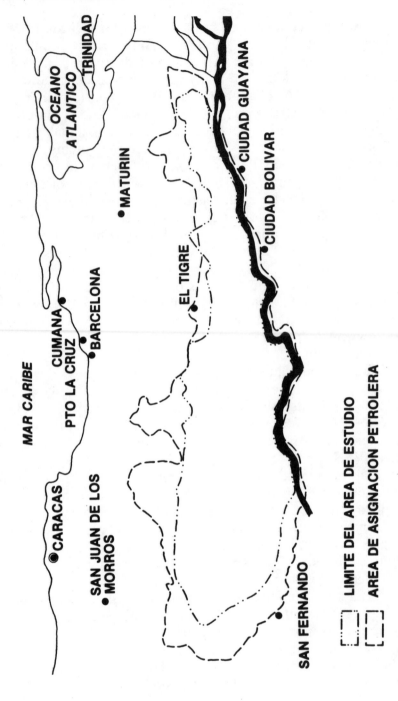

MAP 10.3. Area of CENDES/MARAVEN Study (FAPO)

offered to finance a Prediagnostic Study of the Master Territorial Organization Plan for the Orinoco Heavy Oil Area.[20] This study, published in late 1979, became the basis for attacking the resource-oriented approach of LAGOVEN. The CENDES "reply," covering the area portrayed in map 10.3, received considerable attention in *El Diario de Caracas* and in the newsweekly *Resumen*.[21]

CENDES sought to demonstrate that an integrated regional development approach was superior to one that focused exclusively on isolated, oil industry megaprojects. It implicitly criticized LAGOVEN's almost Pavlovian reliance on Exxon's preferred engineering firms, especially the Bechtel Engineering Group. The CENDES "reply" became an important factor in President Herrera's decision to cancel the Bechtel contract. CENDES pointed out that through Bechtel LAGOVEN was proposing to build a new town near the Monagas community of El Temblador. This so-called "secret oil city" of 30,000 was located about a 90-minute drive from Ciudad Guayana. Ciudad Guayana in 1980 had at least 10,000 vacant apartments.[22] Also, the "secret" nature of the LAGOVEN-Bechtel city led to rumors of a potential CIA takeover of Venezuela's vital Orinoco heavy oil area.

Behind the public polemic and the planning dialogue over the best way to develop FAPO lay MARAVEN's orchestration of its campaign to be included along with the "American sisters." MARAVEN, using the good offices of CORPORIENTE, financed two additional CENDES studies dealing with the area of south Anzoátegui it was disputing with MENEVEN. With great detail these studies focused on the importance of revitalizing local agriculture. They strongly advocated freeing the small farmers from opportunistic middlemen and controlling land speculation. This was seen as a precondition for rational urban growth in FAPO.[23] One interesting fallout of these studies was the uncovering of a land speculation scandal in the MENEVEN-dominated community of El Tigre. It led to the arrest and detention in 1984 of the former president of the bankrupt Banco de los Trabajadores de Venezuela (BTV).

MENEVEN, the veteran operating affiliate in the east, found itself saddled with the liabilities of integrating the closed and fenced-in former oil camps with their surrounding communities and of dealing with the costly prerogatives and privileges accrued over the years by its unionized labor force. In addition, the initial negative reaction of MENEVEN executives to the minister of mines' decision to move its entire headquarters operations to Puerto La Cruz soured relations between MENEVEN and its new headquarters community. While former MENEVEN Vice-President Gustavo Coronel has written with poignancy of the political reasons for that decision, and while the readers of his account in the February 16, 1982 *Wall Street Journal* may have felt sympathy, the good citizens of Puerto La Cruz were insulted.[24] Apparently one key reason that President Herrera imposed the move was COPEI's hope of gaining electoral support in both the city of Puerto La Cruz and the state of Anzoátegui. Nevertheless, considerations relating to the 1983 election did not negate the logic of decentralization. MENEVEN sources, on the other hand, hinted that some COPEI leaders and friends had invested heavily in Puerto La Cruz real estate, and that the real reason for the move was to guarantee profits for their speculative investments.

In contrast to MENEVEN, and with help from CENDES, MARAVEN has pursued a people-oriented approach in order to build grass-roots support in Anzoátegui. MENEVEN, like LAGOVEN, maintains a more aloof project efficiency approach. MENEVEN has offered to build a sewer system for Puerto La Cruz and El Tigre. However, it resists proposals to freeze new construction in its oil camps. Neither MENEVEN nor any government agency has yet developed a comprehensive policy for closing out Venezuela's historic oil company towns. The original plan, to give the senior worker-residents the dwelling they occupied as part of the retirement settlement, has engendered so much jealousy among younger workers as to be an important source of social discord. Also, many of the older workers opted for instant windfall profits and sold their homes to businessmen. The government thus found itself in the position of having to deal a second time with these individuals' needs.

With regard to the oil camp commissaries, a long history of collective bargaining agreements has made them sacred cows—a major obstacle to integrating oil camp and host community. The 1983 collective bargaining agreement signed between PDVSA and its affiliates on one hand and the two oil workers' unions FEDEPETROL (Federation of Petroleum Workers) and FETRAHIDROCARBUROS (Federation of Workers in the Hydrocarbons Industry) on the other included a list of 76 items of primary necessity. These continue to be sold at oil camp commissaries at fixed prices. Black beans, a staple of the Venezuelan diet, were extremely scarce in 1984; they had to be imported by PDVSA in order to meet its collective bargaining agreement. The lifestyle associated with commissary privileges, not surprisingly, continues to be a source of great resentment among non-PDVSA workers.

Regionalizing the operating affiliates of PDVSA and imposing a policy of open communities instead of closed oil camps have forced Venezuela's most efficient economic corporation, PDVSA, to confront the reality of Venezuela's most parochial and corrupt political entity, the provincial district council. One response of PDVSA and of the national political party system has been to upgrade the political and administrative capabilities of the oil-affected district councils. In many cases AD and COPEI have jointly imposed unusually qualified candidates. This facilitated a purging of the old cliques that had dominated local politics over the past 25 years. The beneficiaries were dynamic young businessmen and professionals who had previously shunned local politics.

In 1984 LAGOVEN's president, Alberto Quiros Corradi, signed an agreement with the Institute for the Advanced Study of Administration (IESA) in Caracas. IESA agreed to oversee an upgrading of the administrative capabilities of the three Monagas state municipalities that regularly interact with LAGOVEN.[25] By the end of 1984, IESA was asked immediately to expand its program to the MARAVEN and MENEVEN associated FAPO municipalities. There is now the possibility that the FAPO municipalities will grow in a reasonably harmonious manner, avoiding the boom-and-bust episodes associated with past resource development.

CORPOVEN: Confront Colombia and Not One's Big Sister

CORPOVEN is the newest and smallest "kid sister." Its genesis lies in the difficult merger of the small state oil company, the Venezuelan Petroleum Corporation (CVP), with several small foreign operations. The merger of these distinct corporate cultures began in 1978; while this was in progress, CORPOVEN wisely avoided battles over turf with its big sisters.

Without a firm corporate identity and lacking the powerful resources of a distant former transnational "mother," CORP-OVEN opted to specialize in an area that its big sisters ignored in their drive to dominate heavy oil—the search for new light oil reserves. CORPOVEN's focus on light oil exploration, and the growing geopolitical concerns Venezuela was having in the west, offered the opportunity to confront Colombia along the border rather than the sisters in the east. While not totally relinquishing its exploratory activities in FAPO, CORPOVEN has concentrated its attention along the west coast of Lake Maracaibo, an area close to the turbulent Colombian frontier, and in the Arauca River valley separating Colombia from Venezuela. Both CORPOVEN and the Colombian State oil enterprise have recently announced significant finds of new light oil reserves in the Arauca area.[26]

CORPOVEN takes great pride in having secured the Arauca Valley for Venezuela. There is now a dramatic Venezuelan presence in the southern part of Apure State. CORPOVEN's community integration policy parallels that of MARAVEN in the south of Anzoátegui; it seeks to reinforce existing local communities by creating "open" suburbs and good schools rather than constructing isolated and fenced-in compounds. In the Arauca Valley, CORPOVEN has also lobbied for an increased Venezuelan military presence along the frontier with Colombia.

CONCLUSION

During the years of the petroleum bonanza (1973-81), windfall oil profits enabled Venezuela to postpone addressing the problems associated with making progress toward the goals of social justice and economic productivity. Failure to manage the petrobonanza meant that Venezuela neither achieved social justice nor improved productivity with its huge oil profits. In this context the warning of Juan Pablo Pérez Alfonzo, the father of OPEC, is relevant. He warned his fellow countrymen that Venezuela could "as easily die from over-eating as from starvation." Severe constraints placed on the state's fiscal capacity since 1982 have forced Venezuela to face a new challenge, that of austerity and the need to work hard.

The awesome separation that existed between millions of average citizens of the *país nacional* and the luxurious lifestyle of the 100,000 employed in the privileged *país petrolero* was certain to undermine any serious effort at economic revitalization on the basis of hard work alone. Ending the economic isolation of those living on the oil economy from the rest of the national economy, and breaking down the fences that separated and segregated the "oil camps" from their host communities, may prove to be an important factor in stimulating economic recovery.

The regionalization of the oil affiliates is advancing alongside the standardization of wages for petroleum and nonpetroleum workers. In addition, in 1981, PDVSA issued a "Buy Venezuelan, Hire Venezuelan" decree. The oil industry will no longer be allowed to function as a benign foreign-oriented Gulliver bearing the gifts of income and technology to a nation of backward Lilliputians. The nationalized oil industry is to become a principal instrument for the nation's comprehensive development, not just a source of its revenues.

The MARAVEN versus MENEVEN and LAGOVEN dispute in FAPO between 1979 and 1982 led to the politicization of the Orinoco project. Broad policy statements by politicians seeking social justice and nationalism replaced the controlled press releases of PDVSA technicians. In the urbanized COLM, the Ministry of Urban Affairs was given coordinating powers. In FAPO, the Ministry of Environmental Affairs won the right to coordinate and plan comprehensively. The PDVSA had been reduced to a respected and crucial public enterprise; it was no longer a territorial technocracy.

In planning for FAPO, the Ministry of Environmental Affairs focused on the unity of the region, not on the tasks delegated to individual corporations. In 1982, in response to grass-roots pressures, the boundaries of FAPO were changed to include the entire area of all districts that would be affected by heavy crude development, expanding FAPO's size to 82,000 square kilometers.[27] The only reason the FAPO area was not joined with that of CVG in a joint Orinoco River Basin development was that Andean and Zulian interests feared competition from such an all-encompassing entity.

In summary, the politics of regionalizing PDVSA is converting this powerful public enterprise not only into a good citizen of Venezuela but also into a good citizen of the communities in which it does business. Eventually, when the affiliates are administratively decentralized, they may also provide, through the extension of local taxation, added income for the increasingly important district council governments.

NOTES

1. There is a good brief discussion on the history of state oil enterprises in Gustavo Coronel, *The Nationalization of the Venezuelan Oil Industry from Technocratic Success to Political Failure* (Lexington, Mass.: Heath, 1983), pp. 237–56.

2. See David E. Blank, *Venezuela: Politics in a Petroleum Republic* (New York: Praeger, 1984).

3. Lloyd Rodwin, ed., *Planning Urban Growth and Regional Development: The Experience of the Guayana Program of Venezuela* (Cambridge, Mass.: MIT Press, 1969).

4. David E. Blank, "The Regional Dimension of Venezuelan Politics," in *Venezuela-at-the-Polls: The Elections of 1978*, ed. Howard Penniman (Washington, D.C.: American Enterprise Institute, 1980).

5. David J. Myers, "Caracas: The Politics of Intensifying Primacy," in *Latin American Urban Research*, vol. 6, ed. Wayne Cornelius (Beverly Hills, Calif.: Saga Publications, 1978), p. 245.

6. See Alan Turner, "New Towns in the Development World: Three Case Studies," in *International Urban Growth Policies: New Town Contributions*, ed. Gideon Golany (New York: Wiley-Interscience, 1978), and Alan Turner and Jonathan Smulian, "New Cities in Venezuela," in *Town Planning Review* (Liverpool, U.K.) 42, no. 1 (1971): pp. 3–27.

7. *Washington Post*, "Heavy Oil Project Sparks Controversy in Venezuela" and "Petroleum Flows in Orinoco Valley Like Blackstrap Molasses in January," January 27, 1980.

8. Coronel, *Nationalization of the Venezuelan Oil Industry*, pp. 113–15.

9. Ibid. p. 113.

10. Ibid. p. 115

11. Ibid.

12. Ibid., p. 90.

13. Francisco Mieres, "La desnacionalización de la industria petrolera venezolana" in *Petróleo y ecodesarrollo en Venezuela*, comp. Dorathea Mezger (Caracas: ILDIS, 1981), pp. 77–79.

14. Francisco Mieres, "El papel del petróleo venezolana en la perspectiva de la crisis energética," in *Petróleo y Venezuela*, coord. Marcos Kaplan (Mexico City: Universidad Autonona de México, Edeforeal Nueva Imagen, 1981), p. 256.

15. Coronel, *The Nationalization of the Venezuelan Oil Industry*, p. 80.

16. República de Venezuela, Consejo Supremo Electoral (CSE), *Resultados electorales 1978*, Tomo III, Zulia.

17. Ministerio del Desarrollo Urbano (Mindur) Consejo Municipal del Distrito Bolívar Estado Zulia, *Plan de ordenación territorial de la costa oriental de Lago de Maracaibo*, February 1979, 4 vols.

18. MARAVEN, *Resumen de actividades, 1982* (Caracas: MARAVEN, 1983), pp. 34–35.

19. The Institute of Cultural Affairs (ICA) is a less provocative offshoot of the Saul Alinsky approach to community organization. While Alinsky's disciples sense the need for a conflict situation in order to spark popular conscious raising, that of the ICA focuses on less provocative participatory community problem solving. For more information on the ICA write to its Chicago address: 4750 North Sheridan Road, Chicago, IL 60640, telephone (312) 769-5635.

20. Universidad Central de Venezuela-CENDES (Centro de Estudios Del Desarrollo), *Estudio de prediagnóstico para el plan maestro de ordenamiento territorial del área de la Faja Petrolífera del Orinoco* (1976).

21. "El Estudio del CENDES Sigue Engavetado," *El Diario de Caracas*, November 23, 1979.

22. Blank, "The Regional Dimension of Venezuelan Politics."

23. CENDES-MARAVEN-CORPORIENTE, *"Estudio del impacto socioeconomico en el area Zuata"* (1983), and *"Investigación subsistema regional sur Anzoátegui* (July 1982) (Both mimeo.).

24. "Conflict at Venezuela's Oil Company," *Wall Street Journal*, February 16, 1982.

25. Instituto de Estudios Superiores de Administración, *Projecto de desarrollo gerencial para concejos municipales venezolanes* (Caracas, June 1984).

26. See "De bojoven a CORPOVEN," in *Numero*, October 3, 1982.

27. Ministerio del Ambiente y de Los Recursos Naturales Renovables, *Esquema de ordenamiento territorial de la Faja Petrolífera del Orinoco* (Caracas, June 1982).

11

Educational Policy

Steven Ellner

One of the outstanding achievements of post-1958 Venezuelan democracy has been to incorporate large numbers of Venezuelans into the education system at all levels. The existence of an educated public, in turn, has served to fortify the nation's democracy, permitting it to attain a degree of stability and multidimensional participation that was not possible in previous eras, when the large majority of Venezuelans were illiterate.

In addition to the natural compatibility between education and democracy, a number of specific societal characteristics have shaped education policy since the early 1970s. Unlike Venezuela's neighbor, Colombia, where political apathy has prevailed, Venezuela's two main establishment parties, Democratic Action (AD) and the Social Christians (COPEI), represent mass bases that are easily mobilized and highly participative. Pressure from below channeled through political parties influenced how Presidents Pérez and Herrera spent the windfall in government revenue that followed the 1973 OPEC oil price hikes. The money has not gone exclusively to ambitious infrastructural and industrial projects, as some developmentalists would have preferred, nor has it been absorbed mainly by the privileged sectors and well-placed individuals—the flagrant cases of administrative corruption notwithstanding. Much of the money has been funneled into programs of general welfare. This is reflected by the increase in the overall education budget, which after 1973 kept pace with increases in general government expenditures.

Similarly, allocations within education also have been highly sensitive to popular pressure. The universities have been most favored, since it is in the area of higher education in which the clamor has been the greatest and growth most difficult to control. The response of government authorities and planners to this dilemma has been a two-pronged strategy of restructuring the system of higher learning and renovating the elementary and secondary schools. Renovation seeks to channel youth into nonuniversity pursuits, thus holding in check the university population. Nevertheless, this approach has confronted important obstacles, the most outstanding of which is the persistence of young Venezuelans in demanding the "right" to a university education. The government and university administrators frequently have yielded to these pressures by increasing outlays in order to allow the universities to accommodate more students and retain those of low academic standing. This has been at the expense of support for research, library facilities and laboratories. Appeasement rather than repression has been the rule during the last ten years. It explains the relative tranquility that prevailed on campus in contrast to the turbulance of the violence-ridden 1960s.

NEW GOALS AND TENDENCIES

The keystone of government education policy throughout the ten years following the overthrow of Pérez Jiménez in 1958 was expansion of the system, without major regard for quality. The AD government viewed this approach as part of the democratic process because it incorporated the popular classes. Upon assuming power in 1969, the COPEI government criticized previous policy for subordinating qualitative to quantitative objectives. During his first year and a half in office, President Caldera issued 15 decrees to renovate education, particularly at the secondary level.

Throughout the next decade, however, quantitative indexes remained a major area of concern. The government attempted to expand preschool education beyond middle- and upper-income groups, an objective embodied in the 1980 education law that made attendance obligatory for all children of eligible age. As

TABLE 11.1. Student Enrollment at Different Levels of the Venezuelan Education System, 1969–81

Education level	1969–70	1970–71	1971–72	1972–73	1973–74	1974–75
Preschool	44,463	50,159	71,853	86,247	93,113	152,266
Elementary[a]	1,781,102	1,874,410	1,938,879	1,996,961	2,024,148	2,113,004
Secondary[a]	437,458	498,346	561,919	633,179	694,432	761,186
Adult literacy	16,482	20,419	13,787	12,477	8,437	10,680
Higher education[b]	70,816	85,675	95,294	115,462	159,269	193,264
Universities	66,218	80,598	88,505	107,541	145,462	165,238
Autonomous[c]	54,419	60,753	70,762	88,598	116,706	139,501
Experimental[c]	7,063	6,952	10,244	12,000	13,396	7,611
Private	4,736	12,293	7,499	6,943	15,360	18,126
Institutes and university colleges	4,598	5,077	6,921	13,807	28,024	36,063

[a]Following the 1979–80 academic year, government statistics were based on the "Basic and Diversified" school populations.

[b]Due to diversity of sources, statistics under subheadings do not always exactly add up.

[c]After 1973, UDO is considered an autonomous university.

Sources: Boletín Estadístico, OPSU-CNU (May 1982); *Seperta Estadística*, OPSU-CNU (August 1980); *Memoria y Cuenta*, Ministerio de Educación (1981–82).

Table 11.1 indicates, the 937 percent increase between 1969 and 1981 in the number of preschool children outstripped that of other educational levels. The rate of illiteracy for those over 15 years of age declined from 37 percent in 1960 to 24 percent in 1970 and to 16 percent in 1980. The AD government, which took office in February 1984, has promised to reduce it still further. On the other hand, the mere 44 percent increase in the elementary school population between 1969 and 1980 is clearly unsatisfactory. It means that nearly half of all youth fail to go beyond the sixth grade. Most of those who left primary schools were dropouts, with the highest percentage withdrawing in the first year. An estimated 10 percent were children from rural areas and barrios who were never incorporated into the system in the first place. The problem is likely to become more serious since the 1980 education law raises the level of mandatory education to the ninth grade. In so doing it adds three years to what traditionally had been the last year of obligatory schooling for more than a century.

1975-76	1976-77	1977-78	1978-79	1979-80	1980-81	1981-82	Percentage Increase (1969-70 to 1981-82)
224,600	284,957	329,019	328,927	344,287	421,183	461,017	937%
2,228,042	2,329,552	2,435,858	2,492,564	2,567,849	—	—	—
828,495	906,955	939,187	979,505	1,012,759	—	—	—
11,871	9,906	26,250	46,162	36,662	15,845	28,652	74%
221,581	247,518	865,671	282,074	298,884	307,998	330,986	367%
185,518	202,422	218,392	320,719	238,601	244,636	259,453	292%
155,163	164,436	159,910	175,030	177,735	186,751	195,333	259%
10,992	20,501	39,289	35,499	34,178	35,178	35,877	408%
19,363	17,476	19,193	20,190	24,649	25,754	28,243	496%
—	45,096	47,279	51,355	60,283	63,362	71,533	14,557%

Government policy after 1969 attempted to confront the problem of massification of the university population by channeling youth into alternative areas of education. The Fifth National Plan (1976–80) intended to stabilize enrollment in the government-supported universities while increasing attendance in alternative types of higher learning institutes and the private universities. Government concern stemmed from the fact that the public university student population, after having increased by about 350 percent in the 1950s and again in the 1960s, continued to climb at an equal pace into the mid-1970s (see Table 11.1). The ratio of university students to the overall population in Venezuela exceeded that in many developed nations. Exploding university enrollments diverted money from other levels of education. The outlay for higher education, 22 percent of the education budget in 1961, reached 40 percent by the late 1970s, a figure that also was quite high by Latin American standards.

In spite of these expenditures, Venezuelan universities have not been able to accommodate all interested youth. While in the 1960s the unfortunate high school graduate was one who was assigned to study a major that was not his first choice, in the 1970s he had to wait up to three years to be admitted. The existence of large numbers of these "waiting for space students" represented a grave political problem, especially since the nation's constitution of 1961 guaranteed all youth the right to a free university education. At the beginning of almost every semester the *pre-inscritos* on different campuses went on hunger strikes and occupied buildings, in some cases holding university officials hostage.

Policymakers were also disturbed by the fact that while an inordinate number of high school students chose university track programs, the country faced a scarcity of competent nonuniversity-trained technicians. Consequently, they designed structural modifications to make technical fields more attractive. They also introduced vocational courses in the grade school curriculum in hopes that students would gravitate toward technical fields at an early age, rather than select a liberal arts or general science program that entailed a university education.

This strategy encountered cultural and economic obstacles. The government hoped that individual guidance and orientation in the secondary schools would override ingrained prejudices about the prestige of a university degree. Efforts were made to design job-relevant technical courses and confer distinction on technical careers. However, the nation's wage structure, which heavily favors the professional over the technical career, is an economic reality beyond the scope of government action.

A similar strategy of orienting educating toward the nation's productive needs prevailed in the universities. The Office of Planning of the University Sector (OPSU) was created in 1970 to analyze job market trends. OPSU planners hoped to demonstrate the desirability of work in other than the traditionally prestigious areas of medicine, law, and civil engineering. Advocates of this approach deemphasized study of the humanities and attempted to reorient the social sciences toward business administration, public corporate management, and industrial relations, all of which had a direct application in the business world. While a large number of junior colleges were established to train "advanced technicians," university curricula and programs were modified to lay greater stress on subjects directly related to careers. On the political front, COPEI—rhetoric notwithstanding—abandoned its traditional emphasis on the humanistic objectives of education policy and accepted the technical-productivity approach. In doing so, COPEI adopted the orientation in education matters of its main rival, AD.[1]

The career-oriented strategy of decision makers was denounced by some educators and student leaders as "technocratic." Exponents of the liberal arts philosophy maintained that education was part of the process of citizen formation. Opposition to the "technocratic" approach also came from a well-known economist and a recently arrived German sociologist. Their book, *Universidad, dependencia y revolución*,[2] became the bible of those university activists who looked for inspiration to the May 1968 movement in France. According to the authors, the objective of university education in Venezuela was to impart an understanding of Venezuela's condition as a dependent nation, a thesis that implied some concentration on social science courses. Other radicals argued that the emphasis on technical skills and specialization was part of a new international division of labor imposed by the multinationals whereby third world nations increased their industrial capacity while maintaining ties of dependency.

Another area of debate centered around whether it was more important to provide greater opportunities for the underprivileged at all levels or for a reduced group of the most advanced students regardless of their class backgrounds. Those who favored the first approach argued that the democratization commitment of the 1960s initially mandated an opening up of the education system to the underprivileged; subsequently it entailed upgrading their education in order to compensate for natural disadvantages.

One such disadvantage was the system of selection for admission into the state universities based on four different criteria. Although consideration was made for low-income background, by far the most important factor was grades, which penalized the poorer students in the public schools with their more exacting grading policies. It was also argued that the budgetary priorities in favor of the universities represented an indirect subsidy for middle- and upper-income groups, which were disproportionately represented at that level. A strategy of increasing attendance of underprivileged students at higher levels implied diverse policies, including granting scholarships to the poor, upgrading public grade schools, and eliminating exclusionary practices in the universities that weed out mostly students of low-income backgrounds. Gains for youth from the popular classes, it was argued, would translate into the promotion of social equality; in turn, this would fortify the democratic system.

The opposing view held that Venezuela's economic development depends on the training of selected managers and other specialized personnel who know how to select and develop the technology that best suits Venezuelan needs. Due to the paramount importance of this task, elite recruitment must be on the basis of ability alone. Proponents of this position, not surprisingly, opposed using family income as a criterion for selecting students to study abroad in the ambitious and costly Gran Mariscal de Ayacucho Scholarship Plan. In addition, they emphasized the importance of upgrading Venezuelan graduate programs, as well as providing greater support for such top ranking institutions as the Simón Bolívar University (USB). Projections of trends in the nation's human resources reinforced their position by suggesting that there would soon be surpluses in almost all professional fields. This led them to consider that the meeting of critical needs revolved not so much around increasing the number of graduates in priority areas as in improving the quality of those who did graduate.[3]

In short, the government's emphasis on qualitative gains and vocational education after 1969 produced public debate regarding objectives and priorities. One approach prioritized expenditures for disadvantaged students at all levels but especially in the preschool and elementary schools; a second position emphasized support for the most promising students regardless of class background. Critics of education policy in the 1970s deplored the greater emphasis on career selection and preparation on grounds that it detracted from the goal of character formation and failed to instill in the student a proclivity to think for himself.

STRUCTURAL CHANGES AND REFORMS

In the 1970s, the revision of government priorities in the field of education set off a competition for resources among emerging subsystems. At the lower level, preschool units lobbied to establish a separate identity and to avoid being absorbed by the grade schools' administrative apparatus both in the Ministry of Education and in private schools. Many argued that education from preschool to ninth grade should receive the highest priority because those years provided a leveling experience for the underprivileged and transmitted knowledge necessary for all citizens in a democracy. Graduate programs also expanded during these years and received support from those who argued that education should lead to advanced specialization. This attitude was reflected in the Ayacucho Scholarship Plan when it modified its original emphasis by favoring graduate over undergraduate students. Finally, the autonomous universities competed with the more recently created government-controlled "experimental" institutions, as both lobbied intensively for greater funds.

At the same time that components of the system were competing for resources, educational authorities were seeking to integrate them. Thus the first three years of secondary school were merged with the primary schools in order to ease the transition from one to the other. Similarly, universities established basic cycles in the first year or two in order to serve as bridges with the secondary schools. Efforts were also made to coordinate junior college and university studies in order to facilitate the passage from one to the other. In short, structuring and integrating the education system were major governmental concerns in the 1970s and early 1980s.

Preschool Education

While the grade school system incorporated large numbers of underprivileged children in the 1960s, preschool consisted mostly of private institutions serving middle- and upper-class families. In the following decade, however, democratization penetrated to the preschool level; their annual enrollment increases outstripped those of the grade schools and universities. Nevertheless, half of all eligible children remained outside the system. In an effort to reduce this proportion, the Ministry of Education declared preschool education a priority at the same time that the 1980 education law made attendance obligatory. Previously, opposition in the Congress to making preschool education mandatory had revolved around two arguments: A sharp increase in preschool attendance would become an overwhelming financial burden for the state, and the children of poorer parents who resisted preschool education would subsequently be excluded from the grade schools. In practice, however, the obligatory clause of the 1980 law functioned as a statement of intent; preschool attendance did not become a prerequisite for admission into the first grade.

The Herrera Ministry of Education remained committed to preschool education. This came through in its willingness to separate preschool education from higher grade levels, as educators in that area had proposed. They argued that preschool education was faced with unique challenges, not the least of which was the necessity of winning parents over to the idea. Also, when preschool and grade school levels were combined, administrators of the latter took control of the former and assigned it scant resources and attention. For this reason the Herrera government undertook the construction of separate preschool buildings, though by the end of its term only a small percentage of children in preschool education had been placed in these units. Preschool education was also taken out of the office of primary school education and granted autonomous status within the Ministry of Education. In addition, the 1980 law required teachers at that level to obtain a degree in preschool education from institutions of higher learning. While admirable in theory, the lack of programs in this area raised questions about the quality of their training.

Basic and Diversified Education

The reforms of the 1970s in the grade schools sought to renovate the system by incorporating such practices as student self-evaluation, the granting of opportunities to catch up for students who failed to achieve established objectives, parent participation in academic planning, and cognitive training. These changes were accompanied by a new rhetoric that deemphasized quantitative concerns and stressed individual creativity and self-realization. Nevertheless, the basic structural modifications obeyed a more concrete imperative: the need to channel students away from the universities and to place greater emphasis on technical training. Secondary schools had been geared solely to prepare students for university study. It mattered little that 20 percent of those who graduated never pursued postsecondary education.

The two pillars of the new structure, basic and diversified education, had been discussed at UNESCO and other education conferences as far back as the 1960s. The governments of Rómulo Betancourt and Raúl Leoni experimented along these lines. However, it was the Caldera administration that implemented diversified education; Luis Herrera Campins refined the system of establishing the "basic schools." In the basic schools the first three years of high school are combined with primary school to form one continuous unified cycle for all students from the first to ninth grades. Graduates of the basic schools then choose between a two-year "diversified cycle" in the humanities or sciences. Its principal objective is to prepare the student for the university. The other option is a two- or three-year diversified technical cycle in one of the commercial, industrial, or agricultural fields (see Figure 11.1).

The new system's major innovation is the option for technical graduates to study at the university because of their solid academic formation in the basic school. Regardless of whether a large number of the technical students choose this alternative, it enhances the prestige of the technical track and encourages students to enroll in it. Under the previous system the technical student's preparation was inferior because of the poor quality of the technical schools (which the diversified technical cycles were intended to replace) and because students received only six years of education before the beginning of technical training, rather than nine. Consequently, technical graduates under the old system were denied the title of *bachiller* (important for the prestige that it conferred) and the right to enroll automatically in postsecondary education. Under the new system the technical graduate, unlike those in the humanities and sciences, receives a title in a *specificarea* (electricity, mechanics, and so on). This allows him to seek employment in that field while attending an institution of higher learning. Special advantages for students in technical education were designed to check the 1960s trend that saw the ratio of university track to technical track students increase substantially.

The vocational objectives of the basic school are woven into

FIGURE 11.1. Simplified Version of Modification in the Education Structure after 1969 (numbers correspond to grades; arrows refer to options)

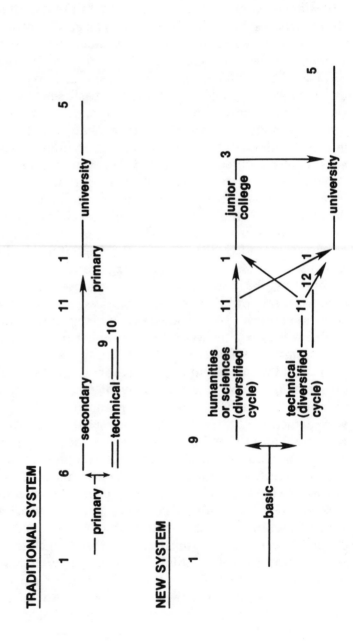

its phases of from two to four years. Each phase provides an increasingly greater emphasis on work habits and experiences. A set of courses entitled "Formation for Work" was designed to establish a permanent relationship between work and education. In its final division during the eighth and ninth grades this course seeks to approximate "the world of work." The program's description claims that its subjects correspond to the key sectors of the regional economy; instructors are drawn from relevant sectors within the community.

Increased emphasis on relevance to the workplace led to modification in curricula and programs that had remained unchanged since the 1940s. The new programs invite community input and initiatives.[4] This focus also underlines a new series of social science courses known as "Thought, Social Action and National Identity" (PASIN). In the lower grades, PASIN courses begin with observable phenomena in the community and regional environments; then they apply what has been learned to wider geographical environments. In addition, the departmental system, whereby classes have distinct teachers for individual subjects, has been implemented for all but the first few grades.

One important example of experimentation in education policy was President Herrera's creation in 1979 of the Ministry for the Development of Intelligence. It was presided over by Luis Alberto Machado, whose recently published *Revolución de la inteligencia* won international acclaim. The ministry sponsored numerous seminars, the best known of which was entitled "To Learn Is to Think." It prepared teachers to replace the rote system with methods intended to foster "intellectual dexterity."

Evaluation of the post-1969 reforms turns on their capacity to upgrade teacher proficiency. Teachers in those grades converted to the departmental system are expected to attain knowledge and develop pedagogic skills in their specialty. Also, the novel ideas associated with the basic schools required assimilation of previously unknown educational concepts. The challenge was, and is, especially great in technical education. At the time of the abolition of separate technical schools, only 19 percent of their instructors possessed degrees from institutions of higher learning and many had terminated their studies at the same school in which they were teaching.

As of the mid-1970s a significant number of postsecondary

education graduates either were unable to find employment as teachers or were offering classes on a part-time basis. At the same time 67 percent of the high school teachers did not hold required degrees. The proportion of non-degree–holding teachers had approached 86 percent in the early 1960s and dropped to roughly 50 percent two decades later. Three conditions explain the persistence of this situation in a saturated market: (1) Education graduates generally refused work in rural districts, (2) many non-qualified teachers were hired at a time when shortages still existed and were given tenure while receiving in-service training, and (3) a number of nonqualified party loyalists were placed as teachers on the basis of political influence in the Ministry of Education. The system of *concursos*, whereby an impartial jury selects the most eligible candidate for the position, could have neutralized such clientelistic practices, but it functioned on a very limited scale until the late 1970s.

At the time of the passage of the 1980 education law, elementary school teachers (*maestros*) were for the most part graduates of secondary level normal schools without any post-secondary experience. The percentage of elementary school teachers who lacked even the degree conferred by normal schools declined significantly in the democratic era, from 49 percent in 1961 to 13 percent in 1982. This compared favorably with most other Latin American countries.

One of the most far-reaching reforms in the 1980 law required all elementary teachers to acquire a degree from an institution of higher learning. When implemented, this reform would eliminate the distinction between *maestro* and *profesor*. It was criticized, however, on grounds that it would create a shortage of elementary school teachers, as lower class youth, then the principal source of elementary teachers, would consider the new requirements too demanding. Nevertheless, the present surplus of graduates of institutions of higher learning in education—estimated at 10,000 by one professional association—suggests that the state can afford to stiffen standards. Not only would the less prestigious term *maestro* be replaced by the more generic word *docente*, but differences in material benefits would be eradicated. Another goal was to inculcate among elementary teachers the sense of pro-fessionalism characteristic of high school teachers, the *profesores*. Training in the field of higher education was offered by a variety of institutions, each one with different requirements and standards. They included the University Institute of Professional Improvement, run by the Ministry of Education and generally criticized for its academic shortcomings and poor administration, several universities whose education programs varied between four and five years, the five-year pedagogic institutes, and the three-year "university college," which trained supervisory personnel. Those who drafted the 1980 law were conscious of the need to coordinate these institutions and integrate them into a single hierarchy.

While the post-1960 grade school reforms met with general approval some criticism has been leveled at the pace of their implementation. Critics claimed that preparatory measures should have been taken to prepare for the new system. For example, the new vocational emphasis mandated immediate attention to the quantity and quality of school workshops, and developing joint evaluations and participation implied stimulating feelings of responsibility in the student, his family, and the community at large. Because this was not done, AD criticized the basic schools and diversified cycles as "improvised," thus raising doubts about the extent to which COPEI-initiated changes will be retained by the present Lusinchi government.

Although education policy has been generally continuous since the early 1960s, both AD and COPEI have identified themselves with different facets of the system. This leads to uncertainty regarding the longevity of individual reforms. The AD government of Carlos Andres Pérez, for instance, reopened the technical schools that diversified education was intended to replace. This was justified on the grounds that the diversified technical cycle had encouraged students with no intention of going to the university to act like university track students. Attaining the goals of national educational planning was thus made more difficult. However, opponents pointed out that a student who entered technical school after having completed the sixth grade lacked sufficient maturity to choose a career. All of this leaves in doubt whether Lusinchi will support continuing with the technical schools. Similarly, the Ministry for the Development of Intelligence created by Herrera Campins was attacked as being a parallel structure rather than a subordinate component of the Ministry of Education. One of President Lusinchi's first acts was its abolition.

There is no timetable for implementing regulations that require *maestros* to acquire a degree and all Venezuelan youth to graduate from the basic school. Both measures appear to be medium- or long-range goals rather than legal obligations. Because basic school education is compulsory, in effect it obliges school authorities to retain rather than dismiss failing students, thus assuring that a greater number of youth will remain in the system until the ninth grade. One argument favoring the basic school was that the concept of a single unified system to form all Venezuelans argued strongly in favor of making the first nine grades obligatory. Planners believed that the rate of egression during the first nine years would be considerably reduced if they were thought of as a single unit. Consequently, some educators opposed proposals to break up the basic school into three individual phases. They feared that the existence of phases would erode the system's unity and thus undermine perceptions that it should be obligatory.[5]

Another fundamental goal—channeling a greater number of students into technical fields—has yet to be realized. Since the diversified education system took shape, the number of students opting for the three-year technical cycle has been less than 10 percent. With 90 percent of all students, the humanities and sciences remain the preferred courses of study. However, less than half of their students manage to graduate. On the other hand, more than 70 percent of the technical and education students receive degrees.[6] Coupled with a lingering prejudice against the technical fields, this higher rate of graduation contributes to a general feeling that the quality of their education is low and not likely to improve. Other factors contribute to the reluctance of students to enroll in the technical tracks. Some are discouraged by the fact that most technical degrees require three years of study rather than two. In addition, the high degree of specialization of each technical track suggests to students interested in such fields as engineering that the more general two-year science track keeps a greater number of options open for a longer time.

Institutions of Higher Learning

The diversification of university models in the 1970s reflected widespread disenchantment with the existing structure and a determination to experiment with new ones. Policymakers generally held the autonomous university structure responsible for the university violence of the 1960s, increasingly viewing it as an inflexible barrier to necessary change. Consequently, they placed newly created institutions of higher learning directly under the Ministry of Education. These new schools, including the "experimental" universities, were designed to test and evaluate new systems. In addition, a proliferation of "short career" institutes reduced higher education study from five to approximately three years. They were designed to lower costs while producing the "advanced technicians" that projected economic development demanded. National planners also reversed a long-held bias against private universities and encouraged their growth. Between 1969 and 1981 the rate of increase in the student population of the private universities was nearly double that of state institutions (see Table 11.1). Also, the number of private universities increased from three to five.

The advanced technicians, graduates of university institutes of technology and university colleges, are distinguished from middle-level technicians in that they possess sufficient scientific background to engage in research. Since 1979 the nonuniversity institutions of higher learning have mushroomed from a handful to about 80; presently they constitute 22 percent of the postsecondary student population (see Table 11.1). Nevertheless, except for the commercial and education track university colleges, these institutions operate below capacity. In the pedagogic institutes, whose student population remained stagnant after 1975, vacancies were due to the emergence of a national surplus of secondary school teachers.

Spokesmen for the pedagogic institutes called for the equalization of conditions throughout higher education, which included the standardization of teacher salaries, student scholarships, and other benefits. A few of the institutions began to implement the rigorous system of *concursos de oposición*, which was practiced in the universities. In the *concurso*, aspirants for teaching openings were hired on the basis of written and oral exams in their specialty. Nevertheless, the disparity in standards between pedagogic institutes and universities blocked plans to integrate the two kinds of institutions. Graduates from the former could not transfer to the latter without losing credits. Many education planners considered integration of the institutes and universities of primary importance. An integrated system would encourage high school graduates to enroll in institutes instead of the overcrowded universities, with the option of transferring to a university at a future date. Some planners, however, warned against the danger of converting the institutions into a veritable primary cycle of university study because they were designed for the job market and not as preparatory schools. They dragged their feet in implementing presidential decrees. Integration was not achieved, and transferring students remained subject to the capriciousness of university "equivalence committees," which lacked established rules when deciding upon the acceptance of credits. In one important case, Venezuela's prestigious Central University (UCV) worked out an arrangement with assorted institutes in the Federal District whereby the latter's curricula and programs conformed to requirements in the corresponding faculty at UCV. The proposed law of higher education sought to generalize the arrangement among institutions of higher learning in each major administrative region.

The experimental universities have introduced alternative approaches and structures that in some cases have been copied by other institutions of higher learning. For instance, the experimental Universidad de Oriente (UDO) established a basic course cycle (*cursos básicos*) for all incoming students,[7] creating campuses in different eastern states under the direction of a centralized structure. Subsequently, these novel arrangements were adopted by other universities. The experimental Simón Bolívar University in Caracas was the most renowned example of a thorough break with Venezuelan university tradition. It was patterned after the archetypal modern university in the developed world. It boasts a departmental system, admissions exams, emphasis on graduate study and research, and virtual absence of political activity on campus. The ease with which the ministry could impose reforms on the experimental universities contrasted with the rigidity of their autonomous counterparts, whose statutes could be modified only with congressional approval. The experimental universities were to be subject to periodic evaluation in order to determine their effectiveness; in practice this requirement has not been carried out.

The economic crunch in the early 1980s led to a competition for funds between the six experimental universities and the five autonomous ones. Representatives of the latter protested the virtually uncontrolled growth of private and experimental institutions because they cut into the education budget. They argued that many of the new private schools subordinated academic standards to considerations of profit and lacked such elementary facets of higher education as libraries, outreach programs, and research activity. Furthermore, the specialties offered by the private institutions seldom corresponded to national priorities, but instead clustered in those fields that did not require additional costs in laboratories and other expensive facilities. Spokesmen for the autonomous universities called on the government to defer approval of new schools. If any were needed they could be included in a new plan based on the economic realities of the 1980s; the plan also would establish mechanisms for government supervision of private universities.

The government-appointed rectors of the experimental universities, in contrast, lobbied to alter the "historic budget" of 1982, which was heavily biased in favor of the larger autonomous universities. Professors and students in the experimental schools lacked the benefits that had long been established in the autonomous universities. This preference in allocations is explained by the makeup of the National Council of Universities (CNU) in which the voting strength of the experimental universities as a bloc is fixed by law and at a level below that of the autonomous universities.

The 1970 Reform of the Law of Universities had greatly amplified the power of CNU. Many considered it a violation of autonomy, including the rector of UCV, Jesús María Bianco, who resigned in protest. The 1970 reform, as well as previous legislation, had infringed on university self-government and the extraterritorial status of the campus. Along with freedom of expression in the classroom, these prerogatives were considered the pillars of university autonomy. Nevertheless, in succeeding years the autonomous universities guarded jealously their decision-making authority and refused to carry out many resolutions of CNU.[8] CNU regulations on student repetition of courses, for instance, were implemented only insofar as they coincided with rules subsequently promulgated by the governing councils of each university. In addition, many individual faculties and universities established their own criteria for student admissions. In some cases they took in more students than authorized by CNU. Finally, some university spokesmen opposed CNU's efforts to equalize professor salaries throughout the university system on the basis that it infringed upon the prerogatives of each autonomous school to arrive at a contractual arrangement with its employees.

Planners have been anxious to break this tradition of entrenched powers in order to impose priorities on the universities that correspond to the demands of the job market. Officially sanctioned studies of national trends in human resource needs were undertaken—including one by MIT in conjunction with the Ayacucho Foundation—but no formal mechanism was created to ensure ongoing research in this area or to integrate its findings into policy planning.[9] The Planning Office of the University Sector (OPSU)—which was in charge of elaborating plans and transmitting information to the universities vis-à-vis CNU—hardly acknowledged the existence of these studies.[10]

The post-1958 period saw a deterioration in conditions for learning in some secondary institutions, due partly to a massive influx of students. Another factor was the increasingly elitist orientation of certain high schools. This trend was a consequence of class structure in that the children of wealthier families possessed the financial resources and academic preparation that went along with being admitted to the most prestigious schools. Several private universities, such as the Catholic University and USB, caught up to or surpassed UCV (and even more so, the other autonomous universities) in general academic ranking. This was demonstrated by the disproportionate attendance at these schools of children from elitist families.[11] Similar to the situation prevailing among the nation's public hospitals and private clinics, high school graduates of working and lower-middle-class families often were forced to wait several years to enroll in the tuition-free autonomous universities. Wealthier youth, in contrast, immediately entered USB and the Catholic University where they received superior academic training.

Within the universities a similar bifurcation process took place. At UCV, the prestigious faculties of engineering and medicine instituted their own admissions exams. Together with law, they required higher high school grade point average than such schools as history, geography, sociology, and philosophy. The depreciation of the value of some degrees also related to the glut of graduates from such faculties as social and economic sciences and the humanities, both of which admitted ever greater numbers of students after· 1958. Finally, AD and COPEI consistently dominated the most prestigious faculties of law, medicine, engineering, and veterinary studies. In contrast, the left was stronger in social and economic sciences and in the humanities. Study in these latter faculties in many instances served as political socialization into radical politics. A university degree per se, however, continues to confer great distinction and opportunities. Nevertheless, bit by bit wide cleavages are opening up between the economic prospects for graduates of different faculties and institutions.

Since the 1960s, policymakers in AD and COPEI have maintained a critical attitude toward the autonomous universities. Autonomy, however, has proved to be an ingrained feature of the universities; efforts to eliminate or restrict it have been unsuccessful. The 1970 Reform of the Law of Universities attempted to restrict autonomy, but it met heavy resistance from the entire university community. Since 1970 the strategy has been to circumvent autonomy by establishing experimental universities controlled by the Ministry of Education. These institutions from the beginning had an ambiguous status; they were to change over to autonomous standing at an unspecified future date. This conversion is made more explicit and immediate in the promised Law of Higher Education that educators drew up during the Herrera administration. Its passage is being debated as of this writing.

The experimental universities were intended to reduce political conflict on campus, but this objective has proved elusive. The incidence of confrontation in proportion to the student population was about the same in the experimental and autonomous schools. Only in the private universities was the percentage substantially lower.[12]

Many leading members of the university community recognize that autonomy in its extreme form becomes an unhealthy divorce between the university and society. Nevertheless, they defend autonomy in theory because it represents a guarantee against undue government intrusion in the universities and safeguards academic freedom. Universities and individual faculty need protection in a variety of situations. In the partisan democracy of the 1970s and 1980s, the Ministry of Education has invariably appointed militants of AD and COPEI as rectors in the experimental institutions. Seldom has the ministry taken into account the preferences of professors and students, thereby creating bad feelings between the government and the universities. It is for this reason that university autonomy, in spite of its potential dangers, remains relevant and will not be easily eliminated by those who favor more centralization.

Graduate Studies and Research

Advances in the areas of university research and graduate programs were made possible by financing that flowed from increasing oil revenues during the 1970s. More funds allowed the universities to hire additional full-time professors whose obligations included teaching as well as research. In addition, the significant increase in scholarship money allowed many professors to pursue graduate education abroad. A UCV study revealed that the typical research-oriented professor dedicated a third of his work time to research, held a graduate degree, was in his 30s, and enjoyed full-time status. It was noted that the professor's devotion to research had been shaped by his experience in foreign graduate schools. However, the study also concluded that unless he was properly stimulated and rewarded, he would return to the traditional work pattern of holding several jobs.[13] Education policymakers, aware of the need to provide greater incentives for graduate study and research, mandated in the proposed Law of Higher Education that a doctoral degree be a prerequisite for promotion above the rank of assistant professor.

As greater resources stimulated academic research in the 1970s, economic crisis in the early 1980s threatened to reduce it to a minimum. Participants in graduate research were thus most vulnerable to budgetary cuts. In hopes of securing outside sources of finance, efforts were made to link university research with the needs of public and private entities. The government issued decrees ordering the bureaucracy to contract universities to carry out needed research. In addition, private business was urged to collaborate with university research institutes in the planning and implementing of research projects. However, the bureaucracy ignored these decrees. Businessmen harbored suspicion toward the university community stemming from the 1960s; at that time students and professors generally viewed cooperation with business as compromising the independence of academic institutions. Consequently, few entrepreneurs contracted out their research to the universities.

Many of the 24 research institutes at UCV, as well as those at other universities, fail to report their activities to the academic community and the public at large. They are not regularly accountable to any higher body. Furthermore, the faculties in which they are housed ofen refuse to cooperate with UCV's research planning unit (the Council for Scientific and Humanities Development) on grounds that its activities represent an abridgment of their own autonomy. This rejection of imposition from outside the faculty also undermines efforts to establish priority areas of research, which, in any case, are considered a violation of the investigator's liberty to choose his own area of pursuance. A similar absence of centralized authority and priority areas of study characterizes graduate programs. Many of these are frequently the result of individual initiatives and have only superficial linkages to a university.[14] The recent formation of a Ministry for Science and Technology, and the issuance of regulations for graduate study programs to be enforced by CNU, are intended to overcome autarchy and isolation in priority areas of advanced study and research.

Scholarship Program

The Gran Mariscal de Ayacucho Scholarship Plan, one of the costly projects initiated by Carlos Andrés Pérez, was also made possible by the windfall in oil revenue. Prior to its initiation, student aid programs were handled by the state planning agency (CORDIPLAN). Subsequently they were placed under the separate Ayacucho Foundation. The foundation became a showpiece of AD's modernizing efforts. While students were sent to 20 countries, in which 20 languages were spoken, more than half studied in the United States; another 15 percent went to England. The foundation was conscious of the cultural dislocations this entailed. For instance, it attempted to ease their impact by furnishing students with current Venezuelan publications. President Pérez himself met with students and listened to their grievances in New York, London, and Rome. The selection of recipients was officially based on grade point average, family and cultural background (as determined by place of residence and public or private status of their high school), and preferred area of specialty. The criteria for selection soon came under public criticism. Some claimed that political party affiliation entered too much into consideration; others argued that class background should enter more into selection to study only in Venezuela. Foreign study for them should be available on the basis of merit alone. Still others claimed that while family income should be a factor, the classification of applicants according to their region of origin and the type of high school they attended were not accurate socioeconomic indicators.[15]

The Ayacucho Plan was inspired by the classic example of Japan, which sent large numbers of young people abroad to study for extended periods in an effort to master Western technology. The foundation consulted MIT in designating priority areas of study on the basis of Venezuela's projected needs in the area of human resources. The foundation's preoccupation with future trends influenced all educational planning.

The program's greatest success most likely will be in foreign graduate studies; comparable opportunities are not readily available in Venezuela. The experience of Venezuelan university professors in graduate programs abroad has stimulated research interest at their own institutions and enhanced comprehension of research methodologies. In contrast, money was spent less wisely on foreign undergraduate education, particularly for those who had never been away from home and were psychologically ill-prepared for a foreign learning experience. Furthermore, Venezuelan undergraduate programs in the same areas were probably undermined by the exit of capable students. Influenced by budgetary constraints in the late 1970s, the foundation altered its priorities to favor graduate students, followed by individuals who aspired to study in Venezuelan institutes and university colleges.

Nonformal Education

The National Open University (UNA) was created in 1977 in response to the failure of the established education system to meet national demands for a university education. UNA was inspired by the English Open University that sought to offer motivated adults high-quality education outside of the classroom. It relied heavily on audiovisual aids and supplementary material. Under the system, teachers in the early semesters worked with students individually in order to familiarize them with the school's philosophy of independent study and to promote learning skills; subsequently they are left largely on their own. While other universities eliminate less committed students by establishing a minimum course load, UNA, which is designed for adults with family and work obligations, allows students to advance at their own pace. Venezuelan defenders of this independent approach, both at UNA and the smaller Universidad Simón Rodríguez, maintain that it is less expensive and academically more effective; it forces the student to search for his own answers unbound by ties to any particular authority.

UNA now faces obstacles stemming from competition for declining resources, prejudice against innovation, and pressure from those who have been excluded. UCV's School of Education opposed UNA at its inception on grounds that the most urgent task of the moment was not to educate adults but to relieve pressure from recent high school graduates who were demanding admission to the already overcrowded traditional universities. Indeed, UNA was forced to address this problem by reducing the minimum age of its students from 21 to 18. A large number of these younger students hoped eventually to transfer to the traditional universities. Nevertheless, by far the heaviest concentration of UNA students is in the 21- to 29-year-old age bracket. This is in accordance with UNA's objective of attracting mainly young working adults.

In anticipation of an attendance avalanche, UNA designed an introductory course to serve as a prerequisite for entrance into the general studies phase. The course was intended to prepare students for the system of independent study while weeding out the unmotivated and incompetent. Nevertheless, suspicion about UNA's quality and prestige limited enrollment to less than the school's capacity. At the same time, UNA was forced to redraw plans and reduce the number of fields it offered from 17 to 9. Its television broadcasts were limited to two half-hour weekly programs. In 1980–81 UNA's student population was 5,752, far below the 50,000 figure that its founders had optimistically hoped to reach within a few years.

EDUCATIONAL POLICY AND POLITICAL RIVALRY ON CAMPUS

The university upheavals labeled as the "Academic Renovation" were inspired by the French movement of May 1968. They capped off a decade of intense student activism that included armed confrontation on campus and student participation in the guerrilla insurgency. Although the left retained control of the student movement in the early 1970s, it modified its antigovernment rhetoric on campus and downplayed militant university struggle. During this period the student mood wavered between moderation and apathy. This was evident in the student elections at the Central University for the Federation of University Centers (FCU) in which the abstention rate steadily mounted. FCU lost some of its prestige due to accusations of misuse of student funds, as well as its failure to play a major role in struggles around such issues as scholarship benefits and practices designed to limit the student population.

In spite of reduced student electoral participation, university politics continued to draw national attention and to command the interest of the political parties. University elections were viewed as barometers of general sentiment regarding national issues, even though the student body was hardly representative of the Venezuelan electorate. This perception took on great importance in 1976 and 1977. In university elections the Movement toward Socialism (MAS), which had been the major student force since its founding in 1971, suffered defeats at UCV, the University of the Andes (ULA), the University of Carabobo (UC), and elsewhere at the hands of the Movement of the Revolutionary Left (MIR). These setbacks were attributed to MAS's opposition to leftist unity. MIR, in contrast, preached the importance of uniting against the domination of AD and COPEI. As a result, MAS modified its position and took initiatives by establishing round table discussions in order to achieve leftist unity.

In another example of how campus electoral contests held broader political implications, AD increased its showing in student elections during the early 1980s, culminating in the 1983 balloting at UCV in which it outpointed COPEI by 16 percent. Nevertheless, it remained well behind a leftist coalition headed by MAS. Over the last 20 years (since the split in AD which gave rise to MIR) COPEI was consistently the largest centrist party in student politics; its eclipse by AD was interpreted as a repudiation of the unpopular COPEI government of Luis Herrera Campins and a presage of the outcome of the upcoming presidential elections.

Party interest in university politics derived from a second consideration. University officeholders were able to dispense such favors for their party's clients as scholarships, admissions certificates, faculty appointments, and tenure. The value of these benefits was considerably enhanced after 1973, when the outlay for university education increased in proportion to the growth of the government revenue.

The parties of the militant left also participated in clientelistic practices on campus in spite of their lack of high administrative positions. In the 1960s several university rectors had received leftist electoral backing, including the twice-elected Jesús María Bianco of UCV. Bianco's departure in 1970, the result of controversy arising from his support for the renovation movement, ushered in a new stage in which COPEI (especially at UCV) and AD dominated the university rectorships. Only ULA remained a bastion of leftist influence. In the universities, as well as on the cultural front, the two establishment parties have been more generous in relation to leftist participation than in other areas. University authorities have granted more opportunities to the left than have their counterparts in housing, labor unions, public programs, and—to cite the most extreme case—the armed forces. Consequently, the universities have become an important prop for the militant left. This is reflected in the large number of the top leftist political leaders who hold academic positions at UCV.

The intervention of political parties in university government was often cited as a root cause of the failure of these institutions to maintain high academic standards and to take full advantage of the abundant resources that were available. (It is a moot point whether the leftist parties, with their weak representation in the rectorships but greater weight at lower levels, deserve a significant share of the blame.) Nevertheless, the political fractions at the universities maintained greater autonomy from their corresponding parties than was the case in labor unions or professional associations. Rectors and other leading university officials, for instance, were frequently considered "sympathizers" of a given party rather than outright party militants.

In university elections, a group of independents often steps forward to criticize the major candidates for being too closely attached to the parties. In the 1976 rectoral elections at UCV, Bianco and another ex-rector were mentioned as possible candidates for the independents. Again in 1980, a slate of independent leftists attacked the UCV fractions of the leftist parties, as well as those of AD and COPEI, for failing to recognize the role of independents and for taking orders blindly from their respective parties.

University autonomy and open admissions policy are two potentially explosive issues that the major parties (AD, COPEI, and MAS) have in recent years been reluctant to uphold as absolute principles. At the nation's first "experimental" university, UNO, student mobilizations were organized by the left, along with support from COPEI. They succeeded in pressuring the government of Rafael Caldera into granting veritable autonomy. Elsewhere, as discussed earlier, autonomy had been the university community's response to threats of government intrusion during the oppressive 1950s and the violent 1960s. The more tranquil setting of the early 1970s ruled out violent government-university showdowns and thus took some of the intensity and urgency out of the movement for autonomy. Consequently, despite the proliferation of nonautonomous institutions in the 1970s, the political parties did not mount a vigorous campaign for their conversion to autonomous status, as had occurred in UDO.

The universities came under heavy attack in the 1970s for perpetuating waste and failing to maintain high academic standards. AD, COPEI, and such leftists as educator and presidential candidate Luis Beltran Prieto Figueroa accepted the idea that the government had the right to ensure that its money was being wisely spent and that accordingly the universities should not be completely insulated from outside interference. Higher education was perceived as a mechanism for training talent to carry out national development plans. On this basis they rejected the idea of absolute autonomy.[16] Although MAS never formally conditioned its support for autonomy, the party maintained that the autonomous universities had abused their privileged status by refusing to deal with the flagrant and frequent violations of regulations by students, professors, and employees. In contrast, the more militant leftists continued to adhere to the notion prevalent in the 1960s that only by struggling to maintain absolute independence from the state could the universities avoid being utilized as an instrument of neocolonial domination.

During the 1970s AD and COPEI also failed to uphold the principle of free open admissions that had been considered so important as to have been written into the constitution of 1961. AD, COPEI, and, by the early 1980s, MAS proposed that tuition payments be required from all but the very poor. The *masista* rector of ULA went so far as to declare that free admissions policy, while long considered a revolutionary banner, was really a reactionary practice in that it ended up by subsidizing the well-to-do.[17] In theory, the three parties continued to defend the right of all students to receive a university education. Nevertheless, their leaders warned that the university could not open its doors to everyone and maintain academic standards at the same time. Unlike the smaller organizations of the militant left (such as the Socialist League and the Committees of Popular Struggle), AD, COPEI, and MAS accepted the use of admissions exams in the more demanding faculties as a mechanism to weed out applicants. These same exams had sparked student protests in the 1960s when they were first implemented in the Faculty of Medicine at UCV and elsewhere.

The parties of the far left usually controlled the *comités de preinscritos*, which were established on campus by those high school graduates who had been turned down at the university. The *comités'* all-or-nothing approach of demanding admission for its entire membership was generally rejected by the student leaders of AD, COPEI, and MAS. They spurned the belligerent tactics employed by the *comités* and accused the radical fringe of trying to gain recruits among high school graduates who, in their desperation to gain entrance into the university, were susceptible to calls in favor of the use of force.

In response to the student population explosion and the harsh criticisms of the universities for absorbing enormous sums of money without producing commensurate results, bold solutions have been offered that divide the university organizations of AD, COPEI, and MAS. These divisions correspond to differences in the concerns and attitudes of professors—with their interest in tightening standards in order to avoid an uncontrolled expansion in the student population—and students—who opposed stringent measures to limit enrollment. Internal tensions have manifested themselves as a result of controversy over the policies of the dean of the UCV Faculty of Engineering, Piar Sosa. These policies have alienated his fellow AD members in the student movement. Sosa's no-nonsense approach includes strict enforcement of rules on repeating courses; he was criticized because they do not provide enough alternatives for those facing suspension. Traditionally, university authorities have been lax in enforcing these ordinances, and thus Sosa's resolve along with his implementation of admissions exams have sparked disturbances. Early in 1984 many important AD student leaders at UCV openly criticized Sosa's call for charging tuition in a vain attempt to block his bid to repeat as the party's candidate in the elections for university rector.

In summary, after the renovation upheavals of 1969–70, the universities were relatively calm while the main parties on campus shied away from such heavily charged banners as open admissions and university autonomy. AD, COPEI, and MAS were in general agreement regarding the magnitude of the problems that had arisen because of university mismanagement. The *masistas*, who as Communist guerrillas in the 1960s had viewed the university in terms of its direct usefulness for the revolutionary cause, in the 1970s emphasized the importance of upgrading academic standards. This attitude was embodied in their slogan "Study and Struggle," which was also adopted by MIR. More immediately, the perennial crisis faced in most universities toward the end of each year concerns the exhaustion of funds. It serves to unite temporarily the university community. At these moments college protests of any type receive broad support on campus because they bring pressure on the government to grant emergency funds to the institution. Naturally, given outstanding ideological differences, a general consensus on how to spend these funds is not to be reached. Nevertheless, the common focus of the main parties on issues of waste and corruption, rather than on radical transformation, reduces the intensity of interparty conflict on campus.

CONCLUDING REMARKS ON THE PLACE OF EDUCATION IN VENEZUELAN SOCIETY

Modern Venezuelan democracy has provided a propitious setting for the expansion of the nation's education system. In the 1960s, democratization of education entailed opening up educational opportunities for working-class youth, a low priority item during the dictatorship of the previous decade. In the 1970s, the university aspirations of young Venezuelans, which the student organizations of political parties lobbied for and channeled along nonviolent lines, pressured the government into allotting a greater share of the education budget to higher learning than most educational planners considered desirable.

Regardless of their ideological persuasion, educators argued that university expenditures should be reduced in order to provide greater opportunities in the elementary and secondary schools. Nevertheless, this consensus was not easily implemented in new policies. The influx of oil revenue after 1973 created a revolution of rising educational expectations. An ever greater number of working-class youth (though very few from the marginal sector) avidly pushed for admission to the universities. Behind their steadfastness was a simple socioeconomic reality: In developing countries children of working-class families who do not acquire professional credentials are generally condemned to permanent underprivileged status.

In addition to increasing the numbers of its citizens receiving an education, improvements by Venezuela's democratic governments in other areas have not been duplicated in most developing nations. Of course, they were made possible by the boom in oil revenues. Under the Ayacucho scholarship program Venezuela placed more students in foreign universities than any other Latin American nation. Universities were able to increase the number of full-time (*dedicación exclusiva*) professors, an advance that long has been called for by Latin American educators. Similarly, professional salaries were made attractive not only by Latin American standards but by those prevailing in the industrial North. Other changes were embodied in regulations that awaited implementation, predicated on a continuously rising oil revenue. Not only was preschool education declared mandatory, but differences in remuneration between primary and secondary school teachers were to be eliminated. Democracy, which in the context of the Venezuelan education systems means greater opportunities for working-class youth, would be served by these advances.

Implementation of these impressive achievements is jeopardized by the return of a buyer's market for oil and by the resultant fall in government revenue. The inauspicious economic situation faced by Jaime Lusinchi during his first year in office contrasted with the situation encountered by his two predecessors. This new juncture raises important interrogatives about the future of education policy and its contribution to the nation's democratic life. In the first place, the continuity of progress for the basic schools and diversified cycles, both products of *copeyano* governments, are uncertain. A persisting feature of Venezuelan democracy throughout the alternating AD-COPEI administrations of the last 15 years has been the failure of each to carry out plans developed when they were in the opposition.

Preuniversity education may also sustain significant budgetary cuts due to the greater political influence of postsecondary institutions. Such an ordering of budgetary priorities will weaken Venezuelan democracy because basic education was intended to provide all Venezuelans with knowledge that is essential to make informed political choices. On the other hand, austerity induced by declining government revenue may force the universities to take stringent measures to limit admissions, thus negating another principle dear to Venezuelan democracy and sanctified by law, namely, the right of all to a university education. Restricting enrollment in the universities and reducing student benefits may also provoke a level of discord on campus capable of threatening the political order. This might be one important consequence of a Lusinchi administration decision to abolish university autonomy.

Nevertheless, abandonment of established principles and increases in political instability are not inevitable, even granted the impending cutbacks in funding for education. Austere measures, if intelligently carried out, can eliminate bureaucratic waste rather than prejudice quantitative or qualitative gains. Furthermore, such innovative approaches as nonformal education demonstrate that a potential exists for reducing costs while maintaining standards. Streamlining and creative renovation demand efficacious administration, far superior to the record of the 1970s. Whether or not the economic realities of the 1980s force an improvement in pedagogic administration will determine how well Venezuelan education performs in the years ahead.

NOTES

1. Centro de Reflexión y Planificación Educativa, *La educación en Venezuela*, VII, *La educación en Copei* (Caracas, 1979), pp. 26–27.

2. Héctor Silva Michelena and Heinz Rudolf Sonntag, *Universidad, dependencia y revolución* (Mexico: Siglo Veintiuno Editores, 1970).

3. Peter P. Gabriel, "La escasez de recursos humanos en Venezuela: Mitos y realidades," in *Venezuela 1979: examen y futuro* (Caracas: Editorial Ateneo de Caracas, 1980), pp. 323–24; UNESCO *Educación Superior en Venezuela*, II, *Apuntes para un análisis de la educación superior Venezuela* (Caracas: Consejo Nacional de Universidades, n.d.), p. 63.

4. Ministerio de Educación, *La revolución educativa* (Caracas, 1976), p. 39.

5. Centro de Reflexión y Planificación Educativa, *La educación Venezuela*, XI, *Educación básica, filosofía* (Caracas, 1982), p. 14.

6. Consejo Nacional de Universidades, *Informador universitario* 3, no. 29 (May 1978): 7.

7. The system of *cursos básicos* was designed to introduce new students to university study and reduce differences in their academic preparation. In practice, it has also served to weed out less qualified students prior to reaching higher grade levels.

8. UNESCO, *Educación superior*, p. 22.

9. Center for Policy Alternative, MIT, "Mercado laboral de docentes de educación pre-escolar, primaria y media en Venezuela" (June 1977), p. 64 (mimeo.).

10. G.E.R. Burroughs, *Education in Venezuela* (London: David Charles Archon Books, 1974), p. 101.

11. Orlando Albornoz, *La formación de los recursos humanos en el área educación* (Caracas: Monte Avila Editores, 1981), p. 179.

12. "Algunos cuadros estadísticos y primeras inferencias sobre los conflictos ocurridos entre 1976–1977," *Cuadernos de educación* (Caracas) (September–November 1979): 119–32.

13. Angel Hernández, "Estrategias para el desarrollo de la investigación universitaria," *Universidad nuestra* (Caracas) 7 (June 1981): 30.

14. D. F. Maza Zavala, *Universidad, ciencia y tecnología* (Caracas: UCV, 1979), p. 124.

15. Humberto Ruiz Calderón, *Plan de Becas Ayacucho: Mito y realidad* (Mérida: Formateca, 1979), pp. 84–94.

16. Luis Beltran Prieto Figueroa, *El estado y la educación en América Latina* (Caracas: Monte Avila Editores, 1977), p. 25.

17. Javier Duplá, *La educación en Venezuelan* (Caracas: Centro Gumilla, 1983), p. 25.

12

Agriculture

Donald L. Herman

During most of its history, rural Venezuela has experienced extreme concentration of landownership based on very large estates, the *latifundia*, that for the most part are inefficiently operated and absentee-owned. While some of these holdings concentrate on the production of commercial crops, such as sugar, coffee, and cotton, others are inadequately exploited, with large tracts of land lying idle or given over to cattle raising. Adjacent to the *latifundia* one might find a small number of medium-sized farms and a larger number of *minifundia*. The latter are five- to ten-acre plots that support a peasant family at subsistence or less than subsistence level, and they contribute nothing to agricultural and economic development.

Such a land tenure system gives rise to several identifiable groups: *latifundistas*, large agroindustrialists (food processing, marketing, fertilizers, and farm implements), commercial farmers who may own a tractor and other machinery, and *minifundistas* and landless laborers. Some of the landless laborers have squatted on public or private lands, but most work for the large estates as seasonal laborers, tenants, sharecroppers, or resident peons. Others are migratory squatters (*conuqueros*) who live in the mountainsides and destroy much of country's soil resources through the slash-and-burn method. The *minifundistas* and landless laborers comprise the peasant class, a majority of the rural population who live in extreme poverty, ignorance, and dependence.

This type of land tenure system is an obstacle to development. Economically, the land is not used efficiently because the *latifundia* are either excessively labor-intensive or modern technology is practically nonexistent. Furthermore, the average agricultural tenant and laborer have so little money income that they have almost no purchasing power and cannot contribute to the consumer market. Socially the system gives rise to rigid social stratification, and landownership determines who has power and prestige. Politically, the peasants might be brought to the election polls and ordered to vote for the landowners' candidates, but they do not participate in the public services that only benefit the rural elite. Culturally, the peasants comprise a subculture dependent upon the protection of the *latifundistas*.

In addition to the negative effect of the land tenure system, Venezuela has two other problems, a tropical climate and poor agricultural land.[1] The llanos, which comprise one-third of the country's landmass and yield the highest percentage of crops, are intermittently parched and flooded. Although much of the dry, barren soil can be made productive by irrigation, major projects take at least 20 years as well as considerable investment to attain the desired results. Because of its warm temperatures the country cannot grow basic feed grains such as soy or wheat, commodities that are essential for agricultural self-sufficiency. The hot, humid climate also accounts for a variety of diseases and pests that can ruin harvests. Furthermore, the country's geography is only moderately suited to agricultural production, and a mere 2 percent of its land surface is currently devoted to crop raising. Andean and coastal range topography limits farming to the valleys and gentle slopes, but population density is often high in these areas, forcing farmers to cultivate less suitable lands that suffer from erosion poor soil fertility, and low productivity.

Thus the agricultural problems involve both land and people. Foremost, perhaps, is the need to improve the efficiency of the agricultural sector so that Venezuela is no longer dependent upon other countries for its foodstuffs. The solution to this problem may partly depend on the alleviation of peasant exploitation. It is unlikely that any progress will be made until and unless the leaders of Venezuela address three matters: *the development of a clear agricultural policy*, which may require changes in the political structure through a democratic reform movement, revolution, or even military coup led by a left wing faction; *agrarian reform*, which may require the distribution of land to the peasants, along with significant investments, including technical training and the extension of credit; and the *integration of agriculture into the larger economy*, which may require planning and an overall strategy for improving the trade balance, particularly the reduction of the importation of such large quantities of agricultural products.

The deep interdependence of political, economic, and social factors raises serious questions: What is the impact of democracy on agriculture? Is it more difficult to initiate reform in a democracy, or is it easier because of a broadening of the base? Specifically, what do the records of AD and COPEI reveal concerning these questions? Conversely, what impact does agricultural policy have on these democratic regimes? It will be shown that improvement in basic conditions of human life and an increase in agriculture's contribution to national development can strengthen a regime in particular and democracy in general.

BACKGROUND

The Gómez Era

The government encouraged extreme land concentration in fewer hands and the *latifundistas* provided paternalistic benefits while at the same time forcing the peasants into a virtual serfdom.[2] The first national Agricultural Census of 1937 indicated that 4.4 percent of the *latifundistas* held 78 percent of the land and 95 percent of the *minifundistas* held 22 percent. A rudimentary commercial agriculture also began to spread, but it led to a further squeezing of the peasant labor force, accompanied by a depersonalized landowner-peasant relationship and a reduction of the goods and services formerly provided by the *latifundistas*. In 1928, the government established the Agricultural and Livestock Bank (BAP) to provide credit for most cash-crop producers. However, due to a high percentage of foreclosures the government became a major landowner, holding approximately 25 percent of the arable land by 1945. By the end of the Gómez period, the *latifundistas* and cattle ranchers of the llanos dominated the rural area. Without any type of agrarian reform, the peasants were becoming increasingly impoverished. Furthermore, the agricultural foundation of Venezuela had been replaced by the petroleum industry and its related manufacturing enterprises. A new elite was poised to challenge the power of the *latifundistas*.

The Trienio

From 1936 to 1945, the ORVE-PDN-AD under Rómulo Betancourt included the agricultural sector in an effort to establish unions closely tied to the party. Cadres went into the countryside promising to give "land for him who works it" and to emancipate the peasants from the landlords. Thus they began to forge an alliance between the challenging political urban elite and the peasant masses, who comprised a majority of the population. In return for political support, the urban elite promised the peasants a change in rural power relationships and a marked improvement in their condition. On the eve of the 1945 October revolution, approximately 100,000 peasants had been organized in local unions.

Although the López Contreras and Medina Angarita governments established several agricultural colonies, Venezuela had not experienced an agrarian reform policy until AD seized power.[3] In a sense, the Betancourt junta instituted a de facto agrarian reform prior to President Gallegos' 1948 election and the Revolutionary Government Junta included an agrarian article in the 1947 constitution. It called for the progressive economic and social emancipation of the peasants, the basis for the expropriation of private property to be the social function of land, and the state to provide credits and take other steps to help the peasants increase production.

The newly created Corporación Venezolana de Fomento (CVF, Venezuelan Development Corporation) focused its investments on agriculture, and BAP used its additional funds to concentrate on the small landholder. The peasant syndicate was one of the principal vehicles to carry out the agrarian reform, and peasant union leaders acquired local rural power, thereby obtaining credit, public works, and land for syndicate members. In November 1947, the Federación Campesina Venezolana (FCV,

Venezuelan Peasant Federation) was incorporated into the CTV, thereby achieving formal national organization status for the peasant union movement.

One month before his government was overthrown, President Gallegos signed an agrarian reform law. Among its stipulations were expropriation of private land and compensation to the owners, granting landownership to peasant colonies, granting communally owned land to peasant cooperatives, and selling land for a minimal amount to individuals. The Instituto Agrario Nacional (IAN, National Agrarian Institute) was created to administer the law which proved to be a forerunner for subsequent AD policy.

During the *trienio*, agricultural production for several important products increased; however the agrarian reform expanded the number of *minifundia* that averaged 2.2 hectares (1 hectare = 2.47 acres). A peasant union movement, incorporated into the AD political apparatus, articulated peasant interests. Except for COPEI strength in the Andean states, strong AD peasant support in the elections indicated a high degree of perceived regime legitimacy in the rural areas. Nevertheless, because AD chose to concentrate on the problems of the rural majority and set budget priorities accordingly, other groups joined the traditional elites in opposition to the *adecos*.

The Pérez Jiménez Dictatorship

Except for a few colonization projects on government-owned land, the dictatorship abandoned the land distribution and credit programs. Peasants were dislodged from the holdings they had acquired, and almost all the land that had been used for the AD agrarian reform program came under private control, including the former Gómez holdings, which reverted to his heirs and claimants on his estate. The land distribution process came to a halt, and the government shifted attention away from the peasants and small to medium-sized farmers and decided to concentrate on commercial agriculture. The low levels of spending on agricultural-rural development during 1950-57 exemplified the government's neglect of this sector, and agricultural imports rose to more than 20 percent by 1957. The relatively small percentage of investments was limited to large-scale, capital-intensive projects such as the sugar central. Nevertheless in spite of the drastic shift in governmental priorities, the growth rate of agricultural product for 1951-57, as illustrated in Table 12.1, was 4.5 percent; this was approximately 1 percent higher than the country's population growth rate. As part of the liquidation of the AD agrarian reform, the dictatorship destroyed the FVC and created its own peasant confederation; however, very few peasant syndicates belonged. The AD clandestine resistance included many national and state leaders of the peasant union movement who would receive strong peasant loyalty in the postdictatorial period.

The Betancourt–Leoni Era

After the Pérez Jiménez dictatorship was overthrown, the rural vote proved to be a significant factor in Rómulo Betancourt's return to power. However, the demographic situation had changed, and the peasants who comprised approximately 50 percent of the population during the *trienio* were slightly less than one-third by 1960. Nevertheless, the Betancourt government coalition proposed instituting major changes in the rural area. Modernization was hindered by agricultural stagnation while economic changes made demands on agriculture that could not be met by the old land tenure system. Socially, the new governing elite wanted personal freedom for the peasant. They promised to eliminate social and legal injustices, lower rural unemployment, and raise the standard of living and quality of life of the rural masses. The political objectives would assure stability and political democracy through the mobilization of peasant support.[4]

We must distinguish between terms. Land reform refers to title distribution, and agricultural reform involves technological services, such as the extension of education, credit, and irrigation facilities. Both terms are subsumed under the concept of agrarian reform.[5] Unlike the *trienio* period, when agrarian reform was exclusively an AD policy, the 1960 Agrarian Reform Law was a multiparty effort through which the political leaders hoped to create a new class of small family farmowners. The Punto Fijo agreement had committed the principal parties to support agrarian reform and President Betancourt chose the COPEI agricultural specialist, Víctor Giménez Landínez, to be the minister of agriculture and livestock. Thus the Betancourt government's agricultural policy basically bore an AD-COPEI imprimatur.

The content of the agrarian reform emphasized the well-being of the rural population and the necessity for social change. The social function of land required that it be in the hands of those who worked it. The land was to be distributed justly among the people, protecting the individual peasant family and the concept of private property. As a result, the peasant would be a defender of justice and order and contribute to a climate of harmony.[6] Although it is virtually impossible to separate the socioeconomic components of the Agrarian Reform Law, Betancourt wanted to provide the poorer peasants with better schools and housing, rural dispensaries, and so forth. He hoped to keep the peasants on the land by making the rural area more attractive.

In part the program's implementation was affected by the 1958-59 spontaneous land invasion to which the government responded with large-scale land distribution. However, during the latter part of the Betancourt regime and throughout the Leoni administration, the government shifted to a controlled and centralized process of integral agrarian reform in which the physical consolidation of reform-created settlements led to economic objectives becoming more important. After 1962 the rate of distribution slowed steadily. Although President Leoni did not abandon the idea of social change, he concentrated more on the infrastructure, such as irrigation projects, technical training, and education.

The administration distributed government-owned land (*tierras baldías*) and privately owned land through expropriations, concentrating on the latter after mid-1961, for which former landowners received cash and government bonds. The policy of providing the peasants with free land grants led to disagreement within the peasant union leadership. Some believed that it would have been psychologically better for the peasants to pay a minimum amount. The individual peasants or cooperative settlements received provisional title that was to become definitive after they demonstrated they could farm the land properly. By 1967, the Leoni government began to issue a small number of definitive titles with certain restrictions. The peasants had to obtain IAN permission to sell the land and, if it were not used properly, the land might revert. Realistically the great majority of the peasants never received definitive title, and to this day 90 percent of the land belongs to the government. Nevertheless, the peasant can work the land with his family and pass it on to his sons.

Several institutions were charged with implementing the agrarian reform program. The reactivated IAN expropriated and redistributed land to the peasants, paid the former landowners, and provided the necessary agricultural equipment such as tractors. The Ministry of Agriculture and Livestock (MAC) directed planting efforts and provided technical assistance and instruction. BAP acted as a credit agency and also provided funds for irrigation. Other government agencies included the Ministry of Education and the Ministry of Health. The Leoni administration established additional agencies that included the Foundation for the Application of Applied Research to Agrarian Reform (CIARA) and the Bank of Agro-Livestock Development (BANDAGRO). In 1968 the government initiated the Program of Directed Credit oriented toward rehabilitating the nonsolvent beneficiaries with the IAN.

Through the reconstituted FCV the peasant union movement established linkages with the government and political parties, particulary with AD. Some FCV officials served in the Congress and as political party leaders, and others received responsible positions with IAN, BAP, and MAC. Local peasant leaders acted as brokers, receiving and shaping peasant demands and ultimately passing them to the state and natinal levels. Undoubtedly peasant unionization in an area had a positive effect on local land distributions and the number of families settled.

Implementation involved serious problems. The growing number of government agencies and autonomous institutes resulted in a burgeoning bureaucracy with overlapping responsibilities. In addition neither BAP nor MAC had sufficient funds; the latter in particular, lacked trained and skilled personnel. The process of providing peasant families with titles was very slow, and marketing facilities to transport the peasants' production to main highways were woefully inadequate. Furthermore, how does one measure the peasants' commitment and contribution to the goals of agrarian reform? As one scholar who interviewed a number of peasants during the early 1960s remarked, "I may observe once again that among the greatest handicaps to the full development of the Venezuelan agrarian reform has been the tendency of the peasants to look to the government for everything."[7]

Adecos and *copeyanos* point to the successes of the agrarian reform. The guerrilla movement of the early 1960s did not receive significant peasant support, the peasants were integrated into the country's political-socioeconomic groups and institutions, and their living conditions improved in an absolute sense.[8] The statistical evidence assembled in Table 12.2 indicates that output increased markedly during the 1959-68 period. Land redistribution began and the government made notable investments in the infrastructure. Agricultural production increased 150 percent, allowing for inflation, as exemplified by the significant rise in corn, rice, coffee, yuca, sesame, hogs, cattle, eggs, and milk. By 1962, agricultural imports declined by 10 percent and agricultural exports increased by 15 percent.[9]

Nevertheless the negative side of the ledger is evident. Peasant leaders continued to complain about such specific inadequacies as land, proper housing, medical facilities, credit, sanitary drinking water, and roads. Furthermore the expanding economy increased the gap between classes and intensified rural stratification. On the one hand, 65 percent of the farms were too small for economical, efficient production and this depressed income and living standards. On the other, the medium-sized to large unit commercial farms operated on a comparatively high technological level, produced the lion's share of profitable crops, and competed with the peasants for credits, investments, services, and markets.[10] At the end of the Leoni government, a survey published by the U.S. Agency for International Development (USAID) indicated that 79 percent of all cultivated land was in the hands of fewer than 2 percent of all proprietors. By contrast, two-thirds of all landholders owned less than 3 percent of all cultivated land. The same survey further indicated that only one-fourth of those listed as farmers or farmworkers owned any land at all. Thus, in the Venezuelan transformation that led to an increasing commercialization of agriculture, rapidly expanding urbanization, and politicization of the masses, the peasants only benefited somewhat from the changes that took place. Demographic changes and the resultant

TABLE 12.1. Growth of Agricultural Products

Period of Government	Percentage
Pérez Jiménez (1951–57)	4.5%
Betancourt (1959–64)	5.6
Leoni (1964–69)	4.4
Caldera (1969–74)	3.3
Pérez (1974–79)	4.7
Herrera (1979–82)	1.1

Sources: Venezuelan Central Bank, *Economic Reports*, and CORDIPLAN, *Plan of the Nation*.

decline in peasant bargaining power intensified the problem of maldistribution of the country's wealth.

The Caldera Government

Caldera's agricultural policy in COPEI's electoral program called for greater consolidation of the agrarian reform process. It called for a slowdown in the distribution rate of land, future land distribution to come primarily from the public rather than from the private sector, and an emphasis on greater productivity. The Fourth National Plan (1970-74) stipulated that while productivity would be increased by helping current peasant settlements, the government would emphasize technical assistance for the small and medium-sized farmers. A subsequent MAC statement (Table 12.3 profiles the institutions responsible for agricultural development) showed that the government wanted to develop further the agroindustrial sector and increase efficiency and exports.[11] The national plan proposed a new program and agency, the Integral Program of Agricultural Development (PRIDA) and the Agricultural Marketing Corporation (CMA).

After a period of AD-COPEI political maneuvering, the Congress approved PRIDA, including increasing investments for the agricultural sector and the approval of a supplemental loan from the Inter-American Development Bank. The money would be used to reorient the agrarian reform "from a social process of

TABLE 12.2. Growth of the Value of Total Agricultural
Production, Animal and Vegetable

Period of Government	Total (%)	Animal	Vegetable
Betancourt	31.7%	60.1%	20.1%
Leoni	29.3	45.4	18.5
Caldera	18.7	30.1	7.3
Pérez	29.4	32.3	29.9
Herrera (first four years)	8.0	14.8	2.0

Sources: BCV, *La economía venezolana en los ultimos treinta y cinco años*, 1978; BCV, *Informe económico*, 1979; BCV, *Series estadísticas*, 1981 and 1982.

distributing the land to an economic process that would increase production—credits, housing, electricity, water, roads, and warehouses."[12] The funds would be applied in four zones: Andes, Central-West, Central, and Northeast. The programs comprising PRIDA were peasant settlements, agricultural research, extension programs, additional credits, construction of silos, drainage, roadways, and a peasant-training program. MAC was responsible for coordinating the various activities with IAN, BAP, CIARA.

In 1970 President Caldera announced the creation of CMA to stimulate the agrarian commercialization process and to absorb the marketing functions previously performed by BAP.[13] Under the authority of MAC, CMA's principal responsibilities were to purchase the products from the farmers at fixed prices, temporarily store the products or bring them to central locations, and to sell the products to consumers at subsidized prices. CMA also established producers' commercial and cooperative associations. Through its subprogram of consolidation of peasant settlements, IAN grouped 124 settlements in the four regions. The investments were used exclusively to finance the necessary infrastructure for the settlements' consolidation. Under the subprogram of agricultural extension, MAC created 200 agencies to provide technical assistance to these settlements. BAP's subprogram of agicultural extension was to assure to financing of infrastructural consolidation in the settlements, and CMA's subprogram of silos was introduced in several states.[14]

During the Caldera government, the sources of financing the

TABLE 12.3. Institutions Responsible for Agricultural Development

Function	Primary Institutions	Collaborative Institutions
Planning and coordination	CORDIPLAN	MAC-IAN-ICAP
Land		
Distribution	IAN	IAN-ICAP-BANDAGRO
Consolidation	MAC	IAN-ICAP-BANDAGRO
Irrigation and drainage	MOP	MAC-IAN
Production perspectives	MAC	IAN-BANDAGRO-CMA
Zoning	MAC-MARNR	IAN-FCA
Resources productivity	MAC	IAN-ICAP-BANDAGRO-FCA-MH-private associations
Rural occupation	MAC	IAN-ICAP-MOP-state governments-private associations
Rural mechanization	MAC	IAN-ICAP-BANDAGRO-FCA-state governments-private associations
Military small farms	MD	MAC
Cooperatives	MAC	IAN-ICAP-state governments-private associations
Capital resources		
Peasant credits	ICAP	FCA
Industrial credits	BANDAGRO	FCA-official banks-private associations
Direction of investments	FCA	IAN-ICAP
Financial mechanisms	FCA	IAN-ICAP-BANDAGRO-state governments
Marketing		
Warehousing	CMA	IAN
Classification	CMA	
Transport	CMA	Private associations
Secondary roads		MAC-IAN-MARNR-state governments

Price policy	MH-MAC	CORDIPLAN-MAC-IAN-CMA-MF
Basic and technological education	MAC	IAN-ME-MD
Research	MAC	IAN-ME-private associations
Exports		
Parity prices	MAC	CMA-ICE
Promotion	MAC	CMA-ICE
Financing		official banks
Conservation of natural renewable resources	MARNR	MAC-IAN-MD-private associations
Industries	MF	MAC-IAN-BANDAGRO-FCA-CMA
Statistics	MAC	CORDIPLAN-OCEI-IAN-ICAP-BANDAGRO-FCA-ICE-MARNR-MH

Source: George Kastner, María Teresa Tello, et al., *El reto de alimentarnos* (Caracas: Instituto de Estudios Superiores de Administración, 1982).

agricultural sector changed. BAP began to deal exclusively with credits for the peasants and the small and medium-sized producers. BANDAGRO serviced the private agroindustrial, livestock, forestry, and fishing sectors. Also, for the first time, private banks contributed to financing agricultural development.

As with its predecessors, the result of the Caldera government's policies were mixed. Compared to the previous administration, credits for the overall agricultural sector decreased; however at the same time, credits for BANDAGRO increased from 136.5 million bolivars in 1970 to 421.6 million in 1973. Through 1971 the government could point to increases in agricultural production, investments, and credits; but in 1972 heavy rains adversely affected agricultural performance. Production of sorghum, rice, cacao, sesame, and coffee, products whose output is aimed primarily at meeting domestic demand, posted significant increases but production of corn, beans, and potatoes declined due to bad weather and official pricing policies that discouraged their cultivation. According to the Inter-American Development Bank:

> During 1970-73 the area of cultivated farmland declined 14 percent while real gross investment was at a standstill having recorded in 1973 a level similar to the 1970-72 average. This situation was reflected in insufficient domestic output that had to be supplemented by imports, that on the average accounted for 24 percent of the total supply of farm products at current prices in that period.[15]

Furthermore, agriculture's share of the gross domestic product (GDP) decreased from 5.46 percent during the Leoni period to 3.59 percent during the Caldera period, whereas it employed 22 percent of the employed population.

At the time Caldera left office a study of Venezuelan agriculture appeared by Meir Merhav, the Israeli economist, that seemed to parallel the Caldera government's thinking in several respects.[16] Merhav pointed out that the peasant sector was the most deprived and the gap between the peasants and other sectors was increasing. The peasant class was marginal, economically superfluous, and it could not satisfy Venezuela's agricultural needs; the growing demand for food required that agricultural production increase 5 percent per year. Merhav also criticized the shortcomings of agricultural policy implementation. "Venezuela is rich in all resources except one: the human resource with the capacity of organization and administration."

Merhav believed that Venezuela must adjust its price structure to world market prices because the necessary agricultural growth rate will be maintained only if a substantial percentage of that growth were directed to the world market through exports. Since the peasant sector cannot even increase production enough to satisfy the domestic market, Merhav's answer was to develop the agroindustrial sector. The peasants must be incorporated into the sector that will determine the future of Venezuelan agriculture. As President Caldera's minister of agriculture and livestock stated, "I want the peasant to become a farmer, sitting on a tractor and working, rather than with hat in hand looking for a government handout."[17]

The Pérez Government

Agricultural policy in the Fifth National Plan (1975–79) called on peasants and farmers to produce enough food so that imports might be reduced while also supplying primary materials for industry. The peasants' standard of living would rise so that they would become consumers of benefits and services. The government would increase investments in the infrastructure—roads, hydraulic works, and irrigation. CMA would establish equitable prices for producers and consumers and the agrarian reform would establish new peasant industries and cooperatives. President Pérez also stated that he wanted "equilibrium in the agricultural economy by means of coexistence, among the organized sectors that represent the interests of peasant producers, and those that represent the capitalist enterpreneurs of the rural areas."[18] With a dramatic rise in petroleum income, the government began an accelerated agricultural investment program. It provided credit for both short-term and long-term investment, encouraged imports of improved breeds of livestock and poultry, and provided subsidies on such items as fertilizer, certified seed, and chemical pesticides.

Early in his administration, Pérez signed the Law of Remission and Consolidation of the Agricultural Debt. The law cancelled small farmers' debts and consolidated agroindustrialists' obligations; IAN subsequently assumed the cancelled debts. Although admitting that the president probably cancelled the debts because he believed it was the right thing to do, critics quickly pointed out that the government thereby encouraged a lackadaisical attitude among the small farmers toward their financial obligations. Another innovation involved private banks. A new law required the banks to keep 20 percent of their funds for agricultural investments or send the money to the Central Bank. The funds would be invested in production, transport, warehousing, and in the mechanization of agrolivestock products. The government hoped to raise 6,000 million bolivars annually and thus multiply the credits of ICAP, BANDAGRO, and other credit institutions. The administration also created additional agricultural organizations, such as the Fund for Agricultural Investigation (FIA), Fund for Agro-Livestock Development (FDA), Fund of Agro-Livestock Credit (FCA), and the Institute of Agro-Livestock Credit (ICAP). The FCA financed the fiscal infrastructure at the large-farm level and made funds available to private banks, and the ICAP financed agrarian reform for the small peasant producers.

The government's agricultural policy met with limited success. Pérez pointed to such accomplishments as the repair of old aqueducts, construction of new ones, and increased rural medical facilities. He complained that during the previous administration housing construction had concentrated on the suburban communities of medium and large cities, almost totally abandoning the rural zones. His minister of agriculture and livestock pointed to the increase of agricultural production over the five-year period, 4.5 percent annually in spite of heavy rains in 1976, and to other statistics such as 14 percent more calories and 20 percent more proteins for the rural population and increased land distribution compared to the Caldera government.[19]

Nevertheless, the debit side of the ledger cannot be ignored. In spite of the dramatic increase in investment funds, agricultural output grew at only a slightly higher rate than the previous five-year period (approximately 1 percent). Critics also complained that massive government expenditures came too quickly, too easily, and without the expertise needed to guarantee an effective use of the funds. Programs suffered from inadequate organization and planning; such heavy spending financed a wasteful bureaucracy while subsidizing inefficient farmers. Furthermore, although the president stated that his predecessor spent too much money to import agrolivestock products, under the Pérez governemtn food imports from the United States grew from 500 million bolivars in 1970 to more than 2 billion bolivars by 1979.[20] Stimulated by the largest rise in income and purchasing power of any previous period, food imports strained the capacity of Venezuela's port facilities.

Various factors caused the food import substitution policy to fail. The price of imported food is cheaper than Venezuelan-produced products and the rural sector cannot meet the increasing urban demand. More livestock requires additional feed grains that Venezuela cannot grow in adequate supply because of its tropical climate. Products such as powdered milk must be imported because poor people do not have refrigerators to keep locally produced milk. The situation led one agricultural expert to remark that Venezuela exemplifies a double dependency on petroleum exports and food imports.[21]

A study analyzing the condition of the country's poor reported that of the approximate 150,000 rural families, only 20 percent had access to mechanization. Almost 80 percent of the agrarian credit went to large commercial farmers and agroindustry, and the small and medium-sized peasant holdings received only 10 percent of state credit. Since more than 80 percent of the national income went to the cities, peasant inequality manifested itself in the urban-rural dimension as well as within the rural sector. The authors concluded that the peasant condition within the country was relatively worse.[22]

The Herrera Government

As stated in the Sixth National Plan (1981–85), the government's agricultural policy set higher production goals to be supported by increased agricultural credit, expanded storage facilities, deregulated food prices at retail, reduced duties on many important foods, and producer incentive prices for some products. The government hoped that agriculture would reach the level obtained in other sectors of the economy, thereby reducing disequilibrium and contributing to a lower inflation rate. Furthermore, by modernizing the rural communities and providing them with the fiscal infrastructure, necessary services, and access to cultural and recreational facilities comparable to those of the urban sector, the rural population would be incorporated into the country's socioeconomic development, progressively eradicating rural marginality and reducing the exodus to the cities. The government's strategy was, simply, growth accompanied by a better distribution of income.[23]

President Herrera addressed himself to the related problems of price controls and subsidies. Minimum farm prices were first instituted by CMA to supervise food imports and oversee price policies. However, instead of protecting the farmer, these minimum prices effectively became maximum levels. Consumer price controls imposed during the 1970s by the Caldera and Pérez administrations made Venezuela more dependent on cheap imports. Price controls and subsidies also put a heavy burden on the state and seriously inhibited modernization efforts. Hoping to move toward a free market economy, Herrera removed all major agricultural subsidies except for milk, promising a food-stamp program for the poorest sectors (that never occurred). Food prices subsequently rose more rapidly and were caught up with international food price increases. Although commercial farmers and agroindustrialists demanded better prices as incentives to invest in new facilities, the government had to worry about the social consequences of implementing food price rises during difficult economic times. By 1981, this concern influenced the government's decision to institute price controls. Thus, rather than allowing market forces to determine supply, demand, and prices, Herrera continued to rely on the preferential-dollar treatment of food imports.

The government believed the farmers must have more incentives to raise production, and therefore increased land distribution and granted more titles than its predecessors. The president also established a private agency of National Agricultural Insurance, funded by the IAN and FCA, to protect the investments of farmers and livestock producers against losses due to adverse climate conditions and disease. The agency also provided life insurance for the small and medium-sized peasant families. In addition, to provide infrastructure for the consolidation of settlements and to obtain credits and socioeconomic promotion for settlement families, the government introduced two new programs, Integral Projects of Agrarian Reform (PIRA) and Integral Rural Areas Development (ARDI).

It hoped that CMA would bring the country closer to food self-sufficiency and obtain the best prices for the producers. In 1981, CMA established a program that encouraged farmers to bring their products to a designated location.[24] Although CMA bought the products (mostly vegetables and some meat), it did not pay the farmers immediately. The farmers understood that they would be paid after CMA sold the products to the consumers, but payment was often delayed from three months to two years. CMA then trucked the products to 16 different cities and sold them during early Saturday morning vegetable fairs, the "popular markets." It charged the consumers slightly more than it paid the farmers or it might charge them a little less, depending on local competition from municipal markets. CMA would sell any remaining products to local hospitals or nutritional institutes at big discounts. CMA paid the farmers (eventually) more than they used to receive and charged the consumers less than they used to pay. By eliminating the middlemen, the farmers dealt directly with the consumers through CMA's services.

I visited two fairs attended by thousands of people in the cities of Maracay and Valencia. They were well organized with a competent administrator in charge, and long lines moved quite well as people entered from one area and left from another. I found opinions quite positive. Consumers liked the fact that prices were fixed and cheaper than they used to be charged in a municipal market, and that the products were fresh. A few did complain, however, that the fairs were located on the city outskirts and were not easy to reach. Without cars, heavy loads had to be carried a considerable distance. According to several Social Christian peasant leaders, "The CMA is the peasant's enemy."[25] According to their view, CMA delayed too long in paying the peasants and the peasants did not receive adequate credits. These critics believed that the peasants were better off selling to middlemen because they were paid immediately. We might add that in spite of the CMA regional fairs and storage facilities, approximately 50 percent of all fruits and vegetables reportedly spoiled before reaching the consumers.

In November 1982, at the government's request, the U.S. Department of Agriculture sent a team of experts to Venezuela who subsequently published a report.[26] The task force pointed out that governmental agencies overgoverned the agricultural sector and recommended less official involvement in the storage, marketing, and distribution of farm products. Instead, the private sectors and the farmers should participate in these activities. In addition, CMA should withdraw from price support programs for basic commodities and allow producers to sell to consumers. The receiving and shipping center (Centro de Acopio) in the state of Mérida, operated by a farmers' association, could be a model for the country. The government should also place a greater emphasis on commercial agriculture because "the time has come to take additional action to transfer federally owned land to commercial farmers in units of sufficient size to be economically viable. Farming must be financially rewarding to attract capital, managerial talent, and labor."[27] This should be encouraged by accelerated land transfer, the security of land titles, and increased investment in irrigation projects to enhance water use.

The task force called for better research and technical information for farmers, as well as long-term governmental planning that would result in a more attractive agricultural investment climate. Other recommendations were to discontinue subsidies on animal feed, install refrigerated storage facilities at major wholesale and distribution centers, redesign retail markets to cut delays in delivery and shipment of perishables, and allow producers to grade their crops, thereby setting prices according to quality rather than uniform, government-set standards.

Although conceived more than a year before the report's publication, the content of the Herrera government's proposed "Long-Term Agricultural Development Plan" (PLANAGRI) was nevertheless influenced by the experts' analysis.[28] The result of an extended survey of agricultural experts, professors, and various technicians, PLANAGRI proposed a 30-year agricultural plan, integrated into an overall national development plan, and co-ordinated by MAC in conjunction with CORDIPLAN and the Ministry of the Environment and Renewable Natural Resources (MARNR). Because AD and COPEI technicians worked on the proposal, PLANAGRI's authors hoped that agricultural develop-ment would have bipartisan, indeed multipartisan, support. Several AD agrarian leaders commented that PLANAGRI was the best idea the *copeyanos* had produced and that the ideal would be the removal of agrarian policy from the political debate.[29] The various PLANAGRI proposals include basing agricultural devel-opment on supply and demand rather than on fixed prices and that 50 percent of the invested capital should come from the state, with the remainder from the private sector and foreign sources. Recognizing that increased world food demand leads to even greater Venezuelan vulnerability, PLANAGRI emphasizes the necessity of food import substitution.

Unfortunately, supporters of the Herrera agricultural policy point to only a few successes. At the end of his term, Venezuela was self-sufficient in poultry, pork, rice, coffee, eggs, and many fruits and vegetables. It was exporting chicken and eggs at competitive prices and impressive gains were made in livestock, dairy, and grain output. The government began to make a conscious effort to remove state institutions from the agricultural production, dis-tribution, and consuming process. Most of the gains were directly attributable to subsidy removals, price relief, and CMA's de-creasing role in importing, storing, and marketing of food. These changes provided better incentive for domestic producers and increased the private sector's role. Although severe weather during 1980–81 contributed to a decline in production, the country recovered by 1982 and the 1983 agricultural production rate was actually more than 4 percent.

Nevertheless, the negative factors outweigh the positive ones and compared to previous periods the argicultural growth rate declined. During the Herrera administration's first four years, agriculture's percentage of the gross domestic product grew only 1.4 percent annually, and although employing approximately 17 to 20 percent of the working population, agriculture contributed only 6 percent to the overall GDP. Furthermore, food imports con-tinued to rise, reaching 60 to 70 percent of the country's total food needs and costing more than $1 billion in 1982. The agricultural growth could not satisfy the expanding urban population and the rapidly developing livestock industry created additional demands for corn, sorghum, and soybean meal. Venezuela was a net exporter of sugar during the 1960s and early 1970s but the country imported 43 percent of its consumption by the end of 1983. Furthermore, the government simply could not solve the basic problems of transportation to the market, irrigation, enough water, and adequate financing and technical assistance. As a result, overall agricultural production declined significantly.

Due to declining petroleum exports, the government faced a budget contraction that naturally affected its agricultural policy. Agencies such as MAC, CMA, BANDAGRO, and ICAP simply did not receive enough money. CMA had to cut 8,000 people from its payroll.[30] Less money was available for commercial loans, or it arrived too late and farmers had to delay planting. The general frustrations contributed to COPEI's poor 1983 electoral performance in the agricultural states of Aragua, Barinas, Cojedes, Guárico, and Yaracuy.

The farmers themselves compounded the problems. Because Pérez had forgiven their loans, many farmers borrowed heavily, hoping that subsequent administrations would do the same. Not only did the small and medium-sized farmers refuse to repay their loans; large producers who contributed to the major political parties were guilty of the same tactic. As a result several companies and agencies, such as farm equipment manufacturers and even BANDAGRO, went into receivership. Some farmers were reluctant to invest in increased production because they were not certain what policies a new administration would bring. This fear to take risks meant that local production of feed grains, such as corn and sorghum, would continue to be inadequate. At the end of the Herrera administration, more than two-thirds of Venezuela's food products continued to be imported at one-third the domestic price.

The Lusinchi Program

During the 1983 electoral campaign, Acción Democrática presented a "Program and Governmental Action (for the) Agricultural Sector" that formed the basis for several proposals and specific legislation of the Lusinchi government.[31] True to their long-standing position, AD and Lusinchi emphasized the need to improve the rural families' condition in housing, sanitation, education, and recreation. Hopefully such steps would slow down the rural exodus. Lusinchi also called for a significant lowering of the proportion of imported foodstuffs by increasing local production of those products with a high degree of dependency such as cereals, corn, sorghum, and sugar. This would be accomplished by a reorientation of the agrarian reform that, in addition to being sensitive to the social content, must emphasize production goals.

Lusinchi wants to combine agricultural reactivation with industrial development, believing that new business ventures in processing and marketing agricultural products will greatly contribute to economic recovery. He also supports a more active state role in the agricultural sector and vertical integration of economic organizations through the "Integrated Collective Peasant Industry" that will diversify and integrate production and provide more administrative and technical assistance. Greater centralization will also result through "Unities of Agro-Livestock Development" that will direct each state's agricultural plan. The head of the national Unity of Agro-Livestock Development will control the activities of IAN, ICAP, BANDAGRO, FCA, and CMA. That person will also direct infrastructure works, as well as animal and vegetable production. Among other proposals are obligatory military service in agro-livestock frontier development programs and a ten-year program to concentrate on increasing production of a variety of agricultural products. The latter would designate 1 million hectares for vegetables and an additional 1 million hectares for new production. The plan apparently would supersede PLANAGRI and the 30-year time span.

Upon assuming office President Lusinchi proposed that the government make credits readily available for new plantings while helping farmers pay their past loans.[32] Apparently the farmers could not expect cancellation of previous debts as had occurred during the Pérez administration. The government also introduced two new laws in the Congress, the Organic Law for Restructuring the Official Agricultural Sector and the Program for Agricultural Development. These laws foresee reorganizing the Ministry of Agriculture and Livestock and putting agricultural development into law regardless of changes in MAC, in agricultural functionaries at the secondary level, or in the government itself.

In March 1984, President Lusinchi asked approximately 25 agencies and institutes, including CMA and its grain storage operations, BANDAGRO, to devise individual reorganization plans within 60 days. If the government were not satisfied, it would offer them for sale to the private sector. CMA and BANDAGRO likely will be dissolved, reorganized, or constituted as another organization with a different name.[33] At the time of this writing CMA continues to be involved in the vegetable fairs, but the government (as its predecessor) wants to turn the operation over to the producers entirely.

Lusinchi has taken other steps to increase agricultural development. The percentage private banks must designate for the agricultural sector has been raised from 20 percent to 22.5 percent. In addition, the government raised consumer beef prices to eliminate the illegal shipment of slaughtered beef to Columbia. (Farmers had been receiving more for their beef because the Venezuelan price was too low.) Toward the end of 1984, the official exchange rate was raised from 4.3 to 7.5 bolivars to the dollar. The cost of agricultural imports will thereby increase considerably; however, the Lusinchi administration hopes to significantly raise domestic agricultural production. In order to aid the adjustment to the new exchange rate, the government periodically designates selected commodities that will remain at the 4.3 preference rate until the end of 1985, while moving the bulk of the agricultural products to the 7.5 rate. Nevertheless, there is serious concern about the inflationary impact on agriculture. The prices of domestically produced grain, oil seed, corn meal, and edible oil will rise considerably. Higher priced animal feed will result in sharp price rises for poultry and pork products.

In all these actions, the government is not following any particular ideology or philosophy. It is simply trying to solve problems and overcome the immediate crisis. As its predecessor, however, the major problem the Lusinchi administration faces is that of budget limitations.

CONCLUSIONS

Dictatorship and Democracy

A comparison of the Gómez and Pérez Jiménez dictatorships to the democratic regime leads to the obvious conclusion that the agricultural policies were significantly different. The Gómez government's policy was based on continuing the practices of Venezuela's past. Land concentration in the hands of the few meant that the *latifundistas'* power was never challenged and semifeudal conditions continued to form the basis of rural life. The Pérez Jiménez government's reversal of the *trienio* agrarian reform resulted in a return to the nineteenth-century Gómez agricultural pattern. Changing conditions during the mid-twentieth-century dictatorship led to such modifications as a more clearly defined emphasis on commercial agriculture, on agro-industry, and an unsuccessful effort to create viable government-controlled peasant syndicates. Both dictatorships assumed an antipeasant policy, and increased income from petroleum exports particularly during the Pérez Jiménez period resulted in declining investments in the agriculture sector.

In contrast to the dictatorships, the democratic regime's agricultural policy led to an attack on Venezuela's historical rural pattern and the *latifundia* system. Agrarian reform and the urban elite-rural alliance held out hope for the peasants that social change was indeed possible in exchange for supporting the regime and political democracy. The effort to incorporate the peasants into the socioeconomic-political system through peasant unions-political parties-governmental linkages theoretically indicated that the peasants would become actors as well as objects of agricultural development. Furthermore, the democratic regime's agricultural policy resulted in a greater governmental involvement in agricultural development through various agencies and institutes.

Although agricultural policy and agrarian reform stood in sharp contrast to the dictatorships' relative neglect, the comparative results were somewhat similar. According to the 1937 Agricultural Census and the 1969 USAID survey, landownership concentration only differed by a few percentage points. The growth rate of agricultural product during the Pérez Jiménez administration with a smaller population was practically the same as that under the democratic regime. Furthermore, the process of petroleum export dependency at the expense of agricultural development accelerated in the postdictatorial period and required a higher percentage of food imports.

Although one might conclude that it made no difference whether the country was under a dictatorship or democracy, we must distinguish between means and ends. The democratic regime's agricultural policy and agrarian reform showed a commitment to alleviate the human condition of the peasants. The disappointing results of agricultural development in no way detracted from that commitment. On the contrary, the effort to improve rural life and enhance agricultural development continued in the post-1958 period. Had Venezuela been governed by a dictatorial rather than a democratic regime, the peasants' condition might have been worse under the military-oligarchical alliance than it was under the urban elite-rural alliance.

AD and COPEI

We can distinguish the major parties' agricultural policies from several viewpoints that include administrations, different governments representing the same political party (Betancourt-Leoni to Pérez and Caldera to Herrera), and philosophical differences in the approach to agricultural problem solving. We recall that the Betancourt agrarian reform was a policy of the AD-COPEI governing coalition. Although COPEI did not participate in the Leoni government, the *copeyanos* remained committed to agrarian reform during the Leoni period. We also recall that Betancourt faced a serious guerrilla movement and that he emphasized social change to win peasant support to increase agricultural production. Giving land to those who worked it (the social function) meant that land redistribution, expropriated primarily from the private sector, was a crucial element in the Betancourt-Leoni program. Toward the end of the Betancourt administration and throughout that of Leoni, consolidation took place and economic objectives became more important.

The first COPEI government emphasized economic objectives to an even greater degree as Caldera shifted from the Betancourt/COPEI-Leoni agricultural policies. By explicitly stressing the economic over the social factor under the rubric of higher production, the government decreased credits for the peasant sector and increased them for the commercial and agroindustrial sectors. Government-owned land rather than the private sector was the source for slower land distribution. In spite of these efforts the results were poor, and the agricultural growth rate continued to fall.

With more funds at his disposal, Pérez hoped to do more to raise the peasants' standard of living, thus somewhat returning to the Betancourt-Leoni principle of emphasizing the social component of agrarian reform. The cancellation of debts and increased land distribution were consistent with this approach. If this effort were successful, rural stratification would decrease, leading to a more equitable socioeconomic balance among peasants, commercial farmers, and agroindustrialists. Although the maldistribution of rural income probably worsened, the increased agricultural product growth rate was almost 1.5 percent higher than during the Caldera administration.

The underlying assumptions of Herrera's agricultural policy were closer to those of the Pérez administration than to those of Caldera. In order to achieve a higher agricultural growth rate plus a more equitable distribution of income he increased the rate of land distributions and the granting of titles. However, he differed from previous administrations in making an effort, albeit limited, to lessen the government's role in agricultural production and marketing. The Herrera government's agricultural output was the lowest of the democratic regimes, and the three AD administrations had a higher productive growth rate than the two COPEI administrations. COPEI defenders can point to such reasons for their relatively poor performance as agrarian reform starting from a lower level, agricultural production growing more rapidly during the early 1960s, more money available to Pérez, budget contraction, and the fact that under Herrera the farmers did not pay back the loans.

The AD and COPEI philosophical differences concern a basic question: How do you take care of the poor peasants? Following a constant theme from the Betancourt-Leoni era, some *adecos* say they want to humanize the rural sector rather than industrialize it. Other *adecos* want to focus on the producers, their social organization, equitable rural income, and rural society rather than on particular products. They take the small approach and are reluctant to emphasize agroindustry. In a sense they advocate integrated rural development that focuses on rural rather than on agricultural development, as well as emphasizing integration. The World Bank defines "rural development ... as a strategy designed to improve the economic and social life of a specific group of people—the rural poor ... ; integrated rural development means the integration of the left out into society and the economy as a whole ... "[34]

Certainly COPEI does not want to turn its back on the rural poor. Nevertheless, a principal COPEI agricultural expert believes that Venezuela should stop playing the "game of agrarian reform" and instead think in terms of an agricultural policy. It is no longer a question of helping the poor peasants but one of producing more, and this means major investments in commercial agriculture and agroindustry.[35] A former COPEI minister of agriculture and livestock believes that agricultural policy should concentrate on those who can use machinery, produce, and repay their loans. The others should look for another way of livelihood.[36] Both these spokesmen point out that those who make the exodus to the cities are younger and more talented. Therefore, it is preferable to develop commercial agriculture and agroindustry not only to increase production but to find jobs and improve the condition of those who remain in the rural sector. Rather than worrying about giving them titles for *minifundia*, the remaining peasants should be transformed into a class of farmers with adequate housing, a decent standard of living, and dignity.

The basic difference between AD and COPEI, whether to focus on rural or agricultural development, is one of emphasis. Both are concerned about peasant welfare and the need to increase agricultural production, but many *adecos* feel more strongly that the latter should not be realized at the expense of the former. Hopefully, as *adecos* and *copeyanos* work together to increase agricultural production and indeed to transform rural society, their philosophical differences will become less important as they turn to more immediate needs of agricultural problem solving.

Impact of Agricultural Policy on the Viability of the Democratic Regime

We can determine the impact of agricultural policy on the viability of the democratic regime by considering whether output has been sufficient to meet Venezuela's needs, whether the goals of agrarian reform have been realized, and whether democracy has reached the rural population. To refine our analysis, we must break down democracy into its economic, social, and political components.

In the economic sphere, agrarian reform did not result in sufficient agricultural development. Although the cumulative annual agricultural growth rate of approximately 4.3 percent over the last 35 years is high compared to most developing countries, it has been insufficient to satisfy the demand generated by accelerated urbanization, the general rise in income, and a very high demographic growth rate (3 to 3.5 percent annually) augmented by illegal immigration, primarily from Colombia.[37] Thus one can question whether the small increase in production justifies the large agricultural investments. Furthermore, agrarian reform did not accomplish its principal goal of establishing the unimodal strategy by which the individual peasant landowner would become a modern agricultural producer within the framework of small-scale farm units. Instead, Venezuela continues to be characterized by the bimodal pattern of agricultural development consisting of numerous *minifundia* and the large farms of 50 hectares and more, the latter accounting for most of the cultivated area and production and enjoying certain privileges such as greater access to credit.[38]

The state controls approximately 65 percent of the economy and has become the modern *latifundista*. It regulates loans, interest rates, prices, imports, exports, and storage facilities for the peasants as well as the commercial farmers. The lack of definitive title requires more than 90 percent of the agricultural producers to go to the official bank for credit because they do not have collateral. Thus the peasants and farmers are totally dependent upon the state. Furthermore, not only are many governmental officials simply poor managers but numerous governmental institutions and an expanding bureaucracy increase the opportunities for corruption. Several officials and peasant leaders told the author that it is often necessary to bribe someone to obtain a loan. Added to these deficiencies is increasing agricultural dependency on imported machinery, equipment, seeds, fertilizers, pesticides, technology, and food. If Venezuela continues to import up to 70 percent of its food, not only the viability of the democratic regime but the sovereignty of the country will be seriously challenged.

According to Jaime Lusinchi's *Social Pact*, "... political liberty only lives and gives its maximum fruits when society is just, egalitarian, [and offers] solidarity." If we conclude that agricultural production has not increased enough to justify the large investments we can raise the same question in regard to the peasants' living conditions. Throughout the period of the democratic regime, Venezuela has continued to demonstrate the traditional rural stratification social system under which the tillers of the land are at the bottom of the ladder. Although agarian reform pushed the peasants a few steps higher and their well-being improved somewhat, the upward social mobility of other societal groups accelerated at a much faster rate and the peasants' relative social condition declined. Inequitable income distribution means that approximately 12 percent of the total 17 percent rural population live in misery, the *marginados* who are literally outside the economy. Indeed, the fruits of political liberty cannot ripen in the arid soil of peasant social injustice.

The political component concerns the effort to have the peasants participate in national events, a process John Duncan Powell noted as crucial to the development of political democracy. The endeavor was doomed from the beginning because the urban reformers wanted to create what *they* considered to be democracy, thereby controlling the timing and extent of agrarian reform, determined more by political pressure than by the genuine social and economic needs of the rural population. For example, many complain that FCV leaders are either government bureaucrats or politicians who do not listen to the peasants' voices and are only concerned with obtaining jobs for their people and delivering the votes. The local elites reinforce the patronage/dependency relationship and, as observed elsewhere, "Patronage further secures the priviledged position of the elite, while the reciprocal dependency further undermines the position of the poor.... Most attempts to organize the rural poor, if they survive at all, are 'captured' by the local elites, who use them to enhance position, power, and wealth more effectively than before."[39] Although the peasants vote in local and national elections, their participation in national events through governmental-political party-peasant organizational linkages is circumscribed by political broker elites who speak in the name of the peasants but act for themselves.

The urban elites broke their promise that rural power relationships would change and the peasants' condition would improve markedly. State paternalism replaced the *latifundia* system and elite control and manipulation became the order of the day. Political peace in the cities was purchased at the cost of misery in the countryside and the decline in peasant electoral strength accelerated the demise of the rural-urban elite alliance. Although peasant rejection of the early guerrilla movement in the early 1960s reflected a limited absolute improvement in living conditions at that time, and the patronage system contributed to a more stable political climate, overall the bimodal agricultural strategy coupled with inadequate output indicate that Venezuela must break the chains of the state paternalistic society. Unless this occurs, agricultural policy will continue to have a negative impact on the viability of the democratic regime and democracy will not reach the rural poor.

Prognosis for the Remainder of the 1980s

As Venezuela faces the remainder of the 1980s, it finds a very different situation than that of the Betancourt-Leoni era. In the former period the government perceived a social necessity to improve the condition of a large rural population; today it must confront an economic necessity of feeding an even larger urban element. The crisis is as great if not greater than that of the early 1960s because a relatively smaller rural population must produce more to feed an expanding urban population. According to a U.S. Department of Agriculture study the country's projected 1990 population will be somewhat less than 21 million, representing a 54 percent rise from 1975, but the birth rate will decline to 2.58 percent.[40]

Venezuela must become self-sufficient as soon as possible because the government will not have as much money for the higher priced agricultural imports. The prospects are not encouraging. Besides expanding the irrigated areas, the government cannot do much about the land-climate problem. Furthermore, projections of production and consumption indicate continued growth in feed grains and meal imports through 1990 and moderate livestock growth. The overall level of self-sufficiency will remain below 50 percent while total import requirements will expand by approximately 1 million metric tons. However, the economic emergency might benefit the peasants somewhat and offset their electoral power decline. The 17 percent rural sector is still a significant voting bloc, and the elite needs the peasants to feed the growing urban population and lessen food import dependency. These developments might lead to a new urban elite-peasant alliance based on economic necessity.

The two approaches to agricultural development transcend AD-COPEI philosophical differences, and economists and technicians have honest disagreements. One school of thought advocates cooperative and collective integrated peasant agricultural industries through which the peasants would be responsible for their own problem solving as they compete with commercial agriculture and agroindustry. The progressive modernization of essentially all farm households would be under a well-conceived, broadly based approach. The social advantages would be realized through improved health and nutrition and a more rapid expansion of employment opportunities that promote higher returns to labor an a narrowing income inequality. Proponents of this view fear that a "crash modernization" program under a labor-saving capital-intensive direction will make it impossible for the great majority of the rural population to participate in the gains in productivity and income.

Nevertheless poverty is such a huge and pervasive problem in rural Venezuela, and the lack of resources so acute, that any distributional adjustment will almost be impossible to implement on a sufficient scale to be of substantial benefit to the poor. This factor lends greater weight to the second school of thought that calls for a resources shift away from the peasants to a greater emphasis on commercial agriculture and agroindustry, thereby increasing agricultural productivity more rapidly. Given the philosophical bent of AD, it will be difficult for the Lusinchi government to opt exclusively for this approach. Scarce capital resources will require deciding upon difficult alternatives such as peasant welfare or commercial and agroindustrial development, and gainful employment of poor farm families or a more rapid increase in agricultural productivity.

The outlook for the peasants is dismal and their relative condition will continue to decline under the present agricultural structure. The government might indeed be forced to shift to a greater emphasis on commercial agriculture and agroindustry. If this does occur, the short-term period will be very difficult for the peasants and their condition will probably worsen even further during the transitional period. However, the continuing numerical decline of the peasant population may hold out a ray of hope. A small percentage of the population, commercial farmers who have incorporated the remaining peasants and the agroindustrialists, will remain in their rural areas, produce more, and live better. Once the peasant class no longer comprises a majority of the rural population, it will be possible for agricultural policy to have a positive impact on the viability of the democratic regime, and the economic, social, and political components of democracy will finally reach rural Venezuela.

In March 1985, the government introduced a plan to turn one-third of existing peasant enterprises into profitable companies. Entitled the integrated Campesino Collective Farm Enterprises (ECACI), the plan anticipates reorganizing 34 promising co-operatives that will receive loans of 2 to 3 million bolivars to expand operations, from planting to marketing. Trust funds will aid in capitalizing the new companies. Believing that the training of peasant leadership is basic to the success of the ECACI project, the IAN drew up a plan to improve rural education from the primary level up, with reports on vegetable gardens, agricultural development theory, and model farms. Volunteers from the national literacy committee began a three-year campaign to teach 600,000 Venezuelans to read and write.

NOTES

1. Scott Swanson, "Agriculture: A Basket Case" *Business Venezuela* (Venezuelan-American Chamber of Commerce and Industry), September/October 1983.

2. John Duncan Powell, *Political Mobilization of the Venezuela Peasant* (Cambridge, Mass.: Harvard University Press, 1971), pp. 15–30.

3. For the *trienio* period, see ibid., pp. 68–85, and Robert J. Alexander, *The Venezuelan Democratic Revolution: A Profile of the Regime of Rómulo Betancourt* (New Brunswick, N.J.: Rutgers University Press, 1964), pp. 26–31.

4. John Duncan Powell, "Venezuelan Agrarian Problems in Comparative Perspective," in *Venezuela: 1969 Analysis of Progress*, ed. Philip B. Taylor, Jr. Papers Prepared for a Conference by Johns Hopkins University and the University of Houston, November 10–11, 1969, Washington, D.C. Applying Samuel Huntington's thesis, Powell believes that the Venezuelan agrarian reform was fundamentally a political phenomenon reflecting the quid pro quo between the urban elite and peasant masses.

5. James W. Wilkie, "Measuring Land Reform," Supplement to the Statistical Abstract of Latin America (Los Angeles: UCLA Latin American Center, 1974), p. iv.

6. Interview with Víctor Giménez Landínez, July, 7, 1971. During the Caldera administration, Giménez Landínez was also director of the IAN.

7. Alexander, *Venezuelan Democratic Revolution*, p. 191.

8. Interview with former President Rafael Caldera, December 15, 1983.

9. See República de Venezuela, "Primer (Segundo, Tercer) Mensaje del Presidente de la República Rómulo Betancourt (Raúl Leoni) al Congreso Nacional" (Caracas: Ministerio de Información y Turismo, 1960–67).

10. See the discussion by Louis E. Heaton, *The Agricultural Development of Venezuela* (New York: Praeger, 1969), pp. 5–57.

11. República de Venezuela, Ministerio de Agricultura y Cría, "La Nueva Estrategía del Desarrollo Agrícola con Especial Referencia al la Política Agro-Industrial" (Acarigua, November 1971).

12. *Seminario COPEI*, December 16–22, 1969.

13. George Kastner, María Teresa Tello, et al., *El reto de alimentarnos* (Caracas: Instituto de Estudios Superiores de Administración [IESA], 1982), pp. 60–61.

14. Oficina Central de Información, *Cuenta ante el país*, Mensaje del Presidente de la República y Exposiciones de los Ministros del Gabinete ante el Congreso Nacional in El Cuarto Año de Gobierno (Caracas, 1973), pp. 431–36.

15. Inter-American Development Bank, *Economic and Social Progress in Latin America*, Annual Report 1974 (Washington, D.C., 1974), p. 428.

16. Meir Merhav, *Hacia una política de desarrollo agrícola y de cambio estructural orientada hacia el exterior* (Caracas: Instituto de Comercio Exterior, 1974).

17. Interview with Miguel Rodríguez, hijo, minister of agriculture and livestock under the Caldera government, December 16, 1983.

18. "Segundo Mensaje del Presidente," 1975, p. 179.

19. Interview with Gustavo Pinto Cohén, minister of agriculture and livestock under the Pérez government, December 12, 1983.

20. L. Jay Atkinson and Oswald P. Blaich, "Venezuela: A Prospective Market for Grain and Livestock Products" (Washington, D.C.: U.S. Department of Agriculture, 1983), p. 2.

21. Interview with Gustavo Pinto Cóhen, December 12, 1983.

22. N.S. Relemberg, H. Karner, and V. Kohler, *Los pobres de Venezuela* (Buenos Aires: Talleres Graficos, 1979), pp. 56–57.

23. IESA; Atkinson and Blaich, "Venezuela: A Prospective Market."

24. Interviews with Celeste E. López, CMA regional administrator in Maracay (Aragua) and Valencia (Carabobo), and Miguel Zapata, national CMA official, December 9–10, 1983.

25. Interview with Víctor Pérez and Héctor Ramos S., Social Christian Agrarian Movement (MASC), Valencia, December 10, 1983.

26. Clarence D. Palmby, Robert W. Long, Stephen Tavilla, T. Kelly White, Jr., and Richard F. Rortvedt, "Report of the U.S. Presidential Agricultural Task Force to Venezuela" (Washington, D.C.: U.S. Department of Agriculture, 1983).

27. Ibid., p. 6.

28. Interview with Nydia Villegas de Rodríguez, minister of agriculture and livestock under the Herrera government, December 9, 1983. See also República de

Venezuela: MAC-MARNR-CORDIPLAN, 1983, and various MAC documents and pamphlets under the same title published between 1981 and 1983.

29. Interview with Rodrigo Rodríguez, Ricardo Bello, and Gilberto Rodríguez, members of the National Agrarian Section of Acción Democrática, December 13, 1983.

30. Interview with Hugo Estrada Ripari, president of CMA under the Herrera administration, December 7, 1983.

31. Acción Democrática, "Programa y Acción de Gobierno Sector Agrícola, Comisión de Agricultura" (Caracas: Marzo, 1983).

32. During February to April 1984, various Caracas newspapers and magazines described the Lusinchi administration's actions.

33. Part of CMA's problem is that it has been charged with corrupt practices. For example, the newspapers reported that its previous director had confiscated 80 million bolivars. He was replaced and the matter was dropped.

34. Bruce F. Johnston and William C. Clark, *Redesigning Rural Development: A Strategic Perspective* (Baltimore: Johns Hopkins University Press, 1982), pp. 248–49.

35. Interview with Luis Marcano Coello, December 13, 1983. Former President Caldera told the author that had his reelection bid been successful, Marcano would have been the minister of agriculture and livestock.

36. Interview with Miguel Rodríguez, hijo, December 16, 1983.

37. Gustavo Pinto Cohén "Venezuelan Agricultural Development: A General View," in *Agroclimate Information for Development*, ed. David F. Cusack (Boulder, Colo.: Westview Press, 1982).

38. For a discussion of the unimodel and bimodal strategies, see Johnston and Clark, *Redesigning Rural Development*, pp. 70–71.

39. Ibid., p. 167.

40. Atkinson and Blaich, "Venezuela: A Prospective Market."

13

Indian Affairs

H. Dieter Heinen and Walter Coppens

Never since the first Spaniards appeared on the Venezuelan coast on July 31, 1498 has change for the area's Indian population been so drastic and rapid as in the last ten years. In contrast to neighboring countries, the oil economy and the resulting boom in the nation's growth centers has kept the pressure off the more than one-third of its territory where some 150,000 Indians have retreated.[1] Furthermore, the "geological imperative"[2] in the search for Amazonian mineral wealth has proceeded on the northern shore of the continent with greater circumspection than elsewhere.

Besides constituting about 90 percent of Venezuela's ethnic variability and speaking some 32 different languages, the indigenous nations[3] of Venezuela are located mainly in sensitive border areas. This may be relevant to geopolitical thinkers but is far removed from the pressing problems of urban areas when half of the country's population of 15,626,955 is concentrated.[4] The Indians constitute less than 1 percent of that total and belong to the so-called "Lowland Indians"[5] populations of the continent's tropical forest, although some live well above the 1,000-meter line. Table 13.1 details Indian administrative units and ethnic subdivisions.

The authors would like to thank Roberto Lizarralde for permission to use the materials contributed to the first edition of the book.

TABLE 13.1. Indian Administrative Units and Ethnic Groups

Administrative Units		Ethnic Groups	
Anzoátegui	4.406	Guajiro (*Wayúu*)	52,000
Apure	5.260	Warao	19.700
Bolívar	21.307	Pemon	11.700
Monagas	2.142	Yanomami	9.400
Sucre	.519	Sanema	2.200
Zulia	59.214	Kariña	7.000
T.F. Amazonas	30.042	Guajibo (*Hiwi*)	7.000
T.F. Delta Amacuro	17.755	Piaroa (*De'arua*)	6.800
		Yaruro (*Pumé*)	3.900
		Yukpa	3.400
		Ye'kuana	3.000
		Paraujano (*Añuu*)	2.600
		Panare (E'ñapa)	2.400
		Curripaco (*Kúrim*)	1.600
		Baríi	1.100
		Baniva	1.100
		Other	5.700
Venezuela	140.645		140.600

Source: Indian census, 1982, manual counting. See Haydée Seijas, "Metodología, operación, y resultados globales del Censo Indígena, 1982," paper presented at the 33nd Annual Convention of the Venezuelan Association for the Advancement of Science, Caracas, October 1983.

As radical change in the Indian areas is unfolding, so are the Indian policies tracing a seemingly contradictory movement to the point where it has been alleged, by Cambridge's Paul Henley among others, that "the absence of a coherent indigenist policy... may in fact be a policy in itself."[6] Thus we will sketch the most important developments on two levels: the highest policy-making sectors in Caracas and the increasing number of actors (at one point we counted more than 20 government agencies involved with indigenous affairs in the state of Bolívar alone). The latter are especially important as the decentralization policies decreed by Carlos Andrés Pérez came to be increasingly implemented from the mid-1970s on. Decentralization has strongly affected indigenous groups, and the consequences of democratic processes and their effects on ethnic groups accompanied by systemic ramification will be addressed in the concluding section.

THE INSTITUTIONAL SETTING

On May 20, 1820 Simón Bolívar updated colonial laws when he decreed that "all *resguardo* land [indigenous land organized on a communal basis according to colonial titles conferred in 1718] should be returned to the *naturales* as legitimate owners," whatever their present holders alleged. However, a series of laws enacted largely during the 1880s turned them into uncultivated waste lands—*tierras baldías*—which were treated as if unoccupied, thereby leaving the indigenous owners without legal protection of their territorial rights. It was in fact the threat of encroachment by Venezuela's neighbors that prompted the 1915 promulgation of the famous Ley de Misiones. Still in effect today, its provisions contradict the constitution by conferring extraterritorial rights through the vast expanses of the Apostolic Vicariates while curtailing the right of free movement.[7] This law, followed by a 1922 convention, entrusted the Capuchin missionaries with "reducing and civilizing" the indigenous peoples.

In more recent times, AD governments have left the Mission Act untouched in order to avoid conflict with the Catholic hierarchy. The COPEI government of Rafael Caldera had drafted a new law but left office before it could be promulgated. That of Luis Herrera Campins did not take up the matter. Accordingly, religious missionary congregations operate on the basis of a February 22, 1967 convention between the Capuchin Order and the Leoni government. The coverage of such other religious orders as the Salesians is subsumed under the convention. The active North American fundamentalist organizations, however, especially the New Tribes Mission (NTM), are regulated by ad hoc decisions without any legal foundations. And although the Judicial Advisory Board on October 30, 1967 attempted to limit the power of the religious missions, more informal attrition in the last 15 years has come from government agencies into such areas as education.

The phenomenon of Catholic missionary affairs has emerged as a new identification with the country, along with the decline of traditional proselytizing activities. There is a newfound role as defenders of Indian values against landowners, mining operations, fundamentalist zealots, and even the occasional excesses of certain government agencies. Earlier, the preponderance of the traditional missionary power structure had been jolted in 1947 with the establishment of the Indian National Commission (CIN), first responsible to the Ministry of Internal Affairs and after 1951 to the Justice Ministry, where an office of church and Indian affairs was created.

Following the 1958 collapse of the Pérez Jiménez dictatorship, a Technical Corps with a sizable budget was established to provide CIN with necessary technical knowledge. The government tried to redefine the power of foreign missionaries through the Judicial Advisory Board of the Justice Department, which stated on April 24, 1959 that "the Indians enjoy full legal status, whatever their degree of civilization. Neither the Indian Commission nor any of the institutions *officially created to civilize and protect the Indians* can therefore claim their legal representation."[8] The power of CIN and especially the Technical Corps was soon curtailed when COPEI's Andrés Aguilar became head of Justice in the Betancourt coalition. At a 1959 interministerial meeting there was criticism of "romanticism." The minister of justice repeated well-worn warnings against "creating a Museum of Indians" and "perpetuating the Indian Commission for a century."

Even the landmark Agrarian Reform Act of 1960 left ambiguous the legal situation of the indigenous population, for it was subsumed under the *campesino* population, even while the act "guarantees and recognizes the right of the indigenous populations which *de facto* retain their communal or extended family status ... to hold the lands, woods, and waterways which they occupy or which belong to them in sites where they customarily dwell, without detriment to their incorporation into national society according to this and other laws." The ambiguity lies in the failure to spell out exactly how the communal life and ethnic values of the Indians can be safeguarded as to their actual land use. There is also little attention to economic relations such as production units and the distribution of the social product by the traditional Indian mechanism of reciprocity.

The Agrarian Reform Act basically altered the nineteenth-century legislation that had eliminated communal land tenure, the *resguardos*. It endorsed the right of collective or individual usufruct, provided that the land had been occupied for at least two years.

This recognition constituted the first step toward acceptance of full-fledged property rights.[9] The act was also one of the first legal documents specifically treating the indigenous population together with the criollo peasantry. Article 77 of the 1961 constitution was also to pledge that the state would delimit "the Exceptive regime required to assume the protection of the indigenous communities and their progressive incorporation into national life." As Bonfil Batalla cogently stated, "The Indian policies of Latin American governments ... had had one final objective common to all, the integration of the Indians. The constitution of Latin American states, due in great measure to its colonial origin ... does not reflect—nor even admit—an undeniable historic fact: the pluri-ethnic character of the societies enveloped by those states."[10]

It is necesary here to distinguish among economic, social, and cultural integration. Most indigenous populations in Venezuela, possibly excepting the Yanomami and a few small groups such as the Hoti, are economically integrated through wage or contract labor and supplies of natural resources and crops. This is not often realized by the political parties, where the pattern of benign paternalism toward the indigenous population unites them. Differences are more a matter of style and short-range political expedience. The Social Christians tend to assign the Indians a theoretically more important role, as with the formation of federations under Caldera and the sponsorship of congresses by Herrera Campins. AD implements a more populist policy in attending to needs of food, housing, education, and health, while striving to integrate organizations into the peasant federation that the party dominates. True to its European middle-class origins, AD ignores the "Indianness" of large sectors of the same Venezuelan peasantry.

During the first COPEI government, large development projects in indigenous areas were organized through the Indigenous Development Unit of the National Agrarian Institute (IAN), which was implementing the 1960 reform. The newly created Comisión para el Desarrollo del Sur (CODESUR), on the other hand, was more concerned about the exploitation of mineral resources such as bauxite (located in the federal territory of Amazonas and in the Cedeño district of Bolívar) than in the local indigenous population. A National Border Council was created on

October 14, 1970 as a dependency of the Ministry of Foreign Affairs. It was responsible for an orderly settling of "empty" spaces in border areas, but was also a direct response to the Guyana uprisings of 1968 and 1969, which involved predominantly Indian populations and caused a large influx of indigenous refugees into Venezuela.

The council was composed of delegates from a host of government agencies and supported by a permanent staff. For the first time a document spelled out coherently how a broader based "human integration" was to be achieved; it was to be understood "as the process of selective integration through which the Nation incorporates all human, cultural and spiritual values that the population of the area may contribute, while ... encouraging the gradual assimilation of the most genuine institutions and values of Venezuelan nationhood" (Article 5, Section 2). The concept of selective integration held that Venezuela is a pluricultural entity including European, indigenous, and African components.[11]

While CODESUR declined under the AD government of Pérez, which took office in March 1974, other development programs experienced new impetus as a consequence of the enormous oil wealth streaming into the country at the time. A high government commission was named to rethink Indian policies and coordinate the activities of such established agencies as the Oficina Central de Asuntos Indigenas (OCAI) and newer entities such as the IAN and the National Border Council. On July 30, 1974 an agreement between OCAI and IAN gave the latter extensive agricultural development responsibilities, while the former concentrated on an education and consciousness-raising program carried out by *promotores indígenas* (mostly bilingual youths uncertain as to what they were to promote).

OCAI also embarked on an enlargement program whereby the three original Coordination Centers (Centros Indigenistas), already grown to a half-dozen, would swell to 21 so-called Nucleos de Acción Indigenista, and be backed by a large intermediate bureaucracy in state and territorial capitals consisting of six Centros Regionales de Acción Indigenista.[12] The Indians immediately and vehemently protested, as did their large delegation to the Forty-first International Congress of Americanists at Mexico City.[13] It was argued that with development projects in indigenous areas increasingly dependent upon such entities as the IAN and the Insituto de Crédito Agrícola y Pecuario (ICAP), the remaining educational functions of OCAI were more logically located at the Ministry of Education.

There was also increasing activity by the Agricultural Development department of the Corporación Venezolana de Guayana (CVG), which, together with Electrificación del Caroní (CVG-EDELCA), took an active interest in the headwaters of the Caroní. This area was the home of some 10,000 Pemón Indians and was crucial to the large Guri Dam. Consequently, in late 1977 OCAI was transferred to the Ministry of Education as the Ministerial Office for Border Zones and Indigenous Peoples (OMAFI). It was directed by Francisco Aurelio Rengifo, a close adviser of President Pérez. Unfortunately for the Indians, and despite Rengifo's sympathy and connections, the Ministry of Education was not geared to large-scale development projects. The OMAFI bureaucracy became the dumping ground for personnel in disfavor with other ministerial sections and insensitive to indigenous affairs. This tendency would continue under the Herrera government.

Rengifo did succeed in initiating an intercultural/bilingual program for indigenous areas whereby more leeway in the official curriculum would be given to special needs of the indigenous and the first years of school were to be taught in the children's native language(s). This entailed a large training program for bilingual schoolteachers, which, while a vehicle for unplanned cultural change, was in some areas successful in preparing an indigenous leadership. In the meantime there was contention over the assignment of border affairs to the Office of Indian Affairs. When Herrera took office in early 1979, the letterhead was changed to Dirección de Asuntos Indígenas (DAI). On September 20, 1979 the new president promulgated Decree 283, instituting the regime of intercultural/bilingual education in indigenous areas.

During the Herrera years, much of DAI's energy went into implementation of Decree 283, training indigenous teachers and unifying the system of symbols used to write the country's Indian languages. There efforts were especially marked under the leadership of Trina de Liendo as DAI head. The IAN was active in promoting projects of so-called integral agrarian development and in helping the flagging movement of indigenous cooperatives, but was never able to form a coherent team. The Herrera years were characterized by a scarcity of qualified manpower in indigenous affairs. Symptomatic was the fact that the OMAFI director under Pérez was recalled from retirement to head a commission on research in the bilingual education program.

Activities of such regional development agencies as the Agricultural Development arm of CVG and the Communities Office of CVG-EDELCA were expanded during the Herrera years. With the shift that followed the overwhelming victory of Jaime Lusinchi in December 1983, a difficult period began. Knowledgeable specialists in Indian affairs were in short supply, and party patronage was evident in early appointments. Rengifo, despite having written the position paper for the AD platform on Indian affairs, did not return to head DAI.

The decisive defeat of the left in 1983 had little impact on Indian affairs, although some of the most articulate spokesmen for the cause come from the nonorthodox left. Doctrinaire Marxists, on the other hand, have always been regarded by the Indians as part of the Western tradition and just as lacking in comprehension as the most reactionary *desarrollistas*. A long-standing AD party pledge has been the creation of an autonomous institute for Indian affairs responding directly to the president or at least to his secretary of government. Despite reports that President Lusinchi will name a commission of experts to organize such an agency, it is doubtful that the expertise will be available for the task, much less to man the key assignments in such a structure.

In the years leading up to 1984, two events of great significance occurred. First was the eruption of diverse forces and sectors into Indian territory, including the Ministry of Youth, the armed forces, the Ministry of Health and Social Assistance, private developers and mining concerns, and even the National Tourist Board. Second was the rise of a new indigenous leadership and a fresh political assertiveness by the Indians. It is to these points that we now turn.

INDIGENOUS AREAS: NEW ACTORS, NEW INDIAN LEADERSHIP

Juan Vicente Goméz, early in the century, called in Spanish missionaries to fend off encroachment by the British. Ever since the fall of the Spanish colonial empire Indian land had been conceived in the public consciousness as wide open spaces and unpopulated wastelands, the *tierras baldías*. For nearly a half-century from the early 1920s, the missions predominated. Slowly, Venezuelan government agencies took their place. The early ones are still active, including the DAI at the Ministry of Education, accompanied by its Comisión Indigenista Nacional (CIN). The IAN remains formally in charge of development programs in indigenous areas and of *dotación de tierras*, the important issuing of formal title to land, which the Indians are still awaiting. The more than 1 million hectares granted to some 100 Indian communities through 1979 was clearly insignificant, given the urgent need to protect Indian lands against encroachment by cattle and mining interests.

Contrary to both benevolent and dogmatic critics,[14] there was never an organized "IAN group." Programs in indigenous areas and the formation of federations, on both a regional and a national level, were carried on by a number of younger government officials, generally in the teeth of their agency heads. This was not a party issue but pitted an older generation of *desarrollistas*, bent on forced technological development in both the industrial and agricultural sectors, against a younger generation wanting to gear development programs to local conditions and popular participation. For example, in June 1972 the IAN commissioned a study of the traditional Warao economy and the implementation of a subsequent development program.[15] Since the Warao were already growing rice for criollo middlemen, the main problem was to convince the Indians that they could go through the rice cycle by themselves. Finally, the Indian cooperative Hobure *Orisaba Yaotamo* ("those who work for each other") was registered in the regional capital of Tucupita in June 1973.[16]

That European-style cooperatives encounter strong conceptual and practical difficulties in the Venezuelan context has been known for some time. Special adjustments to the cultural context have been advocated for the nation's public administration and even for the planning process.[17] After promulgation of the Agrarian Reform Act of 1960, the IAN experimented with a number of organizational forms. When in the early 1970s Venezuelan government agencies, and especially the IAN, debated the question of self-help organizations among the indigenous populations of the country—increasingly exposed to contact situations—it became clear that an entirely new and idiosyncratic organizational form had to be found. On the one hand it was obvious and encouraging that traditional forms of indigenous cooperation were still functioning on the community and sub-community levels. New legal frameworks, however, were needed to help adjust traditional forms of cooperation to the challenges indigenous populations were facing in the regional economy. They also helped to provide indigenous organization with a juridical personality. "Empresas Indígenas" were developed in Venezuela as such a new form.

The structure emphasized a General Assembly, an Administrative Committee, and a Control Mechanism, the Controlling Council, that consisted of the elders who are the traditional leaders of Indian communities. A rather promising example was the Empresa Intercomunitaria Erebato-Nichare-Icutú *Tujumoto*, founded in October 1975, which united in a common enterprise for the first time communities of Ye'kuana and Sanema ethnic affiliations. The organizational mechanisms of the cooperative are the General Assembly, which convenes officially once a year but is repeated during frequent visits between communities. The Administrative Junta consists of president, vice-president, treasurer, and secretary. Each community has individuals in charge of different activities, such as coffee growing. A cattle operation in the Cushime savanna is attended to by different residence groups on a rotational basis. Finally, the Controlling Council is composed of the traditional leaders of the respective communities, the indigenous captain and his lieutenant.

Summing up the Ye'kuana experience, it can be said that while the juridical framework of the Empresa Intercomunitaria is absolutely necessary, the patient work of adaptation of an outside legal framework to local conditions, together with a strong sense of cohesion in the indigenous population, are necessary for the successful continuation of such communal enterprises. Others have been less successful. The internal factions of the government bureaucracy have been reflected in the improvisations of IAN project implementation. At one time, for example, the then foreign affairs minister in the Caldera government barred young IAN officials from access to Indian areas so that land-granting titles had to be given on the basis of outdated maps, making them virtually worthless.

There was an official furthering of Indian organizing efforts during the Herrera years. The yearly Indian congresses on Columbus Day became famous. Starting with Puerto Ayacucho in 1979 and extending to that of 1983 in the Pemon settlement of Kavanayén in Bolívar, the congresses were organized often by maverick governors against the opposition of local party machines—as with the First Warao Congress in Tucupita in 1980.[18] Even though the government obviously tried to control the indigenous organizing effort, much leeway was given to free discussions, and the very concept of *el día de la raza* (Columbus Day) was challenged by the Indians.

In addition to government agencies traditionally active in Indian areas, nearly every official bureaucracy (including PDVSA and the CVG) has developed some supervisory or decision-making function in indigenous lands. The Ministry of Environment and Renewable Natural Resources is supervising National Parks and Forest Reserves; the Ministry of Public Health and Social Assistance, in cooperation with state governments, is creating settlement concentrations; Defense is toying with Brazilian-type garrison townships at the borders; the Justice Ministry is supervising the shrinking activities of traditional missions and is watching helplessly the unregulated expansion of North American fundamentalist mission activities; Energy and Mines is rather indiscriminately granting mining concessions in both Bolívar and the Amazonas territory; the Ministry of Agriculture and Livestock is "supervising" the exploitation of lumber; and even the Ministry of Information and Tourism is overseeing "adventure tourism" in indigenous areas. Petroleum exploration, especially in the Orinoco River delta, affects indigenous regions, as will exploitation of the tar belt. The same is true of the bauxite deposits at Los Pijiguaos near Puerto Ayacucho, which will come on-stream in the near future to furnish raw materials via Interalumina to ALCASA and VENALUM.[19]

The Corporación Venezolana de Guayana itself has also taken a new interest in indigenous zones, as computer projections have consistently shown a food shortage in the Cuidad Guayana area by the mid-1980s. The solution of creating a "breadbasket" for the area by reclaiming large parts of the western Orinoco delta failed for technical reasons (saucer-shaped islands filled with rain water in the wet season despite dams and controlling the annual rise of the Orinoco River). Meanwhile programs for buffalo raising were carried on in the upper and middle Orinoco delta. All such development activities, of course, complicated efforts to deal constructively with Indian problems. And, as noted, many related to Venezuela's projected energy needs for the 1980s.

While these could easily be overestimated, the fact remains that even moderate increases will drastically affect Indian lands, for the economically feasible hydroelectric projects are largely located in the Guayana highlands. The most damaging would have been that at the Para Falls of the Caura River, which would have inundated several Ye'kuana and Sanema villages as well as large Ye'kuana hunting areas in the lower Erebato and Cacada rivers. After maintaining for years a campsite at "La Pava" (*Kuyuji Shodi*), the consulting firm OCOIDESA declared the locale as "not suitable" for a hydroelectric project. A possibly less damaging site at *Seiyato Shodi* on the middle Caura (Medewadi) is under consideration.

In 1981 there was talk that the state electricity company CADAFE would concentrate on distribution and leave actual hydroelectric development to EDELCA, the CVG subsidiary. Thus far, no further steps have been taken. EDELCA's track record regarding Indian communities is not bad. The only Indian community affected by the last phase of the gigantic Guri Dam, La Periquera, is located away from the Pemon Indians' ancestral homeland. EDELCA has taken serious steps to develop a viable "multiple use management plan" for a sizable area inside the La Paragua forest reserve on the southern shore of the lake, which includes the Indian population of La Periquera and anticipates plans for a new indigenous settlement. The Indians would participate in choosing the site and design, with emphasis on swidden agriculture of a type called "improved traditional management." In any case, the next projects to be taken up concern sites below the Guri Dam at Macagua II, Caruachi, and Tocoma.[20] In addition to the Guri Dam project proper, CVG (through its agricultural development arm DDA) and CVG-EDELCA have intensified an interest in the Gran Sabana area of Bolívar state.

The vast regions of Venezuelan Guayana stretch from the

Orinoco River south to the Brazilian border. Part of the Precambrian geological formation of the Guiana Shield, most of this area—especially the highlands of the Gran Sabana—is occupied by Carib-speaking Pemon Indians. On the northern rim of the region, however, where the black waters of the Caroní join the Orinoco, lies one of the major industrial growth poles of the country, based on important iron ore and bauxite deposits and supplied with cheap, abundant hydroelectric power from the highlands of Guayana. The Corporación Venezolana de Guayana is in charge of industrial, urban, and agricultural development, along with its many direct and mixed-capital subsidiaries. Its executives view the Indian territories to the south, especially the Gran Sabana Highlands, as of the utmost strategic importance. This is owing both to the headwaters feeding the hydroelectric Guri project—the Raúl Leoni Dam—and to the potential as an agricultural producer for the burgeoning Cuidad Guayana population, now an estimated 350,000.

The first impulse in the late 1960s was to saturate the area of the Gran Sabana with abundant fertilizer and heavy agricultural machinery at the same time as the indigenous population was enticed into nucleated rural housing developments such as Kamoirán, Yuruaní, and Maurak. As agribusiness-oriented agronomists established themselves after more than 50 years of individualizing missionary activities as the main employer of labor in the area, a state of psychological warfare developed. The Indians refused to practice truck farming and furtively continued swidden agriculture while using the dysfunctional housing of the new settlements only as weekend ritual centers for their syncretistic Aleluya and Chochiman cults.

By the early 1980s, however, the picture had changed dramatically. A new breed of agronomists, ecologists, and geographers had established that (1) swidden agriculture was not impinging on the important headwater systems of the region whose sources were found in savanna areas; (2) limited traditional burning of savanna was, rather, preventive, avoiding major devastating forest fires; (3) important contingents of *conuco* agriculture such as plantains, bananas, and sugarcane were acting as a major water-storing mechanism through their rhizome characteristics on traditional clearings alongside small streams; and (4) exotic new cultigens such as flowers and strawberries were not economically feasible. At the same time, a sudden jump of some 350 percent in the price of fertilizer and other chemical inputs had made truck farming much less attractive. Recent anthropological studies[21] have shown that traditional settlement patterns of small clusters of homesteads tied together in a net of neighborhoods constitute an adaptation to poor soils of the highland savanna environment as compared to the much denser population, articulated into bands and subtribes, of ecosystems such as the Orinoco delta.

Simultaneously, it became evident that a sound base of autosubsistence activities was a necessary condition for truck farming and that a headlong jump into wage labor was creating dependency on government handouts by undermining traditional mechanisms of self-help and reciprocity. As a consequence, the legal and organizational framework of "Empresas Indígenas" has been adopted, and planners are in the process of developing the organizational adjustment based on elements from the original system but tailored to local requirements as expressed by the indigenous populations involved. All these activities are seemingly going on without overall planning. CORDIPLAN, now under Luis Raúl Matos Azocar, is limiting itself to "providing the larger framework," until one or another issue comes to public attention—either by accident or through scandal—and causes a heated headline-making discussion.

Two such major issues may be discussed as symptomatic, one from the early Herrera period and the other pertinent as of March 1984. In late 1979 and 1980 a parliamentary commission of the Chamber of Deputies was conducting hearings on the situation of Venezuela's indigenous population and on the activities of the four Apostolic Vicariates operating with a tenuous extension of the 1964 convention with the Holy See and the 1967 accord with missionary orders, mainly the Capuchins. The parliamentary commission most especially wanted to inform itself about the presence in mineral-rich Amazonas of the fundamentalist New Tribes Mission—unregulated by any agreement whatsoever—and about allegedly heavy-handed methods that lacked respect of cultural values and the private life of indigenous communities. Simultaneously, a military court, assisted by the attorney general, was looking into charges by a high-ranking navy officer that the

Jungle Aviation and Radio Service (JAARS) as a logistical arm of the NTM was engaged in mineral exploration and in running an illegal network of landing strips.

Confusion prevailed. A number of individuals, known antagonists of the NTM because of the latter's proselytizing methods, had vowed to intervene drastically if in a position to do so. Accordingly, when Charles Brewer-Carías became minister of youth under Herrera, action was expected. What happened, however, was that Brewer was summoned to the president's office and subsequently reappeared to state that matters were more complicated than they seemed. To this day, the Venezuelan government has neither taken action against the NTM nor cleared it of compromising charges.

In the meantime the president of the private mining operation MAVA, one Florencio Goméz Muñoz, had quietly applied for extensive mining concessions in Amazonas, amidst Yanomami land. His application had been published in the *Gaceta Oficial* of April 22, 1982 but passed unnoticed. Equally unnoticed had been the granting of concessions by the Ministry of Energy and Mines a few months later (*Gaceta Oficial*, May 26, 1983 and June 9, 1983) that gave at least 45,000 hectares of land in the Orinoco headwaters and 180,000 hectares near Shimada Savanna (*Shimada Woichi*), in the headwater regions of the Padamo and Cuntinamo rivers. A storm broke loose when these facts were denounced by Enzo Ceccarelli, bishop of Puerto Ayacucho, and by several deputies.[22]

When the new Lusinchi minister, Arturo Hernández Grisanti, declared in the press on April 14, 1984 that the concessions had been obtained legally, both the Senate and Chamber commissions for energy and for the environment called for an immediate halt to the mining operation. There were allegations that civil servants of the Ministry of Youth were involved—the interest of former minister Brewer-Carías was well known—and a statement by the environmental commission that the appropriate ministry (Environment and Renewable Natural Resources) had not authorized the exploration. Bishop Ceccarelli was backed by Amazonas territorial governor Rumeno Armas Salazar and joined by four cabinet members. Ultimately, the manner in which this may be resolved will indicate whether housecleaning is proceeding in earnest, or whether much of the furor was designed as a distraction of public attention from the unpopular economic measures enacted by the new Lusinchi regime.

The mining affair remains interrelated with another delicate issue, the creation of the Yanomami Park. Already in 1977 the adverse effect on the heretofore uncontacted Yanomami Indians of irregular casserite mining by Brazilian *garimpeiros* had been denounced by the anthropologists Alcida Ramos and Kenneth Taylor.[23] The ensuing debate in Venezuela produced two not dissimilar proposals, basing themselves on both environmental protection laws and on precedents of awarding title to land to indigenous groups. While one proposal emphasized the former and the second the latter, it would be inexact to draw a sharp line between them. Neither would it be correct to identify one with the Fundación La Salle and the other with the Instituto Venezolano de Investigacion Científica (IVIC), as membership is largely overlapping.[24] The important point is that the Herrera government had not acted on either of the proposals, and that so far no interest has been shown by the Lusinchi government. All this might change with the mining issue in Yanomami territory placed before the Congress. The issue of the Yanomami Park has also been taken up by UNESCO and will be discussed at one of its current meetings.

CONCLUSIONS

Venezuelan democracy at this juncture is facing a great challenge. After five constitutional periods, the project of political democracy has largely been terminated successfully. By voting overwhelmingly for the two major parties of the political spectrum and by defeating both extreme rightists and leftists, Venezuelans have demonstrated that they are aware of this achievement, and want to keep it. At the same time, the possibilities of reformist democracy have been exhausted. The next project, economic democracy, termed by the government a "Social Pact," requires radical changes. In the era of low petroleum prices, ceilings on production, and an enormous external debt, the possibilities of letting white-collar crime proceed while keeping quiet the swelling numbers of the poor are over.

The government has two points in its favor: The *adecos* are adroit in manipulating the Venezuelan masses and have strong grass-roots support, especially in the countryside and middle-sized cities. In addition, the professional and commercial middle classes have not yet run down their reserves so much as to turn against the government. But this can happen in the not too distant future. Paradoxically, the indigenous situation provides a bright light in what is otherwise a dark panorama, for two major reasons. The Indians have rarely if ever received a fair share of the petroleum pie. Rather, incessant meddling in their affairs has produced in effect a net loss. With the exception of the increasing number of urban Indians—such as the 15,000+ Guajiros in the Maracaibo suburb of Ziruma—the more the Indians are left alone, the better off they seem. Seeing their relatives streaming into the country as a consequence of persecution and extreme land grabbing in Venezuela's neighboring states, the Indians are among the staunchest defenders of the democratic system. While complaining loudly, they are well aware that in Venezuela the government pays them a per diem to attend Indian congresses in Caracas to complain about conditions.

The second point holds that prevailing government attitudes support use of the Indian heritage as a means of forming a national identity, and that this posture, while largely nominal, will have an effect on their social standing. Certainly the Indian leadership itself has changed. The predominance of the mission establishment corresponded to the boarding school–educated Indian, who imitated the European peasant outlook held by the missionaries themselves. The indigenous leader corresponding to the authority role of paternalistic government agencies was the bilingual go-between, *el promotor indígena*, the *yadaanawi adeddu adeukano* ("he who speaks the criollo language"), as the Ye'kuana say. He is an alienated individual, both from the missions where he received his education and from his native community, whence he was taken at an early age. He is neither here nor there.

The new indigenous leader, still in his twenties and educated in the country's state colleges and universities, does not feel that he owes anything to anybody. He is without the subservience of the first generation of leaders and without the resentment of the second. He communicates with his peers on a continental level.

While ideologically aware, he is rather pragmatic in his acceptance of the new and his defense of the old; he knows whom he can rely upon and who are false friends trying to use the Indians. For another thing, he will not put up any longer with the lawless situation in the backlands. If the present government is sufficiently farsighted to fulfill his legitimate aspirations to protection from zealots invading his syncretistic privacy of old gods and new Aleluya cults, of keeping avid hands from the gold and diamonds he thinks are rightfully his, and if the military turn to him instead of loosing drunken soldiers on his women, he can be of tremendous help.

The Indians are aware, as are most people in Venezuela, that the military did not bring about economic development in Argentina and are about to give up in Brazil. The armed forces now support a strong democratic tradition in Venezuela, while the left has little to offer. The future of Venezuela will be as idiosyncratic and syncretistic as the Indian present. If the government of Jaime Lusinchi should fail, a new Indian leadership will be the first to turn against him. And at this writing, the *adeco* administration needs all the help it can get.

NOTES

1. Manual counting of the data from the Censo Indígeno of 1982 totaled some 140,645 Indians in six states and the two federal territories; 16 ethnic groups were identified. See Haydée Seijas, "Metodología, operación, y resultados globales del Censo Indígena, 1982," paper presented at the 33 Annual Convention of the Venezuelan Association for the Advancement of Science, Caracas, October 1983.

2. For example, see the writings of Shelton Davis, as in Shelton Davis and Robert Mathews, *The Geological Imperative: Anthropology and Development in the Amazon Basin of South America* (Cambridge, Mass.: Anthropology Resource Center, 1976).

3. This term is preferred by Indian groups today.

4. According to the Censo Nacional, as quoted in Mikel Viana, "El Censo 81 y la dinámica poblacional," *SIC* 46, 459 (1983): 402–05.

5. As opposed to the Highland Indian populations of countries such as Peru, Bolivia, Mexico, and Guatemala.

6. Paul Henley, *The Panare: Tradition and Change on the Amazonian Frontier* (New Haven, Conn.: Yale University Press, 1982), p. 247.

7. See especially Miguel Acosta Saignes, "Sobre la sustitución de la Ley de Misiones," *SIC* 43, 422 (1980): 59–62.

8. Ministerio de Justicia, *Memoria y cuenta del Ministerio de Justicia—1964* (Caracas: Imprenta Nacional, 1964), p. 82. Italics mine.

9. Walter Coppens, "La tenencia de tierra indígena en Venezuela: Aspectos legales y antropológicos," *Antropológica* 29 (1971): 8–15.

10. Guillermo Bonfil Batalla, ed., *Utopia y revolución: El pensamiento político contemporáneo de los indios en América Latina* (Mexico City: Editorial Nueva Imagen, 1984).

11. Daniel de Barandiarán and Walter Coppens, "Ensayos de formulación de una doctrina indigenista venezolana," *América Indígena* 21 (1971): 107–16.

12. Ministerio de Justicia, OCAI, "Creación de los Centros de Acción Indigenista," *Gaceta Indigenista* 3 (Nueva Epoca) (November–December 1974): 1.

13. Confederación Indígena de Venezuela, "Planteamiento de las organizaciones indígenas de Venezuela," in Bonfil Batalla, *Utopia*, pp. 344–47.

14. For the former, see Nelly Arvelo-Jiménez, "Programs Among Indigenous Populations of Venezuela and Their Impact: A Critique," in *Land, People and Planning in Contemporary Amazonia*, ed. Francoise Barbira-Scazzocchio (Cambridge, Mass.: Center of Latin American Studies, 1979), pp. 210–21. For the latter, consult Filadelfo Morales Méndez, "Del morichal a la sabana: Las Empresas Indígenas: Un modelo etnocida de desarrollo. El caso de la comunidad Kariña de Cachama," tesis de ascenso (Caracas: Universidad Central de Venezuela, 1983).

15. Alberto Valdez, *Autogesión Indígena* (Caracas: Fondo Editorial Comun, 1982).

16. Gerald Clarac and Alberto Valdez, "Empresas Indígenas y autogestión en una estrategia desarrollo regional," paper presented at the Forty-second International Congress of Americanists, Paris, August 1976.

17. John Friedmann, *Regional Development Policy: A Case Study of Venezuela* (Cambridge, Mass.: MIT Press, 1966). See also John Friedmann and Barkley Hudson, "Knowledge and Action: A Guide to Planning Theory," *Journal of the American Institute of Planners* 40 (1974): 2–16.

18. Congreso Warao, *Actas del Primer Congreso Warao* (Tucupita: Gobernacián del Territorio, 1980).

19. Part of the CVG holding.

20. CVG-EDELCA, *La empresa de generación hidroeléctrica* (Caracas, 1982), pp. 33–34.

21. Luis Urbina, "Adaptación ecológico-cultural de los Pemón-Arekuna: El caso de Tuauken," M.Sc. thesis (Caracas: IVIC, 1979). Luis Urbina and H. Dieter Heinen, "Ecología, organización social y distribución especial: Estudio de caso de dos poblaciones indígenas, Pemón y Warao," *Antropológica*, in press.

22. *Diario de Caracas*, March 17 and March 27, 1984; *El Nacional*, March 29, 1984; *La Iglesia en Amazonas*, March 1984.

23. Alcida Ramos and Kenneth Taylor, *The Yanoama in Brazil* (Copenhagen: IWGIA, 1979).

24. The present author is not a member of either team. See Comité para la Creación de la Reserva Indígena Yanomami, *Los Yanomami Venezolanos: Propuesta para la creación de la Reserva Indígena Yanomami* (Caracas: Fundación La Salle, 1983). See also Nelly Arvelo-Jiménez, ed., *La Reserva de la Biosfera Yanomami: Una auténtica estrategia para el ecodesarrollo nacional* (Caracas: IVIC, 1983), mimeo.

14

Venezuelan Local Government

Ildemaro Jesús Martínez

The poor performance of local government is one of the most critical problems facing countries in Latin America. Historically, Venezuelan local government was weak, neglected, and able to provide only marginal services. Not surprisingly, therefore, during the first two decades of the democratic regime the level of government closest to the people failed to meet its responsibilities as envisioned in the constitution of 1961. On August 8, 1978 President Carlos Andrés Pérez signed legislation designed to correct the most serious and obvious causes for this failure.[1] The resulting Organic Law of Municipal Government (Ley Orgánica de Régimen Municipal) was passed only after a long process of consultation among the most important political parties, especially Democratic Action (AD), the Social Christians (COPEI), and the Movement Toward Socialism (MAS). This reform represents the great hope of those who believe that local government can become an important vehicle for increasing the responsiveness of rulers to the ruled and for strengthening democracy.

Since passage of the Organic Law of Municipal Government, local governments are receiving greater attention, both for socioeconomic reasons and because they are considered basic building blocks of the entire representative process. This study focuses on these building blocks with the following goals in mind: to sketch briefly the evolution of local government in Venezuela; to discuss the 1978 Organic Law of Municipal Reform and to analyze the most important new offices it created, as well as the problems they were intended to manage. There are important reasons for proceeding in this manner; above all it provides useful categories of feedback for Venezuelan public administrators seeking to upgrade the performances of local government. In addition, this approach directs the attention of social scientists toward analyzing and describing the political significance of local government and of local-national linkages.

THE EVOLUTION OF LOCAL GOVERNMENT

The Spaniards transplanted municipal government forms from Spain to America at the time of the conquest. The conquerors who established villages and cities also designated their mayors and councilmen. Venezuelan municipalities, like their Spanish counterparts, exercised important judicial, religious, and political functions. During the wars for independence, municipal councils throughout Spanish America were centers of rebellion. After the Spanish were defeated, however, the power of the municipal councils declined. Local strongmen called *caciques* exercised power and authority.

In recognition of the political and military autonomy of the *caciques*, federalist forms were written into the Venezuelan constitution of 1864. Venezuelan states received important formal powers similar to those reserved to states in the United States by the U.S. Constitution's elastic clause. When the military strength of a Venezuelan *cacique* waned, however, his state or region seldom exercised any of its constitutionally sanctioned prerogatives. The 1901 constitution imposed by the Andeans took away many of the states' formal but unused powers. Nevertheless, it allowed for the direct election of municipal councilmen. The councilmen, in turn, were to elect the national president, as well as the first and second vice-presidents. This provision was ignored by both Cipriano Castro and Juan Vicente Gómez, who treated the Venezuelan municipality as a centrally controlled subdivision of the national executive. In this context the 1947 constitution was revolutionary. It prohibited national and state authorities from intervening in local affairs. However, the decade of military rule between 1948 and 1958 saw a return to earlier forms of central government domination. In another reversal, the democratic constitution of

1961 increased local autonomy and provided for the popular election of local councilmen.

The constitution of 1961 remains in force at this writing. It organizes Venezuela as a federal republic consisting of 20 states, the federal district, 2 territories, and 72 islands. Each state contains two levels of government, the district (*distrito*) and the municipal (*municipio*) level. The former is by far the more important. There are 202 districts in Venezuela, between 6 and 16 in each state.[2] Districts are divided into municipalities (*municipios*). The constitution declares the districts to be independent of the state in economic and administrative matters, subject only to national laws and regulations. Therefore, the following analysis of Venezuelan local governments begins by describing its most important administrative structures—the district, the municipality, the district council (*consejo municipal del distrito*), and the community committee (*junta comunal*).

Districts are the most significant administrative subdivisions of a state and, as suggested above, the central focus of local government. Territorially defined, a district includes both urban and rural areas, similar to counties in the United States. The principal urban settlement in a district usually is the seat of district government. Like the urban county, the Venezuelan district is empowered to levy and collect taxes, adopt and enforce building and zoning regulations, and provide major services and facilities. Only at the district level do constitutionally sanctioned local decision-making institutions exist.

The municipalities are territorial subdivisions of the districts. While lacking decision-making powers and institutions, municipalities function as the eyes and ears for the district government. Administrators at the municipal level identify needs and suggest programs for each municipality to the district leadership. Venezuelan municipalities, therefore, are not comparable to municipalities in the United States. The latter enjoy a corporate existence that the former lack.

Each district is governed by a district council. Between 1959 and the reforms of 1978, each district council, regardless of the population of its district, numbered seven members. Councilmen were elected directly from party lists by district voters. The council was presided over by a president, who was and is also referred to as a mayor (*alcalde*). Prior to the polarizing election of 1973, the presence on most councils of members from three or four political parties guaranteed an almost annual rotation in the district council presidency. Not only was the presidency itself a prestigious post but its occupant controlled additional patronage.

The community committee is intimately involved in local administration. Appointed by the district council, the community committee has three members. It is responsible for linking the municipality's inhabitants to the district council and for assisting the Ministry of Interior–appointed prefect (*prefecto*) with law enforcement.

Analysis of local government institutions reveals that the meager remnants of Venezuelan federalism in the 1961 constitution reflect more a division of power between national and district governments than one between national and state governments. Most important, although Venezuela in theory is a federal republic with constitutional provisions for some state and local autonomy, in practice almost all power resides in the national government. Decisions are centralized in Caracas.

Article 25 of the 1961 constitution defines the status of Venezuelan districts, stating that they

> constitute the primary and autonomous political entity within the national organization. It is a district responsibility to govern and administer the specific interests of the entity, in particular related to funds and income and to specific matters of local life, such as urban development, supplies, transit, culture, health, social welfare, public credit institutions, tourism, and municipal police.[3]

District government is thus responsible for city planning and urban renewal and for the construction and maintenance of country roads, streets, parks, gardens, markets, aqueducts, and sewers. Additional constitutionally mandated responsibilities include the provision of local police services, fire prevention and extinguishment, public lighting, transit, and the control of public events. Finally, the district councils are charged with the creation and maintenance of schools, libraries, theaters, museums, hospitals, and first-aid centers.[4] The provision of these services is central in maintaining and improving standards of living and in furnishing supportive services for social and political development. However, while the farmers of the 1961 constitution envisioned districts as dynamic governmental entities, the districts have been unable to meet many of their responsibilities.

THE REFORMS OF AUGUST 1978

The Organic Law of Municipal Government was intended to strengthen the district councils and make them more responsive to local demands. One important provision for accomplishing this was to decouple the election of councilmen from voting for state legislators and national congressmen. Another involved the creation of neighborhood associations and their integration into local government. These efforts, however, have been only partly successful, for the high rate of abstention in elections for district councilmen suggests that a large number of voters are either apathetic or alienated. Also, the law contains provisions that attempt to standardize procedures for creating new districts and municipalities and that allow for larger district councils in the more populous areas.

Between 1959 and 1979, district council elections were held in conjunction with elections for the national Congress, the state legislature, and even the presidency.[5] District council campaigns, to the extent they could be separated out, largely reflected problems of a national character; consequently, they responded to directives from the capital city of Caracas. The new law determines that district council elections be separated from national elections. On June 3, 1979 the first separate district council elections in more than three decades took place. Five years later, on May 27, 1984, the second such separate elections held.

Results from the 1979 district council elections favored COPEI, which had won the national elections of December 1978. In the second separate district council elections, the Social Democratic representative, AD, obtained an overwhelming victory. At that time AD had only recently returned to power with its decisive win in the national elections of December 4, 1983. Table 14.1 presents a comparison of the results of the two separate elections for district council, with the last ones held jointly with the national elections of 1973.

TABLE 14.1. District Council Election Results

1973–1984 (in percentages)						
Year	COPEI	AD	URD	United Left	Others	Total
1973	30.24	44.44	3.18	12.50	8.82	100
1979	53.55	35.82	1.02	9.00	0.61	100
1984	23.80	66.20	1.06	6.93	2.01	100

Source: Official statistics of the Supreme Electoral Council.

In 1973, AD gained a plurality with 44.4 percent, in 1979 COPEI won with 53.6 percent; in 1984 AD won again, this time with a majority of 66.2 percent. In these three cases the winning parties had also won the preceding presidential and congressional elections. It is interesting, therefore, that the outcome of district council elections is intimately linked to the results of the national elections, whether together, as in 1973, or separately, as in 1979 and 1984. This suggests that the sheer fact of true local elections has not yet taken hold in the public consciousness—elections based fundamentally on local problems with representatives of the communities themselves as candidates, without impositions from national party commands operating from the capital city of the republic.

The second major innovation introduced by the 1978 reforms involved the organization of neighborhood associations (asociación de vecinos), to which the law devotes ten articles establishing the mechanisms for their formation and operation.[6] For an association to acquire a legal personality, two hundred families must become members. The district councils are required to maintain a register of all legally recognized neighborhood associations located within the boundaries. However, the operation of all neighborhood associations is regulated by the national executive.[7]

The neighborhood associations have been very active from the beginning and have experienced high levels of participation. For example, an association has been established under the name of Federation of Associations of Urban Communities (Federación de Asociaciones de Comunidades Urbanas, FACUR). This federation has become an important pressure group as regards the municipal councils, so much so that open meetings of public sessions are now being held to discuss matters of interest for residents. FACUR also publishes the magazine *Comunidad*, which seeks to become a spokesman for the communities. A neighborhood school (escuela de vecinos) is also operating under the auspices of FACUR; it offers courses for residents on municipal problems and forms of communal organization.

The most important activity currently being undertaken by the neighborhood associations seeks additional changes in local government legislation. It involves a grass-roots movement to assemble and present to the Congress a number of proposals that reflect the feelings of the community concerning ways to increase local political participation. This suggests that the neighborhood associations remain relatively autonomous from the centrally controlled patronage networks of the political parties. Nevertheless, partisans of community level democracy remain fearful that the neighborhood associations may be penetrated and, in some fashion, controlled by the political parties. This sentiment is reflected in opinions publicly expressed by FACUR.[8]

Despite the apparent vigor of the neighborhood associations, Venezuela's democratic leaders are concerned that a great deal of apathy toward local government remains. They see this as reflected in high levels of abstention from voting in the district council elections, even though the vote is obligatory. In the first separate district council elections, the abstention rate was 30 percent; in the second it approached 40 percent.

Popular wisdom asserts that abstention rates in the first two district council elections were high because the candidates for council were chosen by national party leaders who disdained consultation with the local community. Similarly, it is suggested that national elites deliberately discourage the development of local leaders. While these points may have some validity, they are overly simplistic explanations; legal channels and consultative procedures do exist that link the communities to the national power structure. Also, local communities are not without their leaders. Procedures for choosing those leaders date back to the early days of the democratic experiment, and while much remains to be done, community leaders are receiving training on how to defend local interests. All of this is part of a trial and error process that continues to unfold.

Despite the best efforts of those seeking to implement the 1978 reforms, however, a large percentage of the local electorate is either alienated or apathetic. The resulting high level of abstention, in some part, can be attributed to the following reasons:

1. For both the 1979 and 1984 district council elections the closed list system of candidates was used. In other words, each member of the electorate voted only once; this single vote counted for the entire slate of district council candidates offered by each political party. Thus, if a party received one-third of the popular vote, and if the council consisted of fifteen councilmen, the first five names appearing on that party's slate were elected. National party leaders determined who would appear on the list and in which order; the national leadership was under no obligation to respect the wishes of local leaders once they had consulted with them. District council candidates, therefore, were more responsible to the leaders in Caracas who selected them than to the electorate of the district in which they were running for office. Therefore, insensitivity on the part of national leaders to local desires causes the community level electorate to feel that voting in district council elections merely legitimates the arbitrary exercise of power by national party elites.

2. It is almost impossible for feedback from the community to have a direct impact on councilmen who owe their position to Caracas-based party elites. Because there is no local account-ability, many within the community cease to consider councilmen as elected officials before whom it is useful to make demands. Given this mind set, it is not long before even conscientious councilmen become isolated from what their constituents are thinking. This leads to the growth of cynicism, alienation, and apathy on the part of both the governing and the governed.

3. During district council election campaigns the extremely dependent and hierarchical nature of the local political party organizations is exposed for all to observe. On more than one occasion, in the heat of electoral combat, an independent-minded community leader has been given the choice of submitting to party discipline imposed from Caracas or being expelled from his party. This reinforces perceptions of dependency and powerlessness at

the local level. It also results in the national commands from the communities which tell them what they want to hear, regardless of what the community really thinks.

All of the above suggests how and why political messages between the district and national levels of government become distorted. Distortion ensures that effective community communication on behalf of local needs and interests is the exception; if this is not improved it will continue to provoke discontent and possibly produce even greater abstention in the next district council elections.

In addition to changing the procedures for electing district councilmen and creating the neighborhood associations, the 1978 reforms seek to bring order out of the near anarchy that was a consequence of the lack of standardized procedures for classifying and organizing district councils. Until these reforms there were no clearly defined criteria to distinguish urban municipalities from the rural or the large from the small. The 1978 reforms attempt to establish criteria, and a new district council can be created only only if the following conditions pertain: a population of no fewer than 12,000 inhabitants; a populated nucleus of no fewer than 2,500 inhabitants capable of serving as a site for local authorities; the capacity for generating resources sufficient to meet the expenditures of government, administration, and minimum services; and two or more component *municipios*, thus creating a necessary condition for the more encompassing "metropolitan district."

The legislative assemblies of each of the 20 states are empowered to set the boundaries of each district and its component *municipios*. Proposals for creating new districts may spring from the grass roots or from the Caracas establishment. Decisions relating to the creation of new districts are the consequence of both technical and political considerations. One intent of the 1978 reforms was to increase the importance of the former and diminish the capability of the latter to influence the content of decisions.

As of March 1985 there were 202 district councils in Venezuela; they are organized in accord with population criteria illustrated in Table 14.2.

In Table 14.2 one can see that the majority of Venezuelan district councils have a relatively small population base. The 70.8

TABLE 14.2. Districts by Number of Inhabitants

Inhabitants	Districts	Percent
5,000–50,000	143	70.8
50,000–250,000	52	25.7
Over 250,000	7	3.5
	202	100.0

Source: IESA, *Proyecto de desarrollo gerencial para consejos municipales* (June 1984), p. 16.

percent with the lowest population base stands in sharp contrast with the opposite end of the spectrum—the 3.5 percent (seven districts) with over 250,000 inhabitants. There are administrative difficulties at both extremes. In the former case, it is difficult to obtain sufficient financial resources to support governmental activity. In the latter, the condition of gigantism presents problems of control and demand satisfaction. These problems not only derive the need for more and better services, they also relate to the persistence of outmoded administrative and political procedures. Most existing procedures go back to a time in the nineteenth century when even the population of Caracas did not exceed 75,000. Regional cities boasted populations of between 15,000 and 30,000 inhabitants. The administrative and political techniques of that era are inadequate for modern cities of the 1980s.

Returning to the 143 district councils that represent districts with less than 50,000 inhabitants, the revenue problem is extremely serious. Since all but a few are financially insolvent, the framers of the 1978 reforms intended that they should receive revenue from the state and national governments. Because of rivalries and jealousies among national, state, and local governments, the magnitude of revenue anticipated has not materialized. Consequently, some rural district councils hardly function at all. Even many of the 52 medium-sized district council governments lack the funds and skills to perform the tasks assigned to them by the constitution. Their difficulties are compounded by the continuing population exodus from rural and medium-sized districts to the largest metropolitan centers. The ten largest centers already contain 80 percent of the total national population.

Finally, the 1978 reforms provide guidelines for organizing district government. Earlier discussion detailed how the institution exercising maximum local authority within each district is the district council. As pointed out earlier, historically all district councils were composed of seven members. The 1978 reforms varied the size of the councils in accord with the population of the district. District councils are now organized in the following manner:

- Seven councilmen in the districts with 50,000 or fewer inhabitants
- Nine councilmen in districts with 50,001 to 250,000
- Eleven councilmen in districts with 250,001 to 500,000 inhabitants
- Thirteen councilmen in municipalities with 500,001 to 750,000 inhabitants
- Fifteen councilmen in municipalities with 750,001 to 1,000,000 inhabitants
- Seventeen councilmen in municipalities with more than 1 million inhabitants.

In keeping with the above criteria, the number of councilmen elected in the district council elections has grown; where in the pre-reform era there were only seven for each of a smaller number of districts, today we find between seven and seventeen councilmen on the councils of 202 districts. Should the lip service paid to the desirability of increasing grass-roots participation be translated into more responsive organizational forms and procedures at the district level, district councilmen will become increasingly important actors within the democratic system during the late 1980s.

ADMINISTRATIVE STRUCTURE AND PROBLEMS

The most important new offices created by the 1978 reforms of district level government included the municipal administrator and the municipal comptroller. It was intended that those who occupied these offices would be professionals capable of administering the district on a day-to-day basis and of advising councilmen of the implications of their political decisions on financial and personnel matters. While some progress has been made in professionalizing local government at the district level, behavior patterns dating back to the colonial era are not easily changed. The discussion that follows look first at how offices of municipal administrator and municipal comptroller are structured. Attention subsequently focuses on problems associated with the receipt of constitutional grants of funds for the district councils (*situado constitucional*), budgeting procedures, personnel administration, and contracts.

The role of the office of municipal administrator is to implement decisions of the district council. Its size and the technical competence of its staff varies in accord with the population and wealth of the district. Articles 62 through 65 of the Ley Orgánica de Régimen Municipal set forth the requisites for being a municipal administrator at the district level, along with a detailed description of the tasks he is expected to perform.

An important exception in this new arrangement is that the governmental structures sanctioned in the 1978 reforms are obligatory only in those municipalities with more than 50,000 inhabitants. The qualifications of individuals occupying the newly created offices vary in accord with the population. For example, in municipalities with a population of more than 100,000 residents, it is obligatory that a municipal administrator have a degree in higher education, along with experience in public administration. In municipalities with a population from 50,000 to 100,000 inhabitants, it is necessary that, at the least, administrative studies in official institutes or entities recognized by the state have taken place, along with experience in public administration and/or a degree in higher education. In municipalities with a population of less than 50,000 inhabitants, the district council president may exercise the functions of municipal administrator.

The administrator is chosen by the district council by means of a competition; he or she will serve throughout the council's five-year term of office. The administrator's removal is possible only with the agreement of a majority of council members, on the grounds of serious failure. As of March 1985, 59 district governments boasted municipal administrators. In the others, the president of the district council was exercising both administrative and political functions.

Despite the smaller number of municipal administrators in place after six years of reform implementation, several problems have emerged in the 59 districts with a separate office of municipal administration. The most important problem is largely political; its emergence reflects the struggle for power between the elected councilmen who comprise the district councils and the appointed administrator. Historically, the councilmen have enjoyed full power in both the political and administrative realms. For example, decisions on personnel, pay, a cessation of contracts, and the like were made by the council president in conjunction with the other councilmen. Under the reformed system, the administrator becomes the person empowered with all of these prerogatives, thereby depriving the councilmen of some of their powers.

The conflict becomes more pronounced when the council presidency is exercised by an authoritarian personality who wants to keep a tight rein on all political matters, while also invading administrative terrain. Many problems have arisen from this kind of clash, and they will only be resolved satisfactorily when councils and administrators agree on what constitutes a purely administrative prerogative, in contrast to one that is political. The municipal administrator, in the meantime, must come to a realization that many administrative decisions have an important political component, and that the council has every right to expect that in such instances its wishes will be taken into account. These conflicts will take time to resolve, but it must be hoped that ultimately a fuller understanding of the respective roles of the administrator and the council will evolve.

Another change introduced into district-level government involved the creation of the office of municipal comptroller. The 1978 municipal law mandates that the comptroller's office should exist in all district governments having an annual income above 10 million bolivars.

The office of municipal comptroller oversees all the basic control functions associated with district government finance. This includes the safeguarding and handling of income, expense, and municipal property. The office of municipal comptroller is directed by a comptroller who is named by the district council in an open competition. Final selection is by means of a panel composed of councilmen, one representative of the professional organization of public accountants (Colegio de Contadores Públicos), and one representative of the office of the national comptroller (Contraloría General de la República). The municipal comptroller's term of office is for the same five-year period as that of the district council. He can be removed from his position only by penal sentence or administrative condemnation. If a judge declares that sufficient reasons exist to bind him over to legal judgment, the comptroller is suspended from the exercise of his duties until he is found innocent or convicted. In the latter eventuality he is removed automatically.

In this context it is useful to note the role played by the national comptroller's office; it is the right arm and dominant mechanism of financial control on which the national Congress depends. The national comptroller's office is extremely influential in the selection of individual comptrollers at the district level, in the structuring of their offices, and in the preparation of regulations that establish local operational procedures. In addition, the municipal law itself, in Article 71, empowers the national comptroller's office to establish permanent control units within a district when the national comptroller considers this to be necessary. The national Congress also may mandate the creation of permanent control units.

The participation and supervision of the office of the national comptroller in the organization of the district government's comptroller's office clearly constitutes a major instance of national government intervention in local affairs. Many argue that it is a violation of municipal autonomy. Nevertheless, the Caracas bureaucracy considers this intervention necessary if district government is ever to become fiscally responsible. It is pointed out that unless fiscal responsibility is achieved, district councils never can become the important building blocks of democracy envisioned in the 1961 constitution.

Similar reasoning is used to justify two other mechanisms of national government intervention in the finances of district government, the *situado municipal* and the control of general administrative expenses. The *situado municipal* is composed of transferrals from the national government to the districts in order to assist them to cover budgetary shortfalls. In a majority of the districts, as revealed in Table 14.3, the *situado* represents the major source of income spent by the district councils for all kinds of expenses.

In view of the fact that almost 80 percent of most municipalities' budgets historically have gone for current expenses, leaving a very small proportion for capital investment, and considering that the national government is interested in maximizing its ability to construct physical facilities, the framers of the 1978 muncipal reforms devised an innovative procedure for controlling how district governments could use the *situado*. Its stated intention was to coordinate how the districts would invest the funds they receive with the projects programmed by the national bureaucracy and state corporations. Toward this end, the 1978 reform legislation declares that the *situado* to which the districts are entitled will be distributed by the states. However, 50 percent of the *situado* must be delivered to the districts in the form of capital works. This allows the state governors to retain funds for which the district councils have no concrete investment plans. State governors, it should be noted, are appointed by the minister of the interior. Here, once again, we see intervention from Caracas with the

TABLE 14.3. Total Income of Selected District Councils, 1982

District Councils by State	Region	Income from Own Sources	Transferred Income
Sucre	Oriental	67.65%	32.35%
Monagas	Oriental	56.23%	43.77%
Nueva Esparta	Oriental	36.77%	63.23%
Delta Amacuro	Guayana	35.17%	64.83%
Cojedes	Central	32.95%	67.05%
Yaracuy	Centro-Occidental	50.34%	49.66%
Apure	Sur		42.86%
Táchira	Occidental	38.05%	61.95%

Source: Boris Urrutia, *El ingreso público municipal* (Caracas: AVECI, June 1983), p. 86.

intention of controlling district government behavior by means of centralized authority.

The procedure undoubtedly has its positive side in ensuring a certain investment of capital at the community level. On the other hand, however, there is open intervention of the central government in municipal affairs, and one clearly sees the great lack of confidence in municipal management, with the latter considered inefficient in investing the resources that are provided.

The second control mechanism, supervision of generalized administrative expenses, also seeks to orient the mix of district government expenditures more in the direction of capital investment. A provision in Article 123 of the 1978 reform legislation sets upper limits on the percent of the total district budget that can be used for current expenditures, in contrast to capital investments. It stipulates that for all "ordinary income" (income apart from the *situado constitutional*), the following percentages for current expenditures cannot be exceeded:

40% in districts with ordinary income of Bs. 240,000
30% in districts with ordinary income of Bs. 1,000,000
25% in districts with ordinary income of Bs. 5,000,000
20% in districts with ordinary income of Bs. 100,000,000
15% in districts with over Bs. 100,000,000

The national office of the comptroller has the responsibility of overseeing and enforcing this provision of the law. Consequently, the district councils must send annually a copy of their budget to the national office of the comptroller five days after it has been approved.

Provisions for controlling generalized administrative expenditures represent a determined effort by the central government to avoid unnecessary expenses and rationalize expenditures at the district level. Unfortunately, it appears not to be working. According to the most recent annual report of the office of national comptroller, 21 municipalities did not submit copies of their budgets. Moreover, analysis indicated that more than 75 percent of the municipalities were not complying with the percentages set forth in Article 125 of the law; instead they exceeded mandated limitations.

CONCLUSION

During the 26 years of Venezuelan democracy, strengthening of the district councils has remained a high priority item. Political participation has been increased markedly, especially where progress has been made in implementing the 1978 reforms. In this context, the creation of neighborhood associations has been especially important. Also, the separation of municipal and national elections has broken new ground in developing a discernible local political process. Citizens are beginning to feel they can have an impact on who will defend their community interests. However, autonomous district government is not yet a fact. The political parties continue to make decisions in Caracas and impose their candidates on the districts by means of the list system, which was analyzed at great length. On this matter there is great pressure to give local political leaders greater authority; it seems apparent that in the near future the political parties will have to change the electoral law to allow for the election to the district councils of individuals preferred by the community because of their merit and appeal.

Notable progress also is being made on the administrative side. Although the positions of municipal administrator and municipal comptroller have not always functioned as anticipated, their establishment has contributed to separating administrative and political decision making and to rationalizing administrative procedures. All of this is tied to attempts at making way for variety in the structuring of government at the district level in accord with the criteria of population, wealth, and urbanization.

It goes without saying that the search continues for new ways to make district government more supportive of democratic norms and procedures. Flaws remain, but little by little they are being corrected. Indeed, the 1978 municipality law is not the only source of transformation and renewal at the level of district government. Efforts are being carried forward by national associations of municipalities, such as AVECI and FUNDACOMUN. Both continue to lobby for local government reforms that will make the political leaders and administrators closest to the people increasingly responsive to their will.

NOTES

1. *Gaceta Oficial*, no. 2997, August 8, 1978.

2. Calculated from the official election returns for the December 1983 elections of the Consejo Supremo Electoral. The principal subdivisions of the territories and the federal district are known as departments. Excluding the island independencies there are nine departments. The 202 districts are divided into 734 *municipios* (municipalities).

3. In Venezuela the most important district government institution is officially titled the Municipal Council of District X. District councils, therefore, are often popularly referred to as municipal councils. In the hope of avoiding confusion, this chapter will speak only of district councils, by which is meant the municipal council of the district in question.

4. It is important to note that the Venezuelan district is expected to meet rural as well as urban obligations, in contrast to the U.S. concept of the municipality as uniquely urban.

5. The only previous separate district council elections were held during November 1948, several weeks before the military coup that toppled the government of President Rómulo Gallegos.

6. Ley Orgánica de Regimen Municipal, Articles 147–156.

7. Reglamento Parcial No. 1 de Ley Orgánica de Regimen Municipal sobre las Asociaciones de Vecinos, Decreto Presidencial no. 3.130, March 6, 1979.

8. *Comunidad*, magazine published by FACUR, year 1, no. 2.

15

The Foreign Policy of Democratic Venezuela

Charles D. *Ameringer*

The foreign policy of Venezuela during the past 25 years clearly reflects its development as a democratic nation. As José Alberto Zambrano Velasco, the foreign minister of Luis Herrera Campins observed, "Domestic policy and foreign policy are two sides of the coin."[1] At the beginning of the democratic era, the survival of the political order was as much an international problem as a domestic one. Venezuela felt menaced by the presence of dictatorial governments in America, and aggressively sought their elimination by rallying the hemispheric system against them. Later, as its democratic political order became more secure, and with the realization that unresolved economic and social problems constituted more serious threats, Venezuelan foreign policy became more pragmatic and less moralistic. Venezuela valued its position as a democratic nation, but recognized that it might hinder cooperation with certain nations in the struggle to change the international economic order. Finally, the dramatic rise in oil prices in the early 1970s provided Venezuela with the opportunity to realize its developmental goals, along with the muscle to be taken seriously in international affairs. Oil and foreign policy became "indivisible terms," meaning that petroleum became as much a factor as democracy in shaping Venezuelan foreign policy.[2]

In attempting to analyze Venezuela's foreign policy, one must not focus too narrowly upon its democratic political order. The fact that Venezuela is a democratic nation influences the style, substance, and process of its foreign policy, but the degree to which this is so is a matter to be determined, not assumed. There are various theories dealing with the international behavior of Latin American nations, and it would be useful to test them here. Dependency theorists argue that developing countries locked into the Western capitalist mode really have no independent foreign policy, because political subordination is the price one has to pay or is the inevitable result of the unequal economic relationship. A variation of this theme is suggested by Coleman and Quiros, who insist that the foreign policy of developing countries is determined by developmental strategy. They conclude that nondevelopmental goals, relevant for "rich" or industrialized states, are of little use in analyzing foreign policy decision making in Latin America.[3] Ferris and Lincoln, seeking a framework for comparative analysis, have suggested four dimensions of Latin American foreign policy behavior—determinants, process, policy, and consequences—and have identified three issue areas of foreign policy interaction: the military-strategic, the economic-developmental, and the status-diplomatic.[4] It is obvious that an effort to treat the foreign policy of Venezuela as a product of its democratic political order would be unidimensional, yet its democracy is the inescapable ingredient in any discussion of its international behavior.

Setting aside style and substance of foreign policy momentarily, it seems reasonable to expect that a democratic system would have the greatest influence upon the manner in which decisions are made. A democracy by definition provides for popular decision making within a framework of checks and balances. In the case of Venezuelan foreign policy, this is not easy to demonstrate. The only serious study of foreign policy decision making in Venezuela, Cooke's 1968 doctoral dissertation, concluded that the national presidents exercised power and authority in foreign affairs "as in no other area of public policy."[5] Cooke predicted that the increasing complexity and broadening scope of foreign policy problems, along with emerging interest groups and the development of the legislative branch, would diminish the role of the chief executive, but affirmed that the Foreign Ministry, contrary to what one might suppose, did not participate significantly in decision making.

For different reasons, Coleman and Quiros agree. Placing their emphasis upon developmental strategy, they identify a problem of bureaucratic coordination in foreign policy activity, relating that "no longer is it clear which foreign contacts are to be handled by the Foreign Ministry." Overlap is a chronic problem of bureaucracies, but "no other bureaucratic domain has been more frequently invaded than that of foreign relations."[6] This is a general assertion, but seems to apply specifically to Venezuela. According to Tugwell, Venezuela's foreign policy objectives bear directly upon developmental strategy.[7] He demonstrated conclusively the critical role of Juan Pablo Pérez Alfonzo, the minister of mines and hydrocarbons under Rómulo Betancourt, in establishing OPEC and in fashioning generally Venezuela's international oil policy. Skilled personnel and *técnicos* in the oil and finance ministries and in the specialized agencies dealing with trade and planning have replaced the traditional diplomat, diminishing the power and prestige of the Foreign Ministry. Movement toward a civil service has been slow in Venezuelan democracy, and the creation of a career foreign service has proceeded at an even slower pace.

As a result of its democratic order, Venezuela is a dynamic society. In the realm of foreign policy many participants can be identified, including the executive, the legislature, political parties, interest groups, the bureaucracy, the media, and vox populi, but it is more difficult to show the channels through which they move to produce a particular action. Clear lines of initiation, decision, and implementation have not yet been shaped. In fact, in the issue areas identified by Ferris and Lincoln it appears that the mix is distinct for each. In the first edition, this author linked presidential leadership and the conduct of foreign affairs closely. Cooke reached a similar conclusion, although he was dealing with only two presidents of the democratic era. This claim is not based upon a narrow view of the *caudillo* in Hispanic society, but upon the consideration that, given Venezuela's democratic inexperience and the immaturity of its institutional framework, a strong chief executive is in a position to take advantage of the lengthy tradition of personalist rule. The presidents who were forceful and used their constitutional authority broadly (Betancourt, Rafael Caldera, and Carlos Andrés Pérez) took charge and enhanced Venezuela's international position. The presidents who were less skillful as leaders (Leoni and Luis Herrera Campins) witnessed a decline in

Venezuela's international influence. Venezuela has been trying to do many things simultaneously: establish its democratic order, undertake economic development, and share equitably the benefits of growth. It is not surprising that the foreign policy process has been slow to evolve, but because presidents have been at the center of the action, it is convenient to start with them and work one's way outward to identify determinants and measure effectiveness.

The first democratic president, Rómulo Betancourt, assumed an aggressive style in foreign policy. Just as he was fighting to establish democracy within the country, he fought against its foes throughout the hemisphere. Drawing upon his experiences since 1928, during which he spent long periods in exile, he believed that politics were international in scope, with a strong propensity for conspiracy and intervention. The Betancourt doctrine, a nonrecognition policy, contained the essence of his antidictatorial stance. "Regimes which do not respect human rights," he proclaimed, "ought to be subjected to a rigorous *cordón sanitario* and eradicated by the collective peaceful action of the Inter-American juridical community."[8] Essentially, Betancourt condemned right wing dictatorships and broke diplomatic relations with those regimes, even though few other countries of the hemisphere followed his example. He did not stop with diplomatic action, joining with Cuba's Fidel Castro in sponsoring a filibustering expedition against Rafael Trujillo of the Dominican Republic in June 1959, and collaborating with José Figueres of Costa Rica in promoting a coalition movement among Dominican exiles in 1961 in anticipation of Trujillo's overthrow.

Betancourt's fight with Trujillo demonstrated the depth of his feeling against dictators. A year after Betancourt tried to overthrow Trujillo in 1959, Trujillo almost turned the tables in an attempt to assassinate him. Armed with evidence of Trujillo's treachery, Betancourt invoked the Río Treaty. At the Sixth Meeting of Consultation in San José, Costa Rica, in August 1960, the American states condemned the Dominican Republic for "acts of aggression and intervention" and voted to suspend diplomatic relations and impose economic sanctions.[9] Betancourt had succeeded in isolating the hemisphere's longest surviving dictator and he took indirect credit when Trujillo was assassinated in May 1961, but by then he was engaged against a foe at the opposite end of the political spectrum.

Despite Betancourt's victory over Trujillo, Fidel Castro emerged as the most influential leader in the Caribbean and threatened anew Venezuelan democracy. Betancourt resented the young Cuban's challenge and felt betrayed by his failure to comply with the Caracas Pact (July 1958), the agreement under which the Democratic Action party (AD) assisted in the overthrow of Fulgencio Batista. Betancourt continued to support the Cubans who had given him shelter in 1949–52 and with whom he shared ideals and formed close partisan bonds during the years of exile. In turn, Castro related to many Venezuelans, most of them young, who had grown up under the Pérez Jiménez dictatorship and had witnessed its friendly political and economic relations with the United States. These young people went into the streets in the final weeks of the dictatorship and felt cheated by the return to power of Old Guard politicians who "came from outside." The Cuban revolution became their model and Fidel Castro their hero, which heightened tensions and disrupted Venezuela's tender democracy. Betancourt adopted an anti-Castro policy because he abhorred dictatorship, was an anti-Communist, and was determined to fulfill his mandate as the expression of popular sovereignty.[10]

Betancourt's most serious problem in combatting Castro was the impression that he was serving the interests of the United States. As long as Trujillo was alive, he had some leverage by pursuing a "Trujillo first" policy, meaning that he would not cooperate with the United States against Castro until it proved its sincerity by acting to eliminate Trujillo. He resisted U.S. efforts to include complaints against Cuban-Soviet ties on the agenda of the Sixth Meeting of Consultation and forced a separate meeting to deal with those objections. Nonetheless, when the Seventh Meeting convened in San José immediately following the Sixth, and the ministers condemned Soviet intervention and Cuba's "breach" of hemispheric solidarity, it precipitated a crisis within Venezuela's governing coalition. Foreign Minister Ignacio Luis Arcaya, who represented the Democratic Republican Union (URD) in the cabinet, refused to sign the San José declaration, causing Betancourt to recall him and replace him with Marcos Falcón Briceño. This episode demonstrated Betancourt's control over foreign policy. As further evidence, Betancourt made the decision to sever relations with Cuba in November 1961, despite the disruption of the governing coalition and dissension with his own party.[11] He explained that he could no longer maintain "national decorum" and endure Castro's insults.[12]

Following Venezuela's break with Cuba, Betancourt's anti-Castro policy became inseparable from the problem of internal subversion. Terrorism and guerrilla warfare threatened the stability of the Betancourt government during 1962 and 1963, and Betancourt repeatedly accused Cuba of intervention in Venezuelan affairs. Within this context, Venezuela attended the Eighth Meeting of Consultation in Uruguay in January 1962, and voted to exclude Cuba from participation in the inter-American system. The following October, Venezuela strongly supported the United States during the Cuban missile crisis. The escalating conflict between the two countries reached a climax in November 1963, when Venezuelan authorities discovered a three-ton cache of arms on the Caribbean coast near Punta Macama. The Venezuelan government was able to show that the arms came from Cuba and were destined for the FALN for use in a military action to prevent December national elections.[13] Betancourt and his elected successor, Raúl Leoni, used this evidence to achieve the expulsion of Cuba from the Organization of American States and the imposition of additional trade restrictions against the offender (in place since the missile crisis).

The situation eased somewhat when John Kennedy became the U.S. president. Venezuelans generally did not approve of the Latin American policy of the Eisenhower administration and showed their feelings through acts of violence when Vice-President Richard Nixon visited Caracas in May 1958. Betancourt declared that Kennedy was different and, even while Kennedy was president-elect, predicted that he would not tolerate dictators or take Latin America for granted.[14] The two leaders demonstrated their friendship by exchanging visits. When Kennedy came to Venezuela in December 1961, Betancourt praised him as possessing "a philosophy and new concern for Latin American, rooted in the Rooseveltian tradition of the Good Neighbor."[15] Kennedy, for his part, told Betancourt in Washington in February 1963 that he represented "all we admire in a political leader."[16] The Kennedy administration facilitated the extradition of former dictator Pérez Jiménez from the United States and appointed an Hispanic, the Puerto Rican Teodoro Moscoso, as U.S. ambassador to Venezuela. Betancourt confided that he and Kennedy had a direct phone link, "a little sister of the hot-line."[17] The Alliance for Progress gave additional substance to these improved relations.

All along, Betancourt was prepared to be forgiving of U.S. policy, drawing upon a partisan notion that Democrats were different from Republicans. Moreover, he was in awe of the achievements of the Marshall Plan and believed in the capacity of the United States to accomplish similar results in Latin America. He welcome U.S. aid, provided it could be domesticated and made to fit Venezuelan imperatives.[18] What Coleman and Quiros-Varela call the reformist strategy of development helps to explain Venezuelan policy at this stage, whereby Venezuela persuaded the United States to showcase its reformist democracy as the "last alternative" to revolution.[19] However, this interpretation overlooks the broader ideological influence of the AD party in determining Venezuelan foreign policy. Betancourt was at war with Castro during the time that Eisenhower was president and relations were poor with Washington.

Likewise, relations were not always smooth with the United States under Kennedy. Betancourt objected strenuously to the discriminatory practice of setting oil import quotas for Venezuela and not for Mexico or Canada. He told President Kennedy face to face that "Venezuela would continue to be plundered by the United States so long as Venezuelan oil wasn't treated on the same terms as Canadian oil and so long as there was still a scramble for import permits among a few hundred influential vote-catchers in the U.S."[20] Kennedy's assassination apparently prevented him from keeping a promise to correct this "unfair" situation. Betancourt was highly nationalistic in defending the price of Venezuelan oil and encouraged the efforts of Pérez Alfonzo, his minister of mines, to achieve a pricing agreement with the oil-producing states of the Middle East. Venezuela was a founding member, along with Iraq, Kuwait, and Saudi Arabia, of the Organization of Petroleum Exporting Countries (OPEC) in September 1960. No one foresaw then the tremendous impact this arrangement would have upon international affairs and the world's economy.

Betancourt also exhibited his nationalism in the matter of the disputed boundary with British Guiana, soon to be the independent nation of Guyana. If one accepts the premise that democratic states are peaceful, then Betancourt's revival of this conflict in March 1962 would seem uncharacteristic. Betancourt declared that Venezuela had been "despoiled" of a large portion of its national territory by the so-called arbitration of 1899, claiming that U.S. and British diplomats engaged in fraud and deceit and imposed the award upon Venezuela.[21] Betancourt wanted to demonstrate to Venezuela that a democratic government would defend its rights. It is likely that he also wanted to act while the territory was still British, to emphasize that the dispute was with the colonial power and did not affect the achievement of independence by Guyana, which Venezuela supported. Venezuelans generally exhibited a strong Anglophobia.

When Betancourt completed his term in February 1964, he left his personal mark upon Venezuelan foreign policy. He had strengthened Venezuelan democracy by reducing external threats, scoring remarkable victories over his foes, Trujillo and Castro. Venezuela's relations with the United States were improved, although the Alliance for Progress foundered in the wake of President Kennedy's death and the escalation of the conflict in Vietnam. The course that Betancourt set worked for him. He even took pride in the "splendid isolation" of the Betancourt doctrine, but it created problems for his successor, Raúl Leoni, because of the changed international climate of the mid-1960s and the growing importance of economic performance for the health of Venezuelan democracy.

Early in his administration, Leoni discovered the liabilities of the Betancourt doctrine. In April 1964, the Brazilian army overthrew the constitutional government of João Goulart. Venezuela refused to recognize the military regime, even though it lost an important customer for oil and it tended to diminish its influence in international economic affairs. Few governments outside the socialist bloc objected to the removal of Goulart. Leoni did not abandon the Betancourt doctrine because it was a difficult thing to do politically, within the AD party and within the country, where democratic leadership had become a campaign issue. Leoni's foreign minister, Ignacio Iribarren Borges, tried to state it positively, affirming that the policy gave Venezuela "considerable prestige" and that, despite its inconvenience, "its moral and juridical force [was] indisputable."[22]

The policy also applied to Cuba. Although there was a lull in terrorist activity for almost three years following the economic and political ostracism of Cuba in July 1964, Leoni made no effort to normalize relations. In 1967, after Castro threatened to create "new Vietnams" in Latin America, and Venezuelan terrorist groups became active again, Leoni sought additional sanctions against Cuba by the OAS. He also considered an appeal to the United Nations, where he hoped to persuade non-Communist states outside the hemisphere to restrict trade with Cuba. At the Twelfth Meeting of Consultation, convened to hear Venezuela's complaints, the American states, despite greater preoccupation with Ché Guevara's activities in Bolivia, condemned Cuba anew, proclaiming that the Castro government "continued giving moral and material support to the Venezuelan guerrilla and terrorist movement."[23] Leoni probably made political capital with these moves, but they were redundant and did not address the cause of Castro's renewed threat, the disappointing international economic situation.

During Leoni's presidency, it became clear that the United States was unwilling and unable to perform the economic miracle that Betancourt and others of his generation dreamed possible and that, in fact, aid from the United States and other industrialized countries was having undesirable effects in the developing world. The war in Vietnam and racial tensions and youthful rebellion at home were eroding U.S. leadership. In the hemisphere, Leoni sharply reproached President Lyndon Johnson for his intervention in the Dominican Republic and lamented the "lost objectives" of the Alliance for Progress.[24] Under the circumstances, Latin American states moved toward economic integration as a means of achieving development and freeing themselves from reliance upon foreign economic assistance. The earliest scheme, embodied in the Latin American Free Trade Area (LAFTA), followed the customs union approach, which was supposed to promote import-substitution by providing an enlarged market and, hence, attract foreign investment. Venezuela joined LAFTA, but the private sector objected vigorously, which placed a damper on Venezuela's participation.[25] In truth, LAFTA proved counterproductive, mainly because it was based upon a European model of integration, which involved totally distinct circumstances and goals, and because it tended to benefit the already strong economies and facilitate domination by foreign companies (the rise of multinationals).[26] As a result, two smaller industrialized states, Chile and Colombia, proposed a subregional integration plan, made up of the Andean states and designed to defend their interests against the "Big Three" of LAFTA (Argentina, Brazil, and Mexico) and to regulate direct foreign investment and technology transfer.[27]

In August 1966, Leoni met in Bogotá with the presidents of Chile and Colombia and representatives of the presidents of Ecuador and Peru in the first of several conferences leading to the Andean Subregional Integration Agreement (the Andean Pact). The conferees intended to move beyond the customs union approach and to use integration to reinforce developmental strategy, meaning the creation of common institutions for regulation, planning, and policy coordination.[28] Leoni was strongly influenced by the growing number of professional economists and technicians in the Venezuelan bureaucracy. The most prominent, such as José Antonio Mayobre, had experience in international agencies, especially as exiles during the 1950s and particularly in the UN Economic Commission for Latin America (ECLA), where the ideas of Raúl Prebisch prevailed. Leoni was convinced of the wisdom of economic integration, but the concept was not easy to sell, because the gains were nebulous and off in the future, whereas the costs were immediate and painful.[29]

In probably the best example of the influence of pressure group activity upon foreign policy in democratic Venezuela, the Federation of Chambers of Commerce and Production (FEDE-CAMARAS) blocked Venezuela's ratification of the Andean Pact. As noted, the private sector had criticized Venezuelan participation in LAFTA, but both Betancourt and Leoni defied its opposition. With reference to the Andean Pact, agrarian and business leaders were better prepared. They delayed the conclusion of the subregional treaty for over two years and, in the meantime, issued analyses of the proposed arrangement, claiming that it would harm Venezuelan industry in relation to that of Chile and Colombia and that it would sacrifice Venezuela's "special trading relationship with the United States."[30] Leoni was unable to win approval of the idea (professional economists were no match for business leaders in the political arena), and his successor, Rafael Caldera, who represented another political party, did no better when the Andean Pact was finally completed in May 1969.

Despite the fact that Venezuela did not immediately join the Andean Pact, the idea that developing countries could better confront the rich, industrialized nations of the world through common action had been planted, and the *técnicos* would have their day in Venezuelan foreign policy. This concept was already manifest at the international level, where the Leoni administration supported the activities of the Group of 77, the newly formed bloc of developing countries in the United Nations. Venezuela recognized the restraint, even divisiveness, of the inter-American system and intensified its collaboration with the Middle Eastern oil states through OPEC. Leoni endorsed the goals of Betancourt, though he pledged a regular supply of petroleum to consumer countries, a concern that surfaced during the Middle East crisis of 1967 and that was a harbinger of things to come. Leoni even explored the possibility of opening economic contact with the Soviet Union.

Leoni was not a dynamic personality, but he seemed to interpret the signs of his time accurately. Although he did not abandon the Betancourt doctrine, he applied it less rigorously and showed less inclination toward covert action than Betancourt. The pro-U.S. position of Betancourt and faith in the inter-American system faded under Leoni. He was influenced by economists with a third world outlook, and the social democracy of the AD party took on a more European cast. The foreign policy of Leoni served as a transition from that of Betancourt, based upon old friendships and old faiths, to that of Rafael Caldera, based upon a new humanism and new alignments. Some issues remained constant. For example, although Guyana became independent in 1966, Venezuela continued to press its claim in the Esequibo region.

Rafael Caldera, like Rómulo Betancourt, was the founder and dominant personality of a political party, which signified also that he would be an innovator in foreign policy. Caldera replaced the Betancourt doctrine with an entirely new concept for asserting

Venezuela's moral authority, one that did not criticize the political shortcomings of the poor nations but that stressed the obligations of the rich. Caldera rationalized cooperation among Latin American nations regardless of how they were governed, on the basis that Betancourt's adherence to the democratic ideal had played into the hands of the wealthy and powerful. "We must look for what unites us," he insisted, and "not deceive ourselves by emphasizing differences which in substance are not essential but which can easily be exploited by the great interests that seek to divide us in order to be able to manipulate us."[31] If what Caldera called "pluralistic solidarity" appeared unfeeling toward the victims of political tyranny, he justified it with a higher purpose, the attainment of "international social justice." Caldera was an expert in labor law, and he intended to apply the principles of collective bargaining to international affairs. Just as workers discovered strength in numbers, the poor and weak nations of the world might unite to force the rich and powerful states to recognize that "they did not have more rights, only greater responsibilities and obligations."[32]

Caldera demonstrated that Venezuelan democracy was multi-dimensional, which he extended to foreign policy, in the same way that U.S. foreign policy reflected differences between the Democratic and Republican parties.[33] AD, as a social democratic party influenced by Western European concepts of intellectual freedom, tended to believe that social justice was the rational outcome of political democracy. Caldera's COPEI, as a Social Christian party influenced by Hispanic and Catholic thought, was less certain about the perfectability of the individual and stressed the formulation of laws and standards by which one might perform good works and achieve grace. The poor did not have to vote themselves a larger piece of the pie, because the rich must share according to established ethical practices. In any event, as Lombardi has argued, the political philosophies of AD and COPEI came "from abroad."[34] Both of these parties represented international movements, so that as Caldera's policy unfolded, not only did it find new moral underpinnings but it changed its relationships with other countries.

Caldera's pluralistic solidarity, embracing the principles of self-determination and nonintervention, helped to relax tensions, especially in the Caribbean. Caldera refrained from engaging in conspiratorial antidictatorial activities. This worked both ways with reference to Cuba, because terrorism virtually disappeared during Caldera's term. Caldera contributed further to this circumstance through "pacification," by which the Venezuelan government legalized the Communist party and granted amnesty to revolutionary activists. Although Caldera did not fully normalize relations with Cuba, the two countries participated in cultural exchanges in education and sports. A number of factors explain this changed climate but, given the fact that Venezuela had twice demanded and secured the condemnation of Cuba, it seemed strange to have Caldera's foreign minister, Arístides Calvani, remark in April 1973: "There is no reason why when international organizations such as the United Nations recognize Marxism-Leninism, the American states should not do so."[35]

If Caldera's acceptance of ideological pluralism helped to improve relations with Cuba and the socialist countries, his attitude impaired those with the United States. In addition, Caldera chided the United States for its trade and aid policies toward Latin America. He criticized Nelson Rockefeller's study mission to Latin America in 1969, undertaken on behalf of the new U.S. president, Richard Nixon, for being more show than substance and requested cancellation of his planned visit to Caracas, supposedly out of concerns over possible violence.[36] During his own visit to the United States the following year, Caldera expressed deep disappointment that Venezuela's oil exports to the United States had declined over the last decade, while those of Canada had doubled. He complained before the U.S. Congress: "Our people cannot understand being made the object of discriminatory treatment." And he added forcefully, "It is difficult to think that the people who reached the moon are not capable of making a decisive contribution to the development of other countries."[37]

Despite his tough talk, Caldera believed that Venezuela and the United States needed to have a "successful working relationship."[38] This caused the Caracas newsweekly *Resumen* to observe that it was ridiculous to talk like Fidel Castro "if one does not have the slightest intention of acting like Fidel Castro."[39] Caldera responded that, in projecting his message of international social justice, he had to speak frankly, even sternly. "The more developed countries," he stated, "have an obligation to help the developing countries achieve their appropriate objectives, ... not as an act of philanthropy, ... but as a duty."[40] Caldera insisted that he did not wish to alter the "traditionally cordial relations" with the United States, but that a friendship ought not deter him from saying what was necessary.[41]

While Caldera achieved some success as an international spokesman, he was unable to resolve certain nagging problems specific to Venezuela. Under Caldera, Venezuela's relations with its nearest neighbors became strained, a situation that has persisted and has hampered the fulfillment of its larger ambitions. As democracies, Venezuela and Colombia had been good friends for most of the 1960s, but their relations soured by the end of the decade over the issues of illegal immigrants and the location of the maritime boundary in the Gulf of Venezuela. During the decade, close to 500,000 Colombians entered Venezuela illegally in search of jobs and better wages, creating anxiety on the part of Venezuelans fearing competition for jobs and resentment on the part of Colombians charging discriminatory treatment. Until Venezuela experienced economic hard times, the problem persisted. With reference to the Gulf of Venezuela, the armed forces strongly influenced policy, opposing any concessions, essentially on geopolitical grounds,[42] although the possibility of off-shore oil deposits was a factor. Representatives of Venezuela and Colombia met in Rome, in the hope that they might achieve more away from the scrutiny of critics and the press. The talks broke down in 1973, however, ostensibly because Venezuela would not agree to submit the dispute to arbitration.

Venezuela's opposition to arbitration was linked to its chagrin over the 1899 award fixing its eastern frontier and its campaign to overturn that settlement. Betancourt had reopened the issue in 1962; Leoni negotiated the Geneva Accord with Great Britain in 1966, establishing the fact that a dispute existed, without prejudice to Guyana's independence; and Caldera continued the negotiations with the new nation of Guyana. In the talks with Guyana, arbitration again became an obstacle. Venezuela, unwilling to submit to it, agreed to the Protocol of Puerto España, by which the matter was put on hold until June 1982 (under terms of the Geneva

Accord), unless reopened sooner. Venezuela's fears became reality. Although Venezuela had won recognition of its grievance, it now appeared to be the bully, since its claim could be perceived as no longer involving a patch of a colonial empire, but as embracing over one-half of the national territory of a small, third world country.

This situation affected Venezuela's relations with Brazil. Its neighbor to the south had a successful tradition of settling its boundaries through arbitration, making it sensitive to any challenge to the integrity of the process. It sympathized with Guyana and offered to extend financial and technical assistance. Caldera was wary of these moves, suspecting Brazil of seeking to expand into the Caribbean through friendship with Guyana. Brazil had already alarmed him by its activity in the Amazon. In 1966, Brazil's military leaders inaugurated a plan to develop the Amazon, using the armed forces to establish settlements in remote and frontier regions. Caldera responded with an Amazonian development plan of his own (CODESUR), constructing a road through Venezuela's southern wilderness to the Brazilian border and acquiring river patrol craft from the United States (brought back from Vietnam), but the effort was halfhearted. He met these challenges more vigorously in the area of foreign policy, combining two goals, economic development and national security.[43]

In February 1973, Caldera traveled to a number of South American countries: Colombia, Ecuador, Peru, Bolivia, Chile, and Argentina. Although Caldera carried his message of pluralistic solidarity in order to achieve international social justice, the omission of Brazil from his itinerary revealed a move to unite the Hispanic states against the "green giant." Caldera gave substance to this impression by subscribing to the Andean Pact in the course of his trip in the Consensus of Lima, by which Venezuela obtained certain concessions before joining. Caldera had planned well for this action by holding a series of town meetings before departing in order to overcome the objections of the private sector and to appease various special interest groups. Nonetheless, though Venezuela's membership was important for the purposes of economic integration, Caldera's motives were political, designed to enhance Venezuela's influence in the subregion and to contain Brazil.[44] After achieving this success, Caldera met with the president of Brazil, General Emilio Garrastazu Médici, near the remote border town of Santa Elena de Uairén in the Amazon region. The two leaders exchanged decorations and pledges of cooperation and peace, but Brazilian-Venezuelan differences were not overcome.[45]

By the time that Caldera neared the end of his term, he was successfully challenging Brazil and other emerging powers of Latin America for a position of leadership. Although pluralistic solidarity lacked the moral authority of the Betancourt doctrine, it gave Venezuelan foreign policy more flexibility, without necessarily sacrificing its idealism because of the basic goal of international social justice. Caldera moved Venezuela more closely to identification with the third world, reflecting its growing confidence and the declining status of the inter-American system and the troubles being experienced by the United States. He recognized Venezuela's increasing economic power and strove to use it to extend the nation's influence, but, because the energy crisis of 1973–74 came late in his administration, it was his successor who had the economic muscle to achieve "middle power" status.

When the price of oil quadrupled in the energy crisis of 1973–74, Venezuela suddenly had more money than it could handle effectively, and this situation greatly influenced its foreign policy. A new president, Carlos Andrés Pérez, accompanied the flow of petrodollars. Although Pérez represented the return of AD to Miraflores, he was less a kindred spirit of Betancourt and the other founders of his party than was Caldera of COPEI. In effect, he ushered in Venezuelan democracy's second generation of leaders. This was important in foreign policy because it signified a different perception of the United States. Pérez's image of the United States was not the compassion of the New Deal or the awesome display of power in World War II but the neglect of Latin America in the 1950s and the traumas of the Vietnam era. Although not a youth, he affected the youthful style of the times, with his long sideburns, modish clothes, and a general contempt for "old politics." He fit in with a new wave of leaders, energetic and self-confident, like Pierre Trudeau of Canada and Luis Echeverría of Mexico.

Pérez quickly learned that although wealth brought power, it did not make one popular. In fact, Venezuela and the other oil producers were being blamed for the existing international economic malaise. Venezuela was very sensitive to this issue and refused to be made the scapegoat for the economic crisis, seeing it as a ploy by the industrialized nations to divide the developing and third world countries and thus drive down the price of oil. The world's economic ills, Pérez maintained, were not caused by high oil prices but by "a wasteful economic system founded on unjust prices for the raw materials produced by the poor or impoverished countries."[46] Venezuela had no intention of returning to the way things were, and the defense of the new oil prices, imperative for its developmental strategy, became the central feature of its foreign policy. However, Venezuela was aware that the high petroleum prices were hurting the poor countries as much as, if not more than, the rich nations.

As a result, Venezuela undertook to relieve the burden of high oil prices as much as possible from its Latin American neighbors and other countries of the third world. In order to avoid inflation and buy some time, the Pérez administration created the Venezuelan Investment Fund (FIV) for "immobilizing" Venezuela's surplus oil revenue and for promoting public investment and import-substitution programs.[47] Pérez also used this fund to assist poor countries in purchasing oil and developing energy policies. He made bilateral and multilateral funding arrangements with numerous international lending institutions (the IMF, World Bank, Inter-American Development Bank, and regional and central banks) through which Venezuela truly shared its bonanza with other countries. For example, Pérez met with the presidents and chiefs of state of the Central American countries and Panama in Cuidad Guayana in December 1974, where they negotiated financing agreements between FIV and the respective central banks for oil purchases, developmental projects, and marketing strategies for various commodities, particularly coffee.[48] Venezuela made similar arrangements with the small states of the Caribbean, becoming a member of the Caribbean Development Bank and supporting operations of the Caribbean Common Market (CARICOM). Aware of charges that Venezuela was using its economic power for political leverage, Pérez declared, "The oil of Venezuela is the oil of Latin America."[49] He insisted that Venezuela's petroleum was for the welfare of "all our people" and would not be used as a weapon or instrument of persuasion.[50]

At the same time that Venezuela sought to ease its conscience and silence critics through an impressive program of international financial cooperation, it undertook to justify and make permanent its situation through the advocacy of a new international economic order (NIEO). The energy crisis, Pérez affirmed, had exposed the injustice of the existing international economic system, freeing the source of wealth and enabling the producing countries to make the decisions that affected them. Refuting the description of OPEC as a pack of price gougers, Pérez praised it as the third world's "David" that had "successfully challenged" the industrial "Goliaths."[51] The determination to use OPEC's success as a model and, simultaneously, to maintain high oil prices led Venezuela to an active role in the Group of 77 and other UN bodies, the North-South dialogue, and even to flirt with the Movement of Non-Aligned Nations.

Fueled by the high energy prices, Pérez engaged in a peripatetic diplomacy that took him virtually everywhere in the Western Hemisphere and to many of the capitals of Europe and the Middle East. In November 1976, he completed a 12,000-mile trip in 15 days, including a visit to Moscow, making him the first Venezuelan president to journey to the Soviet Union. Wherever he went, he repeated his message of just prices for the products of the developing countries and full participation in international economic decisions. Venezuela wanted not only to determine the price and to control the production of its principal nonrenewable resource but also sought new markets and the means to free itself from reliance upon petroleum revenue. In April and May 1977, Pérez traveled to the Middle East, to the capitals of the Arab members of OPEC, playing the role of mediator between the "price camps." Venezuela looked upon the organization as vital to its "oil lifeline." Hence, although favoring high prices itself, it made unity central to its policy, promoting compromise on pricing decisions and keeping political issues outside. It affirmed that OPEC was an oil cartel, not a political alliance.[52] Matching its global activism, Venezuela under Pérez moved in multiple directions in the hemisphere.

In Latin America, Venezuela promoted solidarity, which

seemed inconsistent with its globalist approach to foreign affairs. In addition to its thrust into the Caribbean and Central America, Venezuela turned its attention to its neighbors of South America. Its special geographic position gave it a Caribbean, Andean, and Amazonian presence, and it could make use of strong historical bonds as well. During Pérez's term, there were a series of sesquicentennials marking major events of the wars of independence, and he took advantage of them to espouse the Bolivarian dream of hemispheric unity. Foreign Minister Ramón Escovar Salom declared that Venezuela's leadership was "not based on oil, but on Bolívar, who preceded oil."[53] Despite intense activity, this phase of Pérez's policy failed, marked by the cancellation of a meeting of Latin American chief executives scheduled to commemorate the one hundredth fiftieth anniversary of Bolívar's First Pan American Conference in Panama.

Pérez persisted in the Venezuelan effort to convert the Andean Pact into a political alliance, and this caused the problem. Whereas Venezuela endeavored to avoid mixing politics and economics in OPEC, its policy toward the Andean Pact lacked similar clarity and cohesion. Although the so-called "spillover" effect cannot be discounted in any economic integration arrangement, Venezuela and the other Pact members seemed to be at odds on the issue of political alignment. Venezuela did manage to raise certain issues and even to rally the Andean states on such matters as an outlet to the sea for Bolivia, support for Panama in gaining control of the Panama Canal, and pressure on Anastasio Somoza to resign. However, aside from using the Pact's mechanisms to finance oil purchases and support energy development, Venezuela's economic performance was disappointing, contributing to a weakened organization. The Pact's industrialization schemes and sectorial planning simply did not mesh with Venezuela's own developmental strategy. But Venezuela alone was not responsible for the Pact's ineffectiveness. Various economic and technical problems plagued it, and Chile's decision to withdraw in 1975 left it "shattered."[54]

Venezuela's principal purpose in joining the Andean Pact, fear of Brazilian expansionism, also seemed to dissipate. Whereas Caldera had been alarmed over Brazil's apparent ambitions, Pérez did not seem concerned and, in fact, had no coherent policy toward Brazil. Relations between the two countries remained cool, mainly because of the nature of Brazil's government. Pérez visited Brazil in November 1977, and Venezuela subscribed to the Amazon Pact (along with Brazil, Colombia, Peru, Bolivia, Ecuador, Suriname, and Guyana) in July 1978. The Treaty for Amazonian Cooperation was not an integration plan, being concerned primarily with conservation and ecological matters. It reflected a recognition on the part of Brazil that it did not have the resources to match its ambitions in the Amazon and a willingness on the part of Venezuela to put the Amazon on the back burner, not a high priority in any case, in order to concentrate on its third world and Caribbean commitments.[55]

As Pérez pursued his goal of leadership over a new hemispheric unity, it was clear that Caldera's scrapping of the Betancourt doctrine facilitated his task. He avoided an issue that could be divisive within his own party and he built upon Caldera's pluralistic solidarity, or, as he preferred, the concept of an "open hemisphere." Pérez's Bolivarian vision signified alignment with the third world (in the search for a new international economic order) and independence from cold war determinants, both of which further undermined the fading inter-American system (OAS). This open hemisphere policy specifically involved relations with Cuba. Following Caldera's lead and consistent with his free-spirited image, Pérez took the initiative to restore Cuba to the Latin American fold. "We must accept ideological differences," he stated, "if we are to join together in the common quest for independent decision-making."[56] Rebuffed in efforts to remove the OAS sanctions against Cuba at the fifteenth consultative meeting in Quito in November 1974, Venezuela achieved a consolation prize the following July in the form of a resolution enabling OAS members to formulate independent policies toward Cuba. By then, Venezuela and Cuba had renewed relations.[57]

As with a number of other initiatives, what seemed like an exciting idea turned out badly. In 1976, Castro's intervention in Angola and the sabotage of a Cuban airliner, allegedly by a Cuban exile group resident in Venezuela, created serious tensions, exacerbated by a flow of persons seeking asylum in the Venezuelan embassy in Havana. When the meeting of Latin American chiefs of state to commemorate Bolívar's 1826 Panama conference was cancelled, apparently because of objections to Fidel Castro's planned attendance, Pérez acquiesced.

Pérez's policy toward Cuba and the open hemisphere concept in general may be understood in the context of his plan to create a solid Latin American front for presenting a common position in international economic affairs. Along with Mexican President Echeverría, Pérez sponsored the Latin American Economic System (SELA), an organization of Latin American states to confront collectively the outside (industrialized) world. The organization excluded the United States, because, as Fagen observed, it implied "the *unionization* of Latin America."[58] Although Venezuela shared the leadership in this enterprise with Mexico, according to Martz, "Without Caracas' unflagging commitment and energetic diplomacy, it is unlikely that the SELA would have seen the light of day."[59] It might be added that this "sharing of leadership" was characteristic of Venezuelan diplomacy, what Tugwell has identified as "consociational." He lists cooperation with Peru in the Andean Pact and Venezuela's general conduct in OPEC as further examples.[60] In many cases, however, Venezuela ended up paying the bill. After 16 months of meetings and negotiations, 23 nations signed SELA's charter on October 18, 1975. They designated Caracas as the seat of the permanent secretariat of the organization, and Venezuela agreed to fund its interim budget. As might be expected, the general thrust of Venezuelan foreign policy did not please the United States.

The United States deeply resented Venezuela's policies. This was true especially during the Nixon-Ford years. OPEC, SELA, the open hemisphere, and the new international economic order represented threats to the old inter-American system. Ironically, the United States contributed to the circumstances about which it complained. In blaming OPEC for inflation and other economic ills, it threatened Venezuela's new wealth, and Venezuela reacted. Venezuela, convinced that an unjust situation had been defeated, took up the struggle with the emotion of a moral crusade. When the United States imposed sanctions on the OPEC countries in the 1974 Trade Act, excluding them (including Venezuela and Ecuador) from the Generalized System of Preferences, thereby making no distinction between OPEC and the Organization of Arab Petroleum Exporting Countries (OAPEC), Venezuela felt humiliated. Venezuela and Ecuador, as members of OPEC, had not participated in the oil embargo by OAPEC, which precipitated the 1973 energy crisis, and Venezuela repeatedly declared that it would not use oil as a political weapon. Tugwell insists that if the United States had recognized the important role Venezuela played in supplying its petroleum needs and had granted it preferential treatment, it might have secured a reliable energy partner, but the United States alienated Venezuela instead.[61]

In order to protect its oil bonanza, Venezuela fought to maintain high prices, sought to reduce its reliance upon the U.S. market for oil exports, and promoted alternatives to petroleum-generated revenue. Even so, looking at events toward the end of Pérez's term, the United States was better off having a nation such as Venezuela as the leader of a more independent or open hemisphere.

Vietnam, Watergate, and OPEC took their toll on the power and prestige of the United States. Its influence in Latin America declined, and countries like Venezuela, Mexico, and Brazil seized their opportunity. None of them represented a threat, but Venezuela offered significant advantages. It had oil and it was a democracy. Its interests were similar to those of the United States, and, although acting independently, it could actually help the United States achieve goals it might not accomplish alone. Although Pérez had struggled against U.S. domination of the hemisphere for three years, he unequivocally hailed the human rights policy of Jimmy Carter. President Carter's policy had its roots in the Betancourt doctrine, and Pérez was thrilled with the U.S. position. Pérez may have muted the Betancourt doctrine for practical reasons, but its spirit remained strong, especially within AD. Pérez visited Washington in June 1977, where Carter welcomed him as a "champion of human rights" and a "leader of the Third World."[62] Returning the visit the following March, Carter referred to Pérez as his "number one advisor on Latin America."[63] During that visit, the United States and Venezuela concluded several agreements on joint energy research and development, and Carter pledged to end Venezuela's exclusion from the Generalized System of Preferences.[64] Despite Pérez's strong support of Panama in the Panama Canal treaty negotiations and his deep involvement in the overthrow of Somoza in Nicaragua, U.S.-Venezuelan relations were cordial by the end of his term.

It was an example of Carter's bad luck that relations improved with Venezuela at a time when the Pérez government was falling into discredit at home. The oil boom had proven too much. As Pérez Alfonzo had remarked, Venezuelan democracy "could die of indigestion as certainly as from hunger."[65] Despite its resolve to divert one-half of its oil revenue to the FIV, the Pérez government yielded to the temptation to use it for ordinary budgetary expenditures, resulting in "a period of extremely wasteful spending."[66] Examples of corruption surfaced, with Betancourt himself writing in September 1977 about a "conspiracy" of multimillion-dollar rackets "contaminating" all levels of Venezuelan society. "Venezuela has now developed its own version of the Mexican 'mordida,'" he charged, "a cut taken by government officials, who, though previously incorruptible in Venezuela, have now started to demanded regular bribes and to sell small-scale favors."[67] The general feeling that, with all the money available, there ought to be more to show for it, applied to foreign policy as well.

When one reviews the many fronts on which Venezuelan foreign policy was active under Pérez, it is breathtaking. Pérez maintained a feverish pace, but the success of his initiatives, especially in the hemisphere, depended on how much he was willing to spend. His efforts at hemispheric unity, relying upon the Bolívarian ideal, came up empty. In fact, Venezuela's democratic reputation was probably a liability, given the resurgence of military dictatorships in Latin America in the 1970s. Only Somoza had fallen, but the rise of the Sandinistas in Nicaragua, coupled with Castro's renewed influence, weakened democracy in Latin America. Pérez had not even made progress with the nagging boundary questions with Colombia and Guyana. Nonetheless, in listing Pérez's lack of specific success, one ought not overlook the general fact that Venezuela had emerged as an influential state in Latin America or that many of his initiatives would win acceptance in the long run.

The problem with Pérez's policy was not inconsistency, as many analysts have concluded, but inexperience and a lack of clear lines of responsibility for policy formulation and implementation. Venezuela's foreign policy had a specific, central concept, its oil lifeline. The energy crisis of 1973 had proven to the satisfaction of Venezuelans what they had suspected all along, that they had been paying for the prosperity of others, and they were not going to let it happen ever again. The implementation of the concept, however, was badly managed, without agreement as to whether Venezuela's course should be political/ideological or economic/technical. For the main part, the economic/technical response prevailed, but it lacked coherence, without systematic coordination among Pérez's most important advisers on foreign economic policy: Manuel Pérez Guerrero, the minister of state for international economic affairs; Valentín Hernández Acosta, the minister of mines and hydrocarbons; and Gumersindo Rodríguez, the chief of the central planning office, CORDIPLAN. Following the oil nationalization on January 1, 1976, the national company, Petróleos de Venezuela functioned as an autonomous agency, giving it a great deal of managerial and administrative leeway, to the extent that it could undertake joint ventures on its own initiative with transnational oil companies. As Blank has written, the democratic management of Venezuela's oil industry created "an element of conflict and a system of checks and balances between the political and managerial roles,"[68] and this influenced foreign policy as well.

The Foreign Ministry did not even play a coordinating role in the conduct of this international economic policy. During Pérez's administration, three different persons served as foreign minister, and only Simón Alberto Consalvi, who took over in the last year, was an influential figure. Bond observed correctly that the Foreign Ministry was "the least professional of all the ministries dealing with foreign policy."[69] Despite the demonstrated need, the Pérez government did little to improve the quality of the diplomatic corps or to develop a career foreign service. These factors, then, help to explain the difficulty in tracing the Venezuelan foreign policy process, but they do not alter the fact that from Venezuela's standpoint, the policy was essentially sound. Luis Herrera Campins, the *copeyano* who successfully campaigned for the presidency in 1978, criticized Pérez's foreign policy as flamboyant, pretentious, and free-spending, but he did not change its essence significantly when he became president. The style came under attack, not the substance.

Herrera Campins made the search for a new international economic order the centerpiece of his foreign policy. In traveling to the Arab countries of OPEC in the first year of his presidency,

Herrera echoed a theme expressed by Pérez five years earlier: the industrialized states and the transnational companies, in a "divide and conquer" tactic, falsely blamed the worldwide inflation on oil prices. He proclaimed that the developing countries and OPEC ought to be "allies."[70] They heeded his appeal, electing Venezuela president of the Group of 77 in September 1980. Foreign Minister Zambrano Velasco stayed on course as well, advising the Group of the need for a strategy to deal with the industrialized nations, in order to revise the international monetary and financial order established at Bretton Woods (the IMF) and make it more just.[71]

The Herrera government continued Venezuelan participation in the Andean Pact and SELA and remained committed to international financial cooperation. In the Andean Pact, Herrera persisted in mixing political and economic goals, although the quest for political unity was not irrelevant to developmental strategy. The Andean Pact was disappointing with reference to its economic performance, but did achieve some success in building common institutions for policy coordination and sectoral programming. Despite structural weakness and political conflicts among member states, the subregional organization approached the kind of unified attitude Venezuela believed essential for facing the outside (industrialized) world, or what Axline referred to as "a manifestation of collective self-reliance."[72] In strictly political matters, such as the overthrow of Somoza in Nicaragua, Venezuela exerted strong influence over the Andean states.

The SELA initiative was less promising, but not because Herrera was any less committed to the idea. The plans for integrated economic development and the sharing of technology among Latin American states cost a great deal of money, and no country, other than Venezuela, seemed willing to contribute significantly. Herrera and José López Portillo, the new Mexican president, shared the leadership as had Pérez and Echeverría, but the poor economic picture by 1982 further hampered their effectiveness. At the meeting in Panama in November 1981 between SELA and the United States, called to identify and analyze economic problems and find means to solve them together, the tone was already softer and less confrontational. The Central American crisis and the mounting debt problem created further obstacles to the development of SELA.

The Herrera government persisted in the policy of international cooperation, especially in the Caribbean, to finance development and oil purchases. The Venezuelan constitution mandated this conduct, and Herrera used the term international social justice once again. He revived the concept of duty, of seeking the "universal common good," as an essential element of Venezuelan foreign policy, adding that economic justice was essential for the promotion and strengthening of democracy.[73] Herrera maintained Venezuela's impressive international giving, at least through the first-half of his term. From 1974 to mid-1981, Venezuela committed a grand total of $7,312,000,000 in programs of international financial cooperation. This figure represented one-sixth of the increase of Venezuela's GNP between 1973 and 1980 and substantially exceeded the guidelines established by the UN General Assembly for developmental aid by developed countries.[74] Venezuela also collaborated with Mexico in providing preferential prices on oil purchases by Central American and Caribbean countries. Herrera and López Portillo signed an agreement to this effect in Costa Rica in August 1980.

Despite Herrera's solidarity with the third world and criticism of the economic policies of the industrialized nations, Venezuela's relations with the United States improved, especially when Ronald Reagan became president. COPEI's pluralistic solidarity fit in better with the Reagan policy of distinguishing between authoritarian and totalitarian regimes than with the human rights policy of Jimmy Carter. More significant, relations with Cuba deteriorated. Whereas Pérez had achieved a reconciliation with Cuba, relations under Herrera became severely strained and unfriendly. The situation started to go awry with the Angola affair in 1976 and hit bottom with the acquittal in September 1980 of four anti-Castro Cubans accused of causing the crash of the Cuban airliner in 1976. However, basic to the problem was the issue of asylum. Large numbers of Cubans had been taking refuge in foreign embassies in Havana, climaxing with the rush of 10,000 onto the Peruvian embassy grounds and the eventual Mariel "boatlift" of 125,000 in April 1980. Although the number in the Venezuelan embassy was relatively small, the embarrassed Castro regime refused to grant them safe conduct, insisting that they were not refugees but common criminals. In the bitter controversy that ensued, both governments withdrew their ambassadors, but Venezuela did not rupture relations because of concern for the safety of the asylees.

The crisis in Central America exacerbated relations with Cuba and tended to identify the Herrera government more closely with U.S. policy. The ever-tightening grip of the Sandinistas in Nicaragua and the Cuban strength there deeply disappointed both AD and COPEI, especially as their respective social democratic and Christian democratic allies lost influence. In El Salvador, Herrera strongly supported his friend and fellow Christian Democrat José Napoleón Duarte. Even after Duarte was ousted, he condemned the "extremism" of the left as much as that of the right and denounced Cuban intervention.[75] Standing up to charges that he was using Venezuelan resources to support unpopular regimes for partisan purposes, to advance the cause of Christian Democracy in Latin America, he criticized the joint Mexican-French statement attacking the electoral process in El Salvador and praised the outcome of the 1982 Salvadoran elections in the face of "terrorist" treats.[76] The influence of political parties upon foreign policy was manifest in the case of El Salvador, as COPEI and the Christian Democratic parties in the region strongly disagreed with the position of AD and the other affiliates of the Socialist International.

Although Herrera's policy in Central America and the Caribbean appeared to harmonize with that of U.S. President Reagan, Herrera insisted repeatedly that the promotion of democracy did not excuse the violation of the principle of nonintervention. Venezuela participated in the meeting of foreign ministers in Nassau in July 1981 with the United States, Mexico, and Canada to discuss the Caribbean Basin Initiative and in the economic summit at Cancún the following October, emphasizing that its position was one of cooperation, not submission. Venezuela welcomed the recognition on the part of the United States that economic and social issues were at the core of the unrest in the Caribbean but insisted that it would not be drawn into the East-West struggle and declared, in fact, that it was vital to prevent the Caribbean from becoming an arena of big power rivalry.[77] Nonetheless, as Cuban actions appeared more menacing, especially when its relations with the revolutionary government of Maurice Bishop of Grenada gave it a presence in the eastern

Caribbean, Venezuela strengthened its ties with the United States by arranging to purchase 24 F-16 jet fighter bombers.

Venezuela's purchase of these expensive, sophisticated aircraft was a dramatic development. Aside from the controversy it caused in Caracas and the alarm it engendered among neighboring states, the sale demonstrated that the United States was prepared to share with Venezuela the task of keeping the Caribbean free of extracontinental influence.[78] Until this time, the U.S. Foreign Military Sales Act had prohibited the sale of such advanced weapons systems to Latin America, so that the Reagan administration, in requesting Congress to approve the sale, was making a strong statement with reference to Venezuela. The narrowing relations between the two countries were abruptly reversed when each reacted differently to Argentina's invasion of the Malvinas Islands in April 1982.

Venezuela proclaimed "absolute solidarity" with Argentina and expressed outrage over U.S. actions in support of Great Britain. Herrera explained Venezuela's position on the basis of Latin American independence and in opposition to colonialism, adding that it was repaying a debt to Luis Drago, the Argentine jurist and foreign minister who supported Venezuela in 1902 when it was a victim of aggression.[79] Venezuela's reaction to this affair totally disrupted the previous course of its foreign policy. It aligned itself with a military regime that only a few months before had been anathema in Caracas, and Venezuela found itself acting in concert with Cuba in the UN. Herrera showed a disposition to reverse his stand on Cuba and to distance himself from the United States, proposing to revamp SELA as a political organization, with the intention of excluding the United States from participation in hemispheric affairs. Among the American states, except for those of Argentina and Cuba, Venezuela's stand was the most vigorous and emotional, even overlooking the detrimental effect it had upon relations with the states of the English-speaking Caribbean. Undoubtedly, Venezuela felt "betrayed " by the United States, that its professions of hemispheric solidarity and friendship for the Hispanic world were insincere and that its true loyalties were with its English kin. Venezuelans generally did not like England (how could it be otherwise toward a country that regarded Drake as a national hero?) and they identified with Argentina as a victim of

English colonialism. The Esequibo claim loomed large in Venezuela's thinking, as a dispute essentially with England, and, although Venezuela denied any intention to resort to military action, it justified Argentina's use of force because Great Britain had refused to negotiate.[80] The furor eventually receded, and Venezuela did not follow up on its statements, mainly because it sustained a second blow in the summer of 1982.

Oil had been a mainstay of Venezuelan foreign policy for a decade. Although Herrera had criticized Pérez for his flamboyance and extravagance, he maintained a hectic pace himself for nearly three years, as petroleum paid the bills and gave Venezuela economic muscle. It even continued to fuel corruption, staining the Herrera administration. However, the signs had been there for a time, as the recession in the industrialized world created an oil surplus, and the price of petroleum declined, despite the efforts of OPEC. Just as the conduct of Venezuelan foreign policy was widely dispersed, so also were economic and financial affairs, with various governmental agencies, including the Central Bank, PDVSA, and the Venezuelan Development Corporation, authorized to borrow and deal directly with foreign banks. With Venezuela rated "triple A" in the international bond market in 1977 by Standard and Poors and Moody, loans were not hard to acquire. Consequently, by 1982 Venezuela had a total foreign debt of more than $30 billion. After a decade of high living, Venezuela experienced austerity, hard times, and even a currency devaluation, extending a depressed spirit to foreign policy.

In the last two years of Herrera's term, foreign policy seemed in disarray. Even tiny Guyana managed to thwart him. In June 1982, Venezuela chose not to extend the Protocol of the Port-of-Spain, and reverted to the Geneva Accord and the procedures prescribed therein for resolving the dispute. Venezuela clearly wanted to go one-on-one with Guyana, but Guyana sought to "internationalize" the dispute, presenting its case before the UN General Assembly in the hope of having it referred to the Security Council or the International Court of Justice. Guyana raised the issue at the conference of Non-Aligned Nations, causing Venezuela to suspend its application for changing its status from observer to full member. Guyana capitalized on the sale of the F-16s to Venezuela, protesting that the planes constituted a direct threat to its territorial integrity and giving particular significance to a visit to Brazil by Prime Minister Forbes Burnham in September 1982. Herrera's reaction to the Malvinas war caused further complications by emphasizing differences between Venezuela and the small states of the eastern Caribbean and by undercutting its power-sharing role in the Caribbean with the United States, which itself was wary of the Burnham government. The dispute threatened to undo all that Venezuela had achieved in the Caribbean in the previous decade.

Herrera was equally ineffective in Venezuela's boundary dispute with Colombia in the Gulf of Venezuela. Venezuela generally had allowed this dispute to drag on for reasons that are not easy to explain, but which may signify a lack of confidence on the part of Venezuelans who believe that Colombians have gotten the better of them historically in frontier adjustments.[81] In addition to the geopolitical and economic concerns, national pride may have been involved. Herrera started the negotiations in secret, then lost his nerve when military leaders objected to any concessions, and left the agreement to its fate in the public arena, much to the mystification of Colombia. "If there is a consensus," the president said in washing his hands, "the Treaty will be signed, if not, it won't be."[82]

A general appearance of ineptness overtook the Herrera administration in its final year. Although Venezuela participated in the Contadora peace initiative, Herrera took a backseat to Colombian President Belisario Betancur. The Contadora Four (Colombia, Mexico, Panama, and Venezuela) played an important role in 1983 in attempting to find a peaceful solution to the Central American crisis, and the inclusion of Venezuela in the group acknowledged its place as a leader. Herrera tended to be one of the least active participants, although in fairness it was Colombia's initiative and Herrera, basically, was committed to Duarte. Nonetheless, it had not been Venezuela's style to be passive. This was especially noticeable in October 1983, when U.S. forces occupied Grenada in a so-called rescue mission that resulted in the overthrow of the revolutionary regime. Venezuela reacted hardly at all, virtually ignoring its stand on the principle of nonintervention, probably because it was relieved to see the Cuban presence removed and because it did not wish to lose any more influence in the eastern Caribbean. Amidst the ruins, the Herrera administration managed one important step, the enactment of the Foreign Service Law. It established procedures for the recruitment, promotion, and rotation of diplomatic personnel, necessary measures for creating a career foreign service.

In the 1983 presidential election, Rafael Caldera, again the COPEI candidate, tried to run by ignoring the Herrera record. The debt crisis and charges of corruption and ineptitude virtually assured the election of the lesser known Jaime Lusinchi of AD. In foreign policy, Venezuela had been on a binge in the Pérez years, and, although Herrera experienced some of the intoxication, he suffered the consequences. Herrera made cutbacks in spending and devalued the bolivar. Now Lusinchi, in the harsh reality of the morning after, has begun a policy of austerity. He has reduced Venezuela's contributions to international organizations and is requiring full cash payments for oil, even from developing countries.[83] For awhile, there was some question as to whether or not Venezuela could afford to send its athletes to the 1984 Summer Olympics. The Lusinchi government has lowered its sights, recognizing the past excesses and the present limitations, and is displaying a levelheadedness that seems to bode well for a strong recovery. The appointment of Isidro Morales Paúl, an expert in the law of the sea, as foreign minister, indicates that Venezuela will at last deal comprehensively and actively with its boundary disputes with Colombia and Guyana and that it will seek to reduce tensions generally in the Caribbean. Venezuela remains vitally interested in the Caribbean, so that its position as a "middle power," despite its economic embarrassment, will require its best efforts in relations with Cuba, the small states of the Caribbean, and its participation in Contadora. Despite its wish to pursue a more modest policy, Venezuela cannot avoid an active role in defense of the price of its oil and, hence, all of the dimensions of policy that that responsibility entails.

Venezuela is taking a responsible approach to the international debt crisis. It is not as badly off as other Latin American states because of its substantial monetary reserve and its oil revenue. The crux of its problem is rescheduling payment, not the inability to make good in the long term. Venezuela is able to observe that its indebtedness may give it as much influence as its wealth did previously. Although Venezuela has resisted any effort to form a "debtors' cartel," it is possible that the debtor countries of the 1980s may achieve changes in the international economic order as substantial as those accomplished by the OPEC countries of the 1970s.

In the past 25 years, the dynamics of international relations have changed greatly. Venezuela's economic muscle enabled it to rise to a position of leadership, but the stability of its political system provided the foundation for its enhanced role, and the existence of its democracy gave it respect. In looking for the determinants of its foreign policy and the process by which decisions were made, one fact stands out: No individual or group totally ran foreign affairs. Venezuelan foreign policy was fashioned in a democratic atmosphere that responded to the influence and pressure of numerous forces, wherein the problem was not that someone was dictating policy but that affairs were frequently managed too loosely. The problems of Venezuelan foreign policy were the problems of a young democracy. Now that Venezuelan democracy has matured, the foreign policy process ought to evolve more routinely, although the Foreign Ministry is still one of the weakest government departments, and the Congress has yet to exert its influence.

Venezuela's petroleum will continue to make it a factor in international affairs, but just as Venezuela made the industrialized states aware of the interdependence of economics in the 1970s, so must Venezuela now approach the development of its resources with a similar rational attitude for the rest of the century. Venezuela and the world have a mutual interest in the sane development of the 700 billion to 800 billion barrels of heavy crude in the Orinoco tar belt. There are many aspects of international affairs beyond Venezuela's power to influence, not just the nuclear arms race or even conflict in Central America; but Venezuelan democracy, in the conduct of foreign policy, has achieved independence and control over Venezuela's destiny as a nation.

NOTES

1. Venezuela, Ministerio de Relaciones Exteriores, *Libro amarillo, 1979* (Caracas: Imprenta Nacional, 1980), p. 3.

2. *Libro amarillo, 1978*, p. 4.

3. Kenneth M. Coleman and Luis Quiros-Varela, "Determinants of Latin

American Foreign Policies: Bureaucratic Organizations and Development Strategies," in *Latin American Foreign Policies: Global and Regional Dimensions*, ed. Elizabeth G. Ferris and Jennie K. Lincoln (Boulder, Colo.: Westview Press, 1981), p. 40.

4. See Elizabeth G. Ferris, "Toward a Theory for the Comparative Analysis of Latin American Foreign Policy," in ibid., pp. 239–57.

5. Thomas M. Cooke, *The Dynamics of Foreign Policy Decision-Making in Venezuela* (Ann Arbor, Mich.: University Microfilms, Inc., 1968), p. iv.

6. Coleman and Quiros-Varela, "Determinants," p. 44.

7. Franklin Tugwell, *Venezuelan Foreign Policy*, U.S. Department of State, External Research Study (March 1976), p. 10.

8. Rómulo Betancourt, *Tres años de gobierno democrático* (Caracas: Imprenta Nacional, 1962) vol. 1, p. 21.

9. *Libro amarillo, 1961*, p. G.

10. See Cooke, *Decision-Making in Venezuela*, p. 136.

11. Ibid.

12. Betancourt, *Tres años*, vol. 2, pp. 167–68.

13. *New York Times*, December 4 and 7, 1963; January 4, 1964; and February 25, 1964.

14. Betancourt, *Tres años*, vol 1, p. 420.

15. Ibid., vol. 2, pp. 173–74.

16. *New York Times*, February 20, 1963, p. 1.

17. Rómulo Betancourt, *Venezuela's Oil*, trans. Donald Peck (London: Allen and Unwin, 1978), p. 58.

18. Betancourt, *Tres años*, vol. 2, p. 139.

19. Coleman and Quiros-Varela, "Determinants," p . 50.

20. Betancourt, *Venezuela's Oil*, p. 62.

21. Betancourt, *Tres años*, vol. 2, p. 328.

22. *Libro amarillo, 1969*, p. xli.

23. *Libro amarillo, 1968*, p. 89.

24. *New York Times*, May 9, 1966, p. 11.

25. Robert P. Clarke, Jr., "Economic Integration and the Political Process: Linkage Politics in Venezuela," in *Contemporary Inter-American Relations*, ed. Yale H. Ferguson (Englewood Cliffs, N.J.: Prentice-Hall, 1972), p. 529.

26. Lynn Krieger Mytelka, *Regional Development in a Global Economy: The Multinational Corporation, Technology, and Andean Integration* (New Haven, Conn.: Yale University Press, 1979), pp. xiv–xv.

27. Ibid., p. 20; and Clarke, "Economic Integration," p. 532.

28. W. Andrew Axline, "Latin American Regional Integration: Alternative Perspectives on a Changing Reality," *Latin American Research Review* 16, no. 1 (1981): 179.

29. Clarke, "Economic Integration." p. 542.

30. Mytelka, *Regional Development*, p. 31.

31.Rafael Caldera, *Solidaridad pluralista de América Latina* (Caracas: Oficina Central de Información, 1973), pp. 187–88.

32. Ibid., p. 119.

33. See Heraldo Muñoz, "Beyond the Malvinas Crisis: Perspectives on Inter-American Relations," *Latin American Research Review* 19, no. 1 (1984): 168.

34. John V. Lombardi, *Venezuela: The Search for Order, the Dream of Progress* (New York: Oxford University Press, 1982), 243.

35. *New York Times*, April 22, 1973, p. 17.

36. *New York Times*, June 2, 1969, p. 1.

37. Rafael Caldera, *International Social Justice and Latin American Nationalism*, trans. Jaime Tello (Caracas: Editorial Arte,1974), pp. 119-20.

38. Donald L. Herman, "Ideology, Economic Power and Regional Imperialism: The Determinants of Foreign Policy Under Venezuela's Christian Democrats," paper presented at the International Studies Association (Toronto, 1976), p. 19.

39, *Resumen* (Caracas), March 3, 1974, p.3.

40. Caldera, *Solidaridad*, p. 123.

41. *New York Times*, June 3, 1970, p. 2.

42. Judith Ewell, "The Development of Venezuelan Geopolitical Analysis Since World War II," *Journal of Inter-American Studies and World Affairs*, 27, no. 3 (August 1982): 309.

43. Robert D. Bond, "Venezuela, Brazil, and the Amazon Basin," in *Latin American Foreign Policies*, ed. Ferris and Lincoln, pp. 155-57.

44. Herman, "Ideology," pp. 18-19.

45. Caldera, *Solidaridad*, p. 97; *Resumen*, March 3, 1974, p. 3.

46. *Venezuela Up-to-Date* 15, no. 4 (December 1974): 16.

47. James H. Street, "Coping with Energy Shocks in Latin America: Three Responses," *Latin American Research Review* 17, no. 3 (1982): 136.

48. Republic of Venezuela, *La cooperación internacional de Venezuela, 1974-1981: Solidaridad en acción* (Caracas, 1981), p. 1.

49. *Venezuela Up-to-Date* 16, no. 1 (January 1975): 4.

50. Ibid.

51. Ibid. 18, no. 3 (Winter 1977-78): 9; see also Robert D. Bond, "Venezuela's Role in International Affairs," in *Contemporary Venezuela and Its Role in International Affairs*, ed. Robert D. Bond (New York: New York University Press, 1977), p. 244.

52. See Franklin Tugwell, "The United States and Venezuela: Prospects for Accomodation," in Bond, *Contemporary Venezuela*, p. 205; and Bond, "Venezuela's Role," ibid., pp. 241-43.

53. *Venezuela Up-to-Date* 16, no. 3 (July 1975): 8.

54. John D. Martz, "Venezuelan Foreign Policy Toward Latin America," in Bond, *Contemporary Venezuela*, p. 193.

55. Bond, "Venezuela, Brazil," pp. 158-61.

56. Quoted in Martz, "Venezuelan Foreign Policy," pp. 173-74.

57. Ibid., p. 174.

58. Richard R. Fagen, "Studying Latin American Politics: Some Implications of a Democratic Approach," *Latin American Research Review* 12, no. 2 (1977): 20.

59. Martz. "Venezuelan Foreign Policy," p. 173.

60. Tugwell, *Venezuelan Foreign Policy*, p. 23.

61. Tugwell, "The United States and Venezuela," pp. 209-10.

62. *Venezuela Up-to-Date* 18, no. 2 (August 1977): 6.

63. John D. Martz. "Ideology and Oil: Venezuela in the Circum-Caribbean," in *Colossus Challenged: The Struggle for Caribbean Influence*, ed. H. Michael Erisman and John D. Martz (Boulder, Colo.: Westview Press, 1982), p. 125.

64. David E. Blank. "Venezuela: Politics of Oil," in *U.S. Influence in Latin America in the 1980s*, ed. Robert Wesson (New York: Praeger, 1982), pp. 84-85.

65. Quoted in ibid., p. 94.

66. Street, "Energy Shocks," p. 137.

67. Betancourt, *Venezuela's Oil*, p. 265.

68. Blank, "Politics of Oil," p. 86.

69. Bond, "Venezuela's Role," p. 253.

70. *Libro amarillo, 1979*, p. 16.

71. *Libro amarillo, 1981*, p. 13.

72. Axline, "Regional Integration," p. 181.

73. *Cooperación internacional de Venezuela*, pp. 2-3.

74. Ibid., pp. 34-35.

75. *Libro amarillo, 1980*, pp. 7-10.

76. *Libro amarillo, 1982*, p. 23.

77. Anthony Payne, *The International Crisis in the Caribbean* (Baltimore: Johns Hopkins University Press, 1984), 1984, p. 120.

78. Philip J. Altinger, "Las implicaciones de la venta de aviones de combate F-16 a Venezuela, por parte de los Estados Unidos," unpublished paper, Georgetown University, April 1984, p. 6.

79. *Libro amarillo, 1982*, p. 13.

80. Ibid., p. 23.

81. Ewell, "Venezuelan Geopolitical Analysis," p. 308.

82. *Libro amarillo, 1980*, p. 11.

83. *New York Times*, July 2, 1984.

16

Venezuelan Democracy: Performance and Prospects

David J. Myers and John D. Martz

This concluding chapter is divided into two parts. The first section centers attention on the performance of Venezuelan democracy, especially since the realigning election of 1973. Performance analysis is concerned with the gap between policy intention and policy consequences. Almond and Powell claim that there are two reasons for this gap: policies pass through an implementing process and are changed during their passage, and policies interact with the social, economic, and cultural processes of the domestic and international environments that they are supposed to affect.[1] Using these insights as starting points, our initial concern is with the four commonly accepted dimensions of political system performance: extractive, distributive, regulative, and symbolic. The shorter second section of this chapter draws upon the preceding discussion and analysis of performance dimensions. It examines them with an eye to discerning what they suggest about the most likely directions of Venezuelan political evolution during the coming decade.

EXTRACTIVE PERFORMANCE

For Venezuela, the very core of the extractive process is the petroleum industry. In 1981, for example, 76.5 percent of ordinary revenues was provided by petroleum; total government income was roughly $22 billion (92,656 million bolivars), of which $16.5

billion (70,866 million bolivars) came from petroleum.[2] For the same year, the total value of Venezuelan exports FOB was $20.078 million, of which 95.1 percent came from petroleum ($19.094; iron provided $170 million, and the remainder of the economy $814 million). Decades-long efforts of *sembrar el petróleo*—to diversify the economy by means of petroleum earnings—continued to be frustrated at every turn. As one measure dramatically demonstrated, the contribution of Venezuela's major commodity to its total value of merchandise exports had actually risen for petroleum. Where the 1970-72 figures had been 88.9 percent, by 1979-1981 it was even higher at 93.5 percent.

While the industry still demonstrated many strengths and a high level of professionalism, the growing politicization described in Martz's chapter helps to simplify the extractive challenges for the system. Crude oil production in 1973—the year in which world market prices quadrupled—totaled 1,228,594,000 barrels. The production of refined oil had also declined from 376,836,000 in 1973 to 360,255,000 in 1979 and 316,090,000 in 1982. To be sure, some of the decline was the result of conservationist impulses, a change in the character of demand, a shifting of production priorities, and the like. At the same time, in conjunction with declining prices on the market, it led to a mid-1980s perspective that bore some ominous indicators.

It can be argued that the nation's extractive capability as regards petroleum will provide economic sustenance for some decades.[3] When the Lusinchi administration took power, Venezuela's proven reserves of crude oil stood at some 20 billion barrels. At the existing rate of production, the nation had the potential for another 26 years. And none of these calculations included the extraordinary deposits of the Orinoco tar belt, which, as time progresses and technology advances, will become increasingly accessible. Reserves of more than 54 trillion cubic feet of natural gas have the potential for another 44 years at the existing production levels. Holdings of iron ore, coal, and other subsoil deposits remain rich, and to a considerable degree have not been adequately tapped.

Even so, petroleum remains crucial. To speak of the extractive capability of the democratic Venezuelan state is not to treat of tax collections and similar means of generating revenue. Neither, if one turns to the international sphere, does the export of manufactured goods hold much promise. This also is true of massive foreign aid programs, loans from the International Monetary Fund, or similar activities. With some $12 billion in foreign reserves as of February 1985,[4] Venezuela hardly qualifies for the preferential treatment given to truly needy developing countries. Returning to the domestic arena, it is inevitable that the agricultural sector come under scrutiny. This in turn directs our attention to Donald L. Herman's findings in his investigation of Venezuelan agricultural policy. It suggests that the regime continues to grapple valiantly with the myriad problems, but with results that are at best mixed.

In stressing performance since the realigning elections of 1973, it is important to recall the policy of the Fifth National Plan adopted by the Pérez administration. Notwithstanding a degree of success, it remains true that agricultural output grew only marginally more than under the previous government. Predictably, the Sixth National Plan elaborated by the Herrera administration set higher production goals while promising greater and more rational means of support. As had Carlos Andrés Pérez earlier, Luis Herrera Campins addressed himself fulsomely to the presumed "solution" of the "agricultural crisis" and, at least implicitly, an improvement in the extractive performance of the Venezuelan state. In the end, however, overall agricultural production declined. Moreover, as Herman aptly remarks, declining petroleum income produced a budgetary contraction that in turn affected support for agriculture. At bottom, Herrera left office with more then two-thirds of Venezuelan food commodities being imported and at one-third the price of domestic production.

In terms of systemic regime types, it is clear that the democratic system has stressed efforts to "reform," revise, and modernize the agricultural sector. It has been concerned with social reforms as well as economic output. At the same time, the nation is now beyond the quarter-century mark in its democratic experience, and the agricultural sector remains a festering sore for policymakers and rural inhabitants as well. Jaime Lusinchi may have elaborated a number of desirable goals and expressed determination to make possible their achievement; however, this, too, is scarcely a novelty on the national scene. The possibility of a shift in emphasis toward even greater impetus for commercial agricultural could indeed enhance systemic extraction with the agricultural sector. However, at this juncture government pledges to alter prevailing patterns are difficult to examine without a healthy dose of skepticism, not to say cynicism.

A broader measure of extractive performance is presented by an overview of gross domestic product. Granting a variety of statistical problems with existing data, at least some general notions can be formed. A return to 1960—virtually the beginning of the democratic era—shows $13,605.9 millions (at the rate of 1980 dollars), which meant GDP per capita of $1,780. A decade later GDP had reached $24,633.6 million, which produced a GDP per capita of $2,296. By 1980, the GDP stood at $36,935.2 million, which meant a per capita GDP of $2,649. For 1982, as the economy began to sag, per capita GDP dropped to $2,538; it fell an additional 5 percent in 1983. This merely reflected prevailing economic realities at the national level, ones that were again intimately tied to the global petroleum markets.

There are those who would argue that, within the context of developmental assessments, the extractive element is not central. In some fashion that is likely true; indeed, our treatment here is itself brief. This perhaps responds to the relative simplicity of the Venezuelan economy over the last quarter-century and beyond. That is, the accumulation and distribution of goods and services, along with the regulative functions, continue to be nourished almost exclusively by the earnings of the petroleum industry. The extractive qualities of the system for all practical purposes are monopolized by petroleum. It may well be that, in the long haul of history, economic performance will be based upon a diversifed complex of both industrial and agricultural productivity. The prevailing perspective today, however, is one in which any Venezuelan government remains extractively dependent upon the petroleum industry. Once again, the world petroleum market and the effective operations of PDVSA and of the Ministry of Mines are the system's developmental linchpin.[5] Any regime, whether democratic or authoritarian, will be shaped and in all probability dominated by this enduring reality.

DISTRIBUTIVE PERFORMANCE

The populist underpinnings and prevailing social justice ideology of Venezuelan democracy ensure that its leaders will aspire to distribute a broad range of money, goods, services, honors, statuses, and opportunities. That these aspirations have been fulfilled in any meaningful sense over the past three decades, as discussed above, reflects the country's good fortune in possessing great reserves of high-quality petroleum. Petroleum revenue proved critical in stabilizing the post-1958 democratic regime during the first decade and a half the state was able to distribute substantial wealth to the have-nots without taxing the haves. Distribution occurred in the form of government jobs, public housing, subsidized food, and subsidized services, especially water, electricity, and medical care.

Following the quadrupling of petroleum prices in 1973, President Carlos Andrés Pérez dramatically increased state subsidies to all segments of the population; in 1979 and 1980, the years in which there was the most to distribute, petroleum revenues exceeded $20 billion. Even given the dramatic reduction in government income that began in 1982, the state's petroleum revenue held at almost $15 billion in 1984. Also, because of the earlier mentioned international reserves, the Lusinchi administration was able to obtain a conditional rescheduling of more than $20 billion of Venezuela's foreign public debt without having to accept the International Monetary Fund austerity measures acquiesced to by Argentina, Brazil, and Mexico.[6] However, while living standards remain higher than in any other Latin American country, the real income of Venezuelans during the last year of the Herrera government was 10 percent lower than it had been when his predecessor, Carlos Andrés Pérez, left office.

During his presidency Pérez used part of the post-1973 petroleum income bonanza to pay for Venezuela's nationalization of the petroleum and iron industries even more went into an imaginative effort to transform the economy. Pérez's Fifth National Plan (1975-80) projected government income of roughly $44 billion. It anticipated creating a complex of state corporations that would industrialize Venezuela and manage its economy. Private enterprise, domestic as well as foreign, was to be permitted only in those economic spheres in which entrepreneurs had demonstrated their capacity to perform efficiently. Profits from the state corporations would be reinvested in the corporations themselves, in diversifying the nation's industrial base, and in improving the quality of life for the average Venezuelan. The Fifth National Plan also emphasized the importance of education and training the state was to provide opportunity for all to learn the skills required in order to operate a rapidly modernizing economy. As Steven Ellner discusses at length, existing educational curricula were transformed, new universities and training institutes were created, and thousands of young Venezuelans were sent abroad to study in the United States, Western Europe, and Japan.

When President Luis Herrera Campins came to office in 1979, he cautioned that the state would have to scale back its developmental and distributive plans. He derided his predecessor's programs as overambitious, incompetently implemented, and shot through with corruption. President Herrera also warned that because loans had been contracted in order to initiate many projects envisioned in the Fifth National Plan, the future distributive capability of the state had been compromised. In his inaugural address he went so far as to proclaim that he had inherited a "mortgaged" country. However, during Herrera's first year in office the diminution of petroleum production related to the Iranian revolution pushed the price of crude, and Venezuela's income from the sale of petroleum, to unprecedented heights. During the Herrera government the Venezuelan state had more resources to distribute than under any chief executive in history. Herrera's Sixth National Plan (1981–1986) projected Venezuela's income from petroleum at more than $20 billion a year.[7]

The distributive performance of the Venezuelan state under the Sixth National Plan was a huge disappointment. In 1981 and 1982, even though the government pumped massive amounts of money into the economy, Venezuela experienced almost no real economic growth. State corporations ran up ever-increasing deficits and public services did not improve. Economists and administrators began to speculate that Venezuela's distributive networks, overloaded by the post-1973 revenue bonanza, were on the verge of breaking down. Confidence in the country's economic potential ebbed. In addition, during late 1982, the international petroleum market softened; Venezuelans began transferring unprecedented amounts of money abroad. Foreign exchange reserves dwindled, and on February 18, 1983, Herrera allowed the bolivar to float. Starting at 4.3/1, the foreign exchange rate between the bolivar and the dollar rose as high as 19/1. Imports declined from

$13.6 billion in 1982 to $6.8 billion in 1983. In the later year, as noted earlier, the gross domestic product fell 5 percent. In other words, significantly fewer goods were available for distribution.

Given the centrality of state subsidies to the standard of living, reduced distributive capability immediately affected the average Venezuelan. Correspondingly, Luis Herrera Campins became the most unpopular president of the post-1958 democratic period. The magnitude and dimensions of his unpopularity are profiled by Myers in his description of how the opposition AD and its presidential candidate swept to power in the national elections of 1983.

Soon after being inaugurated president, Lusinchi attempted to use the state's distributive network to cushion the impact of economic decline.[8] His subsidized food program offered a basket of 33 basic foods—including meat, fish, milk, eggs, fruits, vegetables, potatoes, and oils. It could be purchased through the coupons of a book to be distributed gratis. Some 970,000 indigent families were to be recipients, thereby reaching an estimated 2.5 million persons. All families with income of less than 2,000 bolivars per month were to be included. By midyear, however, the distribution had barely gotten underway, as mechanical and bureaucratic obstacles were encountered. The administration refused to back away from the program even as its implementation proved awkward. Once again, policy designed as a response to human needs foundered because of an overtaxing of the state's distributive capabilities.

The Lusinchi administration, even given problems with the state's distributive networks, turned in a creditable economic performance during the first year in office. The rate of decline in the gross dometic product fell to 1.7 percent, net capital outflows were reduced, and foreign reserves rose to $12.4 billion. Although this kindled some optimism, the watchword was caution. The preliminary outlines of President Lusinchi's Seventh National Plan (1986-91) reflected lowered expectations. Real economic growth was projected at between 2 and 3 percent. Even the best case scenario implied that Venezuelans would do well if, when the plan finished in 1991, they would have regained the standard of living they enjoyed during the late 1970s.

The Seventh National Plan also attempted to address the

problem of the state's finite capacity to distribute wealth. For the first time emphasis was placed on the potential of the private sector to manage the economy and create wealth. President Lusinchi and AD hoped to alter the perceptions of Venezulans concerning the distributive obligations of government. They calculated that by encouraging private economic activity they could avoid, when economic growth resumed, the bottlenecks that had plagued the economy in 1980 and 1981. At that time, as pointed out earlier, it was feared that extreme reliance on state corporations and infrastructure creating bureaucracies had severely stressed Venezuela's distributive capabilities. In other words, distribution networks became paralyzed and retarded economic expansions. The Seventh National Plan not only reversed a quarter-century of thinly veiled hostility toward business, it verged on affirming that whenever an economic activity could be performed efficiently by the private sector it should not be managed by the state.

The Seventh National Plan generated considerable controversy. Businessmen complained that it did not go far enough in shrinking the public sector. They and their allies within the governing party also felt that the plan's generally favorable attitude toward entrepreneurial activity was compromised when the director of the National Planning Agency called for a new anti-monopoly law.[9] On the other hand, many within AD saw the plan as evidence that in the face of economic crisis their party intended to place on hold its historic commitment to achieve a more equitable distribution of wealth. Within a month of the plan's presentation, Luis Raúl Matos Azocar, director of the National Planning Agency (CORDIPLAN), had resigned. Nevertheless, the debate over who would get what, when, and how raged on. It became especially intense during the first half of 1985, as expectations grew that petroleum prices, and with them the wealth-distributing capability of the Venezuelan state, would contract and remain at substantially reduced levels throughout the remainder of the 1980s.

Personal security, including enforcement of the law, is another category of goods that Venezuelans expect their state to create and distribute. Its inability to do this during much of the nineteenth century paved the way for three and a half decades of brutal dictatorial rule between 1899 and 1935. Most initially welcomed an authoritarian order because civil liberties and constitutional guarantees meant little when ongoing civil war had created a situation in which half of the population could expect to die violently. Venezuelans were willing to experiment with democracy only after they no longer feared that political conflict would lead inevitably to a breakdown of civil order.

Civil order teetered on the brink of dissolution during the first decade and a half of post-1958 democracy. It took sustained efforts by three presidents—Betancourt, Leoni, and Caldera—to deflect rightist coups, defeat a leftist insurgency, and institutionalize democratic norms. During the final years of Caldera's presidency, a new security problem, increasing urban crime, moved to center stage. Carlos Andrés Pérez's image as one who would guarantee law and order proved to be an important factor in his successful presidential campaign of 1973. Under Herrera, inertia within the Ministry of the Interior contributed to a deterioration in the efficiency of the various police forces. Violence became more common, and the mafia grew increasingly influential as international organized crime invested in loansharking, prostitution, and the drug trade. Venezuelans perceived themselves less secure under President Herrera, and this contributed to the opposition's victory over the governing Social Christians in 1983.

President Jaime Lusinchi chose Octavio Lepage as his minister of the interior. A close personal friend of the president, Lepage had also held the Interior portfolio during much of the Pérez government. During his first year in office Lepage devoted most of his attention to problems associated with morale and discipline within the various police forces.[10] He also began to explore plans that would enable him to implement a viable civil service regime for the law enforcement community. Here he was hampered by the tradition of paying low salaries to the police and by the lack of resources to increase salaries significantly. Consequently, the Lusinchi government continues to face an extremely difficult, if not impossible, task as it attempts to upgrade and professionalize the police. Unless some improvement takes place, there is little likelihood that the government will be able to provide greater personal security and reduce the penetration of international organized crime.

In addition to wealth and security, Venezuelan democracy has attempted to distribute prestige and status. Both were used to stabilize the democratic regime in the years immediately following the downfall of General Marcos Pérez Jiménez. For example, when implementing the 1961 constitution, General Eleazar López Contreras, a traditional president tied to the traditional oligrachy, received privileges as an ex-president identical to those of Rómulo Gallegos, the first chief executive to be elected by universal suffrage. Also, business interests needed to be reassured. Historically, entrepreneurs distrusted the statist orientation of elected governments. The second Betancourt administration (1959-64) thus made businessmen full participants in the national planning process. Similarly, throughout most of the twentieth century the church perceived itself threaten by the Marxist orientation of AD and URD, especially their commitment to secular education. After 1958 Presidents Betancourt and Leoni provided assistance to church schools. They also attempted to demonstrate that the church and AD were united in their commitment to pluralistic democracy by always including the relevant local clergyman in the president's official party at public events.[11]

The allocations of status and prestige that proved so central in institutionalizing the democratic system continue to this day. In addition, some unions now have received the status of participants in corporations, private as well as public. For the middle classes there are a variety of prizes, medallions, and orders, such as the "Order of Simón Bolívar—First Class." Allocations of status and prestige seem to be taking on new importance as goods intended to legitimate the political system; politicians are gambling that status and prestige can serve as substitutes for wealth, which is in increasingly short supply. The extent to which the former kinds of allocations can be substituted for the latter, and political stability preserved, remains a matter about which little is known.

In conclusion, the post-1958 democratic leadership has been highly skillful in creating and maintaining complex and sophisticated distributive networks. Two of the three basic kinds of distributive networks, however, those allocating wealth and security, seem to be losing capacity. While these losses are not so severe that they threaten the system's stability in the short or medium term, if declines continue unchecked the legitimacy of

Venezuelan democracy will suffer. From this perspective President Lusinchi has chosen wisely in assigning highest priorities to reactivating the economy and professionalizing the police forces.

REGULATIVE PERFORMANCE

Venezuela shares with most of Latin America a fragmented political culture, one in which competing and even incompatible political traditions are at odds with one another. Among the patterns of the past, as Lombardi notes, is a paternalistic style of administration that was institutionalized by three centuries of Spanish colonization. If Venezuela and the other colonies were considered the personal property of the monarch, it was therefore readied for the patron-client system that has endured. By the twentieth century, the nation was prepared to assume the duties and responsibilities of ultimate patron. Sloan has properly observed that there is no strong ideological limitation on statism in Latin America. Rather, "elites are inclined to stress that modernization is essentially an administrative problem rather than a political one."[12]

The creation of a strong central state with a significant regulative capacity marked the long rule of Juan Vicente Gómez. During the half-century since his death, the trend toward ever-greater government involvement has been powerful with both authoritarian and democratic regimes. Government has assumed a highly active role in promoting economic growth, fueled by the petroleum wealth that has enabled it to take control of almost 60 percent of all economic activity. The Venezuelan state thus evolved into one that parallels the description of its counterpart in Southeast Asia. It has become an ideal type "in which the state is the dominant institution in society, guiding and controlling more than it responds to societal pressures ... administrative (bureaucratic) institutions, personnel, and values and style are more important than political and participative organs in determining the behavior of the state and thus the course of public affairs."[13]

During the dictatorial decade preceding the return to limited pluralism in 1958, the centrality of the Venezuelan state continued to grow. This was true not only as regards the military and policy forces but, as Bigler writes, notably included the decentralized public administration. The prevailing inclination toward ever-greater regulatory control by the state and its agencies overrode the divergent approaches of authoritarianism and democracy toward operation of the state. From Rómulo Betancourt through Luis Herrera Campins, administration after administration has expanded the number, scope, and staffing of bureaucracies in hope of rendering them more effective. The early phase of the Lusinchi government, while seeking to cut back on the number of state corporations, is no less inclined to seek a continuing regulatory role of substantial depth and breath. Indeed, it can be argued that Lusinchi has only agreed to shrink the public sector because he feels it is the one way to increase the state's regulative capability.

If the thrust of regulative intention has been consistent for decades, it is also true that a quantitative shift has emerged since the early 1970s—more precisely since the inauguration of Carlos Andrés Pérez. It was the unleashing of the first flood of petro-dollars that provided the wherewithal for a quantum leap in the activities of the state. These combined with Pérez's belief that his administration did indeed represent "the last chance for Vene-zuelan democracy," one result of which was his determined effort to throw millions hastily at the nation's major problems. Earlier analysis profiled how much of this impacted directly on dis-tributive activities; there was also a rapid growth of regulatory personnel and organizations.

While basic constitutional forms were not dramatically altered, as Kelley has written, there was a proliferation of administrative regulations far beyond that previously experienced. The prevailing negative evaluation of most government ministries further encouraged the government elites to extend the structure of independent and semiautonomous state organizations and cor-porations. The renewed effort to prod, stimulate, and ultimately to control the agricultural sector has been documented by Donald Herman. The nationalization of petroleum made of the PDVSA an enormous holding company, one that also sought to operate the industry free from the structures of presumably unimaginative or incompetent bureaucrats in the Ministry of Mines. Even in an area of policy control of as low priority as Indian affairs, the increase of agencies with sweeping regulatory authority was evident, as Heinen and Coppens record.

Without offering a detailed treatment of state control, which goes beyond the limits of space, it can nonetheless be asserted that the dramatic increase of the *carlosandresista* institutional mechanisms reflected a generalized cynicism about the level of performance to that time. The notion was less that of greater intrusion into the daily lives of Venezuelans but, rather, a more efficient and productive capacity. If, for example, the agricultural sector had not responded adequately to the reforms of the 1960s, this was not viewed as demonstrating the inappropriateness of activities and programs directed by the central state. Rather, it suggested that public sector planning should be extended, that new implementing agencies should be created, and, of course, that larger sums of money would be both proper and productive.

If the sheer availability of more income was a factor in post-1973 trends, the realigning character of the elections that year also registered an impact. With a host of political parties swept toward the dustbin of history, AD and COPEI found themselves suddenly dominating the landscape. For AD in particular, the effervescence of a sweeping victory nurtured heady thoughts over the possible establishment of a Mexico-style one-party hegemonic system. Expectations of government jobs and of patronage were extremely high among AD partisans, and the Pérez government made an effort not to disappoint. Even though the bureaucracy rapidly became more bloated, the state proved incapable of satiating the demand for additional employment; this helped to weaken the relationship between the AD president, his government, and the party rank and file. Moreover, the continuing understanding between AD and COPEI over a sharing of bureaucratic posts intensified alienation between AD party members who did not find jobs and the Pérez administration.

Within the bureaucracy itself, rapid increases in personnel blurred lines of authority, increased the number of untrained or incompetent government officials, and fed even further the hunger for improved performance through an enlarged public sector. These weaknesses are analyzed at length in Stewart's chapter.

When Luis Herrera Campins and COPEI reached power in 1979, it was with the promise that things would change. As discussed earlier, however, his effort to stabilize and cool the overheated economy, reduce government controls, and curb official spending proved relatively short-lived. When oil prices again zoomed upward, tendencies evident during the previous five years reappeared and intensified. However, before the *copeyanos* left office, the boom era was over. The analysis of Bond goes far in detailing these developments, and Martz addresses directly the performance of the all-important petroleum industry.

There were a host of basic services that the citizenry found increasingly unsatisfactory during the Herrera period. They mirrored the extent to which the regulative performance of the system was subject to periodic breakdowns. Urban transportation was disrupted by the inability to negotiate collective contracts with the workers, while public fares continued to rise. The much-heralded Caracas metro merely ameliorated a problem regarded by many experts as beyond hope. One urban planning professional denounced failures of the system to avoid such anomalies as planning for 10,000 new middle-class apartments in one high-density area. The project at issue meant that 8 kilometers of cars would be squeezed into a three-lane freeway, extending a distance of 6 kilometers. Within three years movement would be impossible.[14]

Even more directly tied to the regulative as well as distributive capabilities of the democratic system were requirements for the providing of basic nutritional needs. Luis Herrera Campins declared in a December 31, 1981 address to the nation that, to offset declining food production and compensate for rising prices of basic foodstuffs, a system of food stamps would provide a 100-bolivar subsidy to families currently earning less than 1,500 bolivares per month. Some 2.5 million Venezuelans were thus to be assisted. Opponents charged that such bonds would become available only in 1983, just in time to encourage pro-COPEI sentiment as the campaign approached its climax. Ultimately, the program was never fully approved, the extensive bureaucratic apparatus was not established, and there was no such succor for the poor. It was another episode that scarcely did credit to the Herrera government in particular, let alone the performance of the democratic system.

As Herrera departed the presidency, neither admired nor respected by the populace, the manifest economic crisis underlined both the inconstancy of his policies and the looseness with which they were applied. Denunciations of the Herrera performance in office did not center on the uninterrupted commitment to centralized statism but rather on the yawning gap between promises and accomplishments. So it was that when Jaime Lusinchi came to office promising, among other things, to eliminate or reduce government's role in many regulatory activities, it was based on grounds of efficiency, economizing, and a narrowing of the gap between objectives and achievements.

Lusinchi was supported by both political and business elites in his determination to shrink the size of the state, strip away bureaucratic duplication and overlap, and effectively disenfranchise or defenestrate regulations and agencies that were draining the economy. He also sought further to restrict their authority to negotiate foreign loans, which had been an important component in the inflated international debt with which the nation was saddled. At the same time, the new president made apparent his own belief in the central role of the state. Both distributive and regulative elements were writ large in his highly touted "Social Pact" (*pacto social*), which had originally been an ambitious if rather vague 42-page campaign statement.[15]

Lusinchi's Social Pact focused on the business community and its relationship with organized labor. The private sector was to receive strong official encouragement to adopt a variety of measures. These typically included a mandate that employers effectuate an immediate 10 percent hiring increase, which was to produce more than 200,000 new jobs. Additional controls required other business actions designed to help deal with unemployment while the economy was presumably being righted. Business also remained under the rigid control of the government through import-export controls and the regulations of the Banco Central. Preferential exchange rates for the payment of its external debts were either withheld from the private sector or delayed. Similarly, multinational corporations were prevented from repatriating profits during Lusinchi's first year in office. These restrictions raised tensions between AD and the entire private sector. On the other hand, when in January 1985 the Electricidad de Caracas was granted dollars at the pre-1983 rate, a decision that enabled it to satisfy its foreign creditors and prevent bankruptcy, the unions complained that the Lusinchi government was favoring business by selectively applying austerity regulations.

For organized labor, whose support through the Venezuelan Workers' Confederation has been important to Lusinchi in securing both the party nomination and the subsequent electoral victory, favorable treatment also took the form of further government intrusion into its affairs. This included the so-called "Recovery of National Patrimony," announced in March of 1984 by none other than CTV President Juan José Delpino. It called for the employment of an estimated 100,000 jobless in such tasks as street and road repairs, the painting of public buildings, and the like. Participants would be paid 30 bolivars daily—a pittance that, nonetheless, represented a helpful source of support. The program, which was slow to be initiated in practice, was substantially acceptable to the CTV and to the working sector in general. Yet it proffered the possibility of yet greater regulation from the central government.

If the Lusinchi administration was committed to what appeared mutually exclusive objectives, greater social justice and economic austerity, the operational assumptions were true to the cultural tradition of state centralism. Lusinchi's initial determination to reorder many state agencies was, as noted, designed not to eliminate but rather streamline both distributive and regulative performances. And even before the close of his first year in office, it was evident that the obstacles to meaningful accomplishment were enduring. Two examples from diverse policymaking areas are enlightening, and are drawn from both the foreign and domestic spheres.

Regarding the former, Ameringer has sketched the major outlines of recent years, including the presence of ideological factors. This was noticeable under Herrera Campins in the sympathy directed toward successive regimes in El Salvador, where fellow Christian Democrat José Napoleón Duarte stood at or near the center of affairs. AD has been skeptical of *herrerista* policy, and proposed that a more distant and even-handed position be adopted. When former foreign minister Simón Alberto Consalvi became Lusinchi's secretary to the presidency, his views were expected to be decisive. Consalvi, however, quickly became involved in a struggle to maintain access to the president. He never got around to reversing the alleged "*copeyano*-ization" of the foreign ministry and diplomatic corps. The presumably pro-AD independent Isidro Morales Paúl left COPEI partisans or sympathizers in their posts. Only in March 1985 was Morales Paúl replaced by Consalvi as minister. Central American policy was already in some disarray, while diplomatic personnel remained more politicized than in the past. The capacity of the state to regulate its relations with the outside world was suffering in the process.

A very different example—one of many that has a long and unhappy history—lies in the realm of justice. Years of neglect have produced a situation in which more than 75 percent of the 24,000 citizens in prison have never been convicted of a crime. In some cases, prisoners have been waiting up to 14 years for their cases to be heard. This backlog of unconvicted suspects has crammed most prisons to more than twice their capacity, while basic health and sanitation are failing. *El Diario de Caracas* launched a major campaign in November 1984, with its editor fearful that the level of corruption was a growing threat to the democratic system. Minister of Justice José Manzo González, a veteran *adeco* and confidante of Jaime Lusinchi, conceded in addition that Venezuela's trial code was that for a rural country of the late nineteenth century. He established a commission to reform the legal code and redirect attention to the system of justice. In the meantime, the political opposition seized on the issue to attack the government, while the basic regulative function continued to fail the citizenry.[16]

While the system must attempt to improve upon such classically traditional problems, a more contemporary manifestation comes with the rapid rise in cocaine traffic. The government committed itself to "an all-out battle," as Manzo González put it, and promptly created a center for coordination of narcotics intelligence. It negotiated an antidrug trade accord with Colombia and tightened connections with authorities of other countries. It was estimated that Venezuela was becoming an important conduit for international shipments, while as many as 150,000 Venezuelans were regular users. The alleged growth of the mafia, and its ties to members of the police and security forces, further underlined national concern. The Congress adopted a new narcotics law. Yet all of this was accompanied by a dismantling and reorganization of DISIP, the national security policy. Interior Minister Octavio Lepage, in seeking to reduce the influence of pro-COPEI officials, found himself charged with appointing politically sympathetic young officers lacking in the appropriate professional credentials.

While the charges were themselves steeped in partisan politics, the whole situation reflected the inadequacies of regulative agencies. Past shortcomings, more seriously challenged by new threats, were provoking governmental concern that seemed unable to translate itself into meaningful action. As with other areas of crucial public interest in the decade of the 1980s, the democratic system was encountering growing difficulties in providing the level of regulative performance desired by the populace. It is evident that neither military authoritarianism nor democratic pluralism has a corner on wisdom either in policy formulation or implementation. Neither can it be assumed that *adeco* rather than *copeyano* governments might perform more satisfactorily. When all is said, however, regulative performance in areas closest to the daily lives of the Venezuelans cannot be underestimated in importance. Whatever the state of the economy, such basic matters as personal security, the control of crime, and the provision of basic guarantees lie at the very core of public expectations of governmental responsibilities.

SYMBOLIC PERFORMANCE

The idea of Venezuela as an independent political entity goes back to the first century of Spanish colonization. It took on new meaning when the Bourbon reforms organized most of what is present-day Venezuela into the semiautonomous captaincy-general of Caracas. Even Simón Bolívar's vision of Greater Colombia proved less compelling to his countrymen than the idea of Venezuela as a separate and independent state. During the first century and a quarter of independence, however, regional loyalties were almost as strong as those to the nation. Venezuelan leaders of this period were referred to as natives of their region or origin— *caraqueños, andinos, llaneros, orientales*. They often reserved power and wealth exclusively for individuals who shared their region of origin. More recently, however, internal migration and the growth of national communications network have diluted the importance of regional loyalties.[17] Symbols associated with "Venezuela" stand unchallenged in their power to evoke positive affective feelings among all groups except possibly, as Dieter Heinen suggests, the isolated Indian populations of the Guyana Highlands and the Orinoco delta.

The post-1958 democratic regime has sought legitimation by identifying with four broad symbols: liberty and freedom, national self-determination, social justice, and economic development. A burning desire for liberty and freedom sparked the January 23, 1958 revolution, the final curtain to the half-century drama of authoritarian Andean rule. On the morning after General Pérez Jiménez fled, military forces assaulted the headquarters of the infamous Seguridad Nacional (the secret police) and liberated the political prisoners. As hundreds emerged into the morning sunlight, some so weakened by beatings and torture that they had to be carried out of the building, the consequence of Pérez Jiménez's human rights violations were clear for all to see. Widespread outrage and anger led to the burning and looting of homes and businesses belonging to the regime's most prominent figures. Democratic political leaders drew on these feelings when they wrote a broad range of civil liberties and human rights into the constitution of 1961.

Implementing constitutional guarantees of civil liberties and human rights always has presented problems because of the violence endemic to Venezuelan society. Consequently, the 1961 constitution contained provisions for suspending the guarantees when civil order was challenged by groups and individuals intent on overthrowing the government by means of force. During the 1960s, attempts to topple the democratic regime from both the left and right caused Presidents Betancourt, Leoni, and Caldera to suspend constitutional guarantees for long periods. Since 1973, however, the concept of a loyal opposition and the use of popular elections to determine political succession have gained overwhelming acceptance; this has been reflected in a dramatic decline in the number of days during which constitutional guarantees have been suspended. An important indication that Venezuelans perceive democratic governments as having kept their promises to respect civil liberties and human rights appears in public opinion polls. Even when polls profile dissatisfaction with the economic performance of AD and COPEI, they reveal an overwhelming preference for democracy over authoritarian military rule.

Impartial enforcement of the law and respect for the sanctity of contract were symbols associated with civil liberties that the Pérez Jiménez dictatorship ignored with impunity. Not only were the general's political opponents subjected to arbitrary detention, but his friends could purchase interpretations of the law that enabled them to do as they pleased. Also, contracts with the government, especially when they involved payment for services rendered, were almost impossible to enforce until bureaucratic commissions had been dispersed. In addition, Pérez Jiménez's friends received loans that the government then neglected to collect. During the first year of his second government Rómulo Betancourt presided over a major effort to untangle the problems associated with the ousted dictator's selective enforcement of the law as it related to government contracts. Similarly, Betancourt initiated procedures to shield the courts from the exercise of political influence.

Venezuelan democracy has had some success in making law enforcement more impartial and in securing greater respect for the sancity of contracts. Nevertheless, during preparation of President Lusinchi's Seventh National Plan, debate raged over whether to address problems relating to the integrity of the courts. Apparently the judicial system had become highly responsive to the influence of money during the post-1973 petroleum bonanza. Increased petroleum revenue also allowed the state to loan out billions of bolivars in credit to entrepreneurs. Many credits never had been paid back, and the state's efforts to collect outstanding debts were at best haphazard. This led one important official at CORDIPLAN to characterize the Venezuelan state as all-encompassing but powerless. In other words, even though the state in theory controlled most economic activity, it was unable to obtain compliance with its rules and regulations.[18]

Ineffective regulation had an important symbolic fallout. Respect for the state and its institutions suffered because regulations were seldom enforced. This led to a cycle in which perceptions that state institutions were powerless caused individuals to act as if this were the case. Additional attempts were made to circumvent regulations and this placed new strains on the state's regulative capabilities. Consequently, the gap between actual and intended performance became even greater. It was in hopes of breaking this cycle that Luis Raúl Matos Azcar of CORDIPLAN, despite his popular image as the "worker's minister," assigned a high priority to private entrepreneurial activity in the Seventh National Plan.

Nationalism and self-determination are a second important category of symbols to which democratic leaders have appealed in their quest for acceptance. While Pérez Jiménez made some halting attepts to play on nationalistic sentiments, his granting of concessions to the multinational petroleum corporations caused his government to be perceived in most quarters as a tool of foreign interests. The leaders of Venezuelan democracy came to power promising no more concessions to the multinational oil companies. The symbolic importance of their 1976 nationalization of the holdings of Exxon, Shell, Gulf, and a host of smaller companies is obvious. It was an action of which virtually all Venezuelans approved; also, it continues to be a positive factor in the democratic system's persisting legitimacy.

While no other issue can evoke the strong nationalistic sentiments of "control over our petroleum," several others are of considerable importance. They include reducing foreign influence in Venezuela, achieving recognition as a regional power in the Caribbean Basin, and raising Venezuela's profile among the Andean Pact countries. As Lombardi's historical overview suggests, Venezuela has been in a dependency relationship to the North Atlantic since the first Europeans set foot on its shores. Until well into the twentieth century Venezuela's ruling class uncritically attempted to imitate their North Atlantic counterparts. The leaders of AD were the first Venezuelan political elite to search for and give value to national expressions of culture and the arts. While governmental support for Venezuelan culture gathered strength during the 1945–48 *trienio*, this effort was largely abandoned by the Pérez Jiménez dictatorship. During the latter regime, American influence in Venezuela overwhelmed most local expressions of art and culture.

The post-1958 political leadership has given high priority to preserving and nurturing expressions of Venezuelan culture. Each year the National Council of Culture, CONAC, distributes hundreds of millions of bolivars to painters, musicians, dancers, and filmmakers. Works are commissioned and performed throughout the entire country. Despite these efforts, much remains to be done in crafting and transmitting to the general population a positive and coherent image of what it means to be Venezuelan. There continues to be a fascination with all things foreign, and things foreign usually carry greater status than things Venezuelan. This probably is inevitable given Venezuela's comparatively small population and the gap separating the quality of life experienced by Venezuelans from what prevails in the northern industrial countries.

Of the final issues possessing nationalistic symbolism, Venezuela's status in the Caribbean Basin commands greater attention than attempts to increase Venezuelan influence among the Andean Pact countries. Except during the independence movement, Venezuela has interacted more intensely with the Caribbean than with the Spanish-speaking countries of South America's west coast. Venezuela's democratic leaders currently perceive themselves to be locked in an epic confrontation with Fidel Castro's Cuba; the core issue is whether communism or liberal democracy can provide a better quality of life for the people of the Caribbean Basin. AD and COPEI both believe that their capability to dominate Venezuelan party politics, as well as perhaps the future of the democratic system, rides on maintaining their control and influence. Consequently, at one time or another since 1959, Venezuela has aided democratic forces in the Dominican Republic, Nicaragua, Jamaica, Costa Rica, and El Salvador. Even U.S. President Ronald Reagan's September 1983 decision to intervene militarily in Grenada was applauded in Caracas, although with considerable apprehension. AD and COPEI reluctantly concluded that the bloody coup that brought General Hudson Austin to power meant the installation of a pro-Soviet military dictatorship on their front doorstep. Not only would Grenada under communism have been a center from which guerrilla warfare might be reactivated in Venezuela, but MIG 23 aircraft based on Grenada would have been well within range of Venezuela's coastal population centers and oil fields in the states of Monagas and Zulia.[19]

Oil and wealth generated by oil have been the most important resources available to Venezuela in the pursuit of its Caribbean

Basin interests. Under Carlos Andrés Pérez, Venezuela provided millions of dollars in credits that enabled its Caribbean Basin neighbors to purchase petroleum and other Venezuelan goods. In 1981 Venezuela persuaded Mexico to share the costs of continuing and strengthening these programs. Both when acting unilaterally and in concert with Mexico, Venezuela has attempted to use its petroleum wealth to influence the political evolution of Caribbean Basin states along democratic lines. However, like so many programs initiated between 1973 and 1982, assistance to democratic forces in the Caribbean Basin has been cut back because of declining petroleum revenue. Also, Venezuela's new role as a Caribbean power has always been a symbol of questionable value in legitimating the regime. Many ordinary Venezuelans see the strengthening of democratic forces in the Caribbean Basin as a drain on their own state's capability to raise domestic living standards.

Social justice symbols have been used with great regularity in democratic Venezuela. While both AD and COPEI affirm the legitimacy of all classes, they give priority to securing a basic minimum standard of living for the poor. This is the core interpretation of social justice that began to take root in the mid-1920s. As the modernizing generation of 1928 gained influence, political power gravitated from the closed Caracas-Andean elite to mass-based political parties preaching social justice. AD's founders picked up on this theme from their studies of Marxism. Advocacy of social justice also coincided with their self-interest in that it provided an ideological underpinning to efforts that would wrest power from the Caracas-Andean elite. Rafael Caldera and his followers embraced the idea on account of the teachings of the church. However, because of dependence on financing from pro-clerical conservatives sympathetic to the Caracas-Andean elite, COPEI initially muted its advocacy of state intervention on behalf of the poor. This changed when the Social Christians came to power in 1969. They proved to be every bit as aggressive as AD in their efforts to identify themselves with social justice symbols.

The public commitment to secure a basic minimum standard of living for the poor has most often been expressed symbolically in the creation and funding of bureaucracies designed to provide for the poor many services that once were reserved for the wealthy few. AD's first period in office (1945–48) produced an explosive expansion of the bureaucracy for this purpose. The efforts of these revolutionary years were refined during the first decade and a half of the democratic period, as Stewart analyzes. Previously noted efforts by the Caldera government to use bureaucratic programs to further its public identification with social justice goals reflected the broad consensus that had crystallized concerning the importance of social justice as a symbol in legitimating the democratic regime and its institutions.[20]

While it is impossible to examine all institutions of the democratic system that wrap themselves in the cloak of social justice, it is useful to look at a few of the most important. The Ministry of Health and Social Assistance provides free medical care, retirement benefits, and pensions to the disabled. The poor receive services such as water and electricity at nominal costs; they are portrayed as a basic right of all citizens. The Ministry of Education holds out the promise that literacy, technical training, and professional careers will be available to the sons and daughters of the masses. Social justice is also equated with full employment. Consequently money is regularly pumped into the bureaucracy only to ensure that there will be jobs for those who have been trained and educated. Courts in the Ministry of Labor also respond to social justice symbolism when they increase the bargaining power of unions in relation to employers. Finally, the structuring of democratic institutions themselves presents opportunities to participate in shaping the political decisions that affects one's life. Previously, only members of the ruling elite enjoyed these privileges. The present consensus behind the commitment to social justice dictates that they be available to all.

Earlier analysis of the democratic system's capabilities has identified problems and constraints associated with its extractive, distributive, and regulative outputs. In general, symbolic output, especially in the sphere of social justice, has been well received. Poll after poll confirms that Venezuelans see democracy as the best possible government system for them, and their system's symbolic commitment to national self-determination, civil liberties, and social justice is perceived as genuine and valid. However, as suggested throughout this volume, there is growing concern over the operationalization of symbolic commitments. This is particularly relevant in the area of economic development.

It goes without saying that in the twentieth century, skill in stimulating economic growth and development has taken on paramount symbolic importance in legitimating any political order. Venezuela's economic growth in the late 1960s undercut the appeal of insurgents who had labored for more than five years to overthrow the democratic regime by force. During the decade of the oil boom, guerrilla activity descended to the level of occasional banditry. It remains despite the persistence of the *bandera roja* (red flag) guerrilla movement and its efforts to coordinate with the Castroite Army of National Liberation in Colombia. Given AD's historic support in rural areas, only an immense economic disaster would alienate peasants to the point of joining an insurgency against the democratic regime.

Support for AD in the cities never has run as deep as in the countryside.[21] In successive elections since the voter realignment of December 1973, urban voters have supported AD on some occasions; on others they have rallied around COPEI. Most Venezuelans now live in metropolitan areas, and perceptions of economic well-being have been a major determinant of their decision to support one or the other of the major political parties. Despite the economic boom during the Pérez administration, many individuals felt that they had been left out. Combined with COPEI militants, they ousted AD from power and elected Luis Herrera Campins as president. Similarly, AD's landslide election in December 1983 was largely a consequence of the economic downturn under a COPEI government during an election year; the decline in the gross domestic product was roughly 5 percent. The point here is that perceptions about economic well-being and growth have immediate political consequences for the two major political parties in the populous metropolitan areas.

The question remains as to whether continuing economic difficulties may lead to a weakening of the democratic regime's legitimacy. In the short and medium run, the answer would appear to be negative. Public opinion polls suggest that despite extreme dissatisfaction with Herrera government, and some growing doubts concerning Jaime Lusinchi's management of the economy, Venezuelans are not inclined to abandon their democracy. After all, as we have seen, positive perceptions of performance along a number of dimensions are likely to cushion the impact of economic difficulties. The nation's economy remains so closely tied to the world for petroleum, as Venezuelans realize, that it strains credibility to think they would come to believe that either an authoritarian military regime or a Communist dictatorship would solve their economic problems. Indeed, the former proved quite inept in managing the political economy of Brazil, Argentina, and Peru; meantime, the Venezuelan military appears to be satisfied with existing political arrangements.

Venezuelans also seem unlikely to adopt a variant of Cuban communism. Memories of the abortive Castro-supported insurgency during the late 1960s remain strong; more than 80 percent of all Venezuelans hold a negative opinion of communism and Communists. While it seems improbable, therefore, that authoritarian regimes of the left or right will emerge in Venezuela during the coming decade, the political system will not remain stagnant. Our analysis of systems capabilities suggests that some form of pluralism will persist, although it may be significantly different from that which evolved between 1958 and 1983. The final focus of this chapter looks at the most likely variants of pluralism that could emerge in the coming decade. It also discusses and analyzes the conditions that would incline political evolution in the direction of one alternative or the other.

POLITICS AND THE FUTURE

The most likely shape of Venezuela's political system over the coming decade will be an austerity-modified version of the existing limited pluralist arrangement. As the pre-1983 system has been analyzed in detail throughout this volume, it would be redundant and anticlimactic to discuss even its broad outlines yet another time. However, it does seem useful to analyze the possible changes that may occur because of its reduced ability to extract resources from the international environment and continuing difficulties within the distributive and regulative networks. These problems, and the changes they necessitate, were being hotly debated in Caracas during the first months of 1985, as the post-Matos team at

CORDIPLAN was hammering out details of the Seventh National Plan. Also, a small but real possibility exists that belt tightening might force a significant change in the existing regime. As indicated above, we do not believe that either a military authoritarianism or a Marxist-Leninist dictatorship is likely to emerge over the coming decade. Some version of a single-party dominant system that allows for the autonomy of societal interests, a system of hegemonic pluralism similar to that of Mexico, seems the most likely alternative should the present regime give way. The second focus of this closing section briefly looks at how a regime of hegemonic pluralism might emerge in Venezuela, and how it might be structured.

Since 1982 the state has commanded too few resources to permit it to respond to the demands of interest groups by means of increasing economic inputs into the system. Consequently, there is great pressure to do more with less. This is extremely difficult given the tradition of parcelling out resources to every group while demanding neither coordination of their efforts with accepted social, economic, and political goals nor the return of compensatory goods to the state.[22] The Lusinchi government, as we have seen, is talking about the need to abandon assumptions that every increase in the comprehensiveness of regulation leads to greater overall regulative capability. Its inclination is to reduce and simplify regulations and to streamline the bureaucratic maze that has evolved over past decades. There is an emerging consensus that this is the only way the state can increase its capability to stimulate economic growth, regulate behavior, and distribute efficiently the resources that the system extracts. In short, the Lusinchi government believes that while in theory the economic reach of the state has become all-encompassing, in reality it has less control over daily economic decisions than when a greater proportion of total economic activity was in the hands of the private sector and the transnational corporations.[23]

This perception suggests that whichever of the two major parties is in office, elected officials will seek to increase state responsiveness. For public sector corporations, this will translate into a modified form of economic Darwinism. Those that consistently show losses may be offered for sale to private economic interests, be they domestic or foreign. Also, a greater range of economic activity will be open to entrepreneurs, and foreign investors will be offered more attractive terms on which to invest their capital. While these economic policies may reduce the hemorrhage of state revenue into unprofitable economic activities, they also present serious political problems. For example, if business generates large profits by discharging unneeded workers, there will be heavy political demands that those profits fund social programs that support the unemployed. The state's attachment of the profits, which, as Martz analyzes, PDVSA executives were holding for investments in oil exploration and the development of heavy crude reserves, serves as an alarming reminder to business-men of the confiscatory power and inclinations of the Venezuelan state.

Although PDVSA is a state corporation, the transfer of its reserves to the Central Bank created a high level of distrust between its management and the politicians. Similarly, the threat of excessive taxation is an important impediment to the in-vestment of private capital in wealth-producing activities. It lay behind private sector pressures on President Lusinchi to replace the Matos team at CORDIPLAN once the basic direction of its thinking became known. Fears of confiscatory taxation also render businessmen suspicious of any public sector-private sector co-operation that the political leadership may propose. When foreign business interests are involved, there is an additional problem. The concessions needed to attract overseas capital are likely to revive the issue of foreign domination of the economy. This makes it very difficult for Venezuela to attract new investments from the industrial countries on any but extremely unfavorable terms. In turn, this feeds local antiforeign sentiments. Even under the best conditions, therefore, it will be some time before entrepreneurial activity can be expected to generate the quantity of annual income that Venezuela lost when petroleum prices fell in 1982.

Because the government has no alternative but to search for ways to use resources more efficiently, and operates within the Iberian tradition of state centralism, one by-product will be efforts to increase the power of the state. The Pact of Punto Fijo, as we have seen, was never intended to create a classic liberal state. It assumed a central role in regulating component private interests. The 1961 constitution anticipated that it would act as arbiter to adjust the unequal competition for resources between the powerful and not so powerful. In its role as arbiter, the Pact of Punto Fijo state has devised and strengthened cooperative arrangements that, in theory, allow all to lobby on behalf of their legitimate intersts without permitting any single interest to predominate. Consequently, when Jaime Lusinchi's *pacto social* argues that it is necessary to strengthen the state's capacity to regulate, this should not be seen as a fundamental departure from what the leaders of AD, COPEI, and URD agreed to in 1958. Rather, it is an effort by AD to create what the three godfathers of Venezuelan democracy initially intended.

The Pact of Punto Fijo state, like its predecessors, has opted to centralize resource management in order to consolidate political power and stabilize its regime. Consequently, most government decisions have been made by national elites rather than by leaders at the state and local levels. The *pacto social*, despite some protest from regional interests, does not assign high priority to strengthening state and local governments. However, the Lusinchi administration is concerned about the impact of the existing pattern of party-bureaucracy relations on the capacity of the national bureaucracy. Stewart analyzes how, between 1959 and 1983, political parties distributed bureaucratic positions without demanding performance in return; only party loyalty was expected. While this policy strengthened AD and COPEI, it facilitated the exploitation of a state that remained weak and inefficient. For the bureaucracy to function required ever-increasing injections of resources. In an environment with shrinking resources the continuation of this operational style, because it perpetuated a bloated bureaucracy incapable of generating innovations in times of scarcity, constitutes a threat to the viability of the post-1958 regime.

The role of the political parties is being rethought as efforts are made to deal with the consequences of reductions in government income. Between 1958 and 1983 a large number of vertical access channels were created to link societal interests and government. Political parties—above all, the government party—served as intermediaries between interest groups and the government. Few horizontal communication channels developed between interest groups. Therefore, it was almost impossible for expressions of interest to take place away from the vigilance of party or government leaders. This illustrates an important legacy of the old Gómez dictatorship—the heritage of fear when it comes to competing with established political authority.

Avoidance of competition with established political authority causes Venezuelan interest groups to operate quite differently than their counterparts in Western Europe and the United States. They seldom develop cooperative arrangements among themselves because of the lack of horizontal communication channels. They avoid establishing such channels because of the fear that the state will apply sanctions if they are observed using channels that bypass the political elite. Perceiving themselves as having no choice but to use existing vertical channels, Venezuelan interest groups become the captives of political parties. Private problem-solving initiative is thus stifled. However, this is a mixed blessing for the parties. They become so involved in the internal politics of particular interests that they neglect their interest aggregation function. Like the state bureaucracy, party bureaucracies attempt to act in so many diverse circumstances that it is difficult for them to perform efficiently. It is also a situation that may lead to political decay.

While individual Venezuelans overwhelmingly approve of democracy and competitive party politics, it is unclear how long frustrations associated with the post-1982 economic difficulties can fester before either the masses or the political elites will attempt to change the system. The most likely alternative to the present limited pluralist democracy is one that Venezuelan party leaders, journalists, and intellectuals have discussed and debated at great length over the past decade—a variant of Mexico's one-party pluralism. Giovanni Sartori describes this arrangement as "one-party centered and yet displays a periphery of secondary and indeed 'second class' minor parties.... To be sure, these second class parties may be a pure sham, an empty facade.... If so they are irrelevant and should not be counted. However, these peripheral, subordinate parties may be relevant in some substantive respect.... If such is the case, we are still far removed from a predominant party system.... We do have a *sui generis* pattern that I call hegemonic."[24]

The most obvious Venezuelan variant of Sartori's one-party

pluralism would have AD as hegemonic and COPEI and MAS as subordinate but relevant components. Unlike Mexico's Revolutionary Institutional party, however, AD has twice been voted out of office over the past quarter-century. It is no small matter to change from a competitive system in which the government party has lost the past four elections to one in which the opposition has no realistic chance of taking power. While continuing economic difficulties and system performance problems will surely transform Venezuela's limited pluralism, the most likely possibility is that change during the remainder of the twentieth century will not be revolutionary but incremental.

NOTES

1. Gabriel Almond and G. Bingham Powell, *Comparative Politics: A Developmental Approach* (Boston: Little, Brown, 1978), p. 283.

2. The figures have been compiled from PDVSA, government, and international banking reports.

3. It seems to be necessary continually to reassure Venezuelans that this is so. For example, in November 1984 Treasury Minister Manuel Azpúrua stated: "Thanks to government measures we can say with absolute certainty that our oil industry is strong and has the necessary funds to carry out adequately its development projects." *Latin American Weekly Report*, November 9, 1984, p. 5.

4. At the annual Venezuela seminar of the Council of the Americas, during January 1985, Joseph Martin of Chemical Bank projected that Venezuelan reserves would fall only slightly during the remainder of the Lusinchi government, to $10 billion in 1988.

5. "Management and Politics: The Case of Oil," in David E. Blank, *Venezuela: Politics in a Petroleum Republic* (New York: Praeger, 1984), pp. 149-78.

6. As of February 1985 the agreement remained conditional. North American and Western European banks refused to make it final until there was some agreement on how the private sector debt would be repaid. The foreign debt of Venezuela's private sector was just under $19 billion.

7. "Venezuela: The Road to 1985," *Latin American Regional Report: Andean Group*, July 25, 1980, p. 7; "Herrera Government Makes Big Spending Plans for 1980–1985 Period," *Business Latin America*, January 23, 1980, p. 25.

8. *El Nacional* (Caracas), March 1, 1984.

9. Interview with a leading Venezuelan industrialist on January 23, 1985. This was several days after Luis Raúl Matos Azocar, the director of CORDIPLAN, had resigned.

10. "Police Renewal Rebounds on AD," *Latin American Weekly Report*, November 22, 1984, p. 9.

11. Daniel Levine, *Conflict and Political Change in Venezuela* (Princeton, N.J.: Princeton University Press, 1973), pp. 62–144.

12. John W. Sloan, *Public Policy in Latin America: A Comparative Survey* (Pittsburgh: University of Pittsburgh Press, 1984), p. 129.

13. This was Milton J. Esman's description in *Administration and Development in Malaysia* (Ithaca, N.Y.: Cornell University Press, 1972), p. 62. For a discussion of limited pluralism in the Venezuelan context, see "Effective or Limited Pluralism," in José Antonio Gil, *The Challenge of Venezuelan Democracy* (New Brunswick, N.J.: Transaction Books, 1982), pp. 225–75.

14. *El Diario de Caracas*, May 18, 1980, p. 23. As cited by Judith Ewell, *Venezuela: A Century of Change* (Stanford, Calif.: Stanford University Press, 1984), p. 216.

15. "Un pacto para la democracia social," in Jaime Lusinchi, *Frente al futuro* (Caracas: Editorial Arte, 1983), pp. 297–333.

16. A convenient summary of the problem by Jackson Diel appears in the *Washington Post*, November 16, 1984.

17. "Cultural Diversity and Political Cleavages," in Enrique A. Baloyra and John D. Martz, *Political Attitudes in Venezuela: Societal Cleavages and Political Opinion* (Austin: University of Texas Press, 1979), pp. 83–99.

18. Interview by the authors with a high-level planner in CORDIPLAN, January 30, 1985.

19. See figure 2 in David J. Myers, *Venezuela's Pursuit of Caribbean Basin Interests: Implications for U.S. National Security*, Rand Report/R-2994-AF/1 (Santa Monica, Calif, January 1985).

20. Gene E. Bigler, *La política y capitalismo de estado en Venezuela* (Madrid: Editorial Tecnos, 1981), pp. 159–68.

21. Robert E. O'Connor, "The Electorate," in *Venezuela at the Polls*, ed. Howard R. Penniman (Washington, D.C.: American Enterprise Institute, 1980), pp. 59–90.

22. "El petróleo asusta a Venezuela," in Domingo Alberto Rangel, *Fin de fiesta* (Valencia: Vadell Hermanos, 1982), pp. 13–60, and Sanin, *Venezuela Saudita* (Valencia: Vadell Hermanos, 1978).

23. The respected senator from Táchira, Ramón J. Velásquez, as of March 1985, presided over a commission studying governmental reorganization. Candidate Jaime Lusinchi's campaign speech on reforming public administration is reprinted in Lusinchi, *Frente al futuro*, pp. 209–17.

24. Giovanni Sartori, *Parties and Party Systems: A Framework For Analysis* (New York: Columbia University Press 1977), p. 230.

Bibliography:
A Guide to the Study
of Contemporary Venezuela

This bibliography is intended to help those who wish to pursue further research on Venezuela. It is by no means exhaustive; the footnotes to individual chapters are often more complete on particular points, and even those references are selective. My aim has been simply to provide some guidance regarding where to turn first for useful material. I gratefully acknowledge the guidance provided by the authors of each chapter.

David J. Myers

GENERAL INTRODUCTION TO VENEZUELA

Academia Nacional de la Historia. *Fuentes para la historia colonial de Venezuela* (Biblioteca de la Historia). Caracas: Academia Nacional de la Historia, 1962.

Acedo de Sucre, María de Lourdes, and Carmen Margarita Nones Mendoza. *La generación venezolana de 1928; estudio de una élite política.* Caracas: Ediciones Ariel, 1967.

Acosta Saignes, Miguel. *Vida de los esclavos negros en Venezuela.* Caracas: Educaciones Hesperides, 1967.

Arcila Farías, Eduardo. *El régimen de la encomienda en Venezuela.* 2nd ed. Caracas: Universidad Central de Venezuela, 1966.

Brito Figueroa, Federico. *Historia económica y social de Venezuela; una estructura para su estudio.* 2 vols. Caracas: Universidad Central de Venezuela, 1966.

Carrera Damas, Germán. *El culto a Bolívar: Esbozo para un estudio de la historia de las ideas en Venezuela.* Caracas: Universidad Central de Venezuela, 1969.

———. *Sobre el significado socio-económico de la acción histórica de Boves.* Caracas: Universidad Central de Venezuela, 1964.

De Grummond, Jane Lucas. *Renato Beluche, Smuggler, Privateer, and Patriot, 1780–1860.* Baton Rouge: Louisiana State University Press, 1983.

Díaz Sánchez, Ramón. *Guzmán: Élipse de una ambición del poder.* Caracas: Ministerio de Educación, 1950.

Ewell, Judith. *Venezuela: A Century of Change.* Stanford, Calif.: Stanford University Press, 1984.

González, Ginan, Francisco. *Historia contemporánea de Venezuela.* 15 vols. Caracas: Presidencia de la República, 1954.

Grases, Pedro. *Instituciones y nombres del siglo XIX.* Caracas: Seix Barral, 1981.

———. *Preindependencia y emancipación, protagonistas y testimonios.* Barcelona: Seix Barral, 1981.

———, and Manuel Pérez Vila, eds. *Pensamiento político venezolano del siglo xix: Textos para su estudio.* 15 vols. Caracas: Presidencia de la República, 1960–62.

Griffin, Charles C. *Los temas sociales y económicos en la época de la independencia.* Caracas: Fundación John Boulton and Fundación Eugenio Mendoza, 1962.

Grupo de Barbados. *Indianidad y descolonización en América latina: Documentos de la segunda Reunión de Barbados.* Mexico: Editorial Nueva Imagen, 1979.

Levine, Daniel H. "Portraits of Venezuela: Review Essay." *Journal of Interamerican Studies.* May 1981, pp. 203–23.

Lieuwen, Edwin. *Venezuela.* London: Oxford University Press, 1961.

Lombardi, John V. *The Decline and Abolition of Negro Slavery in Venezuela, 1820–1854.* Westport, Conn.: Greenwood Press, 1971.

———. *Venezuela: The Search for Order, the Dream of Progress.* New York: Oxford University Press, 1982.

Moron, Guillermo. *A History of Venezuela.* New York: Roy Publishers, 1963.

Picón Salas, Mariano et al. *Venezuela independiente, 1810–1960..* Caracas: Fundación Eugenio Mendoza, 1962.

Salcedo Bastardo, J. J. *La historia fundamental de Venezuela,* 2d ed. Caracas, 1968.

Vila, Pablo, et al. *Geografía de Venezuela.* 2 vols. Caracas: Ministerio de Educación, 1960, 1965.

VENEZUELA'S POLITICAL SYSTEM

Political History

Alexander, Robert J. *Rómulo Betancourt and the Transformation of Venezuela.* New Brunswick, N.J.: Transaction Books, 1982.

_____. *The Venezuelan Democratic Revolution: A Profile of the Regime of Rómulo Betancourt.* New Brunswick, N.J.: Rutgers University Press, 1964.

Betancourt Rómulo. *Venezuela: Política y petróleo,* 2nd ed. Caracas: Editorial Senderes, 1967.

Blank, David E. *Politics in Venezuela.* Boston: Little, Brown, 1973.

_____. *Venezuela: Politics in a Petroleum Republic.* New York: Praeger, 1984.

Bond, Robert D. "Where Democracy Lives." *Wilson Quarterly* (Autumn 1984): 48-62.

Ewell, Judith. *Indictment of a Dictator.* College Station: Texas A & M Press, 1981.

Levine, Daniel H. *Conflict and Political Change in Venezuela.* Princeton, N.J.: Princeton University Press, 1973.

Lott, Leo B. *Venezuela and Paraguay: Political Modernity and Tradition in Conflict.* New York: Holt, Rinehart and Winston, 1972.

Martz, John D. "The Crisis of Venezuelan Democracy." *Current History* 83 (February 1984): 73-78, 89.

Rangel, D. A. *Gómez: El amo del poder.* Valencia: Vadell Hermanos, 1975.

_____. *Los andinos en el poder.* Mérida: Talleres Gráficos Universitarios, 1966.

Taylor, Philip B. *The Venezuelan Golpe de Estado of 1958: The Fall of Marcos Pérez Jiménez.* Washington, D.C.: Institute for the Comparative Study of Political Systems, 1968.

_____, ed. *Venezuela, 1969: Analysis of Progress.* Houston, Tex.: University of Houston, Office of International Affairs, 1971.

Vallenilla Lanz, Laureano. *Cesarismo democrático: Estudio sobre las bases sociológicas de la constitución efectiva de Venezuela,* 4th ed. Caracas: Tipografía Garrido, 1961.

Velásquez, Ramón J. *Confidencia imaginarias de Juan Vicente Gómez.* Caracas: Ediciones Centauro, 1980.

_____. *La caída del liberalismo amarillo.* Caracas: Ediciones de la Contraloría, 1972.

_____, J. F. Sucre Figarella, and Blas Bruni Celli. *Betancourt: En la historia de Venezuela del siglo xx.* Caracas: Ediciones Centauro, 1980.

Velásquez, Ramón J., et al., eds. *Venezuela moderna.* Caracas: Fundación Eugenio Mendoza, 1976.

Elections and Campaigning

Alvarez, Federico, et al. *La izquierda venezolana y las elecciones del 1973 (un análisis político y polémico).* Caracas: Sintesis Dosmil, 1974.

Baloyra, Enrique, and John D. Martz. *Political Attitudes in Venezuela: Social Changes and Political Opinion.* Austin: University of Texas Press, 1979.

Barthelemy, Francoise. "Venezuela: Les Elections de la Crise." *Problemes d'Amerique Latine* 71 (1984): 5–31.

Bunimov-Parra, Boris. *Introducción a la sociología electoral venezolana.* Caracas: Editorial Arte, 1968.

Davis, C. L., and K. M. Coleman. "Who Abstains? The Situational Meaning of Nonvoting." *Social Science Quarterly* (December 1983): 764–76.

Herman, Donald E., and David J. Myers. "The Venezuelan Election." In *The World Votes—1983.* Edited by Howard E. Penniman. Durham: Duke University Press/American Enterprise Institute, 1985.

Martz, John D., and Enrique A. Baloyra. *Electoral Mobilization and Public Opinion: The Campaign of 1973.* Chapel Hill: University of North Carolina Press, 1976.

Myers, David J. *Democratic Campaigning in Venezuela: Caldera's Victory.* Caracas: Fundación La Salle, 1973.

————. "The Elections and the Evolution of the Venezuela Party System." In *Venezuela at the Polls.* Edited by Howard Penniman. Washington, D.C.: American Enterprise Institute, 1980.

————. "Urban Voting, Structural Cleavages and the Party System Evolution: The Case of Venezuela." *Comparative Politics* 8 (October 1975).

————, and Robert E. O'Connor, "The Undecided Respondent in Mandatory Voting Settings: A Venezuelan Exploration." *Western Political Quarterly* (September 1983): 420–33.

Penniman, Howard, R., ed. *Venezuela at the Polls: The National Election of 1978.* Washington, D.C.: American Enterprise Institute, 1980.

State Organization

Andueza, José Guillermo. "The Congress of Venezuela: A Legal Analysis." *Constitutional and Parliamentary Information* (First Quarter 1980): 11–53.

Brewer-Carías, Allan R. *El régimen municipal en Venezuela*. Caracas: Editorial Jurídica, 1984.

Comisión de Administración Pública. *El congreso de la república de Venezuela*. Caracas: Centro de Investigaciones Administrativas y Sociales, 1967.

Gil Fortoul José. *Historia constitucional de Venezuela*, 4th ed. 3 vols. Caracas: Ministerio de Educacion, 1953.

González, Jesús Alexis, and Dagoberto Duque Zambrano. *El ingreso municipal en Venezuela*. Caracas: Comisión de Estudio y Reforma Fiscal, 1983.

Kelley, R. Lynn. "The Venezuelan Senate: A Legislative Body in the Context of Development." Ph.D. dissertation, University of New Mexico, 1973.

_____. "The Role of the Venezuelan Senate." In *Latin American Legislatures: Their Role and Influence*. New York: Praeger, 1971.

Martínez, Pedro José. "Bases estructurales y priíncipos filosófico-político del orden constitutional venezolano." *Politeia* (1979): 197–245.

Naranjo Ostty, Rafael. *Doctrina y acción juridicas*. Caracas: Gráfica Americana, 1963.

República de Venezuela. *Constitución promulgada el 23 de enero 1961*. Caracas: Secretaría del Senado de la República, 1961.

_____. *Dirección General de Estadística. Décimo censo de población, resultados comparativos*. Caracas: Dirección General de Estadística, 1972.

ACTORS IN VENEZUELA'S POLITICAL SYSTEM

Peasants

Chesterfield, R., and K. Ruddle. "Traditional Agricultural Skill Training Among Peasant Farmers in Venezuela." *Anthropos* 74 (1976): 549–65.

Llonera, B. *El éxodo rural en Venezuela*. Caracas: Ediciones del Cuatricentenario de Caracas, 1966.

Margolies, Luisa, ed. *The Venezuelan Peasant in Country and City*. Caracas: EDIVA, 1979.

Powell, John Duncan. *Political Mobilization of the Venezuelan Peasant*. Cambridge, Mass.: Harvard University Press, 1971.

_____. "Peasant Society and Clientelist Politics." *American Political Science Review* (June 1970): 411–25.

Relemberg, N. S., et al. *Los pobres de Venezuela*. Buenos Aires: El Cid Editor, 1979.

Businessmen

FEDECAMARAS. *Asambleas de FEDECAMARAS.* Caracas, various years.

Friedmann, John. *Venezuela: From Doctrine to Dialogue.* Syracuse, N.Y.: Syracuse University Press, 1965.

Gil Yepes, José Antonio. *The Challenge of Venezuelan Democracy.* New Brunswick, N.J.: Transaction Books, 1981.

Jones, R. J. "Empirical Models of Political Risk in U.S. Oil Production Operation in Venezuela." *Journal of International Business.* Study 15 (Spring/Summer 1984): 81–95.

Rangel, Domingo Alberto. *La oligarquía dinero.* Caracas; Editorial Fuentes, 1972.

Urban Poor

Gilbert A. "Pirates and Invaders, Land Acquisition in Urban Colombia and Venezuela." *World Development* 9 (7) (1981): 657–78.

Karst, Kenneth L., et al. *The Evolution of Law in the Barrios of Caracas.* Los Angeles: Latin American Center, University of California, 1973.

Levine, Daniel H. "Urbanization, Migrants and Politics in Venezuela." *Journal of Interamerican Studies and World Affairs* (August 1975): 358–72.

Peattie, Lisa Redfield. *The View from the Barrios.* Ann Arbor: University of Michigan Press, 1968.

Ray, Talton F. *The Politics of the Barrios of Venezuela.* Berkeley: University of California Press, 1969.

Relemberg, N. S., H. Karner, and V. Kohler. *Los pobres de Venezuela.* Buenos Aires: Talleres Gráficos, 1979.

Students

Arnove, Robert F. *Student Alienation: A Venezuelan Study.* New York: Praeger, 1971.

Hamilton, William L. "Venezuela." In *Students and Politics in Developing Nations.* Edited by Donald K. Emmerson. New York: Praeger, 1968.

McMillan, Douglass F. "Venezuelan University Students as a Force in National Politics." Ph.D. dissertation, University of New Mexico, 1970.

Suárez Naudy F. *Por los legítimos ideales del estudiante venezolano: U.N.R., gestación de una idea revolucionaria.* Caracas: Ediciones Nueva Política, 1973.

Church

Colmenares Díaz, Luis. *La espada y el incensario: La iglesia bajo Pérez Jiménez.* Caracas, 1961.
Febres, Carlos Eduardo. "Religión y Comportamiento Político de la clase obrera en Caracas." *Revista de la Facultad de Ciencias Jurídicas y Políticas* 61 (1981): 247–91.
Levine, Daniel H. *Religion and Politics in Latin America: The Catholic Church in Venezuela and Colombia.* Princeton, N.J.: Princeton University Press, 1981.
_____. "Church Elites in Venezuela and Colombia: Context, Background, and Beliefs." *Latin America Research Review* (Spring 1979): 51–79.
_____. "Democracy and the Church in Venezuela." *Journal of Interamerican Studies and World Affairs* (February 1976): 3–22.
Watters, Mary. *A History of the Church in Venezuela, 1810–1930.* Chapel Hill: University of North Carolina Press, 1933.

Middle Class

Bonilla, Frank. *The Failure of Elites.* Cambridge, Mass.: MIT Press, 1970.

Political Parties

Alexander, Robert J. *The Communist Party of Venezuela.* Stanford, Calif.: Hoover Institution Press, 1969.
Ameringer, Charles D. *The Democratic Left in Exile: The Antidictatorial Struggle in the Caribbean, 1945–1959.* Coral Gables, Fla.: University of Miami Press, 1974.
Bloom, Daniel. "El desarrollo de los partidos políticos en Venezuela: Crecimiento electoral del Partido Social Cristiano (1963–1973) y observaciones sobre la elección presidencial de 1978." *Politeia* 9:287–309.
Borregales, Germán. *COPEI hoy una negación.* Caracas: Editorial Garrido, 1968.
Caldera, Rafael. *Especificidad de la democracia cristiana.* Barcelona: Editorial Nova Terra, 1973.
Ellner, Steve. "Acción Democrática–Partido Communista de Venezuela." Ph.D. dissertation, University of New Mexico, 1980.

————. "Diverse Interests on the Venezuelan Left."*Journal of Interamerican Studies* (November 1981): 483-93.

————. "Factionalism in the Venezuelan Communist Movement." *Science and Society* (Spring 1981): 52-70.

————. "Political Party Dynamics in Venezuela and the Outbreak of Guerrilla Warfare." *Interamerican Economic Affairs* (1980): 3-24.

————. "The Venezuelan Left on the Eve of the Popular Front, 1936-1945." *Journal of Latin American Studies* 2, pt 1 (May 1979).

————. "The Venezuelan Political Party System and Its Influence on Economic Decision Making at the Local Level." *Journal of Interamerican Economic Affairs* (Winter 1982): 79-103.

Herman, Donald L. *Christian Democracy in Venezuela.* Chapel Hill: University of North Carolina Press, 1980.

Herrera Campins, Luis, et al. *Sociedad communitarias y participación.* Caracas: Editorial Ateneo de Caracas, 1979.

Magallanes, Manuel Vicente. *Los partidos politicos en la evolución histórica venezolana.* Madrid: Editorial Mediterraneo, 1973.

Martz, John D. *Acción Democrática: Evolution of a Modern Political Party in Venezuela.* Princeton, N.J.: Princeton University Press, 1966.

Martz, John D. "Los peligros de la petrificación: El sistema de partidos venezolanos y la década de los ochenta." In *Iberoamérica en los años 80; perspectivas de cambio social y politico.* Compiled by Enrique Baloyra y Rafael López Pintor. Madrid: Centro de Investigaciones Sociológicas, 1982, pp. 149-67.

Myers, David J. "Venezuela's MAS."*Problems of Communism* 29 (September-October 1980): 16-28.

Njaim, Humberto. "El sistema venezolano de partidos y grupos de influencia: Consideraciones introductorias."*Politeia* (1978): 181-213.

Oropeza, Luis J. *Tutelary Pluralism: A Critical Approach to Venezuela Democracy.* Cambridge, Mass: Center for International Affairs, Harvard University, 1983.

Petkoff, Teodoro.*¿Socialismo para Venezuela?* Caracas: Editorial Fuentes, 1972.

————. *Tema socialista en venezuela: Razón y pasión del socialismo.* Caracas: Ediciones Centaura, 1973.

Rey Martinez, John C. "El sistema de partidos venezolanos." *Politeia* 1 (1972).

Rivera Oviedo, J. E. *Los social cristianos en Venezuela.* Caracas: Impresos HERMAR, 1970.

Rojas, Juan Bautista, *Los Adecos.* Vols. 1 and 2. Valencia: Vadell Hermanos, 1978.

Tenoro, J. R. Nuñez. *La izquierda y la lucha por el poder en Venezuela.* Caracas: Editorial Ateneo de Caracas, 1979.

Unions and Labor

Alonzo Guzmán, Rafael J. *Estudio analítico de la Ley del Trabajo venezolana.* 2 vols. Caracas: Universidad Central de Venezuela, 1967.

International Labor Office. *Freedom of Association and Conditions of Work in Venezuela.* Geneva, 1950.

Instituto Nacional de Cooperación Educativa. *Testimonios sobre la formación para el trabajo (1539-1970.)* Caracas, 1972.

República de Venezuela, Ministerios del Trabajo. *Memoria.* Caracas: Ministerio del Trabajo, 1958-1970.

U.S. Department of Labor, Bureau of Labor Statistics: *Labor Law and Practice in Venezuela.* Report 386: Washington, D.C.: U.S. Government Printing Office, 1972.

Bureaucracy

Bigler, Gene. *La política y el capitalismo de estado en Venezuela.* Madrid: Editorial Tecnos, 1981.

Brewer-Carias, Alan R. *El proceso de reforma administrativa en Venezuela.* Caracas: Oficina Central de Información, Serie Conceptos, 1970.

_____. *Estudios sobre la reforma administrative.* Caracas: Universidad Central de Venezuela, 1980.

_____. *Introducción al estudio de la organización administrativa venezolana.* Caracas: Editorial Jurídica Venezolana, 1978.

_____. *Política estado y administración pública.* Caracas: Ediciones Conjuntas, 1979.

Cabezas, Ramiro. *Elementos de administración y política tributaria para gobiernos municipales.* Caracas: Editorial FUNDACOMUN, 1973.

Comisión de Administración Pública. *Lineamientos generales de la reforma administrativa.* Caracas: Comisión de Administración Pública, 1970.

Hammergren, Linn. *Development and the Politics of Administrative Reform.* Boulder, Colo.: Westview Press, 1983.

Quero Morales, Constantino. *Imagen objectivo de Venezuela: Reformas fundamentales para su desarrollo.* Vols. I and II. Caracas: Banco Central de Venezuela, 1978.

Stewart, William. *Change and Bureaucracy: Public Administration in Venezuela.* Chapel Hill: University of North Carolina Press, 1978.

_____. *Efficiency, Innovation, and Strategies of Administrative Change.* Washington, D.C.: Pan American Union, 1976.

Military

Avendaro Lugo, José Ramón. *El militarismo en Venezuela: La dictum de Pérez Jiménez.* Caracas: Ediciones Centauro, 1982.

Burggraaff, Winfield J. *The Venezuelan Armed Forces in Politics, 1935-1959.* Columbia: University of Missouri Press, 1972.

Bigler, Gene E., "Professional Soldiers and Restrained Politics in Venezuela." In *New Military in Latin America.* Edited by Robert Wesson. Stanford, Calif.: Hoover Institution Press, 1984.

Carpio Castillo, Rubén. *Geopolítica de Venezuela.* Caracas: Editorial Ariel-Seix Barral Venezolana, 1981.

Fonseca, Jaime. *El militar: Pensamiento y acción.* Caracas: Teniente, 1973.

Gilmore, Robert L. *Caudillism and Militarism in Venezuela, 1810-1910.* Athens: Ohio University Press, 1964.

VENEZUELAN POLICY INTERESTS

Economic Policy

Allen, Loring. *Venezuelan Economic Development: A Politico-Economic Analysis.* Greenwich, Conn.: JAI Press, 1977.

Banco Central de Venezuela. *Informe Económico.* Caracas: Banco Central, various years.

————. *Memorias.* Caracas: Banco Central, various years.

Bitar, S., and E. Troncoso. "The Industrialization of Venezuela, 1950-1980." *Trimestre Económico* 49 (194) (1982): 265-94.

Farley, Rawley. "The Economics of Realism: A Case Study of Economic Change in Venezuela." In *The Economics of Latin America.* New York: Harper & Row, 1972.

Hassen, Mostafa. *Economic Growth and Employment Problems in Venezuela.* New York: Praeger, 1975.

International Bank for Reconstruction and Development. *The Economic Development of Venezuela.* Baltimore: Johns Hopkins University Press, 1961.

Kelley, R. Lynn. "The 1966 Venezuelan Tax Reform." *Inter-American Economic Affairs* 24 (Summer 1970): 77-92.

Levy, Fred D., Jr. *Economic Planning in Venezuela.* New York: Praeger, 1968.

Martínez, Ildemaro. *Finanzas y presupuesto público.* Caracas: Universidad Nacional Abierta, Editorial UNA, 1984.

Martz, John D. "The Frailties of Venezuelan Policymaking." In Steven W. Hughes and Kenneth J. Mijeski. *Politics and Public Policy in Latin America.* (Boulder, Colo.: Westview Press, 1984), pp. 101-17.

Petras, James F., and Morris H. Morley. "Petrodollars and the State: The Failure of State Capitalist Development in Venezuela." *Third World Quarterly* (January 1983): 7-27.

Shoup, Carl, et al. *The Fiscal System of Venezuela.* Baltimore: Johns Hopkins University Press, 1959.

Vidal, G. "The Capitalist State in Venezuela's Marxist Mind." *Problemas del Desarrollo* 11 (42) (1980): 127-53.

Industrial Policy

Coronel, Fernando, and Julie Skueski. "Reproduction Dependency: Auto Industry Policy and Petrodollar Circulation in Venezuela." *International Organization* 36, no. 1 (Winter 1982): 61-94.

Morales J. J. "Industrialization in Venezuela: Past Performance and Outlook." *Barclays Review* (May 1983): 32-36.

Pérez Sánchez, Juan Pablo, and Paul Zaremka. "Accumulation and the State in Venezuelan Industrialization." *Latin American Perspective* Summer 1979, pp. 5-29.

Agricultural Policy

Atkinson, L. Jay, and Oswald P. Blaich. "Venezuela: A Prospective Market for Grain and Livestock Products." Washington, D.C.: U.S. Department of Agriculture, 1983.

Heaton, Louis E. *The Agricultural Development of Venezuela.* New York: Praeger, 1969.

Johnston, Bruce F., and William C. Clark. *Redesigning Rural Development: A Strategic Perspective.* Baltimore: Johns Hopkins University Press, 1982.

Kastner, George, Maria Teresa Tello, et al. *El reto de alimentarnos.* Caracas: Instituto de Estudios Superiores de Administración, 1982.

Martz, John D. "Approaches to Agricultural Policy in Venezuela," *Inter-American Economic Affairs* (Winter 1980): 25-53.

Merhav, Meir. *Hacia una política de desarrollo agrícola y de cambio estructurál orientada hacia el exterior.* Caracas: Instituto de Comercio Exterior, 1974.

Palmby, Clarence D., Robert W. Long, et al. "Report of the U.S. Presidential Agricultural Task Force to Venezuela." Washington, D.C.: U.S. Department of Agriculture, 1983.

República de Venezuela. "Proposición sobre el plan de desarrollo agrícola a largo plazo." Caracas: MAC-MARNR-CORDIPLAN, 1983.

Roseberry, William. *Coffee and Capitalism in the Venezuelan Andes.* Austin: University of Texas Press, 1983.

Soto, Oscar David. *La empresa y la reforma agraria en la agricultura venezolano.* Madrid: Paraninfo S.A., 1978.

Indian Policy

Armellada, Fray Cesareo de. *Fuero indígena venezolano.* Caracas: Universidad Católica Andrés Bello, 1977.

Arvelo de Jiménez, Nelly, "An Analysis of Official Venezuelan Policy in Regard to the Indians." In *The Situation of the Indians in South America.* Edited by Walter Dostal. Geneva: World Council of Churches, 1972.

_____. "Development Programs Among Indigenous Populations of Venezuela: Background, Consequences, and a Critique." *Land, People and Planning in Contemporary Amazonia.* Edited by Francoise Barbira-Scazzocchio. Cambridge, Mass.: Centre of Latin American Studies, 1980, pp. 210-21.

Bonfil Batalla, Guillermo, ed. *Utopia y revolución: El pensamiento político contemporáneo de los indios en América Latina.* Mexico City: Editorial Nueva Imagen, 1981.

Chagnon, Napoleon A. *Yanomamo: The Fierce People.* New York: Holt, Rinehart and Winston, 1968.

Congreso Warao. *Actas del primer Congreso Warao.* Tucupita: Gubernación del Territorio, 1980.

Coppens, Walter. "La tenencia de tierra indígena en Venezuela: Aspectos legales y antropológicos." *Antropológica* 29 (1971): 24-37.

_____, ed. *Los aborigenes de Venezuela.* Caracas: Fundación La Salle, 1980.

Heinen, H. Dieter, and Walter Coppens. "Las empresas indígenas en Venezuela." *América Indígena* 41 (1981): 573-602.

Layrisse, Miguel, and Johannes Wilbert. *Indian Societies of Venezuela: Their Blood Group Types.* Caracas: Fundación La Salle, 1966.

Mosonyi, Esteban Emilio, et al. *El caso Nueva Tribus.* Caracas: Editorial Ateneo, 1981.

Romero Ocando, Eddie. *Un nuevo enfoque en el indigenismo venezolano.* Caracas: Ministerio de Justicia, Dirección de Cultos y Asuntos Indígenas, Oficína Central de Asuntos Indígenas, 1975.

Valdez, Alberto. *Autogestión indígena.* Caracas: Fondo Editorial Comun, 1981.
Wilbert, Johannes. *Survivors of El Dorado.* New York: Praeger, 1972.

Foreign and National Security Policy

Betancourt, Rómulo. *Hacia America latina democrática y integrada.* Caracas: Editorial Senderes, 1967.
Boersner, Demetrio. *Venezuela y el Caribe: Presencia cambiante.* Caracas: Monte Avita, 1978.
_____. "Cuba and Venezuela: Liberal and Conservative Possibilities." In *The New Cuban Presence in the Caribbean.* Edited by Barry B. Levine. Boulder, Colo.: Westview Press, 1983, pp. 91-107.
Bond, Robert, ed. *Contemporary Venezuela and Its Role in International Affairs.* New York: New York University Press, 1977.
_____. "Venezuelan Policy in the Caribbean Basin." In *Central America: International Dimensions of the Crisis.* Edited by Richard E. Feinberg. New York: Holmes & Meier, 1982, pp. 187-200.
Caldera, Rafael, *El bloque latinoamericano.* 2nd ed. Merida: Universidad de los Andes, 1966.
_____. *Justicia social internacional y nacionalismo latinoamericano.* Madrid: Seminarios y Ediciones, S.A., 1973.
_____. *La solidaridad pluralista de America latina.* Caracas: Oficina Central de Informacíon, 1973.
Ewell, Judith. "The Development of Venezuelan Geopolitical Analysis Since World War II." *Journal of Interamerican Studies and World Affairs* (August 1982): 295-320.
Gill, H. S. "Understanding Venezuela's Foreign Policy." *Social and Economic Studies* (September 1978): 350-63.
Gray, William Henry. *Venezuela, Uncle Sam, and OPEC.* Austin, Tex.: O.E.G. Foundation, 1982.
"The Latin American Crisis: Brazil, Venezuela, Argentina." *International Currency Review* (July 1983): 43-78.
Liss, Sheldon. *Diplomacy and Dependency: Venezuela, the United States, and the Americas.* Salisbury, N.C.: Documentary Publishers, 1978.
López Pérez, Eduardo. "Cooperation Among Developing Countries: Some Venezuelan Experience." *Development and Peace* (Spring 1980): 92-105.
Martz, John D. "Venezuelan Foreign Policy and the Role of Political Parties." In *Latin American Nations in World Politics.* Edited by Heraldo Muñoz and Joseph S. Tulchin. Boulder, Colo.: Westview Press, 1984, pp. 133-50.

_____. "Ideology and Oil: Venezuela in the Circum-Caribbean." In *Colossus Challenged: The Struggle for Caribbean Influence.* Edited by E. Michael Erisman and John D. Martz. Boulder, Colo.: Westview Press, 1982, pp. 122-48.

Mendez, Carlos Antonio Romero. "The Role of Venezuela in the Caribbean Since 1958." In *Confrontation in the Caribbean.* Edited by Alan Adelman and Reid Reading. Pittsburgh: University of Pittsburg Center for International Studies, 1984, pp. 149-64.

Myers, David J. *Venezuela's Pursuit of Caribbean Basin Interests: Implications for U.S. National Interests.* Rand-R-2994-AF/1. Santa Monica, Calif., 1985.

Rabe, Stephen G. *The Road to OPEC: United States Relations with Venezuela, 1919-1976.* Austin: University of Texas Press, 1982.

Romero, Aníbal, ed. *Seguridad, defensa y democracia en Venezuela.* Caracas: Editorial Equinoccio, 1980.

Serbin, Andres, ed. *Geopolítica de las relaciones de Venezuela con el Caribe.* Caracas: ASOVAC, 1983.

Tugwell, Franklin. *Venezuelan Foreign Policy.* External Research Study. Washington, D.C.: U.S. Department of State, March 1976.

Education Policy

Acosta Saignas, Gladys. *Investigación sobre materiales de la escuela venezolano.* Caracas: Universidad Central de Venezuela, Facultad de Humanidades y Educación, 1965.

Albornoz, Orlando. *Ideología y política de la universidad latinoamericana.* Caracas: Instituto Societas, 1972.

_____. *La formación de los recursos humanos en el área educación.* Caracas: Monte Avila Editores, 1981.

Bronfenmajer, Gabriela, and Ramón Casanova. "Democracia burguesa, crisis, política y universidad liberal." In *Universidad, clases sociales y poder.* Edited by G. W. Rama. Caracas: Editorial Ateneo de Caracas, 1982.

Dupla, Javier. *La educación en Venezuela.* Caracas: Centro Gumilla, 1983.

Fernández Heres, Rafael. *El ciclo diversificado.* Maracaibo: Fondo Editorial IRFES, 1978.

_____. *Regionalización de la educación en Venezuela.* Caracas: Ediciones Colegio Universitario Francisco de Miranda, 1978.

Maza Zavala, D. F. *Universidad: Ciencia y tecnología.* Caracas: UCV, 1979.

Ribeiro, Darcy. *La universidad latinoamericans*. Caracas: Universidad Central de Venezuela, 1971.

Ruiz Calderón, Humberto. *Plan de becas ayacucho: Mito y realidad*. Caracas: Editorial Ateneo de Caracas, 1979.

Ruscoe, Gordon C. "The Efficacy of Venezuelan Education." In *Venezuela: 1969, Analysis of Progress*. Edited by Philip B. Taylor, Jr. Houston,Tex.: University of Houston, Office of International Affairs, 1971.

Salas Capriles, Roberto. *Interacción educación-industria: Caso venezolano*. Caracas: Fundación Educación-Industria, 1978.

Silvert, Kalman H.,and Leonard Reissman. *Education, Class and Nation: The Experiences of Chile and Venezuela*. New York: Elsevier, 1976.

Petroleum Policy

Adelman, M. A. *The World Petroleum Market*. Baltimore: Johns Hopkins University Press, 1972.

Baloyra, Enrique A. "Oil Policies and Budgets in Venezuela, 1938-1968." *Latin American Research Review* 9, no. 2 (Summer 1974): 28-72.

Blank, David E. "Venezuela: Politics of Oil." In *U.S. Influence in Latin America in the 1980s*. Edited by Robert Wesson. New York: Praeger, 1982.

Coronel, Gustavo. *The Nationalization of the Venezuelan Oil Industry: From Technocratic Success to Political Failure*. Lexington, Mass.: D. C. Heath, 1983.

Gallad, I. Rodríguez, and F. Yañez. *Cronología ideológica de la nacionalización petrolera en Venezuela*. Caracas, 1977.

Lieuwen, Edwin. *Petroleum in Venezuela: A History*. Berkeley: University of California Press, 1954.

McBeth, Brian S. *Juan Vicente Gómez and the Oil Companies in Venezuela, 1908-1935*. New York: Cambridge University Press, 1983.

Martz, John D. "Democratic Politics of Petroleum." In *Politics, Policies, and Economic Development in Latin America*. Edited by Robert Wesson, Stanford, Calif.: Hoover Institution, 1984, 161-88.

Mejía Alarcón, Pedro Estabon. *La industria del petróleo en Venezuela*. Caracas: Universidad Central de Venezuela, Facultad de Economía, 1972.

Mikesell, Raymond F. ed. *Foreign Investment in the Petroleum and Mineral Industries: Case Studies of Investor-Host Country Relations*. Baltimore: Johns Hopkins University Press, 1970.

Pérez Alfonzo, Juan Pablo. *El pentágono petrolero*. Caracas: Ediciones Revista Política, 1967.

―――. *Petróleo: Jugo de la tierra*. Caracas: Ediciones del Arte, 1961.

―――. *Petróleo y dependencia*. Caracas: Sintesis Dosmil, 1971.

―――. *Política petrolera*. Caracas: Imprenta Nacional, 1962.

Philip, George. *Oil and Politics in Latin America*. Cambridge: Cambridge University Press, 1982.

Ravard, Rafael Alfonzo. *Cinco anos de normalidad operativa, 1975–1980*. Caracas: Petróleos de Venezuela, 1981.

Tugwell, Franklin. *The Politics of Oil in Venezuela*. Palo Alto, Calif.: Stanford University Press, 1975.

Uslar Pietri, Arturo. *Petróleo de vida o muerte*. Caracas, 1966.

Vallenilla, Luis. *Auge, declinación y porvenir del petróleo venezolano*. Caracas: Editorial Tiempo Nuevo, 1973.

―――. *Oil, the Making of a New Economic Order: Venezuela Oil and OPEC*. New York: McGraw-Hill, 1975.

Employment and Income Distribution Policy

Jones, Richard C. "Regional Income Equalities and Government Investment in Venezuela." *Journal of Developing Areas* (April 1982): 373–89.

Musgrove, P. "Oil Price Increase and the Alleviation of Poverty: Income Distribution in Caracas, Venezuela in 1966 and 1975." *Journal of Development Economics* (October 1981): 229–50.

Urban and Regional Policy

Acedo Mendoza, Carlos. *Reforma urbana*. Caracas: Editorial FUNDACOMUN, 1974.

Bausch, Thomas A. *The Primate City and Economic Development in Latin America: Caracas, Venezuela, a Case Study*. Ann Arbor, Mich.: University Microfilms, 1968.

Brewer-Carías, Alan R. *Aspectos institucionales del transporte y tránsito en el área metropolitana de Caracas*. Caracas: Editorial FUNDACOMUN, 1972.

Cannon, Mark W., et al. *Urban Government for Valencia, Venezuela*. New York: Praeger, 1973.

Castro Guevara, Julio. *Esquema de la evolución municipal en Venezuela*. Caracas: Editorial FUNDACOMUN, 1972.

Crist, Raymond E. "Development and Agrarian Land Reform in

Venezuela's Pioneer Zone: Social Progress Along the Llano-Andes Border in a Half-Century of Political Advance." *American Journal of Economics and Sociology* (April 1984): 149–58.

Dinkespiel, John R. "Administration Style and Economic Development: The Organization and Management of the Guyana Region Development of Venezuela." Ph.D. dissertation, Harvard University, 1967.

Friedmann, John. *Regional Development Policy: A Case Study of Venezuela.* Cambridge: MIT Press, 1966.

Greenwood, Jonathan C. "Regional Planning in Venezuela: Recent Directions." *Third World Planning Review* (August 1984): 239–53.

Hernández, Omar. *Planificación urbano y el desarrollo urbano no controlado.* Caracas: Editorial FUNDACOMUN, 1973.

Lares, Omar. *Legislación urbanística comparada.* Caracas: Editorial FUNDACOMUN, 1972.

Martínez, Ildemaro Jesús. *Instituciones para el desarrollo: Análisis de Fundacomun en Venezuela.* Caracas: Ediciones IESA, 1974.

Moles Caubert, Antonio, ed. *Estudio de Caracas: Gobierno política.* Vol. 8. Caracas: Universidad Central de Venezuela, 1972.

Myers, David J. *Toma de decisiones sobre renovación urbana en El Conde.* Caracas: Ediciones IESA, 1974.

_____. "Caracas: The Politics of Intensifying Primacy." in *Metropolitan Latin America: The Challenge and the Response.* Edited by Wayne Cornelius and Robert V. Kemper. Vol. VI. Beverly Hills, Calif.: Sage Publications, 1978, pp. 227–58.

_____. "Political Process of Urban Development—Caracas Under Acción Democratica." Ph.D. dissertation, University of California, Los Angeles, 1969.

Mytelka, Lynn Krieger. *Regional Development in a Global Economy: The Multinational Corporation, Technology, and Andean Integration.* New Haven, Conn.: Yale University Press, 1979.

Negron, Marco Antonio. "The Origins of Contemporary Urbanization in Venezuela: Growth Without Accumulation Between 1920 and 1945." *Regional Development Dialogue* (Autumn 1982): 1–28.

Oficina Municipal de Planeamiento Urbano del Distrito Federal. *Plan general urbano de Caracas, 1970–1990.* Caracas: Consejo Municipal del Distrito Federal, 1972.

Pacanins, Guillermo A. *Siete años en la gobernación del Distrito Federal.* Caracas: Tipografía Vargas, 1965.

Rodwin, Lloyd, and Associates. *Planning Urban Growth and Regional Development.* Cambridge, Mass.: MIT Press, 1969.

Torrealba Narvaez, Luis, ed. *Compilación legislativa municipal del Distrito Federal.* Caracas: Consejo Municipal de Caracas, 1972.

Travieso, Fernando. *Cuidad, region y subdesarrollo*. Caracas: Editorial FUNDACOMUN, 1975.

———, and Alberto Urdaneta, eds., "Desarrollo urbano y desarrollo nacional." *Cuadernos de la Sociedad Venezolana de Planificación* (January–March 1971).

POLITICAL DEVELOPMENT AND CHANGE

Acedo Mendoza, Carlos. *Venezuela: Ruta y destino*. 2nd ed. Caracas: Fondo Editorial Comun, 1974.

Albornoz, Orlando. *Desarrollo político en Venezuela*. Caracas: Universidad Central de Venezuela, Consejo de Desarrollo Científico y Humanístico, 1974.

Betancourt, Rómulo. *La revolución democrática en Venezuela*. 4 vols. Caracas: Imprenta Nacional, 1968.

———. *Memoria del último destierro, 1948–1958*. Caracas: Ediciones Centauro, 1982.

Bonilla, Frank, and José A. Silva Michelena, eds. *A Strategy for Research on Social Policy*. Cambridge, Mass.: MIT Press, 1967.

Cardenas Rodolfo José. *El combate político; solo para líderes nuevos*. 2nd ed. Caracas: Editorial Doña Bárbara, 1966.

Centro de Estudios del Desarrollo (CENDES). *Estudios de conflictos y consenso, serie de resultados parciales I: Muestra de líderes sindicales*. Caracas: Universidad Central de Venezuela, CENDES, 1965.

Childers, Victor E. *Human Resources Development: Venezuela*. Bloomington, Ind.: International Development Research Center, 1974.

Davis, C. L. "Political Regimes and the Socioeconomic Model of Political Mobilization: Some Venezuelan and Mexican Data." *Journal of Politics* (May 1983): 422–48.

Fernández, Aníbal, et al. *Modelo demo-economic de Venezuela*. Caracas: IESA, 1975.

Marcel, Granier. *La generación de relevo vs el estado omnipotente*. Caracas: Publicaciones Seleven, 1985.

Matthews, Robert Paul. *Violencia rural en Venezuela, 1840–1858*. Caracas: Monte Avila Editores, 1977.

Velásquez, Ramón J., ed. *1984: ¿A Donde Va Venezuela?* Caracas: Editorial Planeta, 1984.

Silva Michelena, José Agustín. *The Illusion of Democracy in Dependent Nations*. Cambridge, Mass.: MIT Press, 1971.

Index

487

Contributors

John D. Martz, Ph.D., University of North Carolina. He was editor of the *Latin American Research Review* from 1975 to 1980, and his publications include numerous articles and four books on Venezuelan politics. Dr. Martz is professor of political science and head of the Department of Political Science at the Pennsylvania State University.

David J. Myers, Ph.D., University of California, Los Angeles. He recently published *Venezuela's Pursuit of Caribbean Basin Interests* and has conducted social research in Venezuela for almost 20 years. Dr. Myers is associate professor of political science at the Pennsylvania State University.

Charles D. Ameringer, Ph.D., Fletcher School of Law and Diplomacy. The author of the *Democratic Left in Exile: the Antidictatorial Struggle in the Caribbean 1945–1959*, he has published extensively on subjects relating to the Caribbean Basin. Dr. Ameringer is professor of history and head of the Department of History at the Pennsylvania State University.

Enrique A. Baloyra, Ph.D., University of Florida. With John D. Martz, he coauthored *Political Attitudes in Venezuela*, and he has published extensively on the politics of Cuba, Venezuela, and El Salvador. Dr. Baloyra is professor of political science at the University of Miami, Coral Gables.

Gene E. Bigler, Ph.D., The Johns Hopkins University, School of Advanced International Studies (SAIS). He is the author of *La Política y el capitalismo de estado en Venezuela* and served for six years on the staff of the Instituto de Estudios Superiores de Administración (IESA) in Caracas. He currently is a research analyst for Latin American affairs at the USIA and a professional lecturer at SAIS in Washington, D.C.

David E. Blank, Ph.D., Columbia University. He recently published *Venezuela: Politics in a Petroleum Republic* and has conducted research in Venezuela for two decades. Dr. Blank is professor of political science at the University of Louisville.

Walter Coppens, M.A. in anthropology from UCLA and Ph.D. in law from the University of Louvain (Belgium). He is currently director of the Instituto Caribe de Anthropologia y Sociología in Caracas. His most recent book, *Del caualete al motor fuera de borda* examines cultural change among the Indians of southern Venezuela.

Steven Ellner, Ph.D., University of New Mexico. The author of *Los partidos políticos y su disputa por el control del movimiento sindical en Venezuela*, he also has contributed to scholarly journals in Venezuela and the United States. Dr. Ellner is professor of political science at the Puerto La Cruz center of the Universidad de Oriente.

José Antonio Gil, Ph.D., Northwestern University. The author of *The Challenge of Venezuelan Democracy*, he has published extensively on government-business relations. Dr. Gil is professor of public and private sector affairs at Venezuela's Instituto de Estudios Superiores de Administración (IESA) in Caracas.

H. Dieter Heinen, Ph.D., University of California, Los Angeles. He is the author *Oko Warao: We Are Canoe People*, and has conducted extensive field research throughout the Orinoco delta and Amazonas. He has published extensively. Dr. Heinen is professor of anthropology and head of the Anthropology Department of Venezuela's Institute for Scientific Investigation (IVIC).

Donald L. Herman, Ph.D., University of Michigan. He is the author of *Christian Democracy in Venezuela*, and has written extensively on Colombia, Mexico, and Venezuela. Dr. Herman is professor of political science and research associate of the Latin American Studies Center at Michigan State University.

R. Lynn Kelley, Ph.D., University of New Mexico. His dissertation, "The Venezuelan Senate: A Legislative Body in the Context of Development," sparked a continuing interest in Venezuela, and he has contributed to various professional journals. Dr. Kelley is associate professor of political science at Kentucky State University.

John V. Lombardi, Ph.D., Columbia University. His general history, *Venezuela: The Search for Order, the Dream of Progress* was highly acclaimed, and he has published widely on colonial Venezuela. Dr. Lombardi is professor of history and dean of international affairs at the University of Indiana, Bloomington.

Ildemaro Jesús Martínez, Ph.D., Syracuse University. His most recent book is *Finanzas públicas y presupuesto público* and he has designed and coordinated training programs for local government officials and administrators over the past 20 years. Dr. Martínez is professor of public administration at the Instituto de Estudios Superiores de Administración (IESA) in Caracas.

William S. Stewart, Ph.D., University of North Carolina. The author of *Change and Bureaucracy: Public Administration in Venezuela*, he has contributed to scholarly journals and other publications. Dr. Stewart is associate professor of political science at Chico State College, Chico, California.

Enrique Viloria V., Doctor of Administrative Sciences, University of Paris. The author of several books and articles on public administration, he was awarded the Venezuelan Academy of Political and Social Sciences prize for outstanding achievement in 1979. He currently serves as deputy manager for planning and organization at Petróleos de Venezuela.